Lecture Notes in Computer Science

Lecture Notes in Artificial Intelligence   14275

Founding Editor

Jörg Siekmann

Series Editors

Randy Goebel, *University of Alberta, Edmonton, Canada*
Wolfgang Wahlster, *DFKI, Berlin, Germany*
Zhi-Hua Zhou, *Nanjing University, Nanjing, China*

The series Lecture Notes in Artificial Intelligence (LNAI) was established in 1988 as a topical subseries of LNCS devoted to artificial intelligence.

The series publishes state-of-the-art research results at a high level. As with the LNCS mother series, the mission of the series is to serve the international R & D community by providing an invaluable service, mainly focused on the publication of conference and workshop proceedings and postproceedings.

Huayong Yang · Honghai Liu · Jun Zou ·
Zhouping Yin · Lianqing Liu · Geng Yang ·
Xiaoping Ouyang · Zhiyong Wang
Editors

Intelligent Robotics and Applications

16th International Conference, ICIRA 2023
Hangzhou, China, July 5–7, 2023
Proceedings, Part IX

 Springer

Editors
Huayong Yang
Zhejiang University
Hangzhou, China

Honghai Liu ⓘ
Harbin Institute of Technology
Shenzhen, China

Jun Zou ⓘ
Zhejiang University
Hangzhou, China

Zhouping Yin
Huazhong University of Science
and Technology
Wuhan, China

Lianqing Liu ⓘ
Shenyang Institute of Automation
Shenyang, Liaoning, China

Geng Yang ⓘ
Zhejiang University
Hangzhou, China

Xiaoping Ouyang ⓘ
Zhejiang University
Hangzhou, China

Zhiyong Wang
Harbin Institute of Technology
Shenzhen, China

ISSN 0302-9743   ISSN 1611-3349 (electronic)
Lecture Notes in Artificial Intelligence
ISBN 978-981-99-6503-8   ISBN 978-981-99-6504-5 (eBook)
https://doi.org/10.1007/978-981-99-6504-5

LNCS Sublibrary: SL7 – Artificial Intelligence

This Springer imprint is published by the registered company Springer Nature Singapore Pte Ltd.
The registered company address is: 152 Beach Road, #21-01/04 Gateway East, Singapore 189721, Singapore

Paper in this product is recyclable.

Preface

With the theme "Smart Robotics for Sustainable Society", the 16th International Conference on Intelligent Robotics and Applications (ICIRA 2023) was held in Hangzhou, China, July 5–7, 2023, and designed to encourage advancement in the field of robotics, automation, mechatronics, and applications. It aimed to promote top-level research and globalize quality research in general, making discussions and presentations more internationally competitive and focusing on the latest outstanding achievements, future trends, and demands.

ICIRA 2023 was organized and hosted by Zhejiang University, co-hosted by Harbin Institute of Technology, Huazhong University of Science and Technology, Chinese Academy of Sciences, and Shanghai Jiao Tong University, co-organized by State Key Laboratory of Fluid Power and Mechatronic Systems, State Key Laboratory of Robotics and System, State Key Laboratory of Digital Manufacturing Equipment and Technology, State Key Laboratory of Mechanical System and Vibration, State Key Laboratory of Robotics, and School of Mechanical Engineering of Zhejiang University. Also, ICIRA 2023 was technically co-sponsored by Springer. On this occasion, ICIRA 2023 was a successful event after the COVID-19 pandemic. It attracted more than 630 submissions, and the Program Committee undertook a rigorous review process for selecting the most deserving research for publication. The Advisory Committee gave advice for the conference program. Also, they help to organize special sections for ICIRA 2023. Finally, a total of 431 papers were selected for publication in 9 volumes of Springer's Lecture Note in Artificial Intelligence. For the review process, single-blind peer review was used. Each review took around 2–3 weeks, and each submission received at least 2 reviews and 1 meta-review.

In ICIRA 2023, 12 distinguished plenary speakers delivered their outstanding research works in various fields of robotics. Participants gave a total of 214 oral presentations and 197 poster presentations, enjoying this excellent opportunity to share their latest research findings. Here, we would like to express our sincere appreciation to all the authors, participants, and distinguished plenary and keynote speakers. Special thanks are also extended to all members of the Organizing Committee, all reviewers for peer-review, all staffs of the conference affairs group, and all volunteers for their diligent work.

July 2023

Huayong Yang
Honghai Liu
Jun Zou
Zhouping Yin
Lianqing Liu
Geng Yang
Xiaoping Ouyang
Zhiyong Wang

Organization

Conference Chair

Huayong Yang   Zhejiang University, China

Honorary Chairs

Youlun Xiong   Huazhong University of Science and Technology, China

Han Ding   Huazhong University of Science and Technology, China

General Chairs

Honghai Liu   Harbin Institute of Technology, China

Jun Zou   Zhejiang University, China

Zhouping Yin   Huazhong University of Science and Technology, China

Lianqing Liu   Chinese Academy of Sciences, China

Program Chairs

Geng Yang   Zhejiang University, China

Li Jiang   Harbin Institute of Technology, China

Guoying Gu   Shanghai Jiao Tong University, China

Xinyu Wu   Chinese Academy of Sciences, China

Award Committee Chair

Yong Lei   Zhejiang University, China

Publication Chairs

Xiaoping Ouyang   Zhejiang University, China
Zhiyong Wang   Harbin Institute of Technology, China

Regional Chairs

Zhiyong Chen   University of Newcastle, Australia
Naoyuki Kubota   Tokyo Metropolitan University, Japan
Zhaojie Ju   University of Portsmouth, UK
Eric Perreault   Northeastern University, USA
Peter Xu   University of Auckland, New Zealand
Simon Yang   University of Guelph, Canada
Houxiang Zhang   Norwegian University of Science and Technology,
                         Norway
Duanling Li   Beijing University of Posts and
                         Telecommunications, China

Advisory Committee

Jorge Angeles   McGill University, Canada
Tamio Arai   University of Tokyo, Japan
Hegao Cai   Harbin Institute of Technology, China
Tianyou Chai   Northeastern University, China
Jiansheng Dai   King's College London, UK
Zongquan Deng   Harbin Institute of Technology, China
Han Ding   Huazhong University of Science and Technology,
                         China
Xilun Ding   Beihang University, China
Baoyan Duan   Xidian University, China
Xisheng Feng   Shenyang Institute of Automation, Chinese
                         Academy of Sciences, China
Toshio Fukuda   Nagoya University, Japan
Jianda Han   Nankai University, China
Qiang Huang   Beijing Institute of Technology, China
Oussama Khatib   Stanford University, USA
Yinan Lai   National Natural Science Foundation of China,
                         China
Jangmyung Lee   Pusan National University, Korea
Zhongqin Lin   Shanghai Jiao Tong University, China

Contents – Part IX

Cutting-Edge Research in Robotics

Innovative Design and Performance Evaluation of Robot Mechanisms - II

Design and Analysis of a Novel Ring Truss Deployable Antenna Mechanism

Bo Han[1,2], Zhantu Yuan[1], Yuanzhi Zhou[1], Feng Liu[1], Jiantao Yao[1,2(✉)], and Yongsheng Zhao[1,2]

[1] Hebei Provincial Key Laboratory of Parallel Robot and Mechatronic System, Yanshan University, Qinhuangdao 066004, China
{bohan,jtyao}@ysu.edu.cn
[2] Key Laboratory of Advanced Forging and Stamping Technology and Science, Yanshan University, Ministry of Education of China, Qinhuangdao 066004, China

Abstract. With the development of astronautics, satellite antenna as an important communication equipment has also gradually developed to large scale. In this paper, a novel ring truss deployable antenna mechanism is proposed. The mechanism has three layers of installation points with height differences between them, which can be used to ensure that all the installation points will be distributed on the profile of the cable network, and this characteristic ensures the mechanism can be utilized to the maximum. Then the degrees of freedom (DOF) and kinematics of the ring truss deployable mechanism are analyzed using screw theory, where the analysis shows that the DOF of the overall ring truss deployable mechanism is equal to one. Following that, the dynamics model about the mechanism unit is established using the second type of Lagrange equations. Based on this dynamic model, the effect of torsion spring stiffness on the deployment process is discussed and the conclusion is verified by simulation.

Keywords: Deployable Mechanism · Ring Truss Antenna · Degree of Freedom · Dynamics · Screw Theory

1 Introduction

With the development of communication technology and astronautics, space satellite antennas inevitably need to become larger. But constrained by the launch vehicle storage volume system, the traditional solid surface antenna can no longer meet the current growing communication demand. Therefore, the deployable satellite antenna, which can occupy less storage volume after folding and can be deployed to form a larger available area after the satellite reaches its expected position, has received the attention of many scholars and research institutes. Many scholars have conducted research on deployable mechanisms. Kim et al. proposed a deployable truss structure that can be stored in a flat form [1]. Chen et al. designed and studied a new type of planar antenna support mechanism [2]. Wang et al. presented a novel three-limb deployable mechanism using a set of metamorphic mechanism modules, which had potential applications in providing support to the large curved surface deployable membrane structures [3].

H. Yang et al. (Eds.): ICIRA 2023, LNAI 14275, pp. 3–15, 2023.
https://doi.org/10.1007/978-981-99-6504-5_1

There are many types of deployable antennas, including umbrella deployable antenna [4–6], parabolic deployable antenna [7–9], ring truss deployable antenna [10–13]. Among them, the ring truss deployable antenna has more comprehensive advantages in profile accuracy and quality. With the increase of antenna aperture, the surface accuracy of single-layer ring truss deployable antenna decreases seriously, so the novel ring truss deployable mechanism with higher stiffness is needed to be proposed as the support platform of large deployable antenna. After You first designed and fabricated a double ring truss deployable antenna with higher stiffness, this configuration has received a lot of attention and has been studied intensively. Han et al. studied the configuration synthesis of the ring truss deployable mechanism based on the screw theory [13]. Cao et al. presented a topological structure design and kinematic analysis of a novel double-ring truss deployable satellite antenna mechanism [14]. Meng et al. proposed novel basic units with good composability and deployable performance to construct regular polygonal prisms and ring truss deployable mechanisms [15].

This paper proposes a novel ring truss developable mechanism with the following advantages. Firstly, the height difference of the mechanism allows the integrated assembly between the mechanism and the cable net profile. Secondly, the degree of freedom (DOF) of this mechanism is equal to one, which facilitates the calculation of its movement and the deployment control. Thirdly, the prismatic joint (P joint) and the synchronous joint are prone to cold welding [16] under the extreme environment in space, while the proposed mechanism uses only revolute joints (R joints) between the components, which reduces the probability of mechanical failure. In summary, this mechanism has excellent potential for application in the aerospace field.

2   Ring Truss Deployable Mechanism Configuration Design

The proposed ring truss deployable mechanism in this paper evolves from a conventional double ring topology. First, an intermediate cable network installation layer is added by inserting triangles between the inner and outer layers, and then the resulting topology is further simplified by removing unnecessary connections in the inner layer and keeping only the points to obtain the final ring topology, which is shown in Fig. 1.

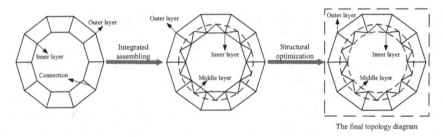

Fig. 1. Evolutionary flow of the multi-layer ring topology diagram

As shown in Fig. 2, the components are represented by capital letters, and the R joints are indicated by the capital letters with labels, and the mechanism unit is symmetrical about the line F_1C_3. The l indicates the length of the linkage, and the subscript letter indicates the start and end of the linkage. When replacing the linkage of the mechanism unit in Fig. 2 with a non-equal length scissors mechanism, the geometric compatibility of the mechanism unit is required to ensure that the resulting multi-loop mechanism is fully closed. The final configuration of the topology in Fig. 1 includes five sets of unequal-length scissors mechanisms, and there are various solutions to the problem for adjusting the rod lengths to form a closed-loop mechanism. In this paper, the design of the mechanism is carried out under the special condition that all five groups of scissors have the same angles, because it can ensure that all scissors mechanisms reach the maximum deployment angle at the same time. And the following three conditions need to be met when designing the mechanism (Fig. 3):

$$l_{A_1F_1} = l_{A_2F_2} \tag{1}$$

$$l_{B_1F_2} = l_{B_2F_3} \tag{2}$$

$$\frac{l_{A_1F_1}}{l_{A_1A_3}} = \frac{l_{B_1F_2}}{l_{B_1B_3}} = \frac{l_{F_3C_1}}{l_{C_1C_3}} \tag{3}$$

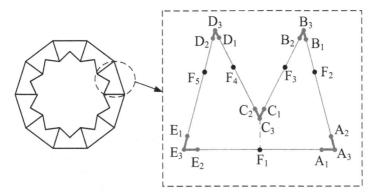

Fig. 2. Ring truss deployable mechanism unit

There are height differences between the three installation points of this ring truss deployable mechanism, and they can be located on the reflective cable network by adjusting the rod length, as shown in Fig. 4. By using this mechanism, the cable network and the support platform can be assembled, compared with other ring truss deployable mechanisms, this mechanism can maximize the utilization of the mechanism without adding additional components. When the ring truss deployable mechanism is deployed, the mechanism can be maintained by installing pretend locking mechanisms in the R joints.

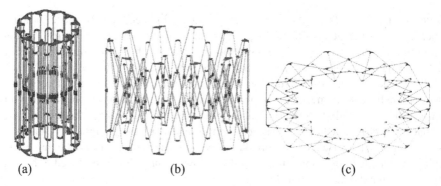

Fig. 3. Ring truss deployable mechanism (a)Folded state, (b) Semi-developed state, (c) Developed state.

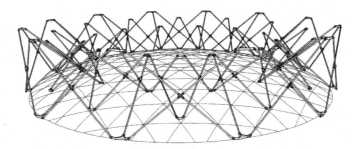

Fig. 4. Ring truss deployable mechanism with cable network

3   DOF Analysis

The O-XYZ coordinate system is established on the component E, and the origin O is located on the point E_3 as shown in Fig. 5. Based on graph theory and screw theory, the components are represented by circles, the R joints are represented by straight lines, and the symbols on the lines represent the screw coordinates of the R joints, e.g., the R joint between components E and E*A is $\$_1$. This mechanism unit includes five groups of scissor mechanisms with different rod lengths and five groups of connections, totaling twenty components and twenty-five joints.

The coordinates of the R_1 joint between the linkage EA* and the component E is:

$$r_{20} = \left(l_{E_3E_2} \ 0 \ 0 \right) \tag{4}$$

The direction of R_1 joint is:

$$S_{20} = \left(0 \ 1 \ 0 \right) \tag{5}$$

According to the screw theory, the screw coordinates of the R_1 joint can be obtained:

$$\$_{20} = \left[0 \ 1 \ 0 \ 0 \ 0 \ l_{E_3E_2} \right]^{\mathrm{T}} \tag{6}$$

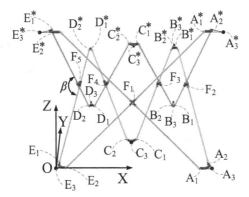

Fig. 5. Unit coordinate system

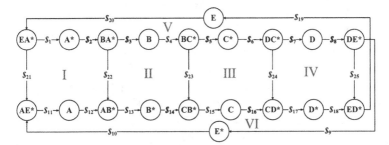

Fig. 6. Screw topology of a ring truss deployable mechanism unit

Similarly, the expressions of other R joints shown in Fig. 6 can be obtained. Using ω to denote the value of the angular velocity, the corresponding screw constraint equations can be established for the six closed loops of I–VI in Fig. 6, as follows:

$$\begin{cases} \omega_1\$_1 + \omega_2\$_2 + \omega_{22}\$_{22} - \omega_{21}\$_{21} - \omega_{11}\$_{11} - \omega_{12}\$_{12} = \mathbf{0} \\ \omega_3\$_3 + \omega_4\$_4 + \omega_{23}\$_{23} - \omega_{22}\$_{22} - \omega_{13}\$_{13} - \omega_{14}\$_{14} = \mathbf{0} \\ \omega_5\$_5 + \omega_6\$_6 + \omega_{24}\$_{24} - \omega_{23}\$_{23} - \omega_{15}\$_{15} - \omega_{16}\$_{16} = \mathbf{0} \\ \omega_7\$_7 + \omega_8\$_8 + \omega_{25}\$_{25} - \omega_{24}\$_{24} - \omega_{17}\$_{17} - \omega_{18}\$_{18} = \mathbf{0} \\ \omega_{11}\$_{11} + \omega_{12}\$_{12} + \omega_{13}\$_{13} + \omega_{14}\$_{14} + \omega_{15}\$_{15} + \omega_{16}\$_{16} \\ +\omega_{17}\$_{17} + \omega_{18}\$_{18} - \omega_{25}\$_{25} + \omega_9\$_9 + \omega_{10}\$_{10} = \mathbf{0} \\ \omega_1\$_1 + \omega_2\$_2 + \omega_3\$_3 + \omega_4\$_4 + \omega_5\$_5 + \omega_6\$_6 \\ +\omega_7\$_7 + \omega_8\$_8 + \omega_{25}\$_{25} + \omega_{19}\$_{19} + \omega_{20}\$_{20} = \mathbf{0} \end{cases} \quad (7)$$

where ω_i represents the angular velocity of R_i joint and $\mathbf{0}$ is a 6×1 matrix. Equation (7) can be simplified to the following equation:

$$\mathbf{MN} = \mathbf{0} \quad (8)$$

where

$$\mathbf{N} = \begin{bmatrix} \omega_1 & \omega_2 & \omega_3 & \dots & \omega_{23} & \omega_{24} & \omega_{25} \end{bmatrix}^{\mathrm{T}} \quad (9)$$

$$
\begin{cases}
\mathbf{M}_1 = \left(\$_1 \; \$_2 \; 0 \; 0 \; 0\right) \; \mathbf{M}_2 = \left(0 \; 0 \; 0 \; 0 \; 0\right) \\
\mathbf{M}_3 = \left(-\$_{11} \; -\$_{12} \; 0 \; 0 \; 0\right) \; \mathbf{M}_4 = \left(-\$_{21} \; -\$_{22} \; 0 \; 0 \; 0\right) \\
\mathbf{M}_5 = \left(0 \; 0 \; \$_3 \; \$_4 \; 0\right) \; \mathbf{M}_6 = \left(0 \; 0 \; -\$_{13} \; -\$_{14} \; 0\right) \\
\mathbf{M}_7 = \left(0 \; -\$_{22} \; 0 \; 0 \; 0\right) \; \mathbf{M}_8 = \left(0 \; 0 \; 0 \; 0 \; \$_5\right) \\
\mathbf{M}_9 = \left(\$_6 \; 0 \; 0 \; 0 \; 0\right) \; \mathbf{M}_{10} = \left(0 \; 0 \; 0 \; 0 \; -\$_{15}\right) \\
\mathbf{M}_{11} = \left(-\$_{16} \; 0 \; 0 \; 0 \; 0\right) \; \mathbf{M}_{12} = \left(0 \; 0 \; -\$_{23} \; \$_{24} \; 0\right) \\
\mathbf{M}_{13} = \left(0 \; \$_7 \; \$_8 \; 0 \; 0\right) \; \mathbf{M}_{14} = \left(0 \; -\$_{17} \; -\$_{18} \; 0 \; 0\right) \\
\mathbf{M}_{15} = \left(0 \; 0 \; 0 \; -\$_{24} \; \$_{25}\right) \; \mathbf{M}_{16} = \left(\$_{11} \; \$_{12} \; \$_{13} \; \$_{14} \; \$_{15}\right) \\
\mathbf{M}_{17} = \left(\$_{16} \; \$_{17} \; \$_{18} \; \$_{19} \; \$_{20}\right) \; \mathbf{M}_{18} = \left(\$_{21} \; 0 \; 0 \; 0 \; 0\right) \\
\mathbf{M}_{19} = \left(\$_1 \; \$_2 \; \$_3 \; \$_4 \; \$_5\right) \; \mathbf{M}_{20} = \left(\$_6 \; \$_7 \; \$_8 \; \$_9 \; \$_{10}\right) \\
\mathbf{M}_{21} = \left(-\$_{21} \; 0 \; 0 \; 0 \; 0\right)
\end{cases}
\tag{10}
$$

$$
\mathbf{M} = \begin{bmatrix}
\mathbf{M}_1 & \mathbf{M}_2 & \mathbf{M}_3 & \mathbf{M}_2 & \mathbf{M}_4 \\
\mathbf{M}_5 & \mathbf{M}_2 & \mathbf{M}_6 & \mathbf{M}_2 & \mathbf{M}_7 \\
\mathbf{M}_8 & \mathbf{M}_9 & \mathbf{M}_{10} & \mathbf{M}_{11} & \mathbf{M}_{12} \\
\mathbf{M}_2 & \mathbf{M}_{13} & \mathbf{M}_2 & \mathbf{M}_{14} & \mathbf{M}_{15} \\
\mathbf{M}_2 & \mathbf{M}_2 & \mathbf{M}_{16} & \mathbf{M}_{17} & \mathbf{M}_{18} \\
\mathbf{M}_{19} & \mathbf{M}_{20} & \mathbf{M}_2 & \mathbf{M}_2 & \mathbf{M}_{21}
\end{bmatrix}
\tag{11}
$$

The screw constraint matrix $\mathbf{M}$ is a 36×25 matrix, and the DOF of the deployable mechanism unit is equivalent to the zero-space dimension of the screw constraint matrix $\mathbf{M}$, which can be calculated by MATLAB software.

$$
rank(\mathbf{M}) = 24
\tag{12}
$$

The number of columns in the matrix $\mathbf{M}$ is 25, and the DOF of the deployable mechanism unit can be obtained as 1.

When this units are used to form a ring truss expandable mechanism, the strategy of shared edge lines is adopted. In this case, each unit has two sets of scissors mechanisms occupied by adjacent units separately at the same time. In the case of the proposed ring truss deployable antenna mechanism in this paper, the DOF of the unit is equal to 1, which means that only one parameter is needed to depict the positions and postures of all the components in the unit mechanism. For example, using the scissors mechanism angle β as the generalized coordinate in Fig. 5, the position coordinate of the R_{F1} joint can be expressed as $\left(l_{E_3E_2} + l_{E_2F_1}\cos(\beta) \; 0 \; 0\right)$. The rest of the joints and components of the mechanism unit are expressed in a similar form.

When the edge sharing strategy is used to form a ring truss deployable antenna mechanism, the scissors mechanisms of all units within the ring truss deployable mechanism have the same angle, i.e., there is synchronization between the units. Further, by taking the angle of the scissors mechanism in any one unit as a generalized coordinate, then all the components of the whole ring truss deployable mechanism can be described using this generalized coordinate. The above analysis shows that theDOF of the whole ring truss deployable mechanism composed of this mechanism unit is still equal to one (Fig. 7).

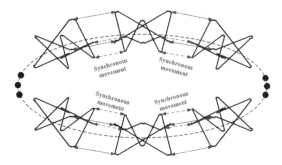

Fig. 7. Synchronous movement of ring truss deployable mechanism

4   Ring Truss Deployable Mechanism Speed Analysis

From the above analysis, it can be seen that this ring truss deployable mechanism has only one DOF, therefore, if the revolute speed of one joints, such as ω_1, is given, the angular velocities of the remaining members can be solved. For example, the screw velocity of each member in the closed-loop I shown in Fig. 6 can all be obtained by vector operation as follows:

$$
\begin{cases}
\mathbf{V}_E = 0 \\
\mathbf{V}_{EA*} = \omega_{20}\$_{20} \\
\mathbf{V}_{A*} = \omega_{20}\$_{20} + \omega_1\$_1 \\
\mathbf{V}_{BA*} = \omega_{20}\$_{20} + \omega_1\$_1 + \omega_2\$_2 \\
\mathbf{V}_{AB*} = \omega_{20}\$_{20} + \omega_1\$_1 + \omega_2\$_2 + \omega_{22}\$_{22} \\
\mathbf{V}_{AE*} = \omega_{20}\$_{20} + \omega_{21}\$_{21} \\
\mathbf{V}_A = \omega_{20}\$_{20} + \omega_{21}\$_{21} + \omega_{11}\$_{11} \\
\mathbf{V}_{AB*} = \omega_{20}\$_{20} + \omega_{21}\$_{21} + \omega_{11}\$_{11} + \omega_{12}\$_{12}
\end{cases}
\tag{13}
$$

where, $\mathbf{V}_i$ denotes the screw velocity of component i.

Similarly, the screw velocities of the remaining components in Fig. 6 can be obtained. According to the characteristics of the screw velocity, the angular velocity vector of each component can be expressed as:

$$
\boldsymbol{\omega}_i = \omega(\mathbf{V}_i)
\tag{14}
$$

where $\omega(\cdot)$ is an operator symbol indicating the first three terms of the vector in the brackets. The centroid linear velocity of the component i can be obtained as:

$$
\mathbf{v}_i = v(\mathbf{V}_i) + \omega(\mathbf{V}_i) \times \boldsymbol{r}_i
\tag{15}
$$

where the $v(\cdot)$ is a vector represents the last three of the screw velocity, ri is a distance vector from the coordinate origin to the centroid of the component.

Since all the units of the ring truss deployable mechanism are identical and the whole ring is highly symmetric about the center, if the coordinate system is established separately for each unit, the velocities of the components in each unit are the same in their own coordinate system during the deployment process. The velocity expressions for all components in a fixed coordinate system can be obtained by transforming the matrix. As in Fig. 8, if a ring truss developable mechanism consists of N basic units, the angle between adjacent coordinate systems X-axis is θ, whose value is equal to $360/N$. Choose O_1-$X_1Y_1Z_1$ as the fixed coordinate system, and the component velocity of the whole ring truss deployable mechanism in the fixed coordinate system can be expressed as:

$$
\begin{cases}
{}^{O_1}v_i = {}^{O_1}_{O_j}R\,{}^{O_j}v_i + \sum_{k=1}^{j} {}^{O_1}_{O_k}R\,{}^{O_{k-1}}v_{O_k} \\
{}^{O_1}\omega_i = {}^{O_1}_{O_j}R\,{}^{O_j}\omega_i + \sum_{k=1}^{j} {}^{O_1}_{O_k}R\,{}^{O_{k-1}}\omega_{O_k}
\end{cases}
\tag{16}
$$

where i represents the component number and j represents the coordinate system number. The expression of the transformation matrix R is:

$$
{}^{O}_{O_j}R =
\begin{bmatrix}
\cos j\theta & -\sin j\theta & 0 \\
\sin j\theta & \cos j\theta & 0 \\
0 & 0 & 1
\end{bmatrix}
\tag{17}
$$

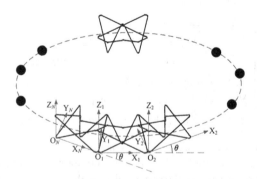

Fig. 8. Speed calculation of ring truss deployable mechanism

The final deployable process of the mechanism is shown in Fig. 9. The figure shows the transformation of the outermost feature points of the ring truss during the development process, and it can be calculated that the ratio of the developed area to the closed area of the ring truss deployable mechanism is 43.6 when $\beta = 100°$.

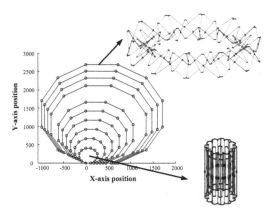

Fig. 9. Kinematic diagram

5   Dynamics Analysis of Ring Truss Deployable Mechanism

The ring truss deployable antenna mechanism is an important large space equipment with strict weight requirement. In order to reduce the weight of the antenna, elastic elements are used as actuations to make the mechanism complete the deployment process, but these passive elements cannot be controlled in real time. In this paper, the dynamics of the passively driven deployable mechanism unit is established according to the second Lagrange equation to study its deployment process.

$$\frac{d}{dt}\frac{\partial E_v}{\partial \dot{\beta}} - \frac{\partial E_v}{\partial \beta} + \frac{\partial E_P}{\partial \beta} = Q \tag{18}$$

where E_v and E_P are the kinetic and potential energies of deployable units and Q is the generalized driving force.

During deployment, all connecting components A, B, C, D, E, A*, B*, C*, D*, E* have only translational motion, linkages A*E, D*E have only rotational motion, and the rest of the linkages have a composite motion of rotation and translation. For example, the kinetic energy of component A and linkage EA* can be expressed respectively as:

$$\begin{cases} E_A = \frac{1}{2}m_A v_A^2 \\ E_{AE*} = \frac{1}{2}J_{AE*}\omega_{AE*}^2 \end{cases} \tag{19}$$

Because the working place of the mechanism unit is in space, there is almost no gravity. The mechanism unit is deployed only by elastic potential energy, and there is no generalized driving force for the whole deployment process, i.e., $Q = 0$. If torsion springs with stiffnesses k_1, k_2, k_3, k_4, and k_5 are added to the R joint F_1, F_2, F_3, F_4, and F_5 of the five groups of scissor mechanisms, respectively, and the initial compression is β_0, the elastic potential energy of the mechanism unit in the initial state can be expressed as:

$$E_P = \sum_{t=1}^{5} \frac{1}{2} k_t \beta_0^2 \tag{20}$$

Substituting Eqs. (19), (20) and Q into Eq. (18) yields the dynamics equations describing the deployment process of the mechanism unit under the passive actuations.

$$(C_{11} + C_{21})\ddot{\beta} + (C_{12} + C_{22})\dot{\beta}^2 + C_3\beta + C_4 = 0 \tag{21}$$

6 Dynamics Simulation

The basic parameters of each component in the unit are shown in Tables 1, 2 and 3. The mechanism dynamics Eq. (21) is a nonlinear higher order differential equation with no analytical solution. The numerical solution is solved by the Runge-Kutta method and the simulation model is established by ADAMS software. Figure 10 shows the deployment of the mechanism unit when using the passive actuation, and the two curves representing the theoretical and simulated displacement values of the component A* coincide exactly.

Table 1. Mass parameters

m_A (g)	m_B (g)	m_{B*} (g)	m_C (g)	m_{AE} (g)	m_{AB*} (g)	m_{BC*} (g)
10.98	5.98	1.94	6.85	53.87	42.74	37.17

Table 2. Rotational inertia parameters

J_{AE} (g*m^2)	J_{AB} (g*m^2)	J_{BC} (g*m^2)
2.836	1.266	0.446

When torsion springs of different stiffnesses are added as actuation, the system has different elastic potentials that affect the deployment process of the mechanism. Combining Eq. (20) and Eq. (21), with the same initial compression, the effect of each torsion spring stiffness on its own driving torque and the driving torque of other torsion springs is:

$$\tau_i = \frac{k_i}{\sum_{t=1}^{5} k_t} \cdot \frac{(C_{11} + C_{21})\ddot{\beta} + (C_{12} + C_{22})\dot{\beta}^2}{2} \tag{22}$$

Table 3. Spring parameter

$k1$ (N·mm/°)	k_2 (N·mm/°)	k_3 (N·mm/°)	k_4 (N·mm/°)	k_5 (N·mm/°)
0.05	0.05	0.05	0.05	0.05

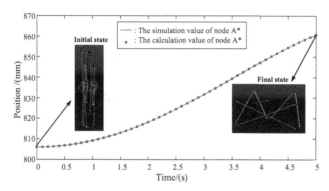

Fig. 10. Displacement simulation and calculation

where τ_i denotes the torque provided by torsion spring i to the mechanism unit.

From Eq. (22), it can be seen that when the total stiffness of the torsion spring remains the same, the total torque provided by the spring for the mechanism is the same and the mechanism has the same deployment process, as shown in Fig. 11. The total stiffness of the torsion springs is set to 0.25 N mm/°, and the stiffness of each of the five torsion springs were taken from Table 4. From Fig. 11, although the spring stiffnesses are different in the five sets of data, the mechanism deployment process identically when maintaining the same total stiffness.

Table 4. Experimental data

k_1 (N·mm/°)	k_2 (N·mm/°)	k_3 (N·mm/°)	k_4 (N·mm/°)	k_5 (N·mm/°)
0.25	0	0	0	0
0.05	0.05	0.1	0	0.05
0.1	0	0.1	0	0.05
0.15	0	0	0.1	0
0	0	0.25	0	0

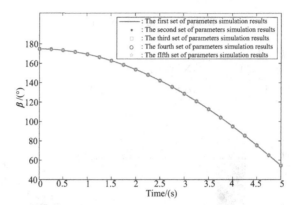

Fig. 11. Five simulation results

7 Conclusion

The ring truss deployable mechanism as the support platform of the ring deployable antenna, the research on it was significant. In this paper, a ring truss deployable antenna mechanism with three layers of cable network installation points was proposed. Following this, the DOF analysis and kinematic were carried out using screw theory, and the results showed that the mechanism has only one DOF. The single DOF feature ensured that the mechanism could deploy without the use of synchronous joints. The subsequent analysis was carried out for the deployment process of the mechanism unit under passive actuation, and the relationship between the deployment process and the total stiffness of the added passive actuation is given.

The proposed ring truss deployable mechanism with high reliability in deployment process can be well applied in the aerospace field and the theoretical analysis method can also be well applied to other deployable mechanisms.

Acknowledgement. This work was supported by the National Natural Science Foundation of China [Grant No. 52105035 & 52075467], the Natural Science Foundation of Hebei Province of China [Grant No. E2021203109], the State Key Laboratory of Robotics and Systems (HIT) [Grant No. SKLRS-2021-KF-15], and the Industrial Robot Control and Reliability Technology Innovation Center of Hebei Province [Grant No. JXKF2105].

References

1. Kim, T.H., Suh, J.E., Han, J.H.: Deployable truss structure with flat-form storability using scissor-like elements. Mech. Mach. Theory **159**, 104252 (2021)
2. Chen, Z.J., Shi, C., Guo, H.W., Liu, R.Q., Deng, Z.Q.: Design and optimization of new space modular planar antenna. Aerosp. Sci. Technol. **123**, 107442 (2022)
3. Wang, S., Huang, H.L., Jia, G.L., Li, B., Guo, H.W., Liu, R.Q.: Design of a novel three-limb deployable mechanism with mobility bifurcation. Mech. Mach. Theory **172**, 104789 (2022)
4. Morozov, E.V., Lopatin, A.V., Khakhlenkova, A.A.: Finite-element modelling, analysis and design of anisogrid composite lattice spoke of an umbrella-type deployable reflector of space antenna. Compos. Struct. **286**, 115323 (2022)

5. Lopatin, A.V., Morozov, E.V.: Modal analysis of the thin-walled composite spoke of an umbrella-type deployable space antenna. Compos. Struct. **88**, 46–55 (2009)
6. Tang, Y.Q., Shi, Z.Y., Li, T.J., Wang, Z.W.: Double-layer cable-net structures for deployable umbrella reflectors. J. Aerosp. Eng. **32**, 04019068 (2019)
7. Guo, J.W., Zhao, Y.S., Xu, Y.D., Zhang, G.X., Yao, J.T.: A novel modular deployable mechanism for the truss antenna: assembly principle and performance analysis. Aerosp. Sci. Techol. **105**, 105976 (2020)
8. Xu, Y., Guan, F.L.: Structure–electronic synthesis design of deployable truss antenna. Aerosp. Sci. Technol. **26**, 259–267 (2013)
9. Guo, J., Zhao, Y., Zhang, G., Liu, E., Liu, B., Xu, Y.: Configuration synthesis and unfolding stiffness characteristics analysis of a truss antenna connecting mechanism based on URU-RR-URU hexagonal deployable unit. Mech. Mach. Theory **177**, 105047 (2022)
10. Sun, Z.H., Yang, D.W., Duan, B.Y., Kong, L.B., Zhang, Y.Q.: Structural design, dynamic analysis, and verification test of a novel double-ring deployable truss for mesh antennas. Mech. Mach. Theory **165**, 104416 (2021)
11. Datashvili, L., Endler, S., Wei, B.: Study of mechanical architectures of large deployable space antenna apertures: from design to tests. CEAS Space J. **5**, 169–184 (2013)
12. Han, B., Xu, Y.D., Yao, J.T., Zheng, D., Guo, X.Y., Zhao, Y.S.: Configuration synthesis of hoop truss deployable mechanisms for space antenna based on screw theory. AIP Adv. **9**, 085201 (2019)
13. Han, B., Xu, Y.D., Yao, J.T., Zheng, D., Guo, L.Y., Zhao, Y.S.: Type synthesis of deployable mechanisms for ring truss antenna based on constraint-synthesis method. Chin. J. Aeronaut. **33**, 2445–2460 (2020)
14. Cao, W.A., Xi, S., Ding, H., Chen, Z.M.: Design and kinematics of a novel double-ring truss deployable antenna mechanism. J. Mech. Des. **143**(12), 124502 (2021)
15. Meng, Q.Z., Liu, X.J., Xie, F.G.: Structure design and kinematic analysis of a class of ring truss deployable mechanisms for satellite antennas based on novel basic units. Mech. Mach. Theory **174**, 104881 (2022)
16. Cao, W.-A., Cheng, P.: Design and kinematic analysis of a novel deployable antenna mechanism for synthetic aperture radar satellites. J. Mech. Des. **144**, 114502 (2022)

Model-Based Performance Enhancement for Compound Twisted and Coiled Actuators

Hao Zhang[1,2], Guilin Yang[1(✉)], Haohao Zhang[1,2], Tianjiang Zheng[1], Tao Chen[1], and Chi Zhang[1]

[1] Ningbo Institute of Materials Technology and Engineering, Chinese Academy of Sciences, Ningbo 315201, China
glyang@nimte.ac.cn
[2] University of Chinese Academy of Sciences, Beijing 100049, China

Abstract. Twisted and Coiled Actuators (TCAs) are a class of new artificial muscles for flexible actuations. However, the existing TCAs are difficult to achieve large output force and long stroke simultaneously, which limits their application. In this paper, a Compound TCA (CTCA) based on spandex fibers and an SMA skeleton is developed. The spandex bundle is spirally wound on the surface of the SMA wire with large number of spiral turns, and the SMA skeleton forms a coil, which can produce additional contraction force for the CTCA owing to the shape memory effect of the SMA wire. To further improve the performance of CTCA, a pre-twisting process for spandex bundle is employed. An analytical model is established for pre-twisting turns based on the elastic rod theory to predict the critical pre-twisting turns with respect to the number of spandex fibers and the draw ratio of spandex bundle. Experiments are conducted to verify the accuracy of the critical pre-twisting turns analysis model. The CTCA fabricated by critical pre-twisting turns exhibits a maximum contraction strain of 44.4 % under load of 350 g and a maximum thermal untwisting torque of 1.44 $N \cdot mm$.

Keywords: Artificial muscle · Compound twisted and coiled actuator · Performance enhancement

1 Introduction

Soft robots have better human-robot interaction safety and environmental adaptability compared to traditional rigid robots due to their high compliance [1–3]. The artificial muscle is the key component to produce motion and force for soft robots [4–7]. Inspired by biological muscles, various types of artificial muscles

This work was supported in part by the Zhejiang Provincial Natural Science Foundation of China under Grants LD22E050008, in part by the National Natural Science Foundation of China under Grants U1909215.

have been developed, including mckibben artificial muscles [8], Dielectric Elastomer Actuators (DEAs) [9], Shape Memory Alloy (SMA) [10]. However, their performances such as output force, strain, fabrication cost, cycle life, and system complexity are still difficut for actual applications.

To overcome such difficulties, polymer fiber-based Twisted and Coiled Actuators (TCAs) are a promising type of artificial muscles due to their large contraction strain, low cost, and long cycle life [11–14]. The TCA is driven by the thermal untwisting torque caused by the twisted fiber [15]. Consequently, the stroke of the TCA is increased with the critical twisting turns (N_c), and the untwisting torque is increased with the fiber diameter (d). To further improvement the performance of the TCA, a new Compound TCA (CTCA) based on spandex fibers and an SMA skeleton is developed, which can has larger N_c and d compared with the conventional TCA configuration [16]. To obtain the designated CTCA configuration, a new compound twisting fabrication process is proposed utilizing the significant stiffness difference between the SMA wire and spandex fibers (ten times). However, due to the small radial stiffness of spandex fiber bundles, radial deformation occurs during compound twisting, resulting in a lower actual N_c than the theoretical value.

In this paper, a pre-twisting process for spandex bundle is proposed to enhance the radial stiffness, which can increase the N_c and d for the CTCA. Therefore, the stroke and output force of CTCA are improved. A critical pre-twisting turns analysis model based on the elastic rod theory is established to predict the critical pre-twisting turns (N_{pc}) with respect to the number of spandex fibers and the draw ratio of spandex bundle. Then, the critical pre-twisting turns analysis model is verified by experimental results, and finally the contraction strain and the thermal untwisting torque of CTCA fabricated by N_{pc} are evaluated.

The rest of this paper is organized as follows. Section 2 presents the thermal contraction principle, fabrication process, and performance enhancement method of the CTCA. A critical pre-twisting turns analysis model is established. In Section 3, both simulation and experimental studies are conducted to validate the proposed critical pre-twisting analysis model and evaluate the performance of the CTCAs. Section 4 presents the conclusion of this paper.

2   Materials and Methods

2.1   Design and Fabrication of CTCA

The configuration of CTCA is shown in Fig. 1, which consists of a SMA wire skeleton and a spandex bundle. The spandex bundle are spirally wound on the surface of the SMA wire skeleton. The N_c is defined as the maximum number of fiber bundle turns wound on the surface of the SMA wire skeleton, which can be written as:

$$N_c = \frac{1}{d},\tag{1}$$

where d is the diameter of the spandex bundle. Spandex is an anisotropic material that exhibits axial contraction when heating. The contraction will cause the spandex bundle and SMA wire compound structure to untwist, and the spring-like structure of the CTCAs can convert the untwisted rotation into the linear contraction.

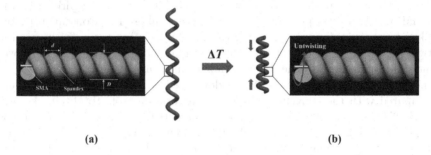

(a)   (b)

Fig. 1. Thermal contraction principle of CTCA. (a) Initial configuration of the CTCA; (b) CTCA contracts when heating.

To obtain the designated CTCA configuration, a new compound twisting fabrication process is proposed, as shown in Fig. 2(a). Utilizing the significant stiffness difference between the SMA wire and spandex fibers, a compound twisting process is employed. First, straighten both the SMA wire and the pre-treated spandex fiber bundle and let them parallel to each other. Then, keep their lengths fixed and twist them together. Since the stiffness of the SMA wire is more than ten times higher than that of the spandex fibers, the SMA wire can twist around its own axis and remain straight, while the spandex fiber bundle is stretched and wound on the surface of the SMA wire.

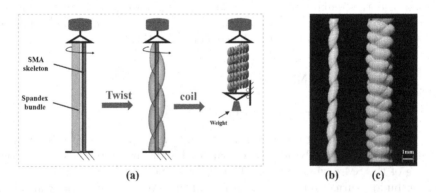

(a)   (b)   (c)

Fig. 2. (a) Fabrication process of the CTCA; (b) optical image of compound twisted fiber structure; (c) optical image of coiled structure.

Due to the low radial stiffness of spandex fiber bundle, it undergo deformation under radial force when twisted with SMA, resulting in N_c being less than the theoretical value. In order to improve the radial stiffness of spandex bundle, a pre-twisting method has been proposed, as shown in Fig. 3. In the initial state, the fiber bundle is oriented uniformly and parallel to the neutral axis. When the fibers are twisted, their orientation tilts relative to the neutral axis, and the fiber orientation angle is denoted as α, while the fiber bundle generates circumferential force $F_{spx} \cos(\alpha)$. The radial stiffness will increase while increasing the pre-twisting number.

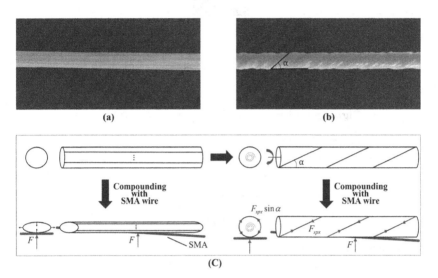

Fig. 3. Performance enhancement principle of CTCA; (a) non-twisted spandex bundle; (b) twisted spandex bundle; (c) spandex bundle and SMA wire compound twisting.

2.2   Analysis Model of Critical Pre-twisting Turns

In order to enhance the driving performance of CTCA, the pre-twisting method is employed. However, there is also a critical value for pre-twisting of spandex bundles. We define this critical pre-twisting numbers as N_{pc}.

Figure 4(a) shows the pre-twisting process of the spandex fiber bundle. A spandex fiber bundle composed of multiple spandex fibers is pre-stretched and fixed in length, and the output shaft of the motor rotates to twist the spandex fiber bundle. When the number of pre-twisting turns exceeds N_{pc}, the spandex bundle will be unstable, and the coordinate system is shown in Fig. 4(b). The spandex bundle subjected to the action of an axial force P and a twisting couple M. According to the constraint condition that one end of the fiber bundle is hinged and the other end is free, the deflection approximation differential equation of the beam can be obtained:

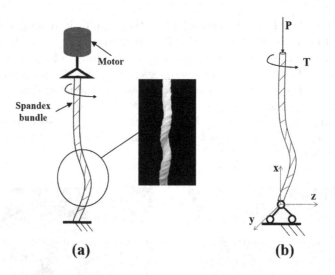

Fig. 4. Spandex fiber bundle pre-twisting instability

$$EI\frac{d^2z}{dx^2} = Pz + T\frac{dy}{dx}. \tag{2}$$

$$EI\frac{d^2y}{dx^2} = Py + T\frac{dz}{dx}. \tag{3}$$

The boundary conditions:

$$z_{x=0} = 0, z_{x=l} = 0, \tag{4}$$

$$y_{x=0} = 0, y_{x=l} = 0, \tag{5}$$

where E and I are the elastic modulus and moment of inertia of the spandex fiber respectively. Solving the differential equations according to the boundary conditions gives:

$$\left(\frac{T}{2\pi EI/_l}\right)^2 = \left(\frac{F}{\pi^2 EI/_{l^2}}\right)^2 + 1. \tag{6}$$

Since the length of fiber bundle is much larger than the diameter, Eq. (6) is simplified as:

$$F = \frac{T^2}{4EI}. \tag{7}$$

For torsional deformation of spandex fiber bundle, we have:

$$\tau = \frac{TD}{2I_p}. \tag{8}$$

$$\gamma = \frac{\pi N_{pc}D}{l}. \tag{9}$$

where τ and γ are the shear stress and shear strain of the spandex fiber, respectively. I_p and D are the polar moment of inertia and diameter of the fiber bundle, respectively. According to the Hooke's law, we have:

$$\tau = G\gamma, \tag{10}$$

where G is the shear modulus of spandex fiber. Substituting Eq. (9) $\sim$ (10) to Eq. (7), N_{pc} can be written as:

$$N_{pc} = \left[\frac{2\sqrt{2(1+\nu)}}{\pi\sqrt{G}}\right]\frac{\sqrt{\sigma\lambda}}{d_0\sqrt{m}}, \tag{11}$$

where $\nu = 0.47$ is the Poisson's ratio of spandex fiber, d_0, m are the diameter and number of polyurethane protofilaments in the spandex fiber bundle, respectively. λ and σ are the stretching rate and the stress generated by the stretching of spandex fiber bundle, respectively.

Since spandex bundle belongs to hyper elastic fiber, its constitutive relation is highly nonlinear. The strain energy function is used to characterize the relationship between the stress and strain in deformation.

$$\sigma_i = \lambda_i\frac{\partial W\left(\lambda_1, \lambda_2, \lambda_3\right)}{\partial\lambda_i}, \tag{12}$$

where $W\left(\lambda_1, \lambda_2, \lambda_3\right)$ is the Helmholtz free energy associated with stretching the elastomer. During deformation of the spandex fibers, only uniaxial stretching occurs. Therefore, (10) become:

$$\begin{aligned}\sigma =&2\left(\lambda^2 - \lambda^{-1}\right)\\&\left[c_{10} + 2c_{20}\left(\lambda^2 + 2\lambda^{-1} - 3\right) + 3c_{30}\left(\lambda^2 + 2\lambda^{-1} - 3\right)^2\right]\end{aligned} \tag{13}$$

where λ is the axial stretch rate of spandex fiber. c_{10}, c_{20}, c_{30} are model parameters in Yeoh model [17].

3 Experiments and Results

3.1 Validation of the Critical Pre-twisting Turn Analyzing Model

To validate the proposed critical pre-twisting turn analyzing model, the experiments have been conducted with five different numbers of spandex fibers m (8, 12, 16, 20, and 24). For the spandex bundle with one out of the five given m, three different draw ratios (1.2, 1.5, and 2.0) are employed. Figure 5(a) shows the N_{pc} of the CTCA from both the theoretical model and the experimental measurement. The three parameters (c_{10}, c_{20}, c_{30}) of Yeoh material model are identified through the spandex uniaxial tensile experiment, which are 0.8079, 0.0158 and 0.0004, respectively, and G is equal to 5.6 Mpa. A good agreement between the simulation and experimental results are obtained under different m and draw ratio conditions. Consequently, the optimum number of pre-twisting turn is obtained, under two inputs, i.e. the number of spandex fibers and draw ratio of spandex, which is plotted in Fig. 5(b).

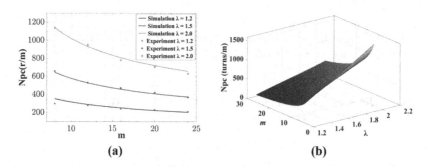

Fig. 5. (a) Simulation and experimental results for the critical pre-twisting turn analysis model; (b) the critical pre-twisting turns with respect to the number of spandex fibers and the draw ratio of spandex bundle.

3.2 Performance Evaluation of CTCA

To evaluate the performance of the CTCAs fabricated by the pre-twisting turns of N_{pc} , an experimental setup is devised. The purpose of these experiments is to measure the contraction displacement of the CTCAs when heated under different loads and the contraction force of the CTCAs under different temperatures. The experimental setup as shown in Fig. 6 consists of a laser displacement sensor (HG-C1400, Panasonic), a load cell (SBT904, SimBaTouch), a programmable DC power supply (HLR-3660D, Heng Hui), a thermocouple (type-T, Omega), and a National Instrument DAQ for data collection.

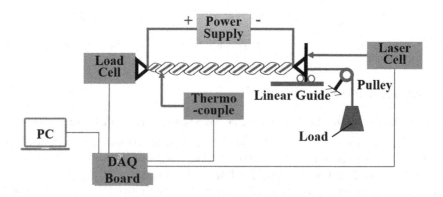

Fig. 6. Schematic diagram of the experimental setup for characterization of the CTCAs.

Two CTCA prototypes are fabricated, and the fabrication parameters and properties of the prototypes are list in Table 1. The experiments are conducted at seven different loads (200, 250, 300, 350, 400, 450, and 500 g). For the particular CTCAs in this experiment, when the SMA skeleton connects to the power supply,

Table 1. Properties of the prototypes with different pre-twisting turns.

Parameter	Initial length of spandex bundle	Spandex fiber number	Draw ratio	Pre-twisting turns	Fabricatio load	Critical twisting turns	Diameter of compound structure
Prototype 1	0.1 m	24	2	0 r/m	900 g	90 r	1.16
Prototype 2	0.1 m	24	2	600 r/m	750 g	130 r	1.36

a square current of 0.5 A lasts for 30 s can heat the CTCAs from 25°C to 55°C, which is measured by the thermal imager. The experimental results are shown in Fig. 7. It can be clearly seen that the contraction strain of CTCA fabricated by critical pre-twisting turns can be significantly increased. The highest contraction strain is peaking at 44.4 %, which is 130.1 % enhancement compared to the CTCA without pre-twisting.

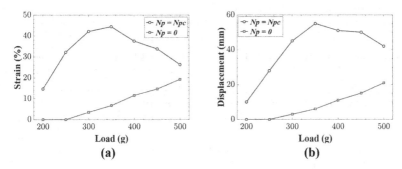

Fig. 7. (a) Contraction displacement versus load at 55°C; (b) contraction strain versus load at 55°C.

To evaluate the thermal untwisting torque performance of CTCA fabricated by critical pre-twisting turns, experiments have been conducted. Because the untwisting torque is very little and hard to measure, the thermal untwisting torque is determined by measurement the contraction force of CTCA. The thermal untwisting torque analysis of the CTCA in heating process is shown in Fig. 8(a). The torque can be written as:

$$T = \frac{\Delta F \cdot D}{2}, \tag{14}$$

where D is the diameter of the CTCA. The experimental results are shown in Fig. 8(b). The relationships between the thermal untwisting torque and the driving temperature are all approximately linear. Furthermore, fabricated by the critical pre-twisting turns significantly increases the torque compared with the conventional configuration, and the maximum increases is 19.7%. It is note that the length of CTCA remains constant during the heating process.

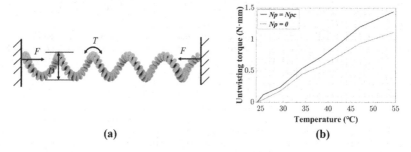

(a)   **(b)**

Fig. 8. (a) Thermal untwisting torque analysis of the CTCA in heating process; (b) the thermal untwisting torque of CTCA with different pre-twisting turns.

4   Conclusions

This paper investigates the configuration design, fabrication, and model-based performance enhancement approach of the CTCA. A new compound twisted and coiled actuator (CTCA) based on the spandex fibers and an SMA skeleton is designed, which has larger critical twisting turns compared with the conventional configuration. The compound twisting fabrication process is also proposed to achieve the designated CTCA configuration. In order to further improve the performance of CTCA, a pre-twisting method is employed to improve the critical twisting turns and diameter of CTCA. A critical pre-twisting turns analysis model based on the elastic rod theory is established to predict the critical pre-twisting turns with respect to the number of spandex fibers and the draw ratio of spandex bundle. The model shows a good agreement with the experimental results. Experimental evaluation has shown that the CTCA fabricated by critical pre-twisting turns achieves maximum contraction strain of 44.4 % and maximum untwisting torque of 1.44 $N \cdot mm$.

References

1. Rus, D., Tolley, M.T.: Design, fabrication and control of soft robots. Nature **521**(7553), 467–475 (2015)
2. Gu, G., Zou, J., Zhao, R., Zhao, X., Zhu, X.: Soft wall-climbing robots. Sci. Robot. **3**(25), eaat2874 (2018)
3. El-Atab, N., et al.: Soft actuators for soft robotic applications: a review. Adv. Intell. Syst. **2**(10), 2000128 (2020)
4. Mirvakili, S.M., Hunter, I.W.: Artificial muscles: mechanisms, applications, and challenges. Adv. Mater. **30**(6), 1704407 (2018)
5. Chen, Y., et al.: Controlled flight of a microrobot powered by soft artificial muscles. Nature **575**(7782), 324–329 (2019)
6. Zhang, J., et al.: Robotic artificial muscles: current progress and future perspectives. IEEE Trans. Robot. **35**(3), 761–781 (2019)

7. Tsabedze, T., Mullen, C., Coulter, R., Wade, S., Zhang, J.: Helically wrapped supercoiled polymer (HW-SCP) artificial muscles: design, characterization, and modeling. In: 2020 IEEE International Conference on Robotics and Automation (ICRA), pp. 5862–5868. IEEE (2020)
8. Alici, G., Canty, T., Mutlu, R., Hu, W., Sencadas, V.: Modeling and experimental evaluation of bending behavior of soft pneumatic actuators made of discrete actuation chambers. Soft Robot. **5**(1), 24–35 (2018)
9. Pelrine, R., Kornbluh, R., Pei, Q., Joseph, J.: High-speed electrically actuated elastomers with strain greater than 100%. Science **287**(5454), 836–839 (2000)
10. Lu, Y., Xie, Z., Wang, J., Yue, H., Wu, M., Liu, Y.: A novel design of a parallel gripper actuated by a large-stroke shape memory alloy actuator. Int. J. Mech. Sci. **159**, 74–80 (2019)
11. Haines, C.S., et al.: Artificial muscles from fishing line and sewing thread. Science **343**(6173), 868–872 (2014)
12. Sun, J., Tighe, B., Liu, Y., Zhao, J.: Twisted-and-coiled actuators with free strokes enable soft robots with programmable motions. Soft Robot. **8**(2), 213–225 (2021)
13. Li, M., Tang, Y., Soon, R.H., Dong, B., Hu, W., Sitti, M.: Miniature coiled artificial muscle for wireless soft medical devices. Sci. Adv. **8**(10), eabm5616 (2022)
14. Higueras-Ruiz, D.R., Shafer, M.W., Feigenbaum, H.P.: Cavatappi artificial muscles from drawing, twisting, and coiling polymer tubes. Sci. Robot. **6**(53), eabd5383 (2021)
15. Zhou, D., Liu, Y., Deng, J., Sun, J., Fu, Y.: Force enhanced multi-twisted and coiled actuator and its application in temperature self-adaptive tensegrity mechanisms. IEEE/ASME Trans. Mechatron. **27**(5), 3964–3976 (2022)
16. Zhang, H., et al.: Design and modeling of a compound twisted and coiled actuator based on spandex fibers and an SMA skeleton. IEEE Robot. Autom. Lett. **7**(2), 1439–1446 (2021)
17. Renaud, C., Cros, J.M., Feng, Z.Q., Yang, B.: The Yeoh model applied to the modeling of large deformation contact/impact problems. Int. J. Impact Eng **36**(5), 659–666 (2009)

Lightweight Design Method of Stacker Column Structure Based on Multi-parameter Sensitivity Analysis

Yuxin Li[1,4], Zhong Luo[1,4(✉)], Wenjie Chen[2,3(✉)], Wenjing Wu[2,3], Mingliang Jin[2,3], Baolong Shi[1,4], and Pengfei Wang[2,3]

[1] School of Mechanical Engineering and Automation, Northeastern University, Shenyang 110819, China
zhluo@mail.neu.edu.cn
[2] Midea Corporate Research Center, Shanghai 201702, Foshan 528300, China
chenwj42@midea.com
[3] Blue-Orange Lab., Midea Group, Foshan 528300, China
[4] Foshan Graduate Innovation School of Northeastern University, Foshan 528312, China

Abstract. Aiming at the problem of mass redundancy of stacker column in traditional empirical design, a lightweight design method of stacker column structure based on multi-parameter analysis and response surface methodology is proposed. Initially, an analysis is conducted on the stacker crane's column structure to uncover its static and dynamic traits, indicating notable rigidity and excessive mass. A multi-parameter sensitivity analysis is conducted by extracting the cross-sectional size parameters of the column and selecting design variables based on the theory related to the moment of inertia. We use a central composite experimental design to generate sample data and create a response surface model. The goal is to optimize the sizing parameters of a column structure by minimizing its mass. The optimization process is bound by certain constraints: the maximum deflection at the top must fall within the permissible limit, and the material stress should not surpass its strength threshold. This method is applied to the lightweight design of a single-column stacker crane of a certain model, and results show that the optimized column weight reduction can reach 50.77%, indicating a significant lightweight effect. This study provides theoretical and technical support for the lightweight design and application of column structures.

Keywords: Stacker column · Sensitivity · Response surface · Lightweight design

1 Introduction

With the vigorous development of automated warehouses, stacker, as its main transportation tool [1], is very important to design its lightweight design while realizing higher and faster. The bending deformation and localized stress concentration occurring in the columns of stacker cranes when subjected to bending moments from various components and the weight of the goods pose a significant challenge to enhancing the transportation

© The Author(s), under exclusive license to Springer Nature Singapore Pte Ltd. 2023
H. Yang et al. (Eds.): ICIRA 2023, LNAI 14275, pp. 26–38, 2023.
https://doi.org/10.1007/978-981-99-6504-5_3

speed and stability of the stacker crane system [2]. Currently, the prevailing approach to meet the stacker's stiffness and strength requirements is to augment the thickness of plates and incorporate numerous stiffened plates. However, this approach leads to unnecessary weight, material inefficiency and elevated manufacturing expenses. Hence, performing static and dynamic characteristics analysis and pursuing lightweight design for stacker crane columns holds significant importance.

In recent years, extensive research has been conducted by scholars on the optimization of column bearing structures. Chan et al. [3] analyzed the static and dynamic properties of a machine tool. By implementing structural modifications, they successfully increased the column's stiffness and improved the overall machine's modal frequency by 26%. Venugopal et al. [4] employed experimental and numerical methods to optimize the design of machine tool column structures, achieving a weight reduction of 17.88% while maintaining satisfactory static performance. Bo et al. [5] utilized a bionic design methodology to optimize the column of a machine tool, resulting in a 5.69% reduction in weight, a 20.65% improvement in stiffness, and a 29.40% enhancement in strength. Jiao et al. [6] utilized the variable density method to optimize the periodic topology of a stacker, introducing an initial lightweight design. Ling et al. [7] adopted a bionic method to optimize the machine tool column structure, leading to a 45.90% decrease in maximum static displacement and a 6.13% reduction in mass. Liu et al. [8] utilized a multi-objective optimization design approach to enhance the vulnerable components of a machine tool, resulting in a 2.76% mass reduction and a 27.38% reduction in deformation. Choudhary et al. [9] optimizes the five regular sections of C, H, I, T and cross with the section shape as the design variable, and the ultimate load of the optimal section can be increased to 6.10 times without sacrificing the material cost.

In conclusion, current efforts in column structure optimization primarily focus on various types of machine tool columns. Typically, the design process involves the selection of column section size parameters or the incorporation of stiffened plate structures, with limited consideration for variables and often relying on self-designed test samples for optimization. Therefore, this study specifically examines the impact of column section size and stiffened plates on the static characteristics of a specific type of stacker crane. Design variables were determined using sensitivity analysis and theoretical principles related to the moment of inertia of sections. The response surface analysis was conducted utilizing a central composite experimental design (CCD), ensuring that the allowable deflection at the top remained smaller than the column height. Through this approach, the column was successfully designed to be lightweight while still meeting the strength requirements.

2 Lightweight Design Method

The conventional finite element simulation process consists of multiple steps, such as creating a geometric model, simplification, meshing, applying loads and constraints, and calculating and analyzing results. However, these steps become time-consuming during the optimization design as modifications to the model necessitate repeating the entire process. Parametric modeling is instrumental in streamlining the iterative design process by allowing automatic updates when modifying geometric parameters.

Since parameters are interdependent, a straightforward combination is not feasible after optimizing a single parameter. Therefore, it is necessary to perform multi-parameter analysis during the optimization process to identify the optimal design scheme that meets the requirements. However, structures often involve numerous design variables, and optimizing all variables simultaneously can be computationally inefficient and burdensome. Hence, it is advisable to initially conduct sensitivity analysis on the simplified model's design variables, exclude unimportant ones, and incorporate relevant cross-section moment of inertia theory to introduce additional design variables. Therefore, the optimization design should be carried out to avoid repeated modeling and simulation operations, and the key variables should be optimized pertinently, which can greatly improve the work efficiency; Besides, this method puts forward a lightweight design evaluation standard for column bearing structure, that is, under the same height, the unit deflection mass ratio is less than 1. At present, the deflection of columns will increase in different degrees while reducing weight, so whether the lightweight design is effective can be judged by the mass ratio of unit deflection, avoiding the phenomenon of mass reduction at the cost of greatly increasing deflection. The lightweight design flow is shown in Fig. 1.

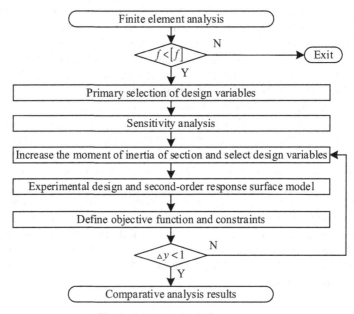

Fig. 1. Lightweight design process

In the lightweight design process of column structures, the main goal is to reduce the column's mass by optimizing the parameters associated with its cross-sectional dimensions. The design is subject to a constraint that restricts the top deflection to an allowable limit and ensures that the maximum stress remains below a predefined threshold. The optimization process focuses on the design variables associated with the section size parameters.

3   Static and Dynamic Characteristics Analysis of Stacker Column

3.1   Analysis of Bearing Deformation of Columns

Structural dimension optimization involves improving the size parameters of a structure while maintaining its topology [10]. This paper will optimize the structure of a stacker column based on Workbench. The allowable deflection of the stacker is H/2000–H/1000, and the height of the column is 7.4 m.

The column is a box structure with weight reduction holes and reinforcing ribs. To enhance calculation efficiency, certain characteristics in the model, such as threaded holes, that have minimal influence on the column's simulation analysis are disregarded. The stacker cargo platform model is simplified as a mass block positioned on top of the column, and the material properties are defined using finite element software, as indicated in Table 1.

Table 1. Material Properties

Project	Performance
Material grade	Q235A
Elastic modulus (Gpa)	210
Density (kg/m^3)	7800
Poisson's ratio	0.30
Yield strength (Mpa)	235

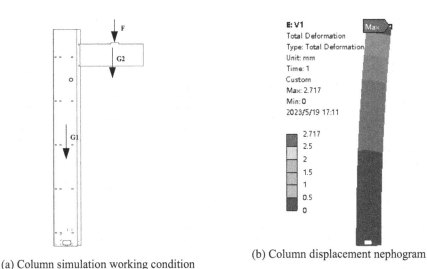

(a) Column simulation working condition

(b) Column displacement nephogram

Fig. 2. Working condition setting and simulation nephogram

Apply a force of F = 14700 N to the top of the cargo platform, which is equivalent to 1.25 times the rated load, and add gravity G1 and G2. The contact between various parts adopts binding constraints to fix the bottom end face of the column. The working conditions, depicted in Fig. 2(a), are established to closely resemble the actual operating conditions. The finite element simulation analysis of the column has minimal impact on calculation results and efficiency due to its simple structure and distinct element types. To ensure efficiency, solid elements and tetrahedral grids with a total of 176,752 grid elements are employed. Figure 2(b) displays the extracted displacement contour after concealing the top cargo platform. The top deflection value is approximately 2.72 mm, significantly below the allowable deflection range of 3.70 to 7.40 mm for the column. The

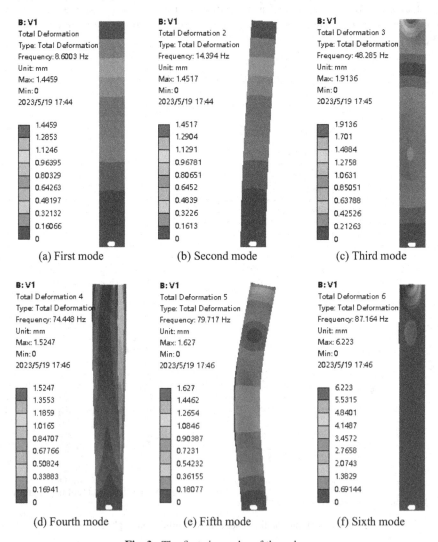

Fig. 3. The first six modes of the column

rigidity is large and the mass redundancy is excessive. Therefore, a lightweight design should be carried out to save the manufacturing cost and reduce the normal working energy loss of the stacker.

3.2 Modal Analysis of Column

Resonance is a critical factor that limits the performance improvement of stacker cranes. As stacker cranes achieve higher speeds and capabilities, the excitation frequency also increases. If the excitation frequency coincides or is close to the natural frequency of the structure, resonance can occur. To prevent this phenomenon, modal analysis can be conducted during the design verification process. The first six modes are shown in Fig. 3.

Figure 3 illustrates the first six natural frequencies of the column: 8.60 Hz, 14.39 Hz, 48.28 Hz, 74.45 Hz, 79.72 Hz, and 87.16 Hz. The axial distance between the two wheels of the stacker used in this paper is 4.7 m. When the stacker runs at the rated speed of 3.3 m/s, the excitation frequency is 0.70 Hz, which is far less than the first frequency of 8.60 Hz. It will not resonate, and the excessive frequency also reflects the stiffness redundancy of the structure, so the structure should be optimized.

4   The Lightweight Design of Column

Response surface methodology is an optimization method that seeks to find the relationship between a target function and various parameter variables by building a response surface that models their interactions [11]. To optimize the column using response surface methodology, the first step involves identifying design variables and selecting an appropriate experimental design approach. This allows for the creation of a second-order response surface model, enabling efficient structure optimization.

4.1   Selection of Design Variables

The columns of the stacker crane model are mainly composed of I-beams, rectangular thin plates, and various reinforcement ribs. There are many dimensional parameters involved, and the existing reinforcement ribs cannot effectively increase the section moment of inertia, which has little effect on reducing deflection. Therefore, the existing stiffened plate in the inner cavity of the column and the local features of the model are all removed, and the rectangular structure of the column is changed into a wedge-shaped structure. The simplified schematic diagram is shown in Fig. 4. To streamline the serial design of the stacker, the total length of the I-beam is kept constant. Seven dimensional parameters are considered as primary design variables: middle plate length, I-beam width, middle plate wedge angle, I-beam short side thickness, middle plate thickness, I-beam long side thickness, and left plate thickness. The range of variation for these design variables is determined according to the manufacturing process. Please refer to Table 2 for a description of the primary design variables for the column structure.

The second-order response surface model was fitted using a sufficient number of sample points to meet the minimum requirement for polynomial terms. Increasing the number of sample points improves the accuracy of the response surface fitting, generally

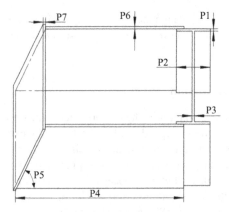

Fig. 4. Simplified schematic diagram of column structure

Table 2. Primary design variables

Design parameters	Describe	Range of change
P1/mm	Thickness of short side of I-beam	5–15
P2/mm	I-beam width	100–200
P3/mm	Thickness of long side of I-beam	5–15
P4/mm	Length of middle plate	700–1500
P5/°	Wedge angle of middle plate	85–90
P6/mm	Middle plate thickness	5–15
P7/mm	Thickness of left plate	5–15

necessitating more than double the minimum number of points. The dataset comprises 7 design variables and 79 selected sample points. Through sensitivity analysis conducted on the obtained sample points from the experimental design, the impact of each design variable on three output parameters (including one target parameter and two constraint parameters) was determined. The outcomes of this analysis are depicted in Fig. 5. So as to realize lightweight design, we should give priority to the variables whose influence on quality is far less than that on maximum deformation, and then exchange the cost of less mass increase for a substantial reduction in maximum deformation. Only P4 in Fig. 5 meets this requirement. Considering that P2 has little influence on quality and great influence on stress, it is decided to keep P2 and P4 as design variables and exclude other variables.

In order to minimize the weight of the column, the sensitivity analysis indicates that decreasing the thickness of each plate is advisable. However, due to practical processing constraints, a 5 mm thickness is chosen for each plate. To improve the moment of inertia of the section and mitigate deflection at the top of the column, two stiffener plates are incorporated at the left end, strategically positioned away from the neutral axis of the

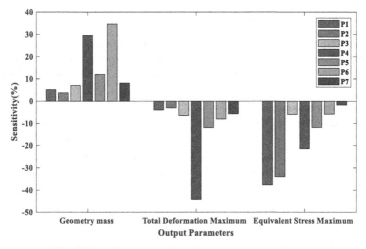

Fig. 5. Sensitivity of each variable to output parameters

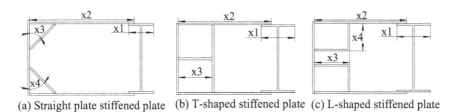

(a) Straight plate stiffened plate   (b) T-shaped stiffened plate (c) L-shaped stiffened plate

Fig. 6. Three different types of stiffened panels

cross-section. This study compares and analyzes three types of stiffener plates (straight plate, T-shaped plate, and L-shaped plate) to maximize their effectiveness, as depicted in Fig. 6. The thickness of the stiffener plates is also set at 5 mm.

Table 3. Selected design parameters

Design parameters	Describe	Range of change
x1/mm	I-beam width	100–200
x2/mm	Length of middle plate	300–1500
x3/°	Angle of upper plate and left plate	0–90
x4/°	Angle of lower plate and left plate	0–90

Initially, a straight plate was used as the stiffener in the optimization. Four dimensional parameters were selected as design variables: I-steel width, middle plate length, upper plate angle, and lower plate angle. See Table 3 for the design parameter description.

4.2   CCD Experimental Design

CCD is an experimental design technique derived from the two-level experimental design [11]. Unlike conventional two-level designs, the Central Composite Design (CCD) incorporates axis points and center points to improve the accuracy of fitting the second-order response surface model. This methodology is particularly useful for evaluating the nonlinear relationship between input and output variables. In this particular study, the CCD experimental design method is employed with 4 design variables and 25 sample points. Three output parameters, specifically column mass, maximum deformation, and maximum stress, are selected based on the results obtained from finite element analysis. For detailed design outcomes, please consult Table 4.

Table 4. CCD experimental design results

Number	Design variable				Weight/kg	Maximum deformation/mm	Maximum stress/MPa
	$x1$	$x2$	$x3$	$x4$	m	f	σ
1	150	900	45	45	959.91	3.86	214.22
2	100	900	45	45	931.13	4.12	179.04
3	200	900	45	45	988.70	3.59	160.40
4	150	300	45	45	613.57	28.67	330.76
5	150	1500	45	45	1306.26	1.84	200.64
6	150	900	0	45	959.91	3.79	214.35
7	150	900	90	45	959.91	3.90	216.02
8	150	900	45	0	959.91	3.79	213.51
9	150	900	45	90	959.91	3.90	215.21
10	114.79	477.48	13.31	13.31	695.75	11.99	175.39
11	185.21	477.48	13.31	13.31	736.29	10.69	217.05
12	114.79	1322.52	13.31	13.31	1183.54	2.29	153.87
13	185.21	1322.52	13.31	13.31	1224.08	1.98	162.52
14	114.79	477.48	76.69	13.31	695.75	12.50	177.27
15	185.21	477.48	76.69	13.31	736.29	11.14	219.86
16	114.79	1322.52	76.69	13.31	1183.54	2.34	154.48
17	185.21	1322.52	76.69	13.31	1224.08	2.00	163.43
18	114.79	477.48	13.31	76.69	695.75	12.50	177.09
19	185.21	477.48	13.31	76.69	736.29	11.14	218.93
20	114.79	1322.52	13.31	76.69	1183.54	2.34	154.54

(*continued*)

Table 4. (*continued*)

Number	Design variable				Weight/kg	Maximum deformation/mm	Maximum stress/MPa
	x1	x2	x3	x4	m	f	σ
21	185.21	1322.52	13.31	76.69	1224.08	2.00	162.54
22	114.79	477.48	76.69	76.69	695.75	13.09	179.17
23	185.21	477.48	76.69	76.69	736.29	11.66	222.04
24	114.79	1322.52	76.69	76.69	1183.54	2.17	153.69
25	185.21	1322.52	76.69	76.69	1224.08	2.01	162.98

4.3 Response Surface Optimization

Response surfaces depicting maximum deformation and maximum stress are constructed based on the response values obtained from the experimental design. These surfaces (Figs. 7 and 8) illustrate the influence of different parameters on deformation and stress. From Fig. 7, it can be observed that increasing the values of x1 and x2 while decreasing x3 and x4 helps reduce deformation. Similarly, Fig. 8 demonstrates that x1 and x2 have a stronger impact on maximum stress compared to x3 and x4.

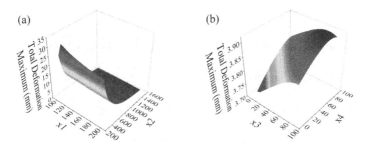

Fig. 7. Maximum deformation response surface

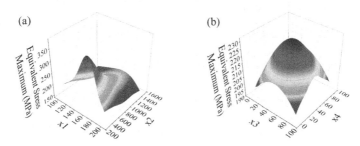

Fig. 8. Maximum stress response surface

The column was optimized using a response surface to minimize mass while meeting deflection and stress requirements (deflection < H/2000, stress < material limit). The column optimization results: x1 = 101.03 mm, x2 = 948.31 mm, x3 = 6.23°, x4 = 15.72°. T-shaped and L-shaped plates were also optimized. The T-shaped results: x1 = 102.59 mm, x2 = 974.47 mm, x3 = 201.01 mm. For the L-shaped: x1 = 121.17 mm, x2 = 960.76 mm, x3 = 51.70 mm, x4 = 51.85 mm. Refer to Table 5 for parameter comparison.

Table 5. Comparison of optimization results of three kinds of stiffened plates

	Straight plate	T-shaped plate	L-shaped plate
m/kg	960.50	1033.90	925.90
f/mm	3.57	3.69	3.69

It can be seen from Table 5 that the effect of an L-shaped stiffened plate is better. For convenience of processing, x1 = 125 mm after rounding the data; x2 = 965 mm; x3 = 55 mm; x4 = 55 mm. Under identical operating conditions, the column was remodeled and simulated. The simulation results, presented in nephogram 9, indicate a maximum deformation of 3.67 mm, which is below the allowable deflection. Furthermore, the recorded maximum stress is 158.17 Mpa, which is notably below the material's strength limit. Table 6 presents the parameters and a comparison of columns pre and post lightweight.

Table 6. Parameters and comparison before and after lightweight

	Before lightweight (a)	After lightweight (b)	Percentage
m/kg	1886	928.50	−50.77%
f/mm	2.72	3.67	34.43%

Note: Percentage = (b − a)/a* 100%

It can be seen from Table 6 that after lightening the column, the weight of the column decreases from 1886 kg before lightening to 928.50 kg after lightening, with a decrease of 50.77%; $y = m/f$; $y(a) = 693.38$, $y(b) = 253$, $\Delta y = y(b)/y(a) = 0.36$ are far less than 1, and the lightweight effect is remarkable (Fig. 9).

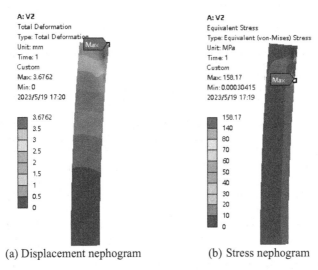

(a) Displacement nephogram　　　　(b) Stress nephogram

Fig. 9. Simulation nephogram

5 Conclusion

Based on the analysis and research of the static and dynamic characteristics of a specific model of stacking crane column, the following conclusion is drawn:

(1) An introduced method for lightweight design of column structures is suitable for multi-parameter structural optimization. Additionally, a lightweight design evaluation standard is proposed specifically for column structures. The effectiveness of the lightweight design is determined by evaluating the mass ratio of unit deflection.

(2) Through sensitivity analysis, the sensitivity of each dimension parameter on the three output parameters is analyzed. The findings indicate that the length of the board has a more significant influence on deformation compared to its thickness. Therefore, when optimizing the structure, it is advisable to prioritize the length of the board as the design variable. Three kinds of stiffened plates are compared, and the results show that L-shaped stiffened plates have better lightweight design effect on columns.

(3) Using the proposed lightweight design method, the column of a specific model stacker crane was optimized. The column weight was effectively reduced by 50.77% through the implementation of lightweight design, while simultaneously maintaining the top-end deflection within the permissible limit and ensuring that the maximum stress remains below the material's strength threshold.

In the follow-up research, the author will further consider the vibration and fatigue analysis, and carry out multi-objective optimization design.

Acknowledgments. This work was supported by the Basic and Applied Basic Research Foundation of Guangdong Province [grant number 2020B1515120015]; the National Science Foundation of China [grant numbers 12272089, U1908217]; and the Fundamental Research Funds for the Central Universities of China [grant numbers N2224001-4, N2003013].

References

1. Geng, J., Lu, Y., Yang, H., Dong, C.: The Design of Stereoscopic Warehouse Stacker' Motion and Control System. Springer, Berlin Heidelberg (2011)
2. Sun, J., Li, J., Ou, D., Li, Y.: Simulation analysis of the stacker column based on high-speed & high-acceleration. In: International Conference on Manufacturing Science and Engineering (2011)
3. Chan, T.-C., Chang, K.-C., Chang, S.-L., Chiang, P.-H.: Simulation, modeling, and experimental verification of moving column precision grinding machine. J. Chin. Inst. Eng. **45**, 54–64 (2022)
4. Venugopal, P.R., et al.: Structural investigation of steel-reinforced epoxy granite machine tool column by finite element analysis. Proc. Inst. Mech. Eng. Part J. Mater. Des. Appl. **233**, 2267–2279 (2019)
5. Bo, W., Mengji, C., Jinfeng, W., Jixin, S., Zhengjie, L.: Fuzzy algorithm based bionic optimization design of boring machine column. Comput. Intell. Neurosci. **2022**, 1–11 (2022). https://doi.org/10.1155/2022/5264781
6. Jiao, H.-Y., Li, F., Jiang, Z.-Y., Li, Y., Yu, Z.-P.: Periodic topology optimization of a stacker crane. IEEE Access **7**, 186553–186562 (2019)
7. Zhao, L., Chen, W.Y., Ma, J.-F., Yang, Y.-B.: Structural bionic design and experimental verification of a machine tool column. J. Bionic Eng. **5**(1), 46–52 (2008). https://doi.org/10.1016/S1672-6529(08)60071-2
8. Liu, S., Guo, Z., Chen, Z.: Finite-element analysis and structural optimization design study for cradle seat of CNC machine tool. J. Chin. Inst. Eng. **39**, 345–352 (2016)
9. Choudhary, P.K., Mahato, P.K., Jana, P.: Cross-section optimization of thin-walled open-section composite column for maximizing its ultimate strength. Proc. Inst. Mech. Eng. Part J. Mater. Des. Appl. **236**, 413–428 (2022)
10. Dong, Y., Yao, X., Xu, X.: Cross section shape optimization design of fabric rubber seal. Compos. Struct. **256**, 113047 (2021)
11. Box, G.E.P., Wilson, K.B.: On the experimental attainment of optimum conditions. In: Kotz, S., Johnson, N.L. (eds.) Breakthroughs in Statistics: Methodology and Distribution, pp. 270–310. Springer New York, New York, NY (1992). https://doi.org/10.1007/978-1-4612-4380-9_23

Optimum Design of 3-UPS/S Parallel Mechanism

Peng Sun[1,2], Yujun Gao[1,2], Chentao Wu[1,2], Shaojiang Feng[1,2], Yunfei Gu[1,2], and Yanbiao Li[1(✉)]

[1] College of Mechanical Engineering, Zhejiang University of Technology, Hangzhou 310023, China
lybrory@zjut.edu.cn
[2] Huzhou Institute of Digital Economy and Technology, Zhejiang University of Technology, Huzhou 313000, China

Abstract. The multi-objective parameters for optimizing the performance of the 3UPS/S parallel mechanism were optimized using the principal component analysis method and space models. This approach comprehensively considered the multi-objective performance of the parallel mechanism. Firstly, the structural characteristics of the mechanism were analyzed, the global kinematic performance index and global static performance index of the mechanism were defined. Then, the influence of the main size parameters of the mechanism on various global performance indicators was analyzed using spatial model technology. The multi-objective parameters of the mechanism were optimized using the principal component analysis method. The comparison of multiple sets of size parameters showed that a higher integrated performance index value corresponds to better global performance, thus verifying the feasibility and correctness of the method. This optimization method provides a new approach for multi-objective parameter optimization of parallel mechanisms.

Keywords: 3-UPS/S parallel mechanism · Kinematic analysis · Static analysis · Multi-objective parameter optimization

1 Introduction

At present, the wrist joint of the humanoid robot arm is usually connected in series. Compared with the series mechanism, the parallel mechanism has the advantages of simple structure, high bearing capacity and small motion inertia [1–3], effectively compensating for the shortcomings of the series mechanism. Due to its position between the palm and the forearm, the wrist joint requires characteristics such as small structure size, large movement space and large bearing capacity, so the parallel structure is the most suitable. In terms of parameter optimization of parallel humanoid wrist joint, Xu Chang

This work was supported by the National Natural Science Foundation of China (Grant No. U21A20122, 52105037, 51975523).

et al. [4–6] used kinematic theory to carry out kinematic analysis of the parallel mechanism, and verified the results with analysis software to obtain the kinematic performance of the mechanism. However, it is difficult to get the equilibrium rule of the mechanism under the action of external force or external torque because there is no statics study and analysis of the mechanism. Zhu Wei et al. [7, 8] optimized the working space of the parallel mechanism and verified that the working space of the mechanism was significantly enlarged and the rotational performance was significantly improved after optimization. But the performance parameters of the mechanism have not been optimized, so the dimensional parameters of the mechanism can not be fully obtained. Zhao Qing et al. [9, 10] adopted the weighted summation method to carry out multi-objective optimization of the parallel manipulator, effectively reducing the joint position following error and improving the control accuracy. However, the weight coefficient of this method was determined manually, which has a certain subjectivity. In this paper, a multi-parameter and multi-objective optimization method is proposed to address the shortcomings of the above-mentioned parallel humanoid wrist joint optimization. Firstly, the kinematic model of the wrist joint was derived by vector method, and the kinematic performance index of the wrist joint was defined. Then, statics is analyzed based on the principle of virtual work, and the regional energy indexes of kinematics and statics are defined. Finally, a multi-objective optimization model of global kinematics and global statics was established. The spatial model technology combined with principal component analysis [11, 12] was used to solve the optimization model, and multiple performance indicators were converted into a comprehensive performance evaluation index, and the comprehensive performance indicators under each structural parameter were obtained. Based on the optimization results, the optimal mechanism size parameters were determined.

2 Kinematic and Static Analysis of Wrist Joint

2.1 Mechanism Model

Humanoid wrist joint be similar to human wrist in size and function. The wrist mechanism in this paper adopts a 3-UPS/S parallel mechanism, which is composed of static platform, dynamic platform and four branch chains. The schematic diagram of the mechanism is shown in Fig. 1. The moving coordinate system is denoted as $O\text{-}XYZ$ (hereinafter referred to as the moving system), which X-axis coincides with oS_1, Z-axis is perpendicular to the moving platform, and Y-axis conforms to the right-hand rule. The static coordinate system is denoted as $O\text{-}XYZ$ (hereinafter referred to as the static coordinate system), which X-axis coincides with OU_1, and Z-axis coincides with O_o, Y The axis follows the right-hand rule. At the initial position, the two coordinates have the same attitude.

Based on the spiral theory for calculating the degree of freedom of the mechanism, the moving platform is only subject to the binding force in the X, Y and Z directions, so the mechanism can realize the degree of freedom of rotation around the X, Y and Z axis in three directions, respectively to achieve the radial/ulnar flexion, dorsolateral extension/flexion and external/internal rotation of the wrist joint.

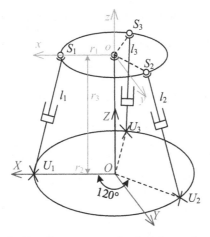

Fig. 1. Coordinate system of wrist joint mechanism

2.2 Kinematic Analysis

In the wrist joint mechanism, the change velocity of the three branch chains l_1, l_2 and l_3 is set as v_1, v_2 and v_3, respectively, and is expressed in vector form $v = [v_1\ v_2\ v_3]^T$. [14, 15]Since the moving platform only rotates around the fixed point o, the input velocity of the branched chain can be obtained

$$v_i = \dot{l}_i = v_{s_i} \cdot e_i = \omega_B \times r_i \cdot e_i = r_i \times e_i \cdot \omega_B = r_i^T \tilde{e}_i H \omega \tag{1}$$

Among them
$$\begin{cases} e_i = \dfrac{l_i}{|l_i|}, e_{i_x} = \dfrac{l_{i_x}}{|l_i|}, e_{i_y} = \dfrac{l_{i_y}}{|l_i|}, e_{i_y} = \dfrac{l_{i_y}}{|l_i|} \\[2mm] \tilde{e}_i = \begin{bmatrix} 0 & -e_{i_z} & e_{i_y} \\ e_{i_z} & 0 & -e_{i_x} \\ -e_{i_y} & e_{i_x} & 0 \end{bmatrix} \end{cases}.$$

In the equation, e_i is the unit vector of the branch l_i stretching direction, $\tilde{e}_i$ is 3×3 antisymmetric matrix. Then the expression for the inverse solution of velocity can be obtained

$$v = J^{-1} \omega_B \tag{2}$$

where, the Jacobian matrix can be expressed as

$$J = \left[\begin{bmatrix} \tilde{e}_1^T r_1 & \tilde{e}_2^T r_2 & \tilde{e}_3^T r_3 \end{bmatrix}^T \right]^{-1} \tag{3}$$

The Jacobian matrix J in Eq. (3) reflects the mapping relationship between the input velocity and the output velocity of the wrist joint mechanism. According to the theory of singular value decomposition of matrices, when the mechanism is not in singular position, it can be obtained

$$\frac{\omega'_{Bx}}{\sigma_{1\omega}} + \frac{\omega'_{By}}{\sigma_{2\omega}} + \frac{\omega'_{Bz}}{\sigma_{3\omega}} = 1 \tag{4}$$

where, $\sigma_{i\omega}(i = 1,2,3)$ represents the singular value of the Jacobian matrix J, and $\sigma_{1\omega} \geq \sigma_{2\omega} \geq \sigma_{3\omega}$.

Equation (3) represents an ellipsoid equation, whose three principal axes are respectively $\sigma_{1\omega}$, $\sigma_{2\omega}$ and $\sigma_{3\omega}$. This implies that when the input velocity vector of the branch is a unit vector, ω_B is located on the ellipsoid, so it can be called the angular velocity ellipsoid. The ellipsoid intuitively represents the kinematic performance of the wrist joint mechanism.

When $\sigma_{1\omega} = \sigma_{2\omega} = \sigma_{3\omega}$, the angular velocity ellipsoid becomes circular, indicating that the wrist joint mechanism exhibits the same kinematic performance in all directions, known as kinematic isotropy. To describe the kinematic performance of the wrist joint mechanism, local angular velocity isotropic evaluation indexes η_ω and local angular velocity transfer evaluation indexes K_ω are defined as follows.

$$\begin{cases} \eta_\omega = {}^{\sigma_{3\omega}}\!/_{\sigma_{1\omega}} \\ K_\omega = {}^{1}\!/_{\sigma_{1\omega}} \end{cases} \tag{5}$$

From the equation, it is easy to know that $\eta_\omega \in [0,1]$, and the closer η_ω is to 1, the better the angular velocity isotropy performance of the wrist mechanism, indicating a superior motion transfer performance. Conversely, the closer η_ω is to 0, the mechanism has a singular position, and the poorer motion transfer performance [16].

2.3 Statics Analysis

The force Jacobian matrix obtained by static analysis of wrist joint mechanism plays a crucial role in the analysis of mechanism performance [17]. To facilitate calculations, certain assumptions are made: each moving member of the wrist joint mechanism is considered rigid, and friction forces of each kinematic pair are ignored. Assuming that the driving force of the whole wrist joint mechanism is $\tau = [\tau_1 \ \tau_2 \ \tau_3]^T$, the generalized force vector acting on the reference point of the moving platform is denoted as F_s, which can be simplified as the force $F = [F_x \ F_y \ F_z]^T$ over the rotation center of rotation, and the moment $M = [M_x \ M_y \ M_z]^T$ acting on the moving platform, therefore, $F_s = [F \ M]^T$.

In this paper, the principle of virtual work [18, 19] is used to obtain the Jacobian matrix

$$G = (J)^T \tag{6}$$

When the wrist joint mechanism is in equilibrium, the torque balance equation is (take the distance from point o).

$$\tau = G \cdot M \tag{7}$$

To obtain the equation by taking the square of the norm on both sides of Eq. (7).

$$\|M\|^2 = \tau^T G^{-1} (G^{-1})^T \tau \tag{8}$$

Assuming that the driving force τ of the wrist joint mechanism is a unit vector, the Lagrange equation is constructed.

$$L = \tau^T G^{-1} (G^{-1})^T \tau - \lambda\left(\tau^T \tau - 1\right) \tag{9}$$

In the Eq. (9), respectively, take partial derivatives to τ^T and λ.

$$\begin{cases} \dfrac{\partial L}{\partial \tau^T} = G^{-1}(G^{-1})^T \tau - \lambda \tau = 0 \\ \dfrac{\partial L}{\partial \lambda} = \tau^T \tau - 1 = 0 \end{cases} \tag{10}$$

From the Eq. (10), we know that $G^{-1}(G^{-1})^T \tau = \lambda \tau$, λ is square $G^{-1}(G^{-1})^T$ of eigenvalue, Therefore, Eq. (8) can also be expressed as

$$\|M\|^2 = \tau^T (G^{-1})^T G^{-1} \tau = \lambda \tau^T \tau = \lambda \tag{11}$$

It can be seen from Eq. (11), the extreme value of $\|M\|$ is square $(G^{-1})^T G^{-1}$ the square root of the maximum and minimum eigenvalue of the $\sqrt{\lambda_{max}}$ and $\sqrt{\lambda_{min}}$.

The generalized force vector can be decomposed into the force passing the center of rotation and the moment acting on the moving platform. Since the force decomposed by the generalized force vector overpasses the center of rotation and does no work, the force Jacobian matrix is only related to the decomposed moment, and G is expressed as

$$G = G_M \tag{12}$$

Therefore, the local torque isotropy evaluation index and the local torque transfer performance evaluation index were defined as

$$\begin{cases} \eta_M = \lambda_{M\,min} \big/ \lambda_{M\,max} \\ K_M = 1 \big/ \lambda_{M\,max} \end{cases} \tag{13}$$

From the equation, it can be seen that $\eta_M \in [0,1]$, and the closer η_M is to 1, the better the moment isotropy of the wrist joint mechanism and the better its static performance[20].

2.4   Regional Energy Index

The four local performance indexes $\eta_\omega, K_\omega, \eta_M, K_M$ defined above will change with the change of the reference point posture of the moving platform at the end of the wrist joint mechanism, that is, the values of these local indexes have different values at different points in the workspace. Therefore, the average value of the local performance index in the workspace of the wrist joint mechanism can be defined as the global index, which is

$$\begin{cases} \overline{\eta}_\omega = \sum_V \eta_\omega \Big/ V \\[2ex] \overline{K}_\omega = \sum_V K_\omega \Big/ V \\[2ex] \overline{\eta}_M = \sum_V \eta_M \Big/ V \\[2ex] \overline{K}_M = \sum_V K_M \Big/ V \end{cases} \tag{14}$$

where V is the workspace of the wrist joint mechanism, $0 \le \overline{\eta}_\omega, \overline{K}_\omega, \overline{\eta}_M, \overline{K}_\omega \le 1$, and the larger the global performance index value, the better the corresponding performance of the wrist joint mechanism.

3   Regional Energy Map

According to the method in literature [21], the equivalent distribution line of the number of wrist joint working space points can be drawn, as shown in Fig. 4. From the analysis of the figure, it can be seen that the regional energy indexes of the wrist joint mechanism are in an excellent region when the dimensionless parameter $Y \ge 2.0$, and $Y_{max} = -\sqrt{3}X + 6$ (Fig. 2).

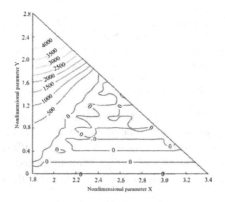

Fig. 2. The atlas of the size of global workspace

From the formula (14), the equivalent distribution lines of the global kinematic performance index and the global statics performance index in a specific region can be calculated, as shown in Figs. 3 and 4. These graphs are an important basis for structural parameter optimization design of wrist joint mechanism based on kinematic and static properties.

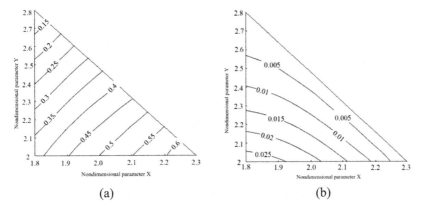

Fig. 3. The atlas of the isotropic performance global angular velocity

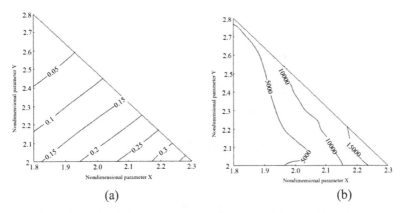

Fig. 4. The atlas of the transmission performance global angular velocity

4 Multi-objective Parameter Optimization of Mechanism

By analyzing the four performance maps obtained in the previous section, it is difficult to determine the optimal size of the wrist joint mechanism because the distribution of each index is inconsistent with the structural parameters of the mechanism. Therefore, it is necessary to determine the optimal size solution by synthesizing each index.

According to PCA method, 50 samples were selected respectively for analysis of the four performance indicators, and their specific values are shown in Table 1.

In order to keep each performance indicator at the same level, Z-score method is adopted to standardize the sample data in Table 1, and the standardized data $Z_i \in R^{m \times 4}$ of each performance indicator is obtained, as shown in Table 2. The standardized formula

Table 1. The raw data of various performance indicators

Sample serial number	$\overline{\eta}_\omega(X_1)$	$\overline{K}_\omega(X_2)$	$\overline{\eta}_M(X_3)$	$\overline{K}_M(X_4)$
1	0.3842	0.0277	0.1420	991.2939
2	0.3703	0.0254	0.1292	1107.0615
3	0.3542	0.0230	0.1161	1245.5557
4	0.3372	0.0206	0.1035	1413.7747
⋮	⋮	⋮	⋮	⋮
47	0.4718	0.0169	0.1910	4135.0131
48	0.4560	0.0146	0.1753	5240.0010
49	0.4394	0.0123	0.1599	6881.8870
50	0.4221	0.0101	0.1454	9452.2808

is

$$
\begin{cases}
Z_{ij} = \left(X_{ij} - \overline{X}_j\right)/s_j \\
\overline{X}_j = \sum_{i=1}^{m} X_{ij}/m \\
s_j^2 = \sum_{i=1}^{m} (X_{ij} - \overline{X}_j)^2/(m-1)
\end{cases}
\tag{15}
$$

Table 2. The Standardized data of various performance indicators

Sample serial number	Z_1	Z_2	Z_3	Z_4
1	0.8300	2.2283	1.0242	−0.1523
2	0.6893	1.9114	0.7926	−0.1522
3	0.5258	1.5855	0.5574	−0.1521
4	0.3542	1.2639	0.3285	−0.1529
⋮	⋮	⋮	⋮	⋮
47	1.7178	0.7618	1.9102	−0.1498
48	1.5576	0.4440	1.6267	−0.1489
49	1.3890	0.1352	1.3481	−0.1477
50	1.2138	−0.1619	1.0868	−0.1456

It can be seen from the analysis of Table 2 that there may exist some correlation among standardized performance indicators, and the correlation coefficient matrix can fully reflect the correlation among performance indicators, which is the primary condition for dimension reduction [22]. The related $n \times n$ order coefficient matrix D is expressed as follows

$$D = \frac{1}{m-1} Z^T Z \tag{16}$$

According to the formula (16), specific values can be obtained as shown in Table 3. The analysis shows that Z_1, Z_2, Z_3 and Z_4 are all positively correlated, but the degree of correlation between the four indicators is different. The correlation coefficient matrix reflects the internal relationships among the four performance indicators, and the principal component is determined based on these internal relationships.

Table 3. The correlation coefficient matrix D of performance indicators

	Z_1	Z_2	Z_3	Z_4
Z_1	1	0.514	0.975	0.062
Z_2	0.514	1	0.524	0.237
Z_3	0.975	0.524	1	0.031
Z_4	0.062	0.237	0.031	1

The eigenvalues and unit eigenvectors of the correlation coefficient matrix D are obtained. Each unit eigenvalue represents the contribution rate of the correlation coefficient matrix to the unit eigenvector corresponding to the unit eigenvalue. Principal component analysis is a statistical method. The basic principle of its selection is not to lose the main information, and the variance of the principal component is an indicator to measure the information. The greater the variance, the greater the amount of information of the principal component [23, 24]. The number of principal components is calculated according to the cumulative variance contribution rate of eigenvalues. The calculation formula is

$$\delta_i = \sum_{i=1}^{p} \lambda_i / \sum_{i=1}^{n} \lambda_i \tag{17}$$

where, λ_i is the eigenvalue of the correlation coefficient matrix, and $\lambda_1 \geq \lambda_2 \geq \ldots \geq \lambda_n \geq 0$, the number of principal components p is usually determined by $\delta_i \geq 85\%$.

The variance contribution rate of the principal component and the cumulative variance contribution rate can be calculated by the formula (17), and the specific values are shown in Table 4. It can be seen from Table 4 that the cumulative variance contribution rate of the first principal component and the second principal component is 88.360%, and its value is greater than 85%, which meets the conditions, indicating that the first principal component and the second principal component reflect the original variables. The 88.360% information provided basically reflects the information contained in all indicators, so the number of principal components is 2.

Table 4. The analysis and calculation results of sample of PCA

Principal component	Eigenvalue	Unit eigenvector	Variance contribution rate (%)	Accumulated variance contribution rate (%)
1	2.778	[0.5778,0.5454, 0.5820, −0.1728]	69.461%	69.461%
2	0.952	[0.1394,0.0113, 0.1425,0.9798]	23.806%	93.267%
3	0.248	[−0.4237,0.8353, − 0.3333,0.0984]	6.200%	99.466%
4	0.021	[0.6901,0.0552, − 0.7315,0.0069]	0.534%	100%

The expression of the first principal component

$$F_1 = 0.5778Z_1 + 0.5454Z_2 + 0.582Z_3 - 0.1728Z_4 \qquad (18)$$

The expression of the second principal component

$$F_2 = 0.1394Z_1 + 0.0113Z_2 + 0.1425Z_3 + 0.9798Z_4 \qquad (19)$$

The eigenvalues and unit eigenvectors of the correlation coefficient matrix are extracted by PCA method, and the number of principal components is determined. Therefore, the global performance evaluation function of wrist joint mechanism can be constructed.

$$F = \sum_{i=1}^{p} \frac{\lambda_i}{\lambda_1 + \lambda_2 + \cdots + \lambda_p} F_i \qquad (20)$$

Based on Eqs. (18), (19) and (20), the comprehensive evaluation expression of the global performance of the wrist joint mechanism is

$$F = 0.4659Z_1 + 0.4091Z_2 + 0.4698Z_3 + 0.1214Z_4 \qquad (21)$$

Finally, the relationship between the comprehensive evaluation index of the wrist joint mechanism and the dimensionless structure size was drawn. As shown in Fig. 5, the isotropy and transfer performance of the wrist mechanism are better when $F \geq 2.5$. The parameter range of the wrist mechanism with better performance can be intuitively determined from the Fig. When the dimensionless parameters $X = 2.0$, $Y = 2.0$ and $X = 2.0$, $Y = 2.05$, the comprehensive evaluation index value of regional energy is greater than 2.5, that means the isotropy and transfer performance of wrist joint mechanism are better than other X, Y combinations.

According to the dimensionless parameters X and Y under the better performance of the selected wrist joint mechanism, the parameters r_1, r_2, and r_3 of the wrist joint mechanism can be calculated. The specific value of parameter n needs to be determined in combination with the actual engineering requirements. In order to verify the correctness of the above selected parameters, several groups of dimensionless parameter combinations with $1.5 \leq F \leq 2.5$ are selected, and the data are compared with the dimensionless parameter combinations with $F \geq 2.5$ the global comprehensive performance index values under each structural parameter are shown in Table 5.

Table 5. The global comprehensive performance indicators of various structural parameters

X	Y	r_1	r_2	r_3	$\bar{\eta}_\omega$	$\bar{K}_\omega$	$\bar{\eta}_M$	$\bar{K}_M$	F
1.8	2.00	0.0485	0.0615	0.2200	0.3842	0.0277	0.1420	991	1.8361
1.9	2.00	0.0390	0.0710	0.2200	0.4467	0.0258	0.1811	1556	2.4214
1.9	2.05	0.0363	0.0682	0.2255	0.4325	0.0234	0.1665	1788	2.0839
1.9	2.10	0.0335	0.0655	0.2310	0.4163	0.0210	0.1515	2080	1.7291
2.0	2.00	0.0295	0.0805	0.2200	0.5011	0.0218	0.2226	2774	2.8597
2.0	2.05	0.0267	0.0778	0.2255	0.4871	0.0193	0.2070	3351	2.5136

According to the comprehensive performance index function, the comprehensive performance index evaluation map is drawn by MATLAB software. After comparison, it is found that Fig. 5 has a high similarity with Fig. 3(a) and Fig. 4(a), which is the same as the overall trend of Fig. 3(b) and Fig. 4(b), which is basically consistent with the conclusion of Table 3. It is easy to obtain from Figs. 3 and 4, when X is larger and Y is smaller, the global angular velocity isotropy index and the global torque isotropy index reach the maximum value, and the global angular velocity transmission performance index and the global torque transmission performance index also achieve large values. Combined with the results of the global comprehensive performance index, it is basically consistent, which verifies the effectiveness of the PCA method in the application of the mechanism. Therefore, the size design of the wrist joint parallel mechanism can refer to the comprehensive global performance map to select the size parameters with better performance.

Finally, based on the results of the above parameter optimization, considering the processability of processing and assembly, the dimensionless parameters $X = 2.0$, $Y = 2.0$ are selected, at which time r_1, r_2, and r_3 are the optimal structural parameters, then the design scheme of the wrist joint mechanism is given, and the model diagram of the wrist joint mechanism is drawn, as shown in Fig. 6. The mechanism is driven by linear motor, which reduces the weight of the whole joint and improves the driving ability of the wrist joint.

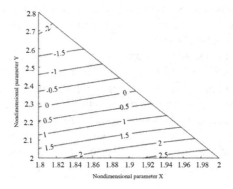

Fig. 5. The atlas of global comprehensive performance evaluation index

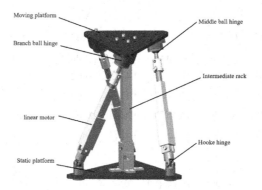

Fig. 6. Parallel anthropomorphic wrist joint mechanism

5 Conclusion

(1) Kinematics analysis of the 3-UPS/S parallel wrist joint mechanism was carried out in this paper, and the evaluation indexes of global angular velocity isotropy, global angular velocity transmission performance, global moment isotropy and global moment transmission performance were defined.

(2) Based on the spatial model technology, the relationship between the regional energy index and the mechanism parameters was shown, and four regional energy maps were drawn, which laid the foundation for the multi-objective structural parameter optimization design of the mechanism.

(3) The principal component analysis method was used to optimize the performance evaluation indexes, and the comprehensive evaluation function of regional energy was obtained, and combined with the spatial model technology, the map of regional energy comprehensive evaluation indexes was drawn. According to the diagram, the dimensional parameters of the wrist joint parallel mechanism with better performance were determined. This optimization method has a certain reference value in the optimization of multi-objective performance parameters of the mecdhanism.

References

1. Hou, Y., Hu, X., Zeng, D., et al.: Biomimetic shoulder complex based on 3-PSS/S spherical parallel mechanism. Chinese J. Mech. Eng. **28**(1), 29–37 (2015)
2. Li, Y., Jin, Z., Ji, S., et al.: Design of mechanical coxa joints based on three-degree-of-freedom spherical parallel manipulators. J. Mech. Sci. Technol. **27**(1), 103–112 (2013)
3. Li, Y., Tan, D., Wen, D., et al.: Parameters optimization of a novel 5-DOF gasbag polishing machine tool. Chinese J. Mech. Eng. **26**(4), 680–688 (2013)
4. Xu, C.: Structure Design and Application of Small 6-DOF Parallel Robot. Beijing University of Posts and Telecommunications, Beijing (2019). (in Chinese)
5. Zhang, C., Li, B., Zhao, X.: Kinematics and working performance analysis of a 3-DOF parallel mechanism. Manuf. Autom. **9**, 54–58 (2017). (in Chinese)
6. Ba, S., Xu, Y., Liu, Y., et al.: Kinematics analysis and simulation of a new 3UPU-PP hybrid mechanism. J. Shanghai Univ. Eng. Sci. **33**(2), 13 (2019). (in Chinese)
7. Zhu, W., Ma, Z., Shen, H., et al.: Kinematics and optimum design of a new SCARA parallel mechanism. Mach. Des. Res. **35**(3), 16 (2019). (in Chinese)
8. Li, H., Zhang, Y., Wang, D.: Comparative analysis of optimization algorithms in workspace optimization of parallel mechanisms. J. Mech. Eng. **46**(13), 61–67 (2010). (in Chinese)
9. Zhao, Q.: High Precision Control of High-Speed Parallel Manipulators. Tianjin University, Tianjin (2017). (in Chinese)
10. Che, L., Cheng, Z., He, B.: 4-PRUR parallel mechanism and its displacement analysis based on differential evolution algorithm. J. Mech. Eng. **46**(23), 36–44 (2010). (in Chinese)
11. Kuroda, M., Mori, Y., Iizuka, M., et al.: Acceleration of the alternating least squares algorithm for principal components analysis. Comput. Stat. Data Anal. **55**(1), 143–153 (2011)
12. Wang, J., Xu, Y., Cao, B., et al.: Ultrasonic face recognition algorithm based on principal component analysis. Computer Eng. Des. **34**(8), 2867–2871 (2013)
13. Huang, Z., Tao, W.S., Fang, Y.F.: Study on the kinematic characteristics of 3 DOF in-parallel actuated platform mechanisms. Mech. Mach. Theory **31**(8), 999–1007 (1996)
14. Huang, Z., Zhao, Y., Zhao, T.: Advanced Spatial Mechanism. China Higher Education Press, Beijing (2006). (in Chinese)
15. Masory, O., Wang, J, Zhuang, H.: On the accuracy of a Stewart platform. II. Kinematic calibration and compensation. In: IEEE International Conference on Robotics and Automation, pp. 725–731. Proceedings. IEEE, Atlanta (1993)
16. Wang, D.: Type Synthesis and Performance Analysis of Parallel Mechanism. Yanshan University, Qinhuangdao (2001)
17. Chambers, W., Mikula, A.: Operational data for a large vertical thrust bearing in a pumped storage application. Trans. Soc, Tribol. Lubricat. Eng. **31**(1), 61–65 (1988). (in Chinese)
18. Zhang, B., Wang, L., Wu, J.: Dynamic isotropic performance evaluation of a 3-DOF parallel manipulator. J. Tsinghua Univ. (Sci. Technol.) **57**(8), 803–809 (2017). (in Chinese)

19. Yang, J., Yu, Y., Du, Z.: Dynamic modeling method of parallel robot with hybrid chains. Chin. J. Mech. Eng. **45**(1), 77–82 (2009). (in Chinese)
20. Zhang, X.: Study of torque isotropy of force sensor based on Stewart structure. Mach. Des. Res. **20**(2), 20–22 (2004). (in Chinese)
21. Gao, F., Liu, X.J., Chen, X.: The relationships between the shapes of the workspaces and the link lengths of 3-DOF symmetrical planar parallel manipulators. Mech. Mach. Theory **36**(2), 205–220 (2001). (in Chinese)
22. Liang, S., Zhang, Z., Cui, L.: Comparison between PCA and KPCA method in dimensional reduction of mechanical noise data. China Mech. Eng. **22**(1), 80–83 (2011). (in Chinese)
23. Zeng, D., Wang, J., Fan, M., et al.: Parameter optimization of parallel mechanisms based on PCA. China Mech. Eng. **28**(24), 2899–2905 (2017). (in Chinese)
24. Wang, W., Chen, X.: Comparison of principal component analysis with factor analysis in comprehensive multi-indicators scoring. Stat. Inform. Forum. **21**(5), 19–22 (2006). (in Chinese)

Kinematic Analysis of Overrunning on a Swing Arm Tracked Mobile Chassis

Song Wang[1,2], Yun Hong[1,2], Fanxuan Li[2], and Duanling Li[2(✉)]

[1] Beijing Key Laboratory of Work Safety Intelligent Monitoring, Beijing University of Posts and Telecommunications, Xitucheng Road No.10. Haidian District, Beijing 100876, China
wongsang@bupt.edu.cn
[2] School of Modern Post (School of Automation), Beijing University of Posts and Telecommunications, Xitucheng Road No.10, Haidian District, Beijing 100876, China
liduanling@163.com

Abstract. Kinematic analysis is carried out for the structure of the swing-arm tracked mobile chassis. Forward and reverse kinematic analysis and modeling are performed for the most important over-barrier motion of the mobile chassis, which is to go over steps as an example. It is analyzed that the coordinates of the center of mass of the mobile chassis and the coordinates of the end of the swing arm are related to the time, the angle of the swing arm and the angle of the body to the horizontal during the process of overstepping. The research results can provide theoretical support for the motion capability of the swing arm tracked robot.

Keywords: Kinematic Analysis · Swing Arm Tracked · Mobile Chassis

1 Introduction

Mobile robot refers to the robot that can complete tasks independently or cooperatively, which is an important branch of robotics. They can be widely applied in various environments and scenarios, such as healthcare, agriculture, manufacturing, exploration, rescue, and other fields [1, 2]. In these fields, mobile robots can reduce the burden of human labor, improve work efficiency, and reduce personnel risks.

The mobile chassis of small ground robots has become a research hotspot due to its small size, low cost, and flexible movement. From the perspective of robot motion, ground mobile robots can be divided into wheeled robots, tracked robots, and legged robots [4]. Wheeled robots achieve movement by controlling the rotation and speed of one or more wheels, so they have good flexibility, maneuverability, and adaptability [5, 6]. However, wheeled robots are susceptible to ground friction and external disturbances, and have high requirements for the road surface, so they cannot cross obstacles or climb high slopes [7, 8]. Legged robots refer to robots that use one or more legs to move. Legged robots have advantages such as flexibility and adaptability, and can move on complex terrains [9–11], but they also have disadvantages such as poor stability, complex control systems, and slow motion speed [12–14]. Tracked robots refer to robots equipped with tracked chassis mechanisms [15, 16], which have received widespread attention

H. Yang et al. (Eds.): ICIRA 2023, LNAI 14275, pp. 53–63, 2023.
https://doi.org/10.1007/978-981-99-6504-5_5

from relevant scholars due to their strong adaptability, high load-bearing capacity, good stability, good obstacle crossing and passing performance, and movement on various complex terrains [17–19].

For tracked robots, the swing arm tracked mobile robot is a new type of robot that combines the swing arm mechanism with the tracked structure [20, 21]. Due to the track leg structure of the swing arm tracked mobile chassis, it has considerable obstacle crossing ability, which makes it widely used in field exploration, search and rescue, and military fields [22, 23]. Therefore, the structure of the rocker tracked mobile chassis is analyzed in kinematics in this paper, which provides theoretical support for the movement ability of the swing arm tracked robots.

2   Basic Structure of Swing Arm Tracked Mobile Chassis

The swing arm tracked mobile chassis can be applied in variable and unstructured environments. Therefore, the body part of the mobile chassis is required to have a certain stiffness that can resist shock and vibration. Therefore, the body structure is a rectangular body structure. The main drive wheels are track driven. The swing arm part is mounted at the front end of the mobile chassis in the forward direction as a moving part of the mobile chassis. The structural design of the swing arm tracked mobile chassis is shown in Fig. 1, 2, 3 and 4.

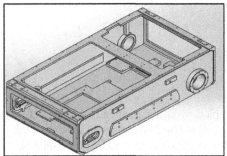
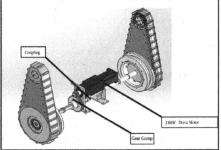

Fig. 1. Welding frame body model   **Fig. 2.** Swing arm structure model

The schematic diagram of the assembled swing arm tracked mobile chassis is shown in Fig. 5.

3   Modeling and Analysis of the Kinematics of a Swing Arm Tracked Mobile Chassis for Obstacle Crossing

$^A\Gamma_B$ and ^AT_B are employed to describe the coordinate transformation of coordinate system $\{B\}$ to coordinate system $\{A\}$. $^A\Gamma_B$ denotes the transformation of two coordinate systems on different components. It is also called moving coordinate transformation. ^AT_B denotes the transformation in which the two coordinate systems have different orientations on the same component. It is also called rotational coordinate transformation.

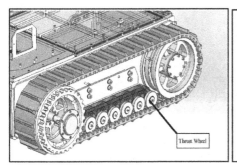
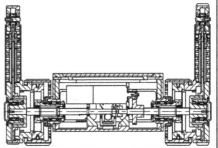

Fig. 3. Main Track Model   **Fig. 4.** Front View of Mobile Chassis

Fig. 5. Overall Structure Diagram

The step of moving the chassis across the step is divided into two steps. The first step is that the swing arm track just touches the top of the step. The second step is that the body is just in contact with the top point of the step. The motion state and coordinate transformation of these two steps are different. These motion state characteristics are decomposed into the motion of some reference points of the moving chassis.

3.1 Phase I Movement Analysis

Firstly, the motion state of the first step is analyzed. The reference point is near the step at a certain distance, the swing arm track is rotated and the end of the swing arm is in contact with the top point of the step.

The meaning of each coordinate system in the figure is following.

(1) $O_G - Y_G Z_G$ is an absolute coordinate system.

(2) $O_O - Y_O Z_O$ is a coordinate system established with the center of mass of the moving chassis as the origin.

(3) $O_A - Y_A Z_A$ is a coordinate system established with the point of contact between the ground and the active wheels of the mobile chassis as the origin.

(4) $O_B - Y_B Z_B$ is a coordinate system locked to the body body, with the origin at the axis of rotation of the active rear wheel.

(5) $O_C - Y_C Z_C$ is a coordinate system locked to the body of the body, with the origin at the axis of rotation of the active front wheel.

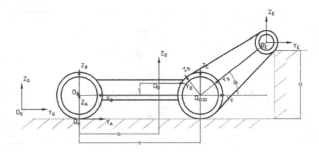

Fig. 6. Analysis of the first stage motion of the mobile chassis over the barrier

(6) $O_D - Y_D Z_D$ is a coordinate system locked to the swing arm track, with the origin at the axis of rotation of the front wheel.

(7) $O_E - Y_E Z_E$ is a coordinate system locked to the end of the pendulum arm, with the pivot out of the end of the arm as the origin.

where, l_1 is the distance between the front and rear active wheel axles. l_2 is the length of the swing arm track. b is the distance from the projection of the center of mass of the mobile chassis on the line of the front and rear active wheel axes to the center of the rear active wheel. H is the height of the step. c is the vertical distance from the center of mass of the mobile chassis to the center line of the front and rear main wheels.

In Fig. 6, the coordinate transformation matrix required for the kinematic analysis of the moving chassis can be derived.

$$
\left\{
\begin{aligned}
&{}^G\Gamma_A = \begin{bmatrix} 1 & 0 & 0 & 0 \\ 0 & 1 & 0 & vt \\ 0 & 0 & 1 & 0 \\ 0 & 0 & 0 & 1 \end{bmatrix} \quad
{}^A\Gamma_B = \begin{bmatrix} 1 & 0 & 0 & 0 \\ 0 & \cos\theta & -\sin\theta & 0 \\ 0 & \sin\theta & \cos\theta & R \\ 0 & 0 & 0 & 1 \end{bmatrix} \quad
{}^B T_O = \begin{bmatrix} 1 & 0 & 0 & 0 \\ 0 & 1 & 0 & b \\ 0 & 0 & 1 & c \\ 0 & 0 & 0 & 1 \end{bmatrix} \\
&{}^B T_C = \begin{bmatrix} 1 & 0 & 0 & 0 \\ 0 & 1 & 0 & l_1 \\ 0 & 0 & 1 & 0 \\ 0 & 0 & 0 & 1 \end{bmatrix} \quad
{}^O T_C = \begin{bmatrix} 1 & 0 & 0 & 0 \\ 0 & 1 & 0 & l_1-b \\ 0 & 0 & 1 & c \\ 0 & 0 & 0 & 1 \end{bmatrix} \quad
{}^C\Gamma_D = \begin{bmatrix} 1 & 0 & 0 & 0 \\ 0 & \cos\theta_1 & -\sin\theta_1 & 0 \\ 0 & \sin\theta_1 & \cos\theta_1 & R \\ 0 & 0 & 0 & 1 \end{bmatrix} \quad
{}^D\Gamma_E = \begin{bmatrix} 1 & 0 & 0 & 0 \\ 0 & 1 & 0 & l_2 \\ 0 & 0 & 1 & 0 \\ 0 & 0 & 0 & 1 \end{bmatrix}
\end{aligned}
\right.
\tag{1}
$$

According to Eq. (1) and the established reference coordinate system, the coordinate change matrix of the end motion of the pendulum arm is calculated as the following metric.

$$
{}^G\Gamma_E = {}^G\Gamma_A \, {}^A\Gamma_B \, {}^B T_C \, {}^C\Gamma_D \, {}^D T_E
\tag{2}
$$

In the process the chassis rotation angle $\theta = 0$, then

$$
{}^A\Gamma_B = \begin{bmatrix} 1 & 0 & 0 & 0 \\ 0 & 1 & 0 & 0 \\ 0 & 0 & 1 & R \\ 0 & 0 & 0 & 1 \end{bmatrix}
\tag{3}
$$

The formula is integrated as follow.

$$
{}^{G}\Gamma_{E} = \begin{bmatrix} 1 & 0 & 0 & 0 \\ 0 & \cos\theta_1 & -\sin\theta_1 & l_2\cos\theta_1 + l_1 + vt \\ 0 & \sin\theta_1 & \cos\theta_1 & l_2\sin\theta_1 + R \\ 0 & 0 & 0 & 1 \end{bmatrix} \tag{4}
$$

In the coordinate system $\{O\}$, the coordinates of the end of the swing arm track of the mobile chassis are $\begin{bmatrix} P_{Ey} & P_{Ez} \end{bmatrix}$. The coordinates of its center of mass in the reference coordinate system $\{O\}$ are $\begin{bmatrix} P_y & P_z \end{bmatrix}$.

The change in the horizontal and vertical coordinates of the end of the swing arm track is shown in the following equation.

$$
\begin{cases} P_{Ey} = l_2\cos\theta_1 + l_1 + vt \\ P_{Ez} = l_2\sin\theta_1 + R \end{cases} \tag{5}
$$

where, v is the movement speed of the moving chassis. θ_1 is the angle of deflection of the swing arm track with respect to the body. R is the radius of the active wheel.

Similarly, the coordinate transformation matrix for moving the center of mass of the chassis can be obtained as follows.

$$
{}^{G}T_{O} = {}^{G}\Gamma_{A}\,{}^{A}T_{B}\,{}^{B}T_{O} = \begin{bmatrix} 1 & 0 & 0 & 0 \\ 0 & 1 & 0 & b + vt \\ 0 & 0 & 1 & R + c \\ 0 & 0 & 0 & 1 \end{bmatrix} \tag{6}
$$

The change in the horizontal and vertical coordinates of the center of mass of the moving chassis during this process is shown in the following equation.

$$
\begin{cases} P_y = b + vt \\ P_z = R + c \end{cases} \tag{7}
$$

The coordinate transformation of the end of the swing arm and the center of mass motion of the mobile chassis in the first stage is simulated. The mobile chassis can travel in accordance with the calculation in stages when performing the movement over the obstacle to avoid the confusion of the action sequence. The mobile chassis can cross the obstacle in a slow and stable manner when performing the movement of crossing the obstacle. It avoids the corresponding impact due to collision with obstacles such as steps (Figs. 7 and 8).

From the figure, it can be seen that the coordinate y of the ground end of the swing arm of the mobile chassis decreases with the increase of θ_1. It increases with the increase of t. When $\theta_1 = 0, t = 1$, the coordinate y of the end of the swing arm reaches the maximum value. At this time, $y_{max} = 1050$ mm. The change of the coordinate z at the end of the swing arm is only related to the change of θ_1. It is not related to the motion time t. The coordinate z increases as θ_1 increases. When $\theta_1 = 0.5\pi$, there is $z_{max} = 430$ mm.

where, $b = 400$ mm, $c = 35$ mm, and substitute the corresponding parameters into Eq. (6) to get the law of change of the center of mass of the moving chassis as shown below.

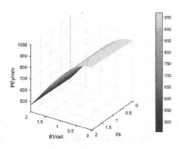

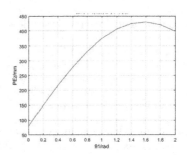

Fig. 7. The relationship between the coordinates y of the end of the swing arm θ_1 and t

Fig. 8. The relationship between the coordinates z of the end of the swing arm θ_1

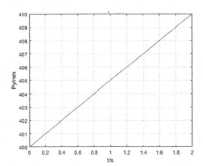

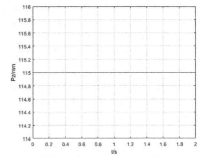

Fig. 9. Center-of-mass coordinates y versus t **Fig. 10.** Center-of-mass coordinates z versus t

As seen in Figs. 9 and 10, the center-of-mass coordinate y of the moving chassis increases linearly. y reaches its maximum value y_{max} at $t = 1$. The center-of-mass coordinate z is independent of the movement time t. The center-of-mass coordinate z is independent of the deflection angle θ_1 of the swing arm track with respect to the body. The center-of-mass coordinate z is also independent of the deflection angle θ_1 of the swing arm track with respect to the body. The center-of-mass coordinate z is constantly equal to 115 mm, and the movement of the chassis in the first stage only affects the absolute center-of-mass coordinate. However, the center of mass remains fixed with respect to the body.

3.2 Phase II Movement Analysis

Subsequently, the motion state of the second step is analyzed. The pendulum arm was rotated and the pendulum arm was in almost complete contact with the step (Fig. 11).

The position and attitude of the end of the swing arm track of the mobile chassis change with the motion of the body of the mobile chassis and the motion of the swing arm track. After coordinate transformation, the coordinate transformation matrix of the swing arm track end can be obtained.

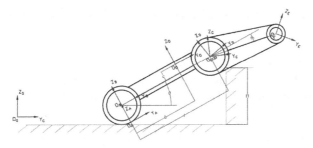

Fig. 11. Analysis of the second stage motion of the mobile chassis over the barrier

$$
{}^{G}T_E = {}^{G}\Gamma_A{}^{A}\Gamma_B{}^{B}T_C{}^{C}\Gamma_D{}^{D}T_E = \begin{bmatrix} 1 & 0 & 0 & 0 \\ 0 & \cos(\theta+\theta_1) & -\sin(\theta+\theta_1) & l_2\cos(\theta+\theta_1)+l_1\cos\theta+vt \\ 0 & \sin(\theta+\theta_1) & \cos(\theta+\theta_1) & l_2\sin(\theta+\theta_1)+l_1\sin\theta+R \\ 0 & 0 & 0 & 1 \end{bmatrix} \quad (7)
$$

The position coordinates of the swing arm track end of the mobile chassis change in the second stage as shown in the following equation.

$$
\begin{cases} P_{Ey} = l_2\cos(\theta+\theta_1)+l_1\cos\theta+vt \\ P_{Ez} = l_2\sin(\theta+\theta_1)+l_1\sin\theta+R \end{cases} \quad (8)
$$

where, θ is the turning angle of the car body of the moving chassis.

Similarly, the change matrix of the position and attitude of the center of mass of the moving chassis with respect to the reference coordinate system can be obtained as shown in the following equation.

$$
{}^{G}T_O = {}^{G}\Gamma_A{}^{A}T_B{}^{B}T_O = \begin{bmatrix} 1 & 0 & 0 & 0 \\ 0 & \cos\theta & -\sin\theta & b\cos\theta - c\sin\theta + vt \\ 0 & \sin\theta & \cos\theta & b\sin\theta + c\cos\theta + R \\ 0 & 0 & 0 & 1 \end{bmatrix} \quad (9)
$$

The coordinates of the center of mass of the moving chassis change in the second stage as shown in the following equation.

$$
\begin{cases} P_y = b\cos\theta - c\sin\theta + vt \\ P_z = b\sin\theta + c\cos\theta + R \end{cases} \quad (10)
$$

The y coordinate of the end of the swing arm track of the mobile chassis is related to the motion time t. The y coordinate of the end of the swing arm track of the mobile chassis is related to the rotation angle θ_1 of the swing arm relative to the body. The y coordinate of the end of the swing arm track of the mobile chassis is related to the turning angle θ of the body. In this paper, the influence of y coordinate by these variables by means of control variables. The results of the simulation experiments are shown in Fig. 12, 13 and 14.

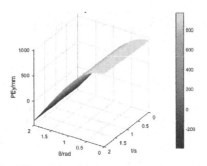

Fig. 12. Relationship between y and θ, t at the end of the swing arm

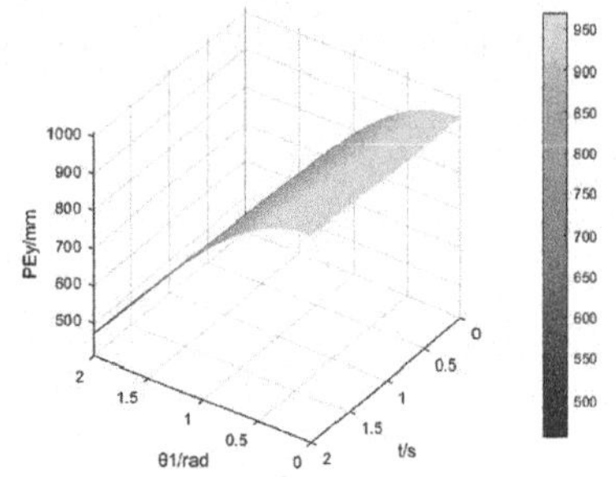

Fig. 13. Relationship between y and θ_1, t at the end of the swing arm

Where θ_1 is a constant, $\theta \in (0, \pi/3)$, $t \in (0, 1)$ the simulation results are shown in Fig. 12. The swing arm track end coordinates y increases with increasing t and decreases with increasing θ. At $t = 1$, $\theta = 0$, y has the maximum value $y_{max} = 900$ mm.

Where θ is a constant, $\theta_1 \in (\pi/9, \pi/2)$, $t \in (0, 1)$ the simulation results are shown in Fig. 13. The swing arm track end coordinate y decreases with increasing θ_1 and increases with increasing t. At $t = 1$, $\theta_1 = 0$, $y_{max} = 960$ mm (Fig. 15).

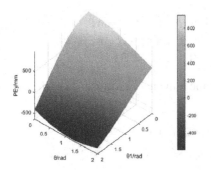

Fig. 14. Relationship between y and θ_1, θ at the end of the swing arm

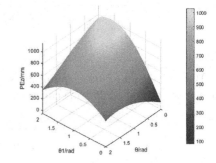

Fig. 15. Relationship between the end coordinates z of the swing arm and θ_1 and θ

Where t is a constant and $\theta_1 \in (\pi/9, \pi/2)$, $\theta \in (0, \pi/3)$ the results are shown in Fig. 14. The swing arm track end coordinate y decreases as θ increases and decreases as θ_1 increases. At $\theta_1 = \pi/9$, $\theta = 0$, y has the maximum value $y_{max} = 850$ mm.

According three graphs, the degree influence of θ on the coordinate y is greater than that of θ_1. The motion time t has the greatest degree of influence on the coordinate y.

The change law of coordinate z at the end of the swing arm track is obtained by substituting the parameters into the formula as shown in the following figure.

Where, the coordinate z of the swing arm track end is independent of the motion time t. It is related to the turning angle θ_1 of the swing arm relative to the body and the turning angle θ of the body. The coordinate z increases with the increase of θ_1 and also with the increase of θ. At $\theta_1 = 30.8°$, $\theta = 59.4°$, z has the maximum value $z_{max} = 946$ mm.

The variation pattern of the moving chassis center of mass coordinates is shown in Fig. 16 and Fig. 17.

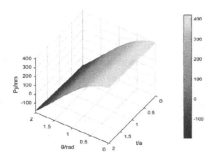

Fig. 16. Relationship between center-of-mass coordinates y, θ and t

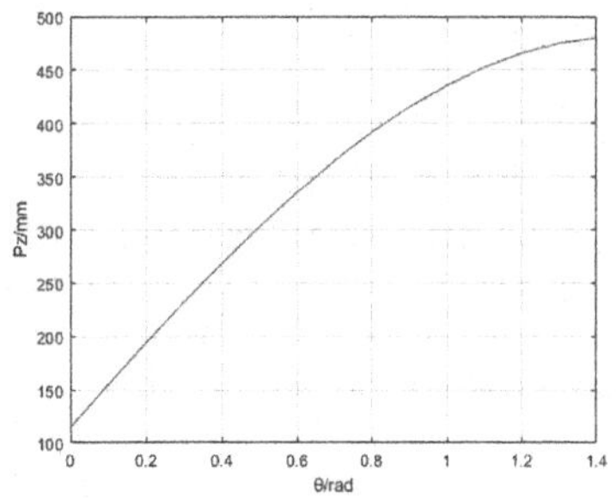

Fig. 17. Relationship between center of mass coordinates z and versus θ

The center-of-mass coordinate y decreases as θ increases. The center-of-mass coordinate y decreases as t increases. At $t = 1$, $\theta = \pi/3$, y has the maximum value $y_{max} = 430$ mm. The center-of-mass coordinate z increases as θ increases. Z_{max} is 478 mm.

The center-of-mass coordinates and the position of the center-of-mass relative to the body in the second stage change with the movement of the moving chassis.

4   Conclusion

The swing arm crawler robot has attracted extensive attention both inside and outside the industry due to its strong obstacle surmounting ability. This paper focuses on the analysis of the structure of the rocker arm crawler mobile chassis from the perspective of kinematics. Taking obstacle crossing as an example, the forward and reverse kinematics analysis and modeling of the most important obstacle crossing motion of the mobile chassis are carried out in this paper. We analyze that the coordinates of the center of mass of the mobile chassis and the end coordinates of the swing arm are related to time, the angle of the swing arm, and the angle of the vehicle body relative to the horizontal plane. The research results of this paper can provide theoretical support for the motion ability of swing arm tracked robots and provide a theoretical basis for the innovation of swing arm tracked robots.

Acknowledgement. This study was co-supported by the National Natural Science Foundation of China (Grant No.62206027, Grant No. 52175019), Beijing Natural Science Foundation (Grant No. 3212009, Grant No. L222038), the Science and Technology Nova Plan of Beijing City (Grant No.Z201100006820122), Xiaomi Foundation / Xiaomi Young Talents Program, the Open Project of the Key Laboratory of Modern Measurement and Control Technology of the Ministry of Education (Grant No.KF20221123201).

References

1. Klančar, G., Zdešar, A., Blažič, S., et al.: Wheeled mobile robotics. Butterworth-Heinemann, From Fundamentals Towards Autonomous Systems (2017)
2. Tzafestas, S.G.: Mobile robot control and navigation: a global overview. J. Intell. Rob. Syst. **91**, 35–58 (2018)
3. Pandey, A., Pandey, S., Parhi, D.R.: Mobile robot navigation and obstacle avoidance techniques: A review. Int Rob Auto J **2**(3), 00022 (2017)
4. Zghair, N.A.K., Al-Araji, A.S.: A one decade survey of autonomous mobile robot systems. Int. J. Elect. Comp. Eng. **11**(6), 4891 (2021)
5. Tagliavini, L., Colucci, G., Botta, A., et al.: Wheeled mobile robots: state of the art overview and kinematic comparison among three omnidirectional locomotion strategies. J. Intell. Rob. Syst. **106**(3), 57 (2022)
6. Básaca-Preciado, L.C., Orozco-García, N.A., Rosete-Beas, O.A., et al.: Autonomous mobile vehicle system overview for wheeled ground applications. Machine Vision and Navigation, 485–533 (2020)
7. Morin, P., Samson, C.: Motion control of wheeled mobile robots. Springer handbook of robotics **1**, 799–826 (2008)
8. Khan, R., Malik, F.M., Raza, A., et al.: Comprehensive study of skid-steer wheeled mobile robots: Development and challenges. Indus. Robo. Int. J. Roboti. Res. Appli. **48**(1), 142–156 (2021)
9. Tenreiro Machado, J.A., Silva, M.: An overview of legged robots. International Symposium on Mathematical Methods in Engineering, 1–40 (2006)
10. Liu, J., Tan, M., Zhao, X.: Legged robots—an overview. Trans. Inst. Meas. Control. **29**(2), 185–202 (2007)
11. Silva, M.F., Machado, J.A.T.: A literature review on the optimization of legged robots. J. Vib. Control **18**(12), 1753–1767 (2012)
12. Zhuang, H., Gao, H., Deng, Z., et al.: A review of heavy-duty legged robots. Science China Technol. Sci. **57**, 298–314 (2014)
13. Bhatti, J., Plummer, A.R., Iravani, P., et al.: A survey of dynamic robot legged locomotion. 2015 International Conference on Fluid Power and Mechatronics (FPM). IEEE, pp. 770–775 (2015)
14. Mahapatra, A., Roy, S.S., Pratihar, D.K., et al.: Multi-legged robots—a review. Multi-body Dynamic Modeling of Multi-legged Robots, 11–32 (2020)
15. Bruzzone, L., Nodehi, S.E., Fanghella, P.: Tracked locomotion systems for ground mobile robots: A review. Machines **10**(8), 648 (2022)
16. González, R., Rodríguez, F., Guzmán, J.L.: Autonomous tracked robots in planar off-road conditions: modelling, localization, and motion control. Springer Science & Business Media (2014)
17. Wang, W., Du, Z., Sun, L.: Dynamic load effect on tracked robot obstacle performance. 2007 IEEE International Conference on Mechatronics. IEEE, pp. 1–6 (2007)

18. Lever, J.H., Denton, D., Phetteplace, G.E., et al.: Mobility of a lightweight tracked robot over deep snow. J. Terrramech. **43**(4), 527–551 (2006)
19. Li, N., Ma, S., Li, B., et al.: An online stair-climbing control method for a transformable tracked robot. 2012 IEEE International Conference on Robotics and Automation. IEEE, pp. 923–929 (2012)
20. Pan, H., Chen, B., Huang, K., et al.: Flipper control method based on deep reinforcement learningfor tracked robot. J. Sys. Simul. https://doi.org/10.16182/j.issn1004731x.joss.22-1105
21. Xie, S., Bao, S., Zou, B., et al.: The research on obstacle-surmounting capability of six-track robot with four swing arms. 2013 IEEE International Conference on Robotics and Biomimetics (ROBIO). IEEE, pp. 2441–2445 (2013)
22. Zhang, J.: Comprehensive evaluation and motion analysis of crawler robot with pendulum arm. AnHui University of Science and Technology (2018)
23. Li, Y.W., Ge, S.R., Wang, X., et al.: Steps and stairs-climbing capability analysis of six-tracks robot with four swing arms. Applied Mechanics and Materials Trans Tech Publications Ltd **397**, 1459–1468 (2013)

Design and Implementation of a Modular Self-reconfigurable Spherical Robot Connected by Magnetic Force

Weihao Wang[1]([✉]), Edwardo E. Fukushima[2], and Naoyuki Kubota[1]

[1] Graduate School of Systems Design, Tokyo Metropolitan University, Tokyo, Japan
23661301@ed.tmu.ac.jp
[2] Graduate School of Engineering, Tokyo University of Technology, Tokyo, Japan

Abstract. This paper proposes a modular self-reconfigurable spherical robot, which modules can independently move for exploration (roll and/or turn), and also can connect with other modules to rearrange themselves into different configurations to overcome obstacles. A module is composed of an external spherical shell and an internal mechanism. The latter is characterized by having: (a) 2-DOF coupled drive rolling/turning motion mechanism; (b) two independent connection mechanism using magnetic force generated/canceled by sets of Permanent Magnets and Pole-piece demagnetization units; and (c) two rotation motion mechanism on which the connection mechanisms are mounted. In this paper, the mechanical design and implementation details and basic control formulation is discussed, followed by experimental verification of each part.

Keywords: Mobile robot · Spherical robot · Modular self-reconfigurable robot · Magnetic connection · Mechanism

1 Introduction

Modular self-reconfigurable robots (MSRR) have been researched extensively in recent years [1, 2, 4, 5]. MSRR system consists of modules, which can rearrange themselves into different configurations according to task requirements. The previous modular self-reconfigurable robots have lots of physical constraints such as: the module connectors are gender-opposite and discrete; the modules need careful trajectories planning to align the connectors while self-assemble.

The modular self-reconfigurable robots can realize the connection/separation and system reconfiguration between modules by docking mechanisms. Therefore, the docking mechanism is one of the most important components of the MSRR system. For example, hooks that are activated by motors [1], or electromagnets. In [3], the author proposed the concept of "the area of acceptance" for MSRR, which is defined as "the range of possible starting conditions for which mating will be successful"; a connector with a larger area of acceptance has a higher success rate when connecting. But it will increase the weight, volume and manufacturing cost of the robot, and the program also be more complex. So, we use magnet to be connector for making the area of acceptance larger as while as keep the weight, volume of connector constant.

This paper proposes a spherical MSRR, which can be connected with fewer physical constraints. Because when spherical modulars are next to each other, the horizontal centers of the spheres must be touched together, and the modulars can easily be connected by magnets. The modules can move independently, be connected/separated without manual assistance and system configurations can be rearranged.

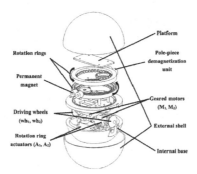

Fig. 1. Assembly exploded diagram of the spherical robot

The robot does not need to be precisely aligned with the specified connector. When it comes to motion performance, a single robot can move on planar surfaces. A group of robots can be rearranged into different configurations to travel through more complicated terrain. The robot system can be extended to more configurations to get more functional requirements, which has great potential to realize a freeform robotic system. The robot has the same basic functions as the most advanced MSRR: module independent motion, connection/separation between modules without manual assistance and system reconfiguration. However, the previous MSRR module needs to plan carefully to trajectories to align the connectors while self-assemble, which increases the difficulty of programming and sometimes requires multiple sensors, which increases the manufacturing cost, weight and volume of the robot. The robot has only two geared motors (M_1, M_2), two rotation ring actuators and magnets for these tasks. In addition, the robot shows better performance than previous MSRR systems in many aspects. But it should be noted that the holding force in tension of the robot is small, which is the weakness of the robot. Although the robot is not competitive in the comparison of holding force in tension, it is sufficient for most tasks. Section 4 introduces the production and basic experiments of the prototype. Finally, conclusions and future work are given in Sect. 5.

2   Mechanical Design

2.1   Robot Design

Figure 1 is the assembly exploded diagram of the robot. This robot is a spherical robot equipped with internal magnets units, which is mainly composed of three parts: plastic spherical shells, single modular driving mechanism and magnetic connection mechanism. The internal driving mechanism consists of two DC motors (M_1, M_2) with planetary reducer gearbox. The magnetic connection mechanisms are made of two servo motors, gears, two sets of permanent magnets and two Pole-piece demagnetization units. It is a non-touch connection between the magnet and the inner surface of the spherical shell, since the internal driving mechanism only touch the inner surface through the two wheels, the magnet and the spherical shell are not in physical contact, so the driving mechanism is easy to move in the spherical shell. The gravity of the internal mechanism is placed in the lower part of the whole. And the bracket of internal mechanism is hemisphere to keep it in balance. The gravity of the robot can be changed through changing the position of the internal mechanism in the spherical shell by controlling two DC motors (M_1, M_2), so that the robot rolling on the plane can be realized.

2.2   Connector

A magnetic connection method is adopted in the robot system. The connector uses the Pole-piece demagnetization unit described in [10]. Figure 2 shows the pole-piece demagnetization unit construction. When the electromagnet part of the pole-piece demagnetization units in the rear of robot is energized, it can generate a reverse magnetic field, so that the magnetic flux of the permanent magnet becomes zero, thus separating the two connected modules. The connectors are divided into four sets: two sets of permanent magnets in the front and two sets of the pole-piece demagnetization units in the rear. Two opposite sets of magnets are used in the front and rear to ensure a stronger connection and the same connection sequence between the modules. The permanent magnets in the front and rear of robot are responsible for connecting the other modules. The electromagnets in the rear of robot are responsible for separating two connected modules. If the rotation rings are made of iron, it can be long-time used, but the center of gravity of the internal mechanism will move up, and the connected magnet will make the friction of two rings rise.

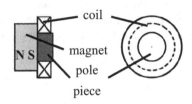

Fig. 2. The pole-piece demagnetization unit in the rear

Fig. 3. The magnetic pole of permanent magnet and pole-piece demagnetization unit

Figure 3 shows the magnetic pole of permanent magnets and pole-piece demagnetization units for connection. The magnetic poles of the front permanent magnet units and the rear pole-piece demagnetization units are opposite to ensure the connection sequence of multiple modules. Figure 4 shows the mechanical structure of the connector. The lower rotation ring (R_1) is driven by lower rotation ring actuator (A_1) through the gear. The upper rotation ring (R_2) is driven by upper rotation ring actuator (A_2) through the gear. Due to the gear transmission, we can precisely control the rotation angle of the rotation rings (R_1, R_2). The origin of coordinate system is located at the center of the spherical robot. The rotation rings are driven by the rotation rings actuators to rotate the magnet for the connection around the Z-axis, which means that the robot can make the other connected robot rotate by the rotation rings at the center of the robot after the connection.

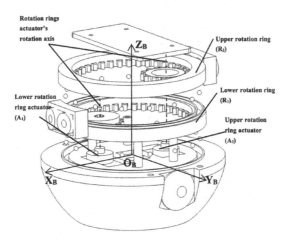

Fig. 4. Exploded diagram of the connection mechanism

The robot is equipped with permanent magnets, the pole-piece demagnetization units and plastic shell, so that the magnetic field can be transmitted to the outside. Therefore, when a robot approaches the internal magnet of another robot, the magnetic attraction is generated. Since the size of the internal magnet is small (the size of the magnet is 10 mm × 10 mm × 8 mm), but the magnetic field strength is large, it can excite a small but strong external magnetic field.

3 Motion of Robot

3.1 Module Independent Motion

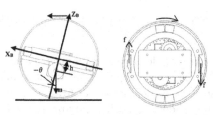

(a) Side view when rolling   (b)Top view when turning

Fig. 5. Motion of the robot (a) Side view when rolling (b) Top view when turning

The robot is essentially a spherical robot, so general movement method of spherical robots is also applicable to this robot. Figure 5 shows the side view of a robot during rolling. The X_B-axis, Y_B-axis and Z_B-axis inertial moment of the spherical shell are I_{xB}, I_{yB} and I_{zB}. When the two driving wheels (wh$_1$, wh$_2$) rotate in the same direction and speed, the internal mechanism moves along the inner surface of the spherical shell, and then the gravity center of internal mechanism is raised, and torque is provided to make robot roll forward. The driving torque τ is given by

$$\tau = hmsin(-\theta) + MR\ddot{\alpha} = I_{yB}\ddot{\alpha}_{yB} \tag{1}$$

where h is the distance from the sphere center to the gravity center of the internal mechanism, m is the mass of the internal driving mechanism, θ is the rolling angle of the sphere, M is the mass of the robot, R is the radius of the robot, I_{yB} is the Y_B-axis inertial moment of the spherical shell and $\ddot{\alpha}_{yB}$ is the Y_B-axis angular acceleration of the spherical shell.

Figure 5(b) shows the top view of a robot during turning. When two wheels rotate in different directions, the friction from the shell will produce a torque around the central axis of the internal mechanism. The internal mechanism will rotate around the axis to change the orientation.

The single module's uphill ability is mainly realized by the driving torque τ. The mass of robot is M. μ is the coefficient of rolling friction. R is the radius of the robot.

According to [14], we can obtain a kinematic model of sphere which adopt the z-y-x Euler angle sequence (φ, θ, ψ) to represent the orientation of the sphere. Define the coordinate rotation matrix $R_z(\varphi), R_y(\theta), R_x(\psi)$. Let the linear velocity v_0 and angular velocity ω_0 of the spherical shell center in $\sum_0$. There are:

$$\begin{aligned} v_0 &= \dot{x}i + \dot{y}j + \dot{z}k \\ \omega_0 &= \omega_x i + \omega_y j + \omega_z k \end{aligned} \tag{2}$$

where the components of ω_0 in $\sum_0$ in three directions are:

$$\begin{cases} \omega_x = \dot{\psi} \cos \varphi \cos \theta - \dot{\theta} \sin \varphi \\ \omega_y = \dot{\theta} \cos \varphi + \dot{\psi} \sin \varphi \cos \theta \\ \omega_z = \dot{\varphi} - \dot{\psi} \sin \theta \end{cases} \tag{3}$$

It is found that this model is also suitable to represent the properties of the robot moving on the flat ground. Assuming $\omega_z = 0$, the kinematics in our notations and coordinate system can be formulated as:

$$q = [x \ y \ \varphi \ \theta \ \psi]^T \tag{4}$$

when, $A(q)\dot{q} = 0$

$$A(q) = \begin{bmatrix} 1 & 0 & 0 & R\cos\varphi & R\sin\varphi\cos\theta \\ 0 & 1 & 0 & R\sin\varphi & -R\cos\varphi\cos\theta \\ 0 & 0 & 1 & 0 & -\sin\theta \end{bmatrix} \tag{5}$$

where φ, θ, ψ are the z-y-x Euler angles. $\omega_x, \omega_y, \omega_z$ are the angular velocities of the sphere about the x_B, y_B, z_B axes, respectively. $\dot{x}, \dot{y}$ are the speed of x and y direction.

3.2 Connection and Separation

Figure 6 from (a) to (d) shows the connection between two robots. In Fig. 7(a), two robots are not touching each other. Next, two robots are touching each other but are not connected in Fig. 6(b). Following Fig. 6(c), robot(A)'s rotation rings (R1, R2) can rotate to find the contact point by rotation actuators (A1, A2) between the two robots, and the internal magnets attract to the robot(B)'s internal magnets to achieve the connection between two modules. As mentioned above, robot(A)'s internal magnet will excite a magnetic field in an area, so there is still a connection force between the modules even if the internal connect point is not precisely adjusted to the other robots connect point. The robot's connectors are fault-tolerant, so the robot doesn't need a complex path planning to align the connector precisely, which to some extent surpasses the existing MSRR system.

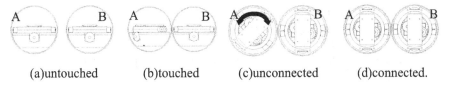

(a)untouched   (b)touched   (c)unconnected   (d)connected.

Fig. 6. Connection between robots

Figure 7 shows the separation between two robots from left to right. In Fig. 7(a), the electromagnet is energized, it can generate a reverse magnetic field, so that the magnetic flux of the permanent magnet becomes zero. Next, the two robots touch each other but

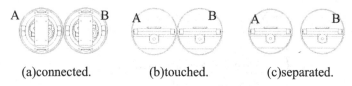

(a)connected.   (b)touched.   (c)separated.

Fig. 7. Separation between robots

are not connected in Fig. 7(b). The robot(A)'s internal driving mechanism is active, and robot(A) move away, the two modulars are separated in Fig. 7(c).

In conclusion, we only control the state of the pole-piece demagnetization units to realize the connector management of robot system, without the need for designated actuator of mechanism to provide this function between two modulars. However, the connection and separation only be achieved on the flat ground.

3.3 Reconfiguration

The combination of multiple robots shows some amazing performance. For MSRR system, we are concerned about how to rearrange these modules to different configurations. The robot has two connect points, there are many ways to arrange the modulars.

According to the data obtained from experiment, the magnetic attraction component in both directions is always positive, which means the other connected robots can move to the left or right from the top view when a robot is immobilized, which means the robot can arrange as a line and then moving like a snake (shown as Fig. 8) [6, 15] or configure as a plane on the water.

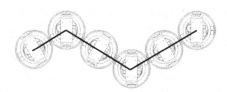

Fig. 8. Top view of snake-shape motion

Figure 9 is a detail of two connected robot connectors. The X-axis is the perpendicular magnetic force direction, and the Y-axis is the parallel magnetic force direction. The contact point of the two robots is taken as the origin, the horizontal direction of the magnetic force is the X-axis, and the vertical direction of the magnetic force is the Y-axis.

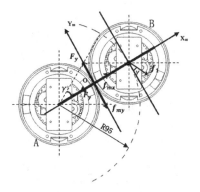

Fig. 9. Top view of connected robots

Figure 9 shows two connected robots (A and B), robot A is fixed to the ground. Next, we analyze the maintain static force balance conditions for two connected robots snake-shape motion on the water. If the two robots in Fig. 10 can keep the static force balance, we have:

$$\begin{cases} F_x = f_{mx} - f_1 \sin \gamma \\ F_y = f_{my} - f_1 \cos \gamma - \mu F_x \end{cases} \tag{6}$$

Spherical shells are made of plastic and the friction coefficient μ is about 0.48. f_1 is the resistance of the fluid on the robot. f_{mx}, f_{my} are the magnetic force in the X-axis and Y-axis. γ is the angle of the water hits the robot.

When the connected robots move on the water, the fluid resistance is:

$$f_1 = \frac{1}{2} \rho C_D U^2 A \tag{7}$$

where ρ is the density of fluid, C_D is the drag coefficient of fluid, U is the speed of fluid, A is the frontal area of robot.

$$\begin{cases} V_{ball} = \frac{4}{3} \pi R_{ball}^3 \\ F_f = \rho_f g V_{ball} \\ G_{ball} = m_{robot} g \end{cases} \tag{8}$$

where m_{robot} the mess of a robot, V_{ball} is the volume of the displaced body of liquid, ρ_f is the density of the fluid, g is the gravitational acceleration.

According to the (8), we can know that $F_f > G_{ball}$, which means the robot can float on the water. It verifies that the connected robots snake-shape move on the water by the buoyancy of the water, making it in a floating state.

After the modulars are numbered, they are controlled by master computer through Wi-Fi. The master computer sends the angle signal to each modulars, make them to turn to the appropriate angle.

Hirose introduced a serpentine curve to control the robot to achieve meandering motion [12]. The following snake-type motion control equation was obtained.

$$\beta_k = -2\alpha_0 \cdot \sin(\frac{(k_n)\pi}{N}) \cdot \sin(\frac{2(k_n)\pi t}{Nl} + \frac{2(k_n)\pi i}{N}) \pm sl \tag{9}$$

α_0 is the angle of initiation, N is the number of modules, k_n is the wave number of the serpentine movement, l is the length of the module, and i is the number of the module. The magnitude of change in unit time of t determines the propagation speed of the serpentine curve in the direction of travel of the waveform.

4   Prototyping and Basic Experiments

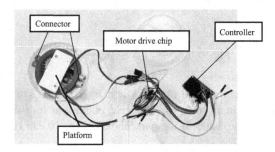

Fig. 10. Prototype of the robot

Table 1. Specifications and Performances of the Prototype

Specification &Performance	Value
Maximum Forward Speed	0.94 Body Length/s
Maximum Steering Speed	46 ± 5 PRM
Time to dock	3 s
Time to undock	0.5 s
Holding force in tension	2.55 ± 0.2 N
Wheel Speed (No Load)	46 ± 5 PRM
Wheel Torque	360 g·cm
Magnetic size	10 × 10 × 10 mm/10 × 10 × 15 mm
Overall Dimensions	95 × 95 × 95 mm
Module Weight	260 g

The prototype is shown in Fig. 10. When the robot closes the shells, we will attach the controller, the motor driven chip and the battery place on the platform. Some specifications and performance of the robot are tested, and the detailed information is shown in Table 1. Numerous experiments have also been conducted to evaluate the performance of the robot in different aspects, i.e., 1) module independent motion, 2) connection motion, 3) connection magnetic force in two directions (Fig. 11).

As Fig. 12 shown, we verified the movement of the robot and show motion of the modular driving mechanism in the spherical shell. When the two motors active, the

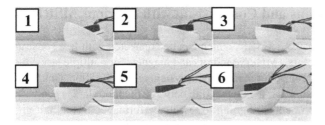

Fig. 11. Experiment of single robot moving on the ground.

center of gravity of the robot will move forward, and rolling moment will be generated, and the spherical shell will roll forward. The robot moves forward.

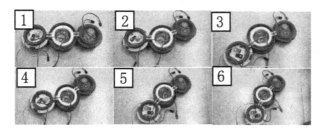

Fig. 12. Experiment of connected motion

Several of prototypes were built and relevant experiments were carried out. The robot controller of prototype is ESP32, motor driven chip is L293D. The servo motor's model is SG90. And the driving motor is planetary gear reduction motor. We measured the forces of connection magnet units along the horizontal and vertical directions to verify that connected modulars will not separate during moving. The results of experiments are showed in Table 2 and experiments are shown as Fig. 13.

Table 2. The Force of Magnetic Connection Along X-axis and Y-axis

Y-axis force (N)	2.43	2.79	2.31	2.62	2.54	2.51	2.70	2.50
X-axis force (N)	2.78	2.86	2.84	2.80	2.79	2.89	2.96	2.90

Table 2 shows the magnetic force between two sets of magnets. Figure 10 shows the magnetic force along the X_m-axis and Y_m-axis. When d = 5 mm (the distance between two sets of magnets when modules connected), the magnetic force reaches the value of 2.55N along the Y_m-axis. When d = 5 mm, the magnetic force reaches the value of 2.85N along the X_m-axis.

As described in Sect. 3.3, each module receives the signal of the rotation angle sent by the master computer in turn, and rotate the front connector ring first, and then rotate the rear connector ring.

5   Conclusions and Comparison with Previous MSRR Systems

This paper proposes a MSRR, which can be connected with less constraints. The robot only has two motors, two servo motors and magnets for multiple tasks: module independent movement, connector management system reconfiguration. Due to the fault-tolerant and freeform connector, the connection between the modulars is genderless and instant. Numerous experiments are going to test its performance to find out great potential to realize a freeform robotic system. We expected that the robot can float on the water and configure to snake shape robot which can move on the water, and the robot can reconfigure to a floating plane.

Table 3 shows the different between the robot and previous MSRR systems.

Table 3. Performances of MSRR modules

Specification	This robot	ATRON	SMORES	M-TRAN III
No. of Actuators	4	**1**	4	2
Ability to Move Independently	**Y**	N	**Y**	N
Holding Force in Tension(N)	2.55	**800**	60	25
Dock Cycle Time (s)	**0.5**	4	2.3	5
Weight (kg)	**0.28**	0.83	0.52	0.42
Data Derived from		[17]	[2]	[1, 17],[20]

References

1. Murata, S., Yoshida, E., Kamimura, A., Kurokawa, H., Tomita, K., Kokaji, S.: M-TRAN: self-reconfigurable modular robotic system. IEEE/ASME Trans. Mechatron. 7(4), 431–441 (2002)
2. Davey, J., Kwok, N., Yim, M.: Emulating self-reconfigurable robots-design of the smores system. In: IEEE/RSJ International Conference on Intelligent Robots and Systems, pp. 4464–4469 (2012)
3. Eckenstein, N., Yim, M.: Area of acceptance for 3d self-aligning robotic connectors: Concepts, metrics, and designs. In: IEEE International Conference on Robotics and Automation, pp. 1227–1233 (2014)
4. Wei, H., Chen, Y., Tan, J., Wang, T.: Sambot: a self-assembly modular robot system. IEEE/ASME Trans. Mechatron. 16(4), 745–757 (2010)
5. Liang, G., Luo, H., Li, M., Qian, H., Lam, T.L.: FreeBOT: a freeform modular self-reconfigurable robot with arbitrary connection point – design and implementation. IEEE/RSJ Int. Conf. Intell. Robots Syst. **2020**, 6506–6513 (2020)
6. Ma, S., Tadokoro, N., Li, B., Inoue, K.: Analysis of creeping locomotion of a snake robot on a slope. In: 2003 IEEE International Conference on Robotics and Automation (Cat. No.03CH37422), vol. 2, pp. 2073–2078
7. Transeth, A.A., Pettersen, K.Y.: Developments in snake robot modeling and locomotion. In: 2006 9th International Conference on Control, Automation, Robotics and Vision, pp. 1–8

8. Yang, M., et al.: Design and analysis of a spherical robot with two degrees of freedom swing. Chinese Control Decision Conf. **2020**, 4913–4918 (2020)
9. Baba, T., Kameyama, Y., Kamegawa, T., Gofuku, F.: A snake robot propelling inside of a pipe with helical rolling motion. In: Proceedings of SICE Annual Conference, pp. 2319–2325 (2010)
10. Hirose, S., Imazato, M., Kudo, Y., Umetani, Y.: Internally balanced magnetic unit. J. Robot. Soc. Japan **3**(1), 10–19 (1985) (in Japanese)
11. Chen, Y., Qiu, Z., Lu, Z., Mao, L.: Numerical simulation of hydrodynamic characteristics of underwater snake-like robot. In: International Conference on Control, Automation and Information Sciences (ICCAIS), pp. 491–495 (2015)
12. Endo, G., Togawa, K., Hirose, S.: Study on self-contained and terrain adaptive active cord mechanism. In: Proceedings of the IEEE International Conference on Intelligent Robots and Systems, pp. 1399–1405, Kyongju, Korea (1999)
13. Bicchi, A., Balluchi, D., Prattichizzo, Gorelli, A.: "Introducing the sphericle": an experimental testbed for research and teaching in nonholonomy. IEEE Int. Conf. Robot. Autom. **3**, 2620–2625 (1997)
14. Mukherjee, R., Minor, M.A., Pukrushpan, J.T.: Motion planning for a spherical mobile robot: revisiting the classical ball-plate problem. ASME. J. Dyn. Sys. Meas. Control. **124**(4), 502–551 (2002)
15. Liljebäck, P., Pettersen, K.Y., Stavdahl, Ø.: A snake robot with a contact force measurement system for obstacle-aided locomotion. IEEE Int. Conf. Robot. Autom. **2010**, 683–690 (2010)
16. 山田浩也, 広瀬茂男, 索状能動体の研究, 日本ロホット学会誌, 26巻, 7号, pp. 801–811 (2008)
17. Jorgensen, M.W., Ostergaard, E.H., Lund, H.H.: Modular atron: modules for a self-reconfigurable robot. IEEE/RSJ Int. Conf. Intell. Robots Syst. **2**, 2068–2073 (2004)
18. Kurokawa, M.H., Tomita, K., Kamimura, A., Yoshida, E., Kokaji, S., Murata, S.: Distributed self-reconfiguration control of modular robot M-TRAN. IEEE Int. Conf. Mechatron. Autom. **1**, 254–259 (2005)
19. Kurokawa, H., Tomita, K., Kamimura, A., Kokaji, S., Hasuo, T., Murata, S.: Distributed self-reconfiguration of m-tran iii modular robotic system. Int. J. Robot. Res. **27**(3–4), 373–386 (2008)

Graph Synthesis of Generalized Parallel Mechanisms with Coupling Sub-chains

Chunxu Tian[1], Luquan Li[1], Zhihao Xia[1], and Dan Zhang[1,2(✉)]

[1] Institute of AI and Robotics, Academy for Engineering and Technology, Fudan University, Shanghai 200433, PR China
chxtian@fudan.edu.cn, dzhang99@yorku.ca
[2] Department of Mechanical Engineering, The Hong Kong Polytechnic University, Kowloon, Hong Kong

Abstract. Over the past few decades, there has been extensive research conducted in both academia and industry on conventional parallel manipulators. However, the exploration of generalized parallel mechanisms with coupling sub-chains has received limited attention. This paper introduces a novel approach to synthesizing parallel mechanisms with additional connecting sub-chains, focusing on number synthesis and graph representation. To develop manipulators with additional constraints, this study constructs contracted graphs with different loops. The contracted graphs are represented by arrays, which denote the connectivity relationships among associated linkages, leading to the discovery of new contracted graphs. Besides, the connective array is introduced to identify isomorphic and invalid contracted graphs, while also analyzing specific contracted graph variations. Furthermore, this paper deduces the evolutionary process of contracted graphs, resulting in the derivation of all available topological arrangements. This innovative method for graph synthesis of parallel mechanisms with coupling sub-chains has the potential to expand the range of available options within the family of generalized parallel mechanisms.

Keywords: Graph Synthesis · Generalized Parallel Mechanism · Coupling Sub-chain · Constructed Graph · Associated Linkage

1 Introduction

Parallel mechanisms exhibit a distinctive feature of linking the platform and the base, or connecting multiple branches within serial kinematic chains [1]. These mechanisms are characterized by their compact structure, high stiffness, strong load-bearing capacity, and the ability to produce combined translational and rotational outputs. Consequently, they find wide-ranging applications in work environment involving multi-force loading, shaking, and polishing of large components. Over the past few decades, the research community has faced the significant and challenging task of designing innovative and practical manipulators. Mechanism type synthesis plays a crucial role in enabling the creative design of parallel mechanisms, and substantial research has been dedicated to this endeavor [2]. Employing various mathematic and mathematical tools, researchers have successfully generated numerous efficient mechanisms [3–5].

© The Author(s), under exclusive license to Springer Nature Singapore Pte Ltd. 2023
H. Yang et al. (Eds.): ICIRA 2023, LNAI 14275, pp. 76–87, 2023.
https://doi.org/10.1007/978-981-99-6504-5_7

So far, the majority of researchers have primarily concentrated on designing conventional parallel mechanisms or spatial kinematic linkages separately. [6]. In general, parallel mechanisms that incorporate coupling sub-chains offer potential advantages such as increased accuracy, stiffness, and greater load-carrying capacity compared to their counterparts. Moreover, they have the ability to achieve specific output motion patterns tailored to specific requirements [7]. Therefore, the introduction of generalized parallel mechanisms (GPMs) with coupling sub-chains is proposed as a means to enhance the performance and functionality of parallel manipulators, and the in-depth study for GPMs has profound academic value and engineering significance. Regarding this type of mechanism, Zeng et al. [8] applied displacement group theory to develop the structural synthesis of multi-loop structures. Zoppi et al. [9] designed a novel interconnected-chains parallel manipulator specifically for manufacturing revolute surfaces. Ding et al. [10] systematically presented a method for addressing the structural synthesis and mobility analysis of two-layer two-loop hybrid mechanisms. Tian [11, 12] proposed the graph and type synthesis of generalized parallel mechanisms with coupling sub-chains by screw theory.

The contracted graph (CG) serves as a fundamental and effective tool for the synthesis of multi-loop mechanisms [13]. Therefore, in order to explore new spatial parallel mechanisms that incorporate interconnected sub-chains, it is essential to initially analyze the CGs [14–16]. However, there are two key considerations that need to be addressed. One pertains to accurately describing the graph, while the other involves identifying isomorphic and invalid graphs. The identification of isomorphism in graphs has remained one of the most challenging problems. Since current isomorphism identification methods heavily rely on personal experience, certain potential mechanisms are inevitably overlooked.

For this reason, the novel graph synthesis method of GPMs with connecting sub-chains are presented in this paper. Accordingly, the remainder of this paper is organized as follows: In Sect. 2, the Euler's equation is introduced into the graph theory and the CGs are constructed. Section 3 covers the geometric mapping, which signifies the arrangements of CGs. Moreover, the evolution process of the CGs is deduced in section 'Geometric Mapping of Contracted Graphs'. Then, the arrays representation and characteristic string of CGs with different loops are conducted, and the isomorphic CGs are identified. Finally, all the evolved contracted graphs are derived through analysing the characteristic strings and conclusions are drawn.

2 Construction of Contracted Graphs

Different from designing new mechanisms through scholars' inspiration and experience, novel mechanisms can be constructed via the number synthesis followed by topological structures. The arrangement of topological structures are derived from the corresponding CGs [12]. For closed-loop topological arrangements, vertices are arranged on the circumference and connected via lines. The CGs are featured by connecting single-degree-of-freedom (DOF) kinematic pairs to links. Using lines (pathes) and vertices (nodes) of geometry to represent serial kinematic chains and basic links [17]. Nothing that basic links are corresponding with six kinds of links as:

- A binary link consists of an L_B link connected to two single-DOF kinematic joints.
- A ternary link comprises an L_T connected to three single-DOF kinematic joints.
- A quaternary link is formed by an L_Q connected to four single-DOF joints.
- A pentagonal link involves an L_{Pe} connected to five single-DOF kinematic joints.
- A hexagonal link is composed of an L_{He} connected to six single-DOF joints.

The configurations of mechanisms are specified by mapping of independent variables, which can be the total number of full-cycle or general mobility F in the mechanism. According to the modified Kutzbach-Grübler formula [18], the formula for calculating general mobility of GPMs can be interpreted as

$$F = \sum_{i=1}^{j} f_i - dL + \zeta - v \tag{1}$$

where L is the number of independent loops, j for the number of kinematic joints, f_i for the allowed DOFs of the ith joint, d for the dimension of task space, ζ denotes the passive DOF, v signifies the redundant constraints.

For a multiple-loop mechanism, we formulate the loop-closure equation above for each independent loop of the mechanism to obtain a set of constraint equations. We note that a multi-DOF joint can be modeled by two or three single-DOF joints. According to *Euler's equation* [19], the calculation of independent loops for the mechanism can be arrived at

$$L = J - N + 1 \tag{2}$$

where N represents the number of links, and J for the number of joints.

If n_k is adopted to signify the number of corresponding basic links, then, the solutions for counting N and J are given as

$$N = n_{LB} + n_{LT} + n_{LQ} + n_{LPe} + n_{LHe} = \sum_{k=2} n_k \tag{3}$$

and

$$J = \tfrac{1}{2}\left(2n_{LB} + 3n_{LT} + 4n_{LQ} + 5n_{LPe} + 6n_{LHe}\right) = \tfrac{1}{2}\sum_{k=2} n_k \tag{4}$$

We now can verify the total number of independent loops in the *GPM*s as follows:

$$L = \tfrac{1}{2}\sum_{k=2} k \cdot n_k - \sum_{k=2} n_k + 1 = \tfrac{1}{2}\left[n_{LT} + 2n_{LQ} + 3n_{LPe} + 4n_{LHe}\right] + 1 \tag{5}$$

where, k represents the number of basic joints connecting to the basic links. Therefore, an immediate consequence of formula (5) is that the number of independent loops in any mechanism can be specified by the parameters of basic links except for binary links. Solving Eqs. (1) and (5) for n_{LB}, yields

$$n_{LB} = 6 + 5(L-1) + F + \zeta - v - \left(n_{LT} + n_{LQ} + n_{LPe} + n_{LHe}\right) = 5L - \sum_{k=2} n_k + \Omega \tag{6}$$

where the coefficient $\Omega = F + \zeta - v + 1$ is calculated to specify the total number of binary links in the topological graph. That is, the particular elements of basic links in the mechanism can be found after providing a set of L, F, ζ and v.

Table 1. Available basic link combinations with $L = 2/3/4/5$.

L	No	n_{LB}	n_{LT}	n_{LQ}	n_{LPe}	n_{LHe}	L	No	n_{LB}	n_{LT}	n_{LQ}	n_{LPe}	n_{LHe}
2	1	$8 + \Phi$	2	0	0	0	4	8	$17 + \Phi$	2	0	0	1
	2	$9 + \Phi$	0	1	0	0		9	$18 + \Phi$	0	1	0	1
3	1	$11 + \Phi$	4	0	0	0	5	1	$17 + \Phi$	8	0	0	0
	2	$12 + \Phi$	2	1	0	0		2	$18 + \Phi$	6	1	0	0
	3	$13 + \Phi$	0	2	0	0		3	$19 + \Phi$	5	0	1	0
	4	$13 + \Phi$	1	0	1	0		4	$19 + \Phi$	4	2	0	0
	5	$14 + \Phi$	0	0	0	1		5	$20 + \Phi$	3	1	1	0
4	1	$14 + \Phi$	6	0	0	0		6	$20 + \Phi$	2	3	0	0
	2	$15 + \Phi$	4	1	0	0		7	$21 + \Phi$	1	2	1	0
	3	$16 + \Phi$	3	0	1	0		8	$21 + \Phi$	2	0	2	0
	4	$16 + \Phi$	2	2	0	0		9	$20 + \Phi$	4	0	0	1
	5	$17 + \Phi$	1	1	1	0		10	$22 + \Phi$	1	0	1	1
	6	$17 + \Phi$	0	3	0	0		11	$22 + \Phi$	0	2	0	1
	7	$18 + \Phi$	0	0	2	0		12	$22 + \Phi$	0	1	2	0

In general, the parallel mechanisms are limited to the structures that are constructed by longitudinal serial-chain linkages of six or fewer joints. In contrast to conventional parallel mechanisms, one of the remarkable features in GPMs is applying latitudinal coupling sub-chains. Consequently, intermediate moving platforms, which can be basic links excluding binary links, must be built-in to generate additional independent loops. In this connection, the number of independent loops L is greater than or equal to 2, that is $L \geq 2$. As a result, by solving Eqs. (3), (5) and (6), we arrive at all sets of acceptable basic links. Table 1 provides the basic link combinations to construct novel structures of GPMs. As for $L = 6$, the feasible combination of basic links has been revealed in the authors' previous work [11, 12].

3   Geometric Mapping of Contracted Graphs

The arrangement of CGs is a basic and effective tool for the graph synthesis of GPMs. In a CGs, vertices are connected with each other by edges, which represents serial sub-chains. Meanwhile, basic links in the CG are corresponding with vertices of geometry. Then, the formative logic of the contracted graph with $(\sum_{k=2} n_k - n_{LB})$ vertices and $(\frac{1}{2}\sum_{k=2} n_k - n_{LB})$ edges can be developed by adding edges and vertices to a lower dimensional form through a particular principle [20].

Table 2. Formative logic and types for One/Two-dimensional forms

Type	Contracted graphs and topological arrangement
1D	I(1, 2) I(2, 2) I(3, 2) I(4, 3)
	I(1⊕1, 2) = I(2, 2); I(2⊕1, 2) = I(3, 2); I(3⊕1, 2) = I(4, 3)
2D	II(1, 3, 3) II(2, 5, 4) II(3, 7, 5) II(3, 8, 6)
	II(1⊕1, 3, 3) = II(2, 5, 4); II(2⊕1, 5, 4) = II(3, 7, 5); II(2⊕1, 5, 4) = II(3, 8, 6)

Noting that the hybrid arrangements of contracted graph that can be divided into two disconnected graphs by splitting one vertex are removed. In a GPM, serial sub-chains and platforms are two types of basic elements. Prior to synthesizing GPMs, it is necessary to determine the acceptable topological arrangement of the corresponding CG. Afterwards, the required structure of the mechanism can be disassembled and configured. As a result, an arbitrary CG can be developed by means of the geometric mapping. In this work, topological arrangements are divided into three types according to the geometrical characteristics. Therefore, the CGs are specified as follows:

- The geometric type I refers to one-dimensional chain, which is formed by serial, parallel, and hybrid topology without coupling sub-chains;
- The geometric type II is corresponding with two-dimensional netted plane, which is constructed by topology;
- The geometric type III is the hybrid form of a three-dimensional netted polyhedron (see Table 3).

Table 3. Formative logic and types for Three-dimensional forms

Types	Contracted graphs and topological arrangements
3D	

III(1, 4, 6, 4)   III(2, 6, 9, 5)   III(3, 8, 12, 6)   III(4, 8, 13, 6)

III(1⊕1,4,6,4) = III(2,6,9,5); III(2⊕1,6,9,5) = III(3,8,12,6); III(3⊕1,8,12,6) = (4,8,13,6)

III(1, 5, 8, 5)   III(2, 8, 12, 6)   III(1, 5, 9, 6)   III(2, 8, 14, 8)

III(1⊕1, 5, 8, 5) = III(2, 8, 12, 6);   III(1⊕1, 5, 9, 6) = III(2, 8, 14, 8);

In Table 2, *P* and *F* respectively denote the moving platform and the fixed base platform, letters *v*, *e*, *p*, and *h* refer to the number of vertices, edges, planes, and polyhedrons, respectively, in geometry. Use I(*e*, *v*), II(*p*, *e*, *v*) and III(*h*, *p*, *e*, *v*) to explain the dimensional forms of the topological arrangements and CGs. Following the formative logic, there are three manners of developing various required geometries, that is, arranging edges I(ý⊕e) of physical one-dimensional forms, arranging planes II(⊕p) of two-dimensional forms, and arranging polyhedron III(⊕h). Significantly, as far as the definition of the end-effector moving platform and the fixed base platform is concerned, different selections result in various topological arrangements. When the connected number of sub-chains in the intermediate moving platform is less than 3, the platform needs to be integrated into the part of sub-chains. For example, the topological arrangement II(1, 3, 3) and I(2, 2) are equivalent and correspond to the same CGs.

4   Isomorphism Identification of Contracted Graphs

After conducting the derivation of spatial CGs, the isomorphism identification becomes the priority among priorities of synthesizing mechanisms. To obtain all potential acceptable CGs and avoid isomorphic units, the CG construction is derived by applying the characteristic strings. Before performing the isomorphism identification, the spatial multi-dimensional CGs are transformed into planar circles. The vertices are distributing around the circumference and connected by edges. The topological arrangement of two vertices and one edge can be viewed as an origami crease mark. Noting that the CGs with any vertex arranged inside the circumference are regarded as invalid structures.

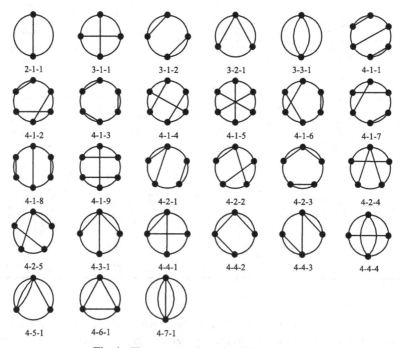

Fig. 1. The contracted graphs with $L = 2/3/4$.

4.1 Arrays Representation

The process of topological evolution can be described in more detail as follows: After arranging two vertices and one edge on CG 2-1-1, CG 3-1-1 and CG 3-1-2 can be obtained; CG 3-2-1 are derived by arranging one vertex and one edge on CG 2-1-1, and one vertex is shared with existing basic link; When arranging one edge on the existing basic link of CG 2-1-1, CG 3-1-1 is derived. Noting that two vertices are shared; Similarly, CG 4-1-1 and CG 4-1-8 are evolved from CG 3-1-2 by adding two vertices and one edge; CG 4-1-2, CG 4-1-6 and CG 4-1-7 are obtained by arranging two vertices and one edge on CG 3-1-1 or CG 3-1-2.

Through the similar analysis, all the evolved CGs can be derived, as shown in Fig. 1. The characteristic string accounts for connection of basic links in a CG and can be signified by connective arrays. Arabic numerals $1, 2, 3, 4, 5, \ldots$ denote basic links distributing around the circumference. Every two-digit number indicates the existence of connection between two corresponding vertices. For the sake of clarity, the intervals arrays are used to denote the corresponding vertices apart in two associative basic links. Therefore, all characteristic strings can be found in Table 4.

4.2 Isomorphism Identification

In most situations, isomorphic CGs can be visually detected by the user. In the alternative, suspicious CGs are capable of being verified by a set of characteristic strings, automatically.

The process of the characteristic string method is described in detail as follows:

- a set of contracted graphs A and B are mutually isomorphic when the connective arrays of these CGs are equivalent by switching the initial basic link.

If the foregoing hypothesis is not true, these CGs are corresponding to different arrangements.

Through analysing a group of character strings intuitively, one can confirm if the two CGs are isomorphic or not. The availability of the proposed isomorphic identification method can be proved via the proof by contradiction, which is a kind of proof that establishes the truth of proposition by supposition. The proof by contradiction of the isomorphism identification is described as the following steps:

1. The first step is to suppose that the proposition is false, namely, CGs A and B are different when the connective arrays are the same by switching the initial basic link.
2. As the above conditional statement being false, one can derived that the second order path arrays, which are obtained from the adjacency matrices of the CGs, are different.
3. Use 4×4 matrices $\boldsymbol{M}_A$ and $\boldsymbol{M}_B$ denote the adjacency matrices of the CGs A and B, which have four basic links. The rows of matrix $\boldsymbol{M}_A$ are list as follows: $row_{A1} = [0, a, b, c]$, $row_{A2} = [a, 0, d, e]$, $row_{A3} = [b, d, 0, f]$, and $row_{A4} = [c, e, f, 0]$. Meanwhile, the rows of the matrix $\boldsymbol{M}_B$ consist of $row_{B1} = [0, b, c, a]$, $row_{B2} = [e, 0, d, a]$, $row_{B3} = [b, f, 0, d]$, and $row_{B4} = [c, f, e, 0]$.
4. All pairs of numbers in the array of CG (x) are the same as that in CG (y) by replacing the numbers in order. Thus, the first order path arrays of CG (x) and CG (y) are the same: $abc.ade.bdf.cef$.

However, the character strings of $A_1{}^2$ and $A_2{}^2$ are identical [21]. We can conclude that the second order path arrays are identical. This reveals CG (x) and CG (y) must be mutually isomorphic. Therefore, there exists a contradiction between the proof and supposition. In other words, the proposition is true. The proof is completed.

Table 4. The process of topological evolution of contracted graphs.

CG	CG	v	e	CG	CG	v	e
2-1-1	-	-	-	4-1-9	3-1-1/ 3-1-2	2/2	1/1
3-1-1	2-1-1	2	1	4-2-1	3-1-2/ 3-2-1	1/2	1/1
3-1-2	2-1-1	2	1	4-2-2	3-1-1/ 3-1-2/ 3-2-1	1/1/2	1/1/1
3-2-1	2-1-1	1	1	4-2-3	3-1-2/ 3-2-1	1/2	1/1
3-3-1	2-1-1	0	1	4-2-4	3-1-1/ 3-2-1	1/2	1/1
4-1-1	3-1-2	2	1	4-2-5	3-1-1/ 3-1-2/ 3-2-1	1/1/2	1/1/1
4-1-2	3-1-1/ 3-1-2	2/2	1/1	4-3-1	3-2-1	1	1
4-1-3	3-1-2	2	1	4-4-1	3-1-1/ 3-2-1	0/1	1/1
4-1-4	3-1-1/ 3-1-2	2/2	1/1	4-4-2	3-1-2/ 3-2-1	0/1	1/1
4-1-5	3-1-1	2	1	4-4-3	3-1-2/ 3-2-1	0/1	1/1
4-1-6	3-1-1/ 3-1-2	2/2	1/1	4-5-1	3-2-1/ 3-3-1	0/1	1/1
4-1-7	3-1-1/ 3-1-2	2/2	1/1	4-6-1	3-2-1	0	1
4-1-8	3-1-2	2	1	4-7-1	3-3-1	0	1

As a result, the connective arrays of the derived contracted graphs are obtained as shown in Table 5. According to the isomorphic identification, a group of isomorphic contracted graphs has the following characteristics: the connective arrays are equivalent after replacing the numbers in order. To observe different groups of connective arrays, the digital span is introduced to distinguish different contracted graphs. And the effectiveness of this method can be proved by the response value [22].

For example, in the contract graph 4-1-2 with connective array (12 35 46), the initial position 1 is replaced by the position 3. Consequently, basic links 2, 3, 4, 5, and 6 are changed to 6, 1, 2, 3, and 4. Then the new contract graph 4-1-6 with connective array (13 24 56) are obtained, as shown in Fig. 2. Similarly, the other isomorphic contract graph 4-1-7 with connective array (13 24 45) can be obtained after replacing positions 2, 3, 4, 5, and 6 by 5, 6, 1, 2, and 3. As it can be seen that the isomorphic contracted graphs in this group have the same digital span as ignoring the order of the array. Similar to the above analysis, the contract graphs 4-1-1 and 4-1-8, the contract graphs 4-1-4 and 4-1-9, and the contract graphs 4-2-2 and 4-2-5, are mutually isomorphic, respectively. Therefore, three groups of isomorphic contracted graphs are obtained as drawn in Fig. 3. In summary, after the relatively simplified analysis, 21 non-isomorphic contracted graphs for $L = 2/3/4$ are proposed and four groups of contracted graphs which are mutually isomorphic are discovered.

Table 5. The connective arrays and digital span of contracted graphs

Type	Connective arrays	Digital span	Type	Connective arrays	Digital span
2-1-1	12	0	4-1-9	14 26 35	2 1 1
3-1-1	13 24	1 1	4-2-1	12 13 45	0 1 0
3-1-2	12 34	0 0	4-2-2	12 14 35	0 1 1
3-2-1	12 13	0 1	4-2-3	12 15 34	0 0 0
3-3-1	12 12	0 0	4-2-4	13 14 25	1 1 0
4-1-1	12 36 45	0 2 0	4-2-5	13 15 24	1 0 1
4-1-2	12 35 46	0 1 1	4-3-1	12 13 14	0 1 1
4-1-3	12 34 56	0 0 0	4-4-1	12 13 24	0 1 0
4-1-4	13 25 46	1 2 1	4-4-2	12 14 23	0 0 0
4-1-5	14 25 36	2 2 2	4-4-3	13 14 23	1 0 0
4-1-6	13 24 56	1 1 0	4-5-1	12 12 13	0 0 1
4-1-7	13 26 45	1 1 0	4-6-1	12 13 23	0 1 0
4-1-8	14 23 56	2 0 0	4-7-1	12 12 12	0 0 0

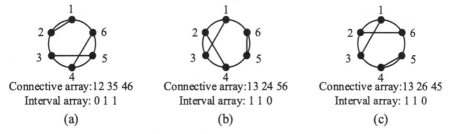

Connective array:12 35 46
Interval array: 0 1 1
(a)

Connective array:13 24 56
Interval array: 1 1 0
(b)

Connective array:13 26 45
Interval array: 1 1 0
(c)

Fig. 2. The group of three mutually isomorphic contracted graphs.

As for the 21 non-isomorphic contracted graphs, the corresponding contracted topological graphs can be obtained by arranging fixed platform and end-effector moving platform on the basic links of the contracted graphs. As a result, 21 contracted topological graphs with $L = 2/3/4$ are derived.

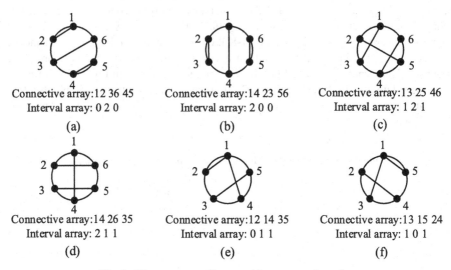

Connective array:12 36 45
Interval array: 0 2 0
(a)

Connective array:14 23 56
Interval array: 2 0 0
(b)

Connective array:13 25 46
Interval array: 1 2 1
(c)

Connective array:14 26 35
Interval array: 2 1 1
(d)

Connective array:12 14 35
Interval array: 0 1 1
(e)

Connective array:13 15 24
Interval array: 1 0 1
(f)

Fig. 3. Three groups of isomorphic contracted graphs.

5 Conclusions

In this paper, the novel graph synthesis method of GPMs with connecting sub-chains has been presented. The Euler's equation has been introduced into the graph theory, and the relationship of associated linkages and independent loops have been established. The proposed connective array method is a feasible and effective method for identifying isomorphic CGs has been proposed. Then the CGs which are mutually isomorphic or isomorphic with themselves have been revealed. Besides, the geometric mapping and formative logic of different dimensional CGs has been deduced. Moreover, the arrays representation of CGs with different loops have been conducted, and the isomorphic CGs have been identified. Finally, 21 non-isomorphic CGs for $L = 2/3/4$ have been derived.

Acknowledgements. This work is founded by National Nature Science Foundation of China (grants 52150710538).

References

1. Gogu, G.: Structural Synthesis of Parallel Robots. Springer (2008)
2. Huang, Z., Li, Q., Ding, H.: Theory of Parallel Mechanisms. Springer, Netherlands, Dordrecht (2013)
3. Wang, Z., Zhang, W., Ding, X.: A family of RCM mechanisms: type synthesis and kinematics analysis. Int. J. Mech. Sci. **231**, 107590 (2022)
4. Meng, Z., Cao, W., Ding, H., Chen, Z.: A new six degree-of-freedom parallel robot with three limbs for high-speed operations. Mech. Mach. Theory **173**, 104875 (2022)
5. Tian, C., Zhang, D.: A new family of generalized parallel manipulators with configurable moving platforms. Mech. Mach. Theory **153**, 103997 (2020)
6. Guo, S., Fang, Y., Qu, H.: Type synthesis of 4-DOF nonoverconstrained parallel mechanisms based on screw theory. Robotica **30**, 31–37 (2012)
7. Tian, C., Zhang, D., Tang, H., Wu, C.: Structure synthesis of reconfigurable generalized parallel mechanisms with configurable platforms. Mech. Mach. Theory **160**, 104281 (2021)
8. Zeng, Q., Fang, Y.: Structural synthesis and analysis of serial–parallel hybrid mechanisms with spatial multi-loop kinematic chains. Mech. Mach. Theory **49**, 198–215 (2012)
9. Zoppi, M., Bruzzone, L., Molfino, R., et al.: A novel 5-DoF Interconnected-Chains PKM for manufacturing of revolute surfaces. In: 4th Chemnitzer Parallel Kinematik Seminar, pp. 20–21. Chemnitz (2004)
10. Cao, W., Ding, H., Chen, Z., Zhao, S.: Mobility analysis and structural synthesis of a class of spatial mechanisms with coupling chains. Robotica **34**, 2467–2485 (2016)
11. Tian, C., Fang, Y., Ge, Q.J.: Structural synthesis of parallel manipulators with coupling sub-chains. Mech. Mach. Theory **118**, 84–99 (2017)
12. Tian, C., Fang, Y., Ge, Q.J.: Design and analysis of a partially decoupled generalized parallel mechanism for 3T1R motion. Mech. Mach. Theory **140**, 211–232 (2019)
13. L.-W. Tsai, Mechanism Design: Enumeration of Kinematic Structures According to Function. CRC press (2000)
14. Gogu, G.: Structural synthesis of fully-isotropic translational parallel robots via theory of linear transformations. Eur. J. Mech.-A/Solids **23**, 1021–1039 (2004)
15. Vucina, D., Freudenstein, F.: An application of graph theory and nonlinear programming to the kinematic synthesis of mechanisms. Mech. Mach. Theory **26**, 553–563 (1991)
16. Lu, Y., Leinonen, T.: Type synthesis of unified planar–spatial mechanisms by systematic linkage and topology matrix-graph technique. Mech. Mach. Theory **40**, 1145–1163 (2005)
17. Lu, Y., Ye, N.: Type synthesis of parallel mechanisms by utilizing sub-mechanisms and digital topological graphs. Mech. Mach. Theory **109**, 39–50 (2017)
18. Huang, Z., Li, Q.C.: General methodology for type synthesis of symmetrical lower-mobility parallel manipulators and several novel manipulators. Int. J. Robot. Res. **21**, 131–145 (2002)
19. Tsai, L.-W.: Robot Analysis: The Mechanics of Serial and Parallel Manipulators. Wiley, New York (1999)
20. Zeng, Q., Fang, Y.: Algorithm for topological design of multi-loop hybrid mechanisms via logical proposition. Robotica **30**, 599–612 (2012)
21. Lu, Y., Lu, Y., Ye, N., Mao, B., Han, J., Sui, C.: Derivation of valid contracted graphs from simpler contracted graphs for type synthesis of closed mechanisms. Mech. Mach. Theory **52**, 206–218 (2012)
22. Xia, Z., Zhang, D., Chen, Y., Tian, C., Liu, J., Wu, C.: A novel 6 DOFs generalized parallel manipulator design and analysis based on humanoid leg. Mech. Mach. Theory **176**, 105029 (2022)

Analysis of Mechanism Elastodynamic Performance in Automatic Excavating Process of Excavating Robot

Liang He[1,3], Fen Wang[1,2(✉)], YaPing Wang[1], Wei Li[1], Jiao Ma[1], Zhenglong Chen[1], and Ganwei Cai[2]

[1] School of Construction Machinery, Hunan Sany Polytechnic College, Changsha, China
414936424@qq.com
[2] School of Mechanical Engineering, Guangxi University, Nanning, China
[3] School of Mechanical and Electrical Engineering, Central South University, Changsha, China

Abstract. The robotization of excavator has become an important development trend, the calculation and analysis of the dynamic performance of excavating robot during the automatic excavation process is the foundation for optimizing the design, fatigue analysis, and vibration research of their working devices. Due to the different elastic angles and curvatures at the connection between the hydraulic cylinder and the hydraulic rod, this paper proposes a hydraulic driving element unit. Taking excavation of foundation pits as an example, the particle swarm optimization algorithm is used to calculate the joint angle values corresponding to the path points, and the joint trajectory is interpolated using a cross difference polynomial. Based on the classic soil bucket model, a finite element model diagram of the hydraulic excavator working device is established, and the first three natural frequencies and dynamic response of the bucket end during the operation process are solved. The calculation trajectory of the bucket tooth tip during excavation of the foundation pit is obtained.

Keywords: Excavating robot · Dynamic response · Trajectory planning

1 Introduction

With the development of electrification, self-driving technology, automatic excavating and other technologies, the robotization of excavator has become an important development trend. It is important to study the dynamic performance of excavating robot in the automatic excavation process.

The dynamic performance of excavator mechanism has been studied a lot, Du J N [1] used step load to simulate load mutation, used fourth-order Runge-Kutta method

---

Supported by organization The National Natural Science Foundation of China(51765005), The Guangxi Science and Technology Major Projects(Gui Ke AA19254021) and the Natural Science Foundation of Changsha City(kq2208085).

H. Yang et al. (Eds.): ICIRA 2023, LNAI 14275, pp. 88–100, 2023.
https://doi.org/10.1007/978-981-99-6504-5_8

to analyze the dynamic response of lifting system of large mining hydraulic excavator, obtained acceleration response, and studied its time domain and frequency domain. Wang X B [2] used the mode superposition method to solve the dynamic response of the working device of mining electric shovel excavator, and analyzed the six typical mode shapes. Wang X B et al. [3] used the beam element model with concentrated mass to be equivalent to the excavator working device, established its dynamic equation with Lagrange method, and solved its dynamic response with numerical software. Guo L X et al. [4] established a three-dimensional finite element model of the excavator's working device, obtained the resonant frequency and vibration mode of the working device system through modal analysis, and solved the dynamic response of the working device under different digging resistance. Bošnjak et al. [5] used a four-degree-of freedom discrete dynamic model to study the influence of structural parameters on the response of the bucket wheel excavator superstructure. Taking four typical geometric configurations of buildings on the upper floor as examples, they determined the influence of structural element stiffness and bucket wheel weight on the system response. The working device model of hydraulic excavator established in the above studies does not consider the particularity of hydraulic components. In previous studies, there is no mechanism dynamics considering the excavation resistance in the process of automatic excavation, therefore, this paper takes this as the starting point to establish the hydraulic component unit, and takes excavation of foundation pit as an example to solve the dynamic responses of the excavating mechanism running along this trajectory.

2   Kinematic Model and Excavating Condition

In this paper, a certain type of excavating robot is taken as an example. Its physical picture is shown in Fig. 1, and its working device motion diagram is shown in Fig. 2, without considering the slewing device. Where *AB*, *HQ* and *QJ* are boom, bucket rod and bucket respectively; *CF*, *DH* and *EK* are boom hydraulic cylinder, bucket rod hydraulic cylinder and bucket hydraulic cylinder respectively, *NK* is connecting rod, *KL* is rocker.

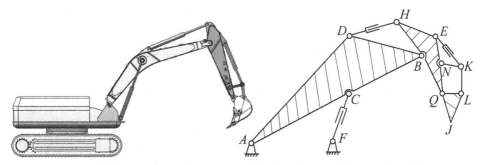

Fig. 1. 3D model of the whole machine   **Fig. 2.** Kinematic diagram of working mechanism

2.1   Forward and Inverse Kinematics of the Working Device

DH parameter method is used to establish the DH coordinate system of the working device of hydraulic excavator, as shown in Fig. 3. The pose expression of bucket tooth tip is obtained through the secondary coordinate transformation, and the DH parameter table is shown in Table 1.

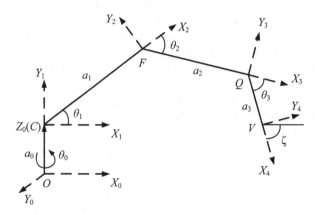

Fig. 3. DH coordinate system of working mechanism

Table 1. D-H parameter table of working device of excavating robot

Joint i	θ_i	d_i/mm	a_i/mm	α_i/(°)
0	θ_0	2760	0	90
1	θ_1	0	6400	0
2	θ_2	0	4190	0
3	θ_3	0	1720	0

According to coordinate transformation calculation, the transformation expression of joint space in position and pose space is finally obtained as shown in Eq. (1).

$$\begin{cases} x = c\theta_0(a_3c\theta_{123} + a_2c\theta_{12} + a_1c_1 + a_0) \\ y = s\theta_0(a_3c\theta_{123} + a_2c\theta_{12} + a_1c_1 + a_0) \\ z = a_3s_{123} + a_2s_{12} + a_1s\theta_1 + d_0 \end{cases} \tag{1}$$

The transformation from pose space to joint space is the process of inverse solution. Firstly, the joint Angle (A_1, B_1, C_1) and the position of the target point (X,Y) are given in the initial state, and then the corresponding joint Angle value (A_2, B_2, C_2) when reaching the target point is inversely solved by particle swarm optimization algorithm based on the principle of stationary joint Angle transformation.

In the solution of particle swarm optimization algorithm, this paper takes the joint Angle corresponding to the target point as the design variable. Taking the minimum sum of joint Angle changes of each joint as the objective function, it can be expressed as: $min(|A_2 - A_1| + |B_2 - B_1| + |C_2 - C_1|)$. The constraint condition is that the positive solution obtained from the optimization result is the same as the coordinate of the target point, but this equality constraint condition is difficult to realize. Therefore, this paper uses the penalty coefficient method to transform the original optimization problem into an optimization problem without constraints, and its final adaptive value function is:

$$F_f = \omega_{ik}((a_3 \cos(A_2 + B_2 + C_2) + a_2 \cos(A_2 + B_2) + a_1 \cos(A_2) - X_2)^2 + (a_3 \sin(A_2 + B_2 + C_2)$$
$$+a_2 \sin(A_2 + B_2) + a_1 \sin(A_2) + d_0 - Y_2)^2) + \min(|A_2 - A_1| + |B_2 - B_1| + |C_2 - C_1|) \tag{2}$$

where is the penalty coefficient, whose value is 10000.

Particle swarm optimization algorithm is used to solve the joint Angle of the target point of the working device. The joint Angle value (°) of the initial point was set as (0, -90, -45), the coordinate of the first target point was set as (6,0, -4), the particle number $N = 20$, the inertia weight, the acceleration factor $C1 = C2 = 1.5$, and the final evolutionary algebra was 150. The inverse kinematic solution results were shown in Table 2.

Table 2. Inverse solution results of kinematics of working mechanism

	Joint angle A	Joint angle B	Joint angle C
Starting point	$-20°$	$-10°$	$-45°$
Target point	$-21.942°$	$-10.553°$	$-45.000°$

2.2 Determination of Excavation Conditions

2.2.1 Mining Trajectory Curves

In this paper, taking excavation of foundation pit as an example, the first three order natural frequencies and time domain diagram of the working device are solved when it works along the corresponding trajectory under this working condition. The excavation path of foundation pit is shown in Fig. 4. The joint angles of the corresponding waypoints are shown in Table 3.

The "4–3–3–3–4" polynomial of Sun Z Y [6] was selected for joint space trajectory planning, and the trajectory curves of each joint were solved by combining the waypoints and joint Angle values in Table 3. The trajectory curves of the joint space of the manipulator, bucket bar and bucket were expressed as follows:

The trajectory curve of the arm joint is:

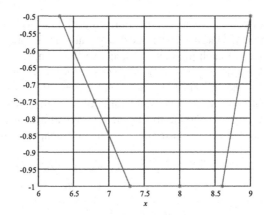

Fig. 4. Mining path diagram

Table 3. Waypoints and joint Angle values

Node sequence number	Tooth tip coordinate point /m	Angle of articulated arm /(°)	Bucket Rod joint angle /(°)	Bucket joint angle /(°)
1	(9, −0.5)	4.1749	−43.8726	−45.0000
2	(8.6, −1)	2.8950	−51.3881	−38.5000
3	(8, −1)	6.2097	−65.9235	−29.4500
4	(7.3, −1)	8.7878	−81.0872	−17.6000
5	(6.8, −0.75)	10.1000	−81.3384	−37.0077
6	(6.3, −0.5)	10.1910	−81.8021	−55.0000

$$\begin{cases} \theta_{11}=0.802t^4 - 1.590t^3 + 4.175(0 < t < 1.5714) \\ \theta_{12} = -1.926(t - 1.5714)^3 + 4.375(t - 1.5714)^2 + 0.659(t - 1.5714) + 2.895(1.5714 < t < 2.6154) \\ \theta_{13} = 0.350(t - 2.6154)^3 - 1.742(t - 2.6154)^2 + 3.446t + 6.210(2.6154 < t < 4.1242) \\ \theta_{14} = -0.048(t - 4.1242)^3 + 0.107(t - 4.1242)^2 + 0.566(t - 4.1242) + 8.788(4.1242 < t < 6.8219) \\ \theta_{15} = -0.012(t - 6.8219)^4 + 0.089(t - 6.8219)^3 - 0.236(t - 6.8219)^2 + 0.258(t - 6.8219) + 10.100 \\ (6.8219 < t < 9.0686) \end{cases}$$

$$(3)$$

The trajectory curve of the Bucket rod joint is:

$$
\begin{cases}
\theta_{21} = 0.678t^4 - 3.006t^3 - 43.873(0 < t < 1.5714) \\
\theta_{22} = 2.128(t - 1.5714)^3 - 4.137(t - 1.5714)^2 - 11.739(t - 1.5714) - 51.388(1.5714 < t < 2.6154) \\
\theta_{23} = 0.039(t - 2.6154)^3 + 2.620(t - 2.6154)^2 - 13.344t - 65.924(2.6154 < t < 4.1242) \\
\theta_{24} = -0.546(t - 4.1242)^3 + 2.828(t - 4.1242)^2 - 3.745(t - 4.1242) - 81.087(4.1242 < t < 6.8219) \\
\theta_{25} = -0.090(t - 6.8219)^4 + 0.568(t - 6.8219)^3 - 1.093(t - 6.8219)^2 + 0.407(t - 6.8219) \\
\quad -81.338(6.8219 < t < 9.0686)
\end{cases}
\tag{4}
$$

The trajectory curve of the bucket joint is:

$$
\begin{cases}
\theta_{31} = -1.063t^4 + 3.348t^3 - 45(0 < t < 1.5714) \\
\theta_{32} = 0.166(t - 1.5714)^3 + 0.053(t - 1.5714)^2 + 8.308(t - 1.5714) - 38.500(1.5714 < t < 2.6154) \\
\theta_{33} = -1.056(t - 2.6154)^3 + 0.581(t - 2.6154)^2 + 8.979t - 29.450(2.6154 < t < 4.1242) \\
\theta_{34} = 0.465(t - 4.1242)^3 - 4.500(t - 4.1242)^2 + 1.194(t - 4.1242) - 17.600(4.1242 < t < 6.8219) \\
\theta_{35} = -0.813(t - 6.8219)^4 + 3.904(t - 6.8219)^3 - 1.664(t - 6.8219)^2 - 14.753(t - 6.8219) \\
\quad -37.008(6.8219 < t < 9.0686)
\end{cases}
\tag{5}
$$

2.2.2 Excavating Resistance

The classical soil bucket model is a mathematical model proposed by Reece [7] to simulate the soil cutting process, as shown in Fig. 5. The basic earthmoving equation (FEE) is based on this model to calculate the digging resistance in the cutting process, as shown in Eq. (6).

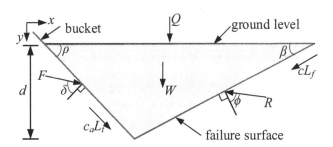

Fig. 5. Classic soil bucket model

Where W is the gravity of movable wedge soil; Q is the gravity of the overloaded part (the soil accumulated above the ground level); L_t is the bucket length; L_f is the length of soil failure surface (the plane on which wedge soil moves); c_a is the adhesion coefficient between soil and bucket; C is the cohesion coefficient between soils. d is the digging depth (the depth of the bucket tooth tip below the ground plane); R is the force of soil to prevent wedge soil movement; φ is the internal friction Angle of soil; β the Angle between ground plane and soil failure surface; ρ is the Angle between the ground plane and the bucket; F is the digging force of the bucket acting on the soil; δ is the Angle between F and the normal direction of the bucket.

$$F = \frac{W + Q + cd[1 + \cot\beta\cot(\beta + \phi)]}{\cos(\rho + \delta) + \sin(\rho + \phi)\cot(\beta + \phi)} + \frac{c_a d[1 - \cot\rho\cot(\beta + \phi)]}{\cos(\rho + \delta) + \sin(\rho + \phi)\cot(\beta + \phi)}$$

(6)

3 Element Elastodynamic Model

3.1 Beam Element

For the hydraulic excavator, a simple three-link mechanism, each rod is simulated by a straight beam with equal section. As shown in Fig. 6, the boom, bucket rod and bucket are modeled by beam elements.

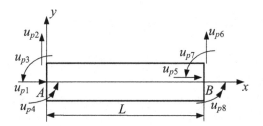

Fig. 6. Beam elements and generalized coordinates

In the Fig. 6, u_{p1}, u_{p5} is the longitudinal displacement at nodes A and B; u_{p2}, u_{p6} is the transverse displacement at nodes A and B; u_{p3}, u_{p7} is the elastic rotation Angle at nodes A and B; u_{p4}, u_{p8} is the curvature at nodes A and B. The above eight generalized coordinate arrays are combined into the element generalized coordinate array of the linkage, as shown below.

$$\mathbf{u}_p = \begin{bmatrix} u_{p1}\, u_{p2}\, u_{p3}\, u_{p4}\, u_{p5}\, u_{p6}\, u_{p7}\, u_{p8} \end{bmatrix}^{\mathrm{T}}$$

(7)

4 Hydraulic Drive Element Unit

The hydraulic driving element is composed of hydraulic cylinder and hydraulic rod, so the hydraulic driving element needs to be simulated by two beam elements. Moreover, they have different material properties, different cross-sectional areas and different length changes, so the elastic rotation Angle and curvature at the connection point of the two elements are different. Figure (a) in Fig. 7 is the hydraulic cylinder unit and its generalized coordinates, and figure (b) is the hydraulic rod unit and its generalized coordinates.

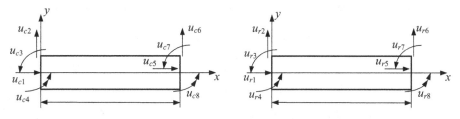

(a) units and generalized coordinates   (b) rod elements and generalized coordinates

Fig. 7. Hydraulic cylinder, rod element, generalized coordinates

Because the horizontal and vertical coordinates of the connection between the hydraulic cylinder and the hydraulic rod are equal, therefore $U_{c5} = U_{r1}$, $U_{c6} = U_{r2}$. The generalized coordinate array of the element at any point on the hydraulic cylinder can be expressed as:

$$\mathbf{u}_c = [u_{c1} \, u_{c2} \, u_{c3} \, u_{c4} \, u_{c5} \, u_{c6} \, u_{c7} \, u_{c8}]^\mathrm{T} \tag{8}$$

The generalized coordinate array of the element at any point on the hydraulic rod can be expressed as:

$$\mathbf{u}_r = [u_{r1} \, u_{r2} \, u_{r3} \, u_{r4} \, u_{r5} \, u_{r6} \, u_{r7} \, u_{r8}]^\mathrm{T} \tag{9}$$

The generalized coordinate array of the element at the connection point of the hydraulic cylinder and the hydraulic rod can be expressed as:

$$\mathbf{u}_{cr} = [u_{c5} \, u_{c6} \, u_{c7} \, u_{c8} \, 0 \, 0 \, u_{r3} \, u_{r4}]^\mathrm{T} \tag{10}$$

5   Finite Element Model of Hydraulic Excavator Working Device

The mechanism and finite element model diagram of excavating robot at a certain moment are established, as shown in Fig. 8. In this paper, the rocker and connecting rod are not considered. The boom and bucket rod are divided into three units, the bucket is divided into two units, and the three hydraulic components are divided into two units. With 1, 2, … indicates the node number. The value can be ①, ②, … Represents the unit number.

Therefore, a total of 13 nodes, 14 units and 52 generalized coordinates are set up in this institution. The generalized coordinate array U of the system is defined by symbols $U_1, U_2, \cdots, U_{52}$, and then U can be expressed as:

$$\mathbf{U} = [U_1 \, U_2 \, \cdots \, U_{52}]^T \tag{11}$$

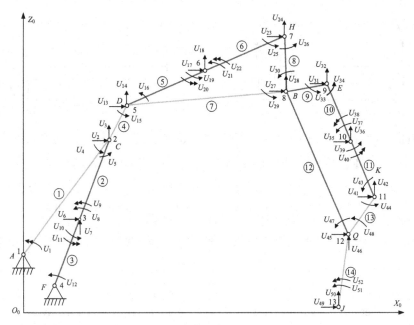

Fig. 8. Finite element model diagram of working mechanism of excavating robot

The model composition matrix $\mathbf{I}_u$ is used to represent the relationship between the unit label and the whole label, which can be expressed as:

$$
\mathbf{I}_u = \begin{bmatrix}
0 & 0 & 0 & 1 & 2 & 3 & 4 & 0 \\
2 & 3 & 5 & 0 & 6 & 7 & 8 & 9 \\
6 & 7 & 10 & 11 & 0 & 0 & 12 & 0 \\
2 & 3 & 4 & 0 & 13 & 14 & 15 & 0 \\
13 & 14 & 16 & 0 & 17 & 18 & 19 & 20 \\
17 & 18 & 21 & 22 & 23 & 24 & 25 & 0 \\
13 & 14 & 15 & 0 & 27 & 28 & 29 & 0 \\
23 & 24 & 26 & 0 & 27 & 28 & 30 & 0 \\
27 & 28 & 30 & 0 & 31 & 32 & 33 & 0 \\
31 & 32 & 34 & 0 & 35 & 36 & 37 & 38 \\
35 & 36 & 39 & 40 & 41 & 42 & 43 & 0 \\
28 & 29 & 30 & 0 & 45 & 46 & 47 & 0 \\
41 & 42 & 44 & 0 & 45 & 46 & 48 & 0 \\
45 & 46 & 48 & 0 & 49 & 50 & 51 & 52
\end{bmatrix} \tag{12}
$$

6 Frequency Characteristics and Dynamic Response Analysis

6.1 Natural Frequency

The natural frequency is an important index reflecting the dynamic characteristics of the robot mechanism. The mechanism needs to avoid resonance in practical application to prevent damage to the mechanism and safety accidents. At the same time, the size of the natural frequency also reflects the stiffness of the robot mechanism [8]. The natural frequency of the mechanism system is determined by its dynamic characteristic parameters, and the natural frequency of the system can be attributed to the problem of finding the following eigenvalues, as shown in Eq. (13):

$$\left[\mathbf{K}^{(i)} - \left(\omega^{(i)}\right)^2 \mathbf{M}^{(i)}\right]\varphi^{(i)} = 0 \tag{13}$$

The cross-sectional area A of the boom, bucket bar, bucket and hydraulic components, the density ρ of the material, the elastic modulus E of the material, the moment of inertia I of the section and the length L of each element are given in Tables 4 and 5. Combining these material parameters, the natural frequency of the excavator working device along the excavation can be calculated.

Table 4. Parameter table of hydraulic excavator working device

	Cross-sectional area (m^2)	density (kg/m^3)	Elastic modulus (N/m^2)	Moment of inertia (m^4)
Rrm	2.6e-1	7.8e3	2.1e11	1.33e-3
Rod	2.2e-1	7.8e3	2.1e11	8.76e-3
Bucket	7.86e-2	7.8e3	2.1e11	2.34e-5
Hydraulic cylinders	3.14e-2	7.85e3	2.1e11	5.97e-5
Hydraulic rod	7.85e-3	7.85e3	2.1e11	4.91e-6

Combined with the parameters in Table 4 and Table 5 and the coordinates of excavating waypoints, the first three natural frequencies of the excavating robot working mechanism along the excavating path are obtained as shown in Fig. 9.

It can be seen from Fig. 9 that the variation range of the first natural frequency is 8.8–10.1 Hz, with an average value of 9.5 Hz; the variation range of the second natural frequency is 12.1–15.6 Hz, with an average value of 14.1 Hz; the variation range of the third natural frequency is 20.3–26.6 Hz, with an average value of 23.2 Hz. It can be seen that when the hydraulic excavator works on this track, its first, second and third order natural frequencies do not change much with the position of the working device.

Table 5. Length of working device unit of excavating robot

The unit number	length /m	The unit number	length /m	The unit number	length /m
1	2.99	6	2.15	11	1.52
2	1.81	7	3.78	12	3.12
3	/	8	0.91	13	0.69
4	0.71	9	0.73	14	1.72
5	/	10	/		

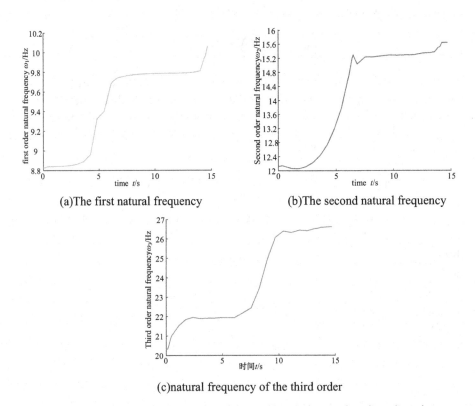

(a)The first natural frequency   (b)The second natural frequency

(c)natural frequency of the third order

Fig. 9. The first three natural frequencies of the working device running along the trajectory

6.2 Dynamic Response Analysis

Newmark method is used to solve the dynamic response of hydraulic excavator during excavation. The solution steps of Newmark method are as follows:

(1) According to the initial conditions x_0 and $\dot{x}_0$, Eq. (14) is used to obtain $\ddot{x}_0$, and the initial values of x_0 and $\dot{x}_0$ in this paper are all 0.

$$\ddot{x}_0 = M^{-1}(F - C\dot{x}_0 - Kx_0) \tag{14}$$

(2) Select appropriate values of Δt, α and β. In this paper, $\Delta t = 0.02s$, $\alpha = \frac{1}{2}$, $\beta = \frac{1}{2}$.

(3) Starting from I = 1, Eq. (15) is used to calculate the displacement vector x_{i+1}.

$$x_{i+1} = \left[\frac{1}{\alpha(\Delta t)^2}m + \frac{\beta}{\alpha\Delta t}c + k\right]^{-1} \times \left\{F_{i+1} + m\left[\frac{1}{\alpha(\Delta t)^2}x_i + \frac{1}{\alpha\Delta t}\dot{x}_i + (2\alpha - 1)\ddot{x}_i\right]\right.$$
$$\left. + c\left[\frac{\beta}{\alpha\Delta t}x_i + \left(\frac{\beta}{\alpha} - 1\right)\dot{x}_i + \left(\frac{\beta}{\alpha} - 2\right)\frac{\Delta t}{2}\ddot{x}_i\right]\right\}$$

(15)

(4) Find the velocity and acceleration vector at time t_{i+1} according to Eqs. (14) and (15), and repeat steps (2)-(3).

$$\ddot{x}_{i+1} = \frac{1}{\alpha(\Delta t)^2}(x_{i+1} - x_i) - \frac{1}{\alpha\Delta t}\dot{x}_i - \left(\frac{1}{2\alpha} - 1\right)\ddot{x}_i \qquad (16)$$

$$\dot{x}_{i+1} = \dot{x}_i + (1 - \beta)\Delta t\ddot{x}_i + \beta\Delta t\ddot{x}_{i+1} \qquad (17)$$

Taking the joint trajectory curve of the excavation excavation as an example, the excavation resistance was taken as the external excitation, and the dynamic response of the end of the working device was obtained by using Newmark method and numerical simulation software, as shown in Fig. 10 (a), (b), (c).

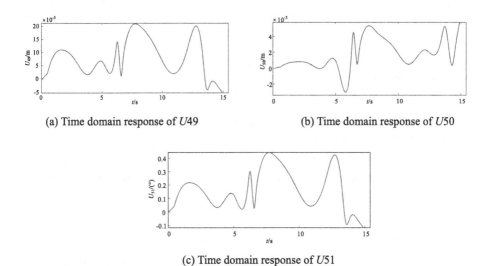

(a) Time domain response of $U49$ (b) Time domain response of $U50$

(c) Time domain response of $U51$

Fig. 10. Time-domain responses of lateral displacement $U49$, longitudinal displacement $U50$ and elastic Angle $U51$ of the end point

7 Conclusion

In this paper, firstly, the forward and inverse solutions of the excavating robot working mechanism are solved, the excavating conditions and their corresponding waypoints are given, and the joint angle value corresponding to the waypoints is calculated by the inverse kinematic solution solution method, and the joint Angle is interpolated by 4–3–3–3-4 polynomial, and the joint curve expression is obtained. At the same time, the digging resistance formula of classical soil-bucket model is adopted. Due to hydraulic cylinder and hydraulic rod joint Angle and curvature elasticity is different, so in this paper, a hydraulic driving element unit, builds the finite element model of hydraulic excavator working device, before working condition of mining as an example, combined with the digging resistance, to the work device along the track, the first three order natural frequency of the operation are, at the same time, take the bucket at the end of the time-domain diagram, It provides a certain theoretical basis for the control of real trajectory of excavating robot.

References

1. Du, J.N.: Dynamic Characteristics Analysis of Hoist System for Electric Mining Shovel. Dalian University of Technology, Dalian (2018)
2. Wang, X.B.: Optimization Design Methods of the Excavating Trajectory for Intelligent Electric Shovels. Dalian University of Technology, Dalian (2019)
3. Wang, X.B., Tong, S.G., Zhang, J., et al.: Research on Dynamics of Hydraulic Excavators Rotating Device System Based on Finite Element Analysis. Mechanical Science and Technology for Aerospace Engineering. **34**(11), 1693–1698 (2015)
4. Guo, L.X., Xie, H.L., Zhou, S.W., et al.: Dynamic response analysis of working device of hydraulic excavator under working impact loading. Appl. Mech. Mater. **16–19**, 39–43 (2009)
5. Bošnjak, S.M., Oguamanam, D.C.D., Zrnić, N.Đ: The influence of constructive parameters on response of bucket wheel excavator superstructure in the out-of-resonance region. Archives of Civil and Mechanical Engineering **15**(4), 977–985 (2015)
6. Sun, Z.Y., Zhang, Y.Y., Li, H., et al.: Time optimal trajectory planning of excavator. J. Mecha. Eng. **55**(05), 166–174 (2019)
7. Reece, A.R.: The fundamental equation of earthmoving mechanics. J. Terrramech. **2**(1), 99 (1965)
8. Dong, C.L.: Modeling and Integrated Design of A Novel 5-DOF Hybrid Robot. Tianjin University, Tianjin (2022)

Measurement and Analysis of End Jitter of Six-Axis Industrial Robots

Hongfei Zu[1(✉)], Mingxu Zhao[1], Zhangwei Chen[2], Jianxin He[3], and Jun Zhou[3]

[1] School of Mechanical Engineering, Zhejiang Sci-Tech University, Hangzhou 310018, China
zuhongfei@zstu.edu.cn
[2] State Key Laboratory of Fluid Power and Mechatronic Systems, Zhejiang University, Hangzhou 310058, China
[3] Changzhou Institute of Inspection, Testing, Standardization and Certification, Changzhou 21 3000, China

Abstract. In this manuscript, the force hammer excitation method was employed to measure and analyze the intrinsic frequency of the six-axis industrial robot. The end jitter of the robot under different working conditions was tested with the help of the end jitter testing platform, and the trajectory that minimized the end jitter amplitude was obtained by comparing the end displacement of different trajectories at the same speed. Furthermore, in order to investigate the impact of each single joint rotation on end jitter, the end jitter caused by independent rotation of each joint was measured, and it was found that the rotation of joint 2 and joint 3 caused larger jitter than others for the tested robot. Finally, the single-joint rotation self-power spectrum was used to derive the dominant frequency in the low frequency range during single-joint rotation and the relationship between end jitter and robot resonance was analyzed.

Keywords: Industrial Robot · End Jitter · Modal Analysis · Self-power Spectrum

1 Introduction

Against the backdrop of the Industrial Revolution, various new scientific and technological advancements have continuously emerged, particularly the rapid development of electronic information technology since the mid-20th century, which has had significant positive impacts on societal transformation. Since the implementation of the reform and opening-up policy in China, there have been remarkable improvements in the industrial economy and scientific and technological levels, leading to substantial progress in societal productivity. Many new scientific and technological achievements have been widely applied across various domains, injecting strong momentum into the nation's prosperity and development. In addition to engineering products such as computers, refrigerators, televisions, automobiles, and mobile phones, industrial robots, representing a new type of advanced and precision technology, have also gradually appeared in industrial, civilian, and military fields, exerting positive and profound influences on modern society's production and lifestyle [1–3].

© The Author(s), under exclusive license to Springer Nature Singapore Pte Ltd. 2023
H. Yang et al. (Eds.): ICIRA 2023, LNAI 14275, pp. 101–109, 2023.
https://doi.org/10.1007/978-981-99-6504-5_9

Industrial robots are widely used in production activities because of their high accuracy, efficiency, high intelligence and adaptability to the environment. In production activities, trajectory accuracy and positioning accuracy are important indicators of measuring the superiority of robotic arms [4–6], and these indicators are increasingly required in industrial production. Moreover, robotic arms with high accuracy indicators are becoming more and more popular in high-end intelligent manufacturing. It has been found that jitter at the end of the robotic arm is a key factor for its poor trajectory accuracy. Both the small overall stiffness of the robot arm and the operating error of each joint motor can cause the actual trajectory of the robot to deviate significantly from the theoretical trajectory. Another phenomenon that cannot be ignored is that when the jitter frequency of the robot end is close to the intrinsic frequency of the robot, resonance will occur, which will cause the jitter to be exceptionally severe. Therefore, it is necessary to study the testing methods for the end jitter of the robot and analyze its sources.

2   System Composition and Measurement Methods

2.1   System Composition

The experiment in this work was conducted on a Bronte 6-axis industrial robot with the model of BRTIRUS0805A. The testing system included a 6-axis industrial robot, an intelligent portable 8-channel data acquisition and analyzer, a force hammer, triaxial accelerometers, and PC-based data acquisition and analysis system [7].The robot is excited by a force hammer and the intrinsic frequency of the robot is acquired by the data acquisition and analyzer. The principle of modal analysis is shown in Fig. 1, and the first five orders of intrinsic frequencies are shown in Table 1. As shown in Table 1, it can be known that the first to fifth order intrinsic frequencies of the robot are 12.5, 17.5, 30, 61.25 and 102.49 Hz, respectively.

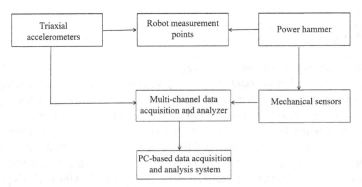

Fig. 1. Schematic diagram of the modal analysis experiment.

Table 1. Robot intrinsic frequency (Hz)

Order/Direction	1	2	3	4	5
Z	12.5	17.5	30	61.25	102.49

2.2 Jitter Measurement at the End of Different Trajectories at the Same Speed

During the test, the initial and target positions of the industrial robot in the global coordinate system (X, Y, Z) were set to be (0, 583, 649.5) and (-150, 700, 800), respectively, and the following three trajectories were tested:

Track 1: The robot moved sequentially in the Z, Y, and X directions from the initial point to the target point, i.e. from (0, 583, 649.5) to (0, 583, 800) to (0, 700, 800) and to (-150, 700, 800).

Track 2: The robot moved sequentially in the Y, X, and Z directions, i.e. (0, 583, 649.5) to (0, 700, 649.5) to (-150, 700, 649.5) and to (-150, 700, 800).

Track 3: The robot moved in the Z, X, and Y directions in sequence, i.e. (0, 583, 649.5) to (0, 583, 800) to (-150, 583, 800) and to (-150, 700, 800).

In the above trajectories, point-to-point linear motion path actions were selected for pose linear command, which means that the six joints of the robot worked together to ensure that the end of the robot moved in a straight line. The experimental setup was to run the above three trajectories at 100% speed to study the impact of different trajectories

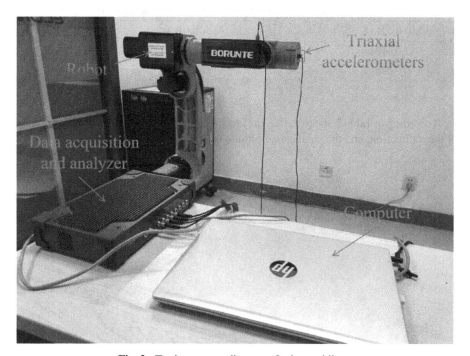

Fig. 2. Testing system diagram of robot end jitter.

on the end jitter of the robot at the same speed. The triaxial accelerometers is placed at the end of the robot and the jitter data of the robot during the motion is acquired by the data acquisition and analyzer. The testing system consists of a robot, triaxial accelerometers, a data acquisition and analyzer, and a computer, as shown in Fig. 2.

The acceleration signal is obtained from the accelerometers [8, 9]. The velocity signal is obtained by integrating the acceleration signal:

$$V(t) = \int a(t)dt \tag{1}$$

Then the velocity signal is integrated to obtain the displacement signal:

$$S(t) = \int v(t)dt \tag{2}$$

3   Results and Discussions

The three-directional displacements measured by the measuring system are shown in Table 2.

Table 2. Jitter amplitude in different directions

Direction	Positive directional displacement (mm)	Negative directional displacement (mm)
X	0.02132	−0.01918
Y	0.01835	−0.02063
Z	0.02612	−0.02556

According to Table 2, the robot has the largest jitter amplitude in z direction, followed by the x direction, and the smallest amplitude is in y direction.

The end jitter at the same speed for different trajectories was analyzed in various ways by processing the experimental data. It is worth noting first that due to the limited stiffness of the robot, abrupt changes in end displacement occur when performing start and stop operations [10]. Triaxial accelerometers collected jitter signals in each direction, and a comparison of the end jitter in the Z-direction for different trajectories is shown in Fig. 3 and Table 3.

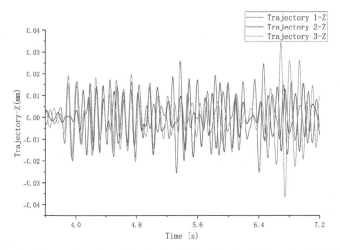

Fig. 3. Comparison of end jitter in the Z-direction for different trajectories

Table 3. Jitter statistics in the Z-axis direction for different trajectories

Tracks	Track 1	Track 2	Track 3
Average value	0.00786	0.00693	0.00802
Peak	0.0261	0.0183	0.0365

In this work, the end jitter of the studied robot was tested, and based on the testing results, it can be found that the end jitter in the Z-axis direction was more concentrated, so it was selected to represent the end jitter of each trajectory for comparison. From Table 3 and Fig. 3, it can be seen that the peak value of end jitter of trajectory 3 is 0.0365 mm, which is 39.8% higher than that of trajectory 1 and 132.5% of trajectory 2, respectively. Among the three different trajectories, trajectory 2 is the smoothest and most accurate one, which is more suitable for practical application in processing production.

Then the end jitter of the robot when each joint rotates at the same angle and speed is measured. As shown in Fig. 4, the amplitudes of the jitter are very small when joint one, four and six rotates separately. Joint five has a large peak of jitter, but overall it is relatively stable. However, the rotation of joint two and joint three has a particularly prominent impact on end jitter.

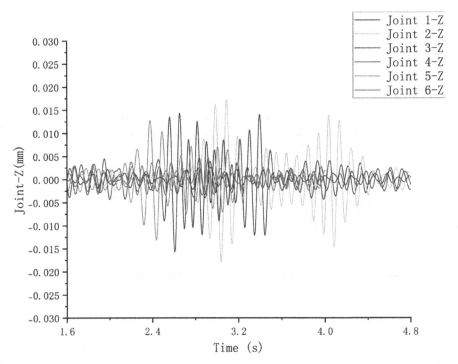

Fig. 4. Comparison of jitter at the end of a single joint rotation in the Z-axis direction.

During the experiment, in addition to time-domain signals, frequency-domain signals represented by the self-power spectrum were also captured and analyzed. The self-power spectrum reflects the frequency domain structure of the signal and is essentially calculated from the spectral function, i.e. the complex spectrum multiplied by its conjugate. As it reflects the square of the amplitude, its frequency domain structure is more distinctive making it more suitable for jitter frequency analysis.

$$S_x(\omega) = \lim_{T \to \infty} \frac{1}{T} |X(\omega)|^2 \qquad (3)$$

where $X(\omega)$ is the spectrum function.

The sampling frequency was set to be 2560 Hz and the number of sampling points was 2048. Through Fig. 5 and Fig. 6, the following results can be obtained: the main frequency of the end jitter when only joint two moves is 10 Hz, it is 11.25 Hz when only joint three moves, and the first-order intrinsic frequency of the robot is 12.5 Hz. The resonance frequency can be interpreted as the frequency band within the floating range of the inherent frequency, and the resonance band should also be considered in practical engineering applications to avoid the resonance band. The general resonance band is taken as 40% of the intrinsic frequency. The empirical calculation of joint two main frequency is lower than the inherent frequency by 20%, and joint three main frequency is lower than the inherent frequency by 10%, which are theoretically in the resonance band. Therefore, it can be inferred that the possible reason for the vibration of joint two and joint three is the resonance caused by the vibration frequency of the reducer or motor of joint 2 and joint 3 being close to the natural frequency of the robot body [11].

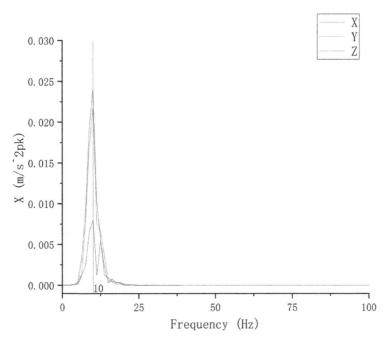

Fig. 5. Self-power spectrum of joint 2 during rotation.

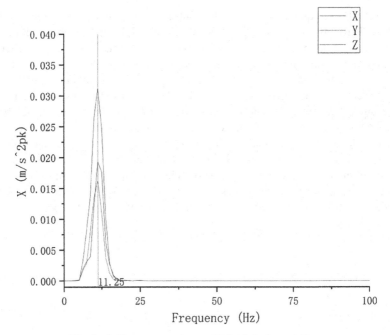

Fig. 6. Self-power spectrum of joint 3 during rotation.

4 Conclusion

The testing of the studied robot in this work showed that the motions of joint two and joint three had the greatest effect on the end jitter. To investigate whether the intense end jitter during the motion of joint two and three was caused by the resonance, the self-power spectrum was analyzed. It was found that the main frequencies of joint 2 and joint 3 during rotation were close to the intrinsic frequencies, so the end jitter was probably caused by the resonance. To reduce the jitter of this robot, it is recommended to replace the gearbox of robot joints 2 and 3, or to move joints 2 and 3 first in trajectory planning. More importantly, the measurement and analysis methods proposed in this article can be extended to other series robots.

Acknowledgment. This work was supported by the "Ningbo High tech Zone 2021 Major Science and Technology Special Project (Major Technological Innovation Project)" (No.: 2021DCX050012).

References

1. Ruishu, Z.: The status and development of industrial robots. Materials Science and Engineering (2018)
2. Gao, H.: Development Status and Trend of Industrial Robot in China. Applied Science and Innovative Research (2021)

3. Li, Z., Liu, S., Wang, S.: Current situation and future of chinese industrial robot development. Int. J. Mechan. Eng. Robo. Res. (2016)
4. Zhang, S., Huang, D.: End-Point regulation and vibration suppression of a flexible robotic manipulator. Asian Journal of Control **19**(1), 245–254 (2017)
5. Cheng, H., Li, W.: Reducing the frame vibration of delta robot in pick and place application: an acceleration profile optimization approach. Shock and Vibration (2018)
6. Der-Ming, K., Lien-Wen, C.: Kineto-elastodynamic vibration analysis of robot manipulators by the finite element method. Comput. Struct. **37**(3), 309–317 (1990)
7. Jong, K.K., Hwan, L.Y., Beom, L.K., Soon, L.C., Yeon, C.J., Ho, K.J.: Estimation of structural displacements for cantilever beam using mode shapes and accelerometers under free vibration. J. Korean Soc. Aerona. Space Sci. (2017)
8. Sensor Research; Studies from Korea Advanced Institute of Science and Technology (KAIST) in the Area of Sensor Research Described (Forecasting the Concentration of Particulate Matter in the Seoul Metropolitan Area Using a Gaussian Process Model). Journal of Engineering (2020)
9. Viviana, M., Yanez Sergio, J., Leonel, Q., Saavedra Flores Erick, I.: Damage detection in steel-concrete composite structures by impact hammer modal testing and experimental validation. Sensors **22**, 3874–3874 (2022)
10. Liu, G.R., Quek, S.S.: The finite element method: a practical course. Butterworth-Heinemann (2013)
11. Benfield, W.A., Hruda, R.F.: Vibration analysis of structures by component mode substitution. AIAA J. **9**(7), 1255–1261 (1971)

Description of Configuration Transformation Matrix of Reconfigurable Mechanism and Automatic Retrieval and Recognition of Motion Mode

Liang Cai[1], Chunyan Zhang[1(✉)], and An Ping[2]

[1] Shanghai University of Engineering Science, Shanghai, China
2623218851@qq.com
[2] Donghua University, Shanghai 201620, China

Abstract. Aiming at the problem of incomplete expression of the configuration description matrix information of reconfigurable mechanisms, a new matrix description method for the topological structure and configuration changes of reconfigurable mechanisms is proposed to effectively describe the compound hinges in the reconfigurable mechanisms. Recognition, determination of multiple components, determination of movement types and orientations, the new matrix description method is used to express the configuration changes of the reconfigurable mechanism, and the mathematical operation of the configuration change law is used as the recognition of the mechanism in different motion modes. Finally, a reconfigurable multi-mode mobile robot is used as a case for analysis and verification. The results show that, compared with the traditional description matrix method, the method proposed in this paper has the characteristics of clear and rich information expression, simple structure, and is conducive to automatic retrieval and recognition of movement modes.

Keywords: Reconfigurable mechanism · Configuration description matrix · Configuration transformation · Mode recognition

1 Introduction

Reconfigurable mechanism is a kind of mechanism which realizes the change of topological structure configuration through reconstruction when the mechanism is performing tasks, including metamorphic mechanism, multi-mode mechanism, bifurcation mechanism and so on. The reconfigurable mechanism, which differs from the traditional mechanism with a relatively fixed number of components and a single functional mode, is distinguished by multiple topologies and multiple motion modes that do not require reassembly. Therefore, reconfigurable mechanisms have great engineering application value in the fields of ground robot technology, aerospace, precision machining and so on.

H. Yang et al. (Eds.): ICIRA 2023, LNAI 14275, pp. 110–123, 2023.
https://doi.org/10.1007/978-981-99-6504-5_10

The configuration change of a reconfigurable mechanism is described using single and double color topologymatrices, and other representation methods. Matrix has attracted the attention and research of experts and scholars as an important method for mechanism and motion pair description, compound hinge recognition, configuration motion chain synthesis, mechanism configuration change analysis, and other fields. Ref. [7] studied the adjacency matrix used to describe the configuration transformation matrix and the azimuth change of the kinematic pair. In Ref. [8], for the identification of composite hinges in the kinematic chain of the mechanism, which is difficult to analyze, an adjacency matrix based on the adjacency matrix between components and components is proposed, and the improved Hamming number is used to determine the isomorphism. However, the information on the type of kinematic pairs and the change of spatial orientation of kinematic pairs cannot be described. Reference [9] used the eigenvalues and eigenvectors of the computer value-added matrix to determine the composite hinge and isomorphism, but the value-added matrix had a large number of non-integer values after solving, and the matrix expression was not simple and could not describe the type information of the component motion pair.

In summary, while the reconfigurable mechanism has made some progress in the use of matrix description, it has not been able to further express the structural characteristics and topological characteristics of the mechanism itself, and cannot simultaneously meet the analysis of composite hinge recognition, multi-component determination, motion pair type and orientation determination in reconfigurable mechanisms.

Based on this, this paper proposes a matrix description method for reconfigurable mechanisms that can clearly describe the structural and topological characteristics. This matrix is used to describe the mathematical operations of the reduction and increase of the number of components and the change of the azimuth information of the kinematic pairs in the process of mechanism reconstruction. The accuracy and uniqueness of this mathematical operation are used to identify the configuration change law of the reconfigurable mechanism to determine its different motion modes. Finally, a reconfigurable multi-mode mobile mechanism is used as a case to verify the correctness of the matrix method analysis.

2 Configuration Matrix of Describing Reconfigurable Mechanism

2.1 Configuration Matrix Element Information of Reconfigurable Mechanism

The use of an unimproved adjacency matrix or incidence matrix based on key points and components can result in issues such as missing information representation of the constitutive matrix and the inability to identify some key features of the mechanism. Taking Fig. 1 motion chain as an example, the components are numbered and the key points are shown in the figure, and its motion chain contains other characteristic elements such as composite hinges and multiple components. Among them, the key points 1, 7, 8, 9, 10, 11, 13 are composite hinges, 3C, 6F are moving pairs,. Using the adjacency matrix A without improvement shown in Eq. (1), whose rows and columns are the component numbers of the kinematic chain, respectively. The adjacency matrix can express the basic information of the kinematic chain, such as whether there is a connection among the components, but it cannot effectively identify and express the type of kinematic pair, the spatial orientation change of the kinematic pair, the composite hinge and other information existing in the mechanism.

$$
A = \begin{bmatrix}
0 & 1 & 0 & 0 & 0 & 0 & 0 & 0 & 0 & 0 & 0 & 0 & 1 & 0 & 0 & 0 \\
1 & 0 & 1 & 0 & 0 & 0 & 0 & 0 & 0 & 0 & 0 & 0 & 0 & 0 & 0 & 0 \\
0 & 1 & 0 & 1 & 0 & 0 & 0 & 0 & 0 & 0 & 0 & 0 & 0 & 0 & 1 & 0 \\
0 & 0 & 1 & 0 & 1 & 0 & 0 & 0 & 0 & 0 & 0 & 0 & 0 & 0 & 1 & 0 \\
0 & 0 & 0 & 1 & 0 & 1 & 0 & 0 & 0 & 0 & 0 & 0 & 0 & 0 & 0 & 0 \\
0 & 0 & 0 & 0 & 1 & 0 & 0 & 0 & 0 & 0 & 0 & 0 & 0 & 0 & 0 & 1 \\
0 & 0 & 0 & 0 & 0 & 0 & 0 & 1 & 1 & 0 & 0 & 0 & 1 & 1 & 0 & 0 \\
0 & 0 & 0 & 0 & 0 & 0 & 1 & 0 & 0 & 1 & 1 & 0 & 1 & 0 & 0 & 0 \\
0 & 0 & 0 & 0 & 0 & 0 & 1 & 0 & 0 & 1 & 0 & 0 & 0 & 1 & 0 & 0 \\
0 & 0 & 0 & 0 & 0 & 0 & 0 & 1 & 1 & 0 & 1 & 0 & 0 & 0 & 0 & 1 \\
0 & 0 & 0 & 0 & 0 & 0 & 0 & 1 & 0 & 1 & 0 & 1 & 0 & 0 & 0 & 0 \\
0 & 0 & 0 & 0 & 0 & 0 & 0 & 0 & 0 & 0 & 1 & 0 & 1 & 0 & 0 & 0 \\
1 & 0 & 0 & 0 & 0 & 0 & 1 & 1 & 0 & 0 & 0 & 1 & 0 & 0 & 0 & 0 \\
0 & 0 & 0 & 0 & 0 & 0 & 1 & 0 & 1 & 0 & 0 & 0 & 0 & 0 & 1 & 0 \\
0 & 0 & 1 & 1 & 0 & 0 & 0 & 0 & 0 & 0 & 0 & 0 & 0 & 1 & 0 & 0 \\
0 & 0 & 0 & 0 & 0 & 1 & 0 & 0 & 0 & 1 & 0 & 0 & 0 & 0 & 0 & 0
\end{bmatrix}
\tag{1}
$$

The incidence matrix A is constructed as shown in Formula (2), whose rows and columns represent the key point number of the kinematic chain and component respectively. The incidence matrix of the kinematic chain can express the relationship between the component and the kinematic pair, and can express the existing multi-component to some extent. However, the information such as the type of kinematic pair, the spatial orientation change of the kinematic pair, and the composite hinge in the kinematic chain cannot be effectively identified and expressed.

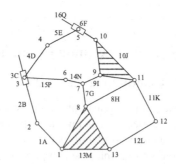

Fig. 1. Motion chain and its components, key point number

Using existing methods to describe the phenomenon, the information cannot be fully and accurately expressed. This paper constructs a new configuration matrix based on the characteristics of the reconfigurable mechanism's configuration transformation to describe the configuration of the reconfigurable mechanism, the connection relationship of the components, the type of the kinematic pair, and the orientation characteristics of the kinematic pair based on the relationship between the key points.

$$
\mathbf{A} = \begin{bmatrix}
1 & 1 & 0 & 0 & 0 & 0 & 0 & 0 & 0 & 0 & 0 & 0 & 0 & 0 \\
0 & 1 & 1 & 0 & 0 & 0 & 0 & 0 & 0 & 0 & 0 & 0 & 0 & 0 \\
0 & 0 & 1 & 0 & 0 & 0 & 0 & 0 & 0 & 0 & 0 & 0 & 0 & 0 \\
0 & 0 & 1 & 1 & 0 & 0 & 0 & 0 & 0 & 0 & 0 & 0 & 0 & 0 \\
0 & 0 & 0 & 1 & 1 & 0 & 0 & 0 & 0 & 0 & 0 & 0 & 0 & 0 \\
0 & 0 & 0 & 0 & 1 & 0 & 0 & 0 & 0 & 0 & 0 & 0 & 0 & 0 \\
0 & 0 & 0 & 0 & 0 & 0 & 1 & 1 & 0 & 0 & 0 & 0 & 0 & 0 \\
0 & 0 & 0 & 0 & 0 & 0 & 0 & 1 & 0 & 0 & 1 & 0 & 0 & 0 \\
0 & 0 & 0 & 0 & 0 & 0 & 1 & 0 & 1 & 0 & 0 & 0 & 0 & 0 \\
0 & 0 & 0 & 0 & 0 & 0 & 0 & 0 & 1 & 1 & 1 & 0 & 0 & 0 \\
0 & 0 & 0 & 0 & 0 & 0 & 0 & 0 & 0 & 1 & 1 & 0 & 0 & 0 \\
0 & 0 & 0 & 0 & 0 & 0 & 0 & 0 & 0 & 0 & 1 & 1 & 0 & 0 \\
1 & 0 & 0 & 0 & 0 & 0 & 0 & 1 & 0 & 0 & 0 & 0 & 0 & 1 \\
0 & 0 & 0 & 0 & 0 & 1 & 1 & 0 & 0 & 0 & 0 & 0 & 0 & 0 \\
0 & 0 & 1 & 0 & 0 & 0 & 1 & 0 & 0 & 0 & 0 & 0 & 0 & 0 \\
0 & 0 & 0 & 0 & 1 & 0 & 0 & 0 & 0 & 1 & 0 & 0 & 0 & 0
\end{bmatrix} \tag{2}
$$

The structural topological characteristic configuration element information of reconfigurable mechanism is described by matrix A:

$$
A = \begin{bmatrix}
E_1 & J_{1,2}^{S_1 S_2} & J_{1,3}^{S_1 S_3} & \cdots & J_{1,i}^{S_1 S_i} & \cdots & \cdots & J_{1,n}^{S_1 S_n} \\
a_{1,2} & E_2 & J_{2,3}^{S_2 S_3} & J_{2,4}^{S_2 S_4} & \cdots & J_{i,j}^{S_i S_j} & \cdots & J_{2,n}^{S_2 S_n} \\
a_{1,3} & a_{2,3} & E_3 & J_{3,4}^{S_3 S_4} & \cdots & & \cdots & \cdots \\
\vdots & \vdots & \ddots & \ddots & \ddots & \vdots & \vdots & \vdots \\
a_{1,j} & a_{2,j} & \cdots & a_{i-1,j} & E_i & J_{i,i+1}^{S_i S_{i+1}} & \cdots & J_{i,n}^{S_i S_n} \\
\cdots & \cdots & a_{i,j} & \cdots & a_{i,j+1} & \ddots & \ddots & \vdots \\
a_{1,n-1} & a_{2,n-1} & \cdots & \cdots & \cdots & & E_{n-1} & J_{n-1,n}^{S_{n-1} S_n} \\
a_{1,n} & a_{2,n} & \cdots & \cdots & a_{i,n} & & a_{n-1,n} & E_n
\end{bmatrix} \tag{3}
$$

where E is the motion pair symbol (revolute pair, moving pair, etc.) at the key point. When the motion pair is a combined motion pair, write it in front and mark the component number to determine the relationship between the combined motion pair and the component.

where $a_{i,j}$ represents the component number between the two key points. When the two key points exist on the same component and the digital value represents the component number; when there is no component connection between two key points, the corresponding element is zero.

$$
a_{i,j} = \begin{cases} p & \text{Construction number between two key points} p = 1, 2, 3 \ldots n \\ 0 & \text{Componentless connection between two key points} \end{cases} \tag{4}
$$

where $J_{i,j}^{S_iS_j}$ represents the motion joint spinor corresponding to the two ends of the component between the two key points, $\$_i$ and $\$_j$ are the motion spinors of the key points S_i and S_j at both ends of the component; if there is no component between the two key points, the corresponding element is zero.

$$J_{i,j}^{S_iS_j} = \begin{cases} J_{i,j}^{\$_i\$_j} & \text{Kinematic joint spinor at both ends of component between two} \\ & \text{key points} \\ 0 & \text{No component between two key points} \end{cases} \quad (5)$$

The key points connected between the components in the kinematic chain shown in Fig. 1 are taken as the rows and columns of the matrix, and the configuration matrix Eq. (6) for describing the reconfigurable mechanism is constructed by the definition of Eq. (4) and Eq. (5).

$$A = \begin{bmatrix} R & J_{1,2}^{S_1S_2} & 0 & 0 & 0 & 0 & 0 & J_{1,8}^{S_1S_8} & 0 & 0 & 0 & 0 & J_{1,13}^{S_1S_{13}} \\ 1 & R & J_{2,3}^{S_2S_3} & 0 & 0 & 0 & 0 & 0 & 0 & 0 & 0 & 0 & 0 \\ 0 & 2 & RP^3 & J_{3,4}^{S_3S_4} & 0 & J_{3,6}^{S_3S_6} & 0 & 0 & 0 & 0 & 0 & 0 & 0 \\ 0 & 0 & 4 & R & J_{4,5}^{S_4S_5} & 0 & 0 & 0 & 0 & 0 & 0 & 0 & 0 \\ 0 & 0 & 0 & 5 & RP^6 & 0 & 0 & 0 & 0 & J_{5,10}^{S_5S_{10}} & 0 & 0 & 0 \\ 0 & 0 & 15 & 0 & 0 & R & J_{6,7}^{S_6S_7} & 0 & 0 & 0 & 0 & 0 & 0 \\ 0 & 0 & 0 & 0 & 0 & 14 & R & J_{7,8}^{S_7S_8} & J_{7,9}^{S_7S_9} & 0 & 0 & 0 & 0 \\ 13 & 0 & 0 & 0 & 0 & 7 & R & 0 & 0 & J_{8,11}^{S_8S_{11}} & 0 & J_{8,13}^{S_8S_{13}} \\ 0 & 0 & 0 & 0 & 0 & 0 & 9 & 0 & R & J_{9,10}^{S_9S_{10}} & J_{9,11}^{S_9S_{11}} & 0 & 0 \\ 0 & 0 & 0 & 0 & 16 & 0 & 0 & 0 & 10 & R & J_{10,11}^{S_{10}S_{11}} & 0 & 0 \\ 0 & 0 & 0 & 0 & 0 & 0 & 0 & 8 & 10 & 10 & R & J_{11,12}^{S_{11}S_{12}} & 0 \\ 0 & 0 & 0 & 0 & 0 & 0 & 0 & 0 & 0 & 0 & 11 & R & J_{12,13}^{S_{12}S_{13}} \\ 13 & 0 & 0 & 0 & 0 & 0 & 0 & 13 & 0 & 0 & 0 & 12 & R \end{bmatrix}$$

$$(6)$$

The configuration matrix (6) can not only express the adjacency matrix and incidence matrix element information, but it can also identify the type of kinematic pairs in the kinematic chain, identify composite hinges, determine multiple components, and change the spatial axis of the kinematic pairs.

2.2 Properties of New Configuration Matrix

The configuration matrix of the reconfigurable mechanism is obtained based on the definition and distribution of each information element in the configuration matrix, which can describe the type of the kinematic pair of the expression component, the identification of the composite hinge, the determination of the multi-component, and the determination of the spatial axis orientation of the kinematic pair.

(1) Description of component motion subtypes: the main diagonal elements of the matrix represent the types of kinematic pairs at the key points of the component (such as revolute pairs, moving pairs, spherical pairs, etc.), including the presence of combined

kinematic pairs. For example, at the key point 3, there is a kinematic pair composed of a revolute pair and a moving pair, and the moving pair is located on the component numbered 3C. The digital number 3 of the component is marked above the moving pair to indicate the relationship between the component and the moving pair. The type of the moving pair at the key point 3 is RP^3. Similarly, the key point 5 kinematic pair type is RP^6.

(2) Composite hinge identification: the lower triangular element of the matrix is the construction number between the two key points. When the row and column element $a_{i,j}$ where the corresponding key point is located in the lower triangular matrix has three or more non-zero and unequal values, it is proven that there is a composite hinge at the key point. If the row and column elements of the key point 7 contain the component numbers 7,9,14, the key point 7 *is* a ternary composite hinge. Similarly, the key points 3,8 and 11 are composite hinges.

(3) Multi-component determination: when the number of the same component number in the lower triangular element $a_{i,j}$ of the matrix is three or more, the component is determined to be a multivariate component. For example, component numbers 10 and 13 appear three times in the lower triangular matrix respectively, which proves that component 10 and 13 are ternary components.

(4) Determination of the orientation of the mechanism motion sub: The upper triangular element $J_{i,j}^{S_i S_j}$ of the matrix describes the spatial position of the kinematic pair at the key point i and the key point j, as well as the motion spinor they represent. If it is the revolute pair R, it refers to the direction of the rotation axis, and the mobile pair P refers to the direction of the moving axis. For example, the triangular element $J_{1,2}^{S_1 S_2}$ on the matrix indicates that the motion screw of the axis direction S_1 and S_2 of the revolute pair at the key point 1 and the key point 2 is $\$_1$ and $\$_2$, and the triangular element $J_{i,j}^{S_i S_j}$ on the matrix determines the spatial position of the kinematic pair at the connection of each component of the mechanism.

3 Mathematical Description of Mechanism Configuration Matrix Transformation

Reconfigurable mechanism configuration is primarily manifested as the reduction of mechanism components, the increase of mechanism components, and the change of the spatial orientation of the mechanism motion pair when self-restructuring and reconstructing by changing its own topology according to the environment and task needs.

3.1 Properties of New Configuration Matrix

When the kinematic pair d between any two adjacent components b and c in the reconfigurable mechanism is consolidated, component b and component c can be equivalent to one new component, reducing the number of components in the mechanism. Corresponding to the configuration matrix of the n × n order mechanism, the key point d of the kinematic pair fails after the consolidation, and the new component label of the components b and c is equivalent to $(n + 1)$. The configuration matrix after the reconstruction of the mechanism is obtained by using the elementary matrix $E^g_{(n-1)\times n}$ and $U^g_{(i,j),n-1}$, where $E^g_{(n-1)\times n}$ is the order unit matrix to eliminate the d-line, which is used to eliminate the row and column elements of the key point, and $U^g_{(i,j),n-1}$ establishes the connection relationship after the key point disappears.

$$
\mathbf{E}^g_{(n-1)\times n} =
\begin{bmatrix}
1 & 0 & \cdots & 0 & 0 & 0 & 0 & \cdots & 0 \\
0 & 1 & \cdots & 0 & 0 & 0 & 0 & \cdots & 0 \\
\vdots & \vdots & \cdots & \vdots & \vdots & \vdots & \vdots & & \vdots \\
0 & 0 & \cdots & 1 & 0 & 0 & 0 & \cdots & 0 \\
0 & 0 & \cdots & 0 & 0 & 1 & 0 & \cdots & 0 \\
0 & 0 & \cdots & 0 & 0 & 0 & 1 & \cdots & 0 \\
\vdots & \vdots & \cdots & \vdots & \vdots & \vdots & \vdots & \cdots & \vdots \\
0 & 0 & \cdots & 0 & 0 & 0 & 0 & \cdots & 1
\end{bmatrix}_{(n-1)\times n}
\tag{7}
$$

$$
\mathbf{U}^g_{(i,j),n-1} =
\begin{bmatrix}
0 & \cdots & 0 & \cdots & 0 & \cdots & 0 \\
\vdots & \cdots & \vdots & \cdots & \vdots & \cdots & \vdots \\
0 & \cdots & 0 & \cdots & J^{S_i S_j}_{i,j} & \cdots & 0 \\
\vdots & & \vdots & & \vdots & & \vdots \\
0 & \cdots & 0 & \cdots & 0 & \cdots & 0 \\
\vdots & \cdots & \vdots & \cdots & \vdots & \cdots & \vdots \\
0 & \cdots & 0 & \cdots & 0 & \cdots & 0
\end{bmatrix}_{(n-1)\times(n-1)}
\tag{8}
$$

Ai is The configuration matrix of the reconfigurable mechanism. When the configuration of the reconfigurable mechanism transits from configuration $g - 1$ to the next configuration g, its mathematical expression is given by:

$$
\mathbf{A}_g = \mathbf{E}^g_{(n-1)\times n}\mathbf{A}_{g-1}(\mathbf{E}^g_{(n-1)\times n})^T + \mathbf{U}^g_{(i,j),n-1}
\tag{9}
$$

where the elementary matrix $\mathbf{E}^g_{(n-1)\times n}$ eliminates the d row and column of the key point d, indicating that the key point d fails. Matrix $\mathbf{U}^g_{(i,j),n-1}$ establishes a new connection relationship matrix after the key point d disappears.

3.2 Configuration Transformation of Increasing Number of Reconfigurable Mechanism Components

The increase in the number of components of the reconfigurable mechanism, such as the expansion of the folded and contracted components after reconstruction, the decomposition of the components, etc. If component d is decomposed into components e and f, E_i is the new kinematic pair, corresponding to the configuration matrix of n_g key points, and the number of components increases when the key point between two components is added as $(n_g + 1)$, and the $(n_g + 1)$ row and column are added to the configuration matrix, which can also be obtained by using the elementary matrix $\mathbf{E}_{(n+1)\times n}^{g+1}$ and $\mathbf{U}_{(i,j),n+1}^{g+1}$ operations.

$$
\mathbf{E}_{(n+1)\times n}^{g+1} =
\begin{bmatrix}
1 & 0 & & 0 & 0 & 0 & & 0 \\
0 & 1 & \cdots & 0 & 0 & 0 & \cdots & 0 \\
& & \cdots & & & & \cdots & \\
\vdots & \vdots & & \vdots & \vdots & \vdots & & \vdots \\
0 & 0 & \cdots & 0 & 0 & 0 & \cdots & 0 \\
0 & 0 & \cdots & 1 & 0 & 0 & \cdots & 0 \\
0 & 0 & \cdots & 0 & 1 & 0 & \cdots & 0 \\
0 & 0 & & 0 & 0 & 1 & & \vdots \\
\vdots & \vdots & \cdots & \vdots & \vdots & \vdots & \cdots & \\
& & \cdots & & & & \cdots & \\
0 & 0 & & 0 & 0 & 0 & & 1
\end{bmatrix}_{(n+1)\times n}
\tag{10}
$$

$$
\mathbf{U}_{(i,j),n+1}^{g+1} =
\begin{bmatrix}
0 & & 0 & 0 & 0 & & 0 \\
\vdots & \cdots & \vdots & \vdots & \vdots & \cdots & \vdots \\
0 & \cdots & 0 & J_{n_g-1,n_g+1}^{S_{n_g-1}S_{n_g+1}} & 0 & \cdots & 0 \\
0 & \cdots & e & E_i & J_{n_g,n_g+1}^{S_{n_g}S_{n_g+1}} & \cdots & 0 \\
0 & \cdots & 0 & f & 0 & \cdots & 0 \\
\vdots & \cdots & \vdots & \vdots & \vdots & \cdots & \vdots \\
0 & & 0 & 0 & 0 & & 0
\end{bmatrix}_{(n+1)\times(n+1)}
\tag{11}
$$

The mathematical expression of the configuration matrix for the increase in the number of components of the reconfiguration of the body configuration g to configuration $g + 1$ is *given by*

$$
\mathbf{A}_{g+1} = \mathbf{E}_{(n+1)\times n}^{g+1}\,\mathbf{A}_g\,(\mathbf{E}_{(n+1)\times n}^{g+1})^{\mathrm{T}} + \mathbf{U}_{(i,j),n+1}^{g+1}
\tag{12}
$$

3.3   Configuration Transformation of Spatial Orientation Change of Motion Pair

In addition to the reduction and increase of the number of components during the reconfiguration, the change of the mechanism topology caused by the change of the spatial orientation of the kinematic subsets will also change the mechanism configuration after the mechanism reconfiguration. When the spatial orientation of the kinematic pair of the mechanism changes, the values \$i and \$j of the kinematic screw in the S_i and S_j directions of the upper triangular element $J_{i,j}^{S_iS_j}$ in the configuration matrix change. Although the change of the spatial orientation of the kinematic pair does not cause the change of the number of components, the configuration of the mechanism is transformed to the next configuration after reconstruction, and the values S_i and S_j of the kinematic screw at the key points cause the mathematical change of the configuration matrix of the mechanism.

4   Configuration Matrix Transformation and Mode Recognition of Reconfigurable Mechanism Motion Modes

Reconfigurable mechanism undergoes multiple conformational changes during task execution, and the sequence of conformational changes follows a specific rule, resulting in a specific movement mode. The mathematical operation of configuration matrix describes the configuration change rule of reconfigurable mechanism in each motion mode, which is the mode recognition of reconfigurable mechanism.

4.1   Initial Configuration Matrix of Reconfigurable Mechanism

As shown in Fig. 2, the initial configuration of the reconfigurable mechanism with multiple motion modes, including the folding mode and rolling mode are all changed on the basis of the initial configuration. The number of components and key points of the reconfigurable mechanism are marked in the diagram. Formula 13 is the initial configuration matrix A1 of the reconfigurable mechanism. From the initial configuration matrix A1, it can be seen that the reconfigurable mechanism has composite hinges (such as key points 1 and 5 are four-element composite hinges), kinematic pair types (such as key points 4,6,11 and 12 are RP combined kinematic pairs) and other structural characteristics.

$A_1 =$

$$
\begin{bmatrix}
R & J_{1,1}^{S_1S_1} & 0 & 0 & 0 & 0 & 0 & J_{1,8}^{S_1S_8} & J_{1,9}^{S_1S_9} & 0 & 0 & 0 & 0 & J_{1,14}^{S_1S_{14}} \\
1 & R & J_{2,3}^{S_2S_3} & 0 & 0 & 0 & 0 & 0 & 0 & 0 & 0 & 0 & 0 & 0 \\
0 & 2 & R & J_{3,4}^{S_3S_4} & 0 & 0 & 0 & 0 & 0 & 0 & 0 & 0 & 0 & 0 \\
0 & 0 & 3 & RP & J_{4,5}^{S_4S_5} & 0 & 0 & 0 & 0 & 0 & 0 & 0 & 0 & 0 \\
0 & 0 & 0 & 4 & R & J_{5,6}^{S_5S_6} & 0 & 0 & 0 & 0 & J_{5,11}^{S_5S_{11}} & J_{5,13}^{S_5S_{13}} & 0 & 0 \\
0 & 0 & 0 & 0 & 5 & RP & J_{6,7}^{S_6S_7} & 0 & 0 & 0 & 0 & 0 & 0 & 0 \\
0 & 0 & 0 & 0 & 0 & 6 & R & J_{7,8}^{S_7S_8} & 0 & 0 & 0 & 0 & 0 & 0 \\
8 & 0 & 0 & 0 & 0 & 0 & 7 & R & 0 & 0 & 0 & 0 & 0 & 0 \\
9 & 0 & 0 & 0 & 0 & 0 & 0 & 0 & R & J_{9,10}^{S_9S_{10}} & 0 & 0 & 0 & 0 \\
0 & 0 & 0 & 0 & 0 & 0 & 0 & 0 & 10 & R & J_{10,11}^{S_{10}S_{11}} & 0 & 0 & 0 \\
0 & 0 & 0 & 0 & 12 & 0 & 0 & 0 & 0 & 11 & RP & 0 & 0 & 0 \\
0 & 0 & 0 & 0 & 13 & 0 & 0 & 0 & 0 & 0 & 0 & RP & J_{12,13}^{S_{12}S_{13}} & 0 \\
0 & 0 & 0 & 0 & 0 & 0 & 0 & 0 & 0 & 0 & 0 & 14 & R & J_{13,14}^{S_{13}S_{14}} \\
16 & 0 & 0 & 0 & 0 & 0 & 0 & 0 & 0 & 0 & 0 & 0 & 15 & R
\end{bmatrix}
$$

$$(13)$$

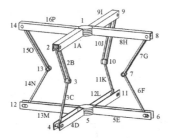

Fig. 2. Initial configuration of reconfigurable mechanism

4.2 Folding Mode Configuration Matrix and Recognition

The reconfigurable mechanism undergoes three configuration changes in the folding mode, from initial configuration change to folding mode configuration 1, and finally to folding mode configuration 2, and its configuration matrix also changes from A1 to A2 and A3, as shown in Table 1.

Table 1. Position name and matrix of folding mode

Folding mode of reconfigurable mechanism		
Configuration position	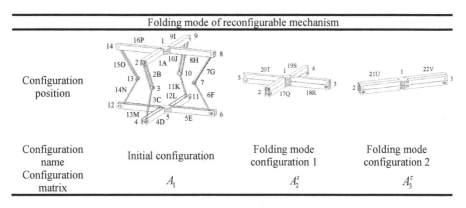	
Configuration name	Initial configuration	Folding mode configuration 1	Folding mode configuration 2
Configuration matrix	A_1	A_2^z	A_3^z

The initial configuration change to folding mode configuration 1 is a case of reducing the number of components; the key points that have been eliminated are 3, 4, 5, 6, 7, 10, 11, 12, 13, the reduced component number is 2, 3, 6, 7, 10, 11, 14, 15, and the new build number is 17, 18, 19, 20. After component reduction and merger, the key points and components of the corresponding institutions are renumbered as shown in Table 1 in the folding mode configuration 1. The mathematical operation from the initial configuration matrix A1 to the folding mode configuration 1 is given by:

$$\mathbf{A}_2^z = \mathbf{E}_{5\times14}^2 \mathbf{A}_1 (\mathbf{E}_{5\times14}^2)^{\mathrm{T}} + \mathbf{U}_{5\times5}^2 \tag{14}$$

$$
A_2^z = \begin{bmatrix} R & J_{1,2}^{S_1 S_2} & J_{1,3}^{S_1 S_3} & J_{1,4}^{S_1 S_4} & J_{1,5}^{S_1 S_5} \\ 17 & RRP & 0 & 0 & 0 \\ 18 & 0 & RRP & 0 & 0 \\ 19 & 0 & 0 & RRP & 0 \\ 20 & 0 & 0 & 0 & RRP \end{bmatrix} \tag{15}
$$

When folding mode configuration 1 is changed to folding mode configuration 2, the number of components decreases further; the eliminated key points are 4 and 5, the reduced component numbers are 17, 18, 19, 20, and the component reduction merged component numbers are 21 and 22, and the key points and mechanisms of the mechanism are renumbered after the change, as shown in Table 1 for folding mode configuration 2. The mathematical operation of the folding mode configuration 1 matrix A_2^z to folding mode configuration 2 matrix A_3^z is given by:

$$
A_3^z = E_{3 \times 5}^3 A_2^z (E_{3 \times 5}^3)^T + U_{5 \times 5}^3 \tag{16}
$$

$$
A_3^z = \begin{bmatrix} R & J_{1,2}^{S_1 S_2} & J_{1,3}^{S_1 S_3} \\ 21 & RRPRRP & 0 \\ 22 & 0 & RRPRRP \end{bmatrix} \tag{17}
$$

The reconfigurable mechanism folding mode changes the configuration three times, and the configuration matrix and operation matrix used in each configuration transformation are the identification features of the different modes of the reconfigurable mechanism. When the mathematical operation of configuration matrix of reconfigurable mechanism satisfies Formula (16), it can be identified that the mechanism is in folding mode.

4.3   Rolling Mode Configuration Matrix and Recognition

The reconfigurable mechanism in rolling mode consists of initial configuration, rolling mode configuration 1, and rolling mode configuration 2, respectively, and its configuration matrix also goes from A_1 to A_2^r and A_3^r in order as shown in Table 2.

The change from initial configuration to rolling mode configuration 1 belongs to the case where the number of components is reduced, the number of key points does not change, and the missing components are numbered 1, 4, 5, 8, 9, 12, 13, 16. After the components are reduced and merged, the new construction numbers are 17, 18, 19, and 20, after the change corresponds to the mechanism key points and components renumbered as shown in Table 1 fold rolling configuration 1. The mathematical operation of initial configuration matrix to rolling mode configuration 1 is given by:

$$
A_2 = A_1 + U_{14 \times 14}^2 \tag{18}
$$

Table 2. Position name and matrix of rolling mode

	Reconfigurable mechanism rolling mode		
Configuration position			
Configuration name	Initial configuration	Rolling mode configuration 1	Rolling mode configuration 2
Configuration matrix	A_1	A_2^r	A_3^r

$A_2 =$

$$
\begin{bmatrix}
R & J_{1,2}^{S_1S_2} & 0 & 0 & 0 & 0 & 0 & J_{1,8}^{S_1S_8} & J_{1,9}^{S_1S_9} & 0 & 0 & 0 & 0 & J_{1,14}^{S_1S_{14}} \\
17 & R & J_{2,3}^{S_2S_3} & 0 & 0 & 0 & 0 & 0 & 0 & 0 & 0 & 0 & 0 & J_{2,14}^{S_2S_{14}} \\
0 & 2 & R & J_{3,4}^{S_3S_4} & 0 & 0 & 0 & 0 & 0 & 0 & 0 & 0 & 0 & 0 \\
0 & 0 & 3 & RP & J_{4,5}^{S_4S_5} & 0 & 0 & 0 & 0 & 0 & 0 & J_{4,12}^{S_4S_{12}} & 0 & 0 \\
0 & 0 & 0 & 19 & R & J_{5,6}^{S_5S_6} & J_{5,7}^{S_5S_7} & 0 & 0 & 0 & J_{5,11}^{S_5S_{11}} & J_{5,12}^{S_5S_{12}} & 0 & 0 \\
0 & 0 & 0 & 0 & 20 & RP & J_{6,7}^{S_6S_7} & 0 & 0 & 0 & J_{6,11}^{S_6S_{11}} & 0 & 0 & 0 \\
0 & 0 & 0 & 0 & 0 & 6 & R & J_{7,8}^{S_7S_8} & 0 & 0 & 0 & 0 & 0 & 0 \\
18 & 0 & 0 & 0 & 0 & 0 & 7 & R & J_{8,9}^{S_8S_9} & 0 & 0 & 0 & 0 & 0 \\
18 & 0 & 0 & 0 & 0 & 0 & 0 & 18 & R & J_{9,10}^{S_9S_{10}} & 0 & 0 & 0 & 0 \\
0 & 0 & 0 & 0 & 0 & 0 & 0 & 0 & 10 & R & J_{10,11}^{S_{10}S_{11}} & 0 & 0 & 0 \\
0 & 0 & 0 & 0 & 20 & 20 & 0 & 0 & 0 & 11 & RP & 0 & 0 & 0 \\
0 & 0 & 0 & 19 & 19 & 0 & 0 & 0 & 0 & 0 & 0 & RP & J_{12,13}^{S_{12}S_{13}} & 0 \\
0 & 0 & 0 & 0 & 0 & 0 & 0 & 0 & 0 & 0 & 0 & 0 & R & J_{13,14}^{S_{13}S_{14}} \\
17 & 17 & 0 & 0 & 0 & 0 & 0 & 0 & 0 & 0 & 0 & 0 & 15 & R
\end{bmatrix}
\tag{19}
$$

When rolling mode configuration 1 is changed to rolling mode configuration 2, the number of components does not change, nor does the number of key points. The mechanism configuration only changes the orientation of the motion subspace, and the values of the rotational quantities $1–$3$, $7–$10$ and $13–$14$ of $J_{1,j}^{S_1S_j}, J_{3,j}^{S_3S_j}, J_{13,j}^{S_{13}S_j}, J_{7,j}^{S_7S_j}$ and $J_{10,j}^{S_{10}S_j}$ in the matrix A2 of rolling mode configuration 1 change, and the corresponding mechanism key points and components are renumbered as shown in the fold-rolling configuration 2 in Table 2. The configuration matrix of the rolling configuration 2 is given by:

$$\mathbf{A}_3 = \begin{bmatrix}
R & J_{1,2}^{S_1S_2} & 0 & 0 & 0 & 0 & 0 & J_{1,8}^{S_1S_8} & J_{1,9}^{S_1S_9} & 0 & 0 & 0 & 0 & J_{1,14}^{S_1S_{14}} \\
17 & R & J_{2,3}^{S_2S_3} & 0 & 0 & 0 & 0 & 0 & 0 & 0 & 0 & 0 & 0 & J_{2,14}^{S_2S_{14}} \\
0 & 2 & R & J_{3,4}^{S_3S_4} & 0 & 0 & 0 & 0 & 0 & 0 & 0 & 0 & 0 & 0 \\
0 & 0 & 3 & RP & J_{4,5}^{S_4S_5} & 0 & 0 & 0 & 0 & 0 & 0 & J_{4,12}^{S_4S_{12}} & 0 & 0 \\
0 & 0 & 0 & 19 & R & J_{5,6}^{S_5S_6} & J_{5,7}^{S_5S_7} & 0 & 0 & 0 & J_{5,11}^{S_5S_{11}} & J_{5,12}^{S_5S_{12}} & 0 & 0 \\
0 & 0 & 0 & 0 & 20 & RP & J_{6,7}^{S_6S_7} & 0 & 0 & 0 & J_{6,11}^{S_6S_{11}} & 0 & 0 & 0 \\
0 & 0 & 0 & 0 & 0 & 6 & R & J_{7,8}^{S_7S_8} & 0 & 0 & 0 & 0 & 0 & 0 \\
18 & 0 & 0 & 0 & 0 & 0 & 7 & R & J_{8,9}^{S_8S_9} & 0 & 0 & 0 & 0 & 0 \\
18 & 0 & 0 & 0 & 0 & 0 & 0 & 18 & R & J_{9,10}^{S_9S_{10}} & 0 & 0 & 0 & 0 \\
0 & 0 & 0 & 0 & 0 & 0 & 0 & 0 & 10 & R & J_{10,11}^{S_{10}S_{11}} & 0 & 0 & 0 \\
0 & 0 & 0 & 0 & 20 & 20 & 0 & 0 & 0 & 11 & RP & 0 & 0 & 0 \\
0 & 0 & 0 & 19 & 19 & 0 & 0 & 0 & 0 & 0 & 0 & RP & J_{12,13}^{S_{12}S_{13}} & 0 \\
0 & 0 & 0 & 0 & 0 & 0 & 0 & 0 & 0 & 0 & 0 & 0 & R & J_{13,14}^{S_{13}S_{14}} \\
17 & 17 & 0 & 0 & 0 & 0 & 0 & 0 & 0 & 0 & 0 & 0 & 0 & 15 & R
\end{bmatrix} \tag{20}$$

Therefore, the multi-mode mobile mechanism in the rolling mode first passes through the matrix transformation $\mathbf{A}_2 = \mathbf{A}_1 + \mathbf{U}_{14 \times 14}^2$ that the components are combined and the key points do not change, and then passes through the spatial orientation change of the motion pair to the component matrix A3. The regular transformation of the configuration matrix A1, A2 and A3 constitutes the motion recognition in the rolling mode.

5 Conclusion

A new description matrix method is proposed for the configuration change of reconfigurable mechanism, which expresses the topological structure relationship of reconfigurable mechanism based on the adjacency relationship of key points between components. The element information of the matrix has the characteristics of representing compound hinge recognition, multi-component, motion pair type and orientation. It has the advantages of further simplification and more comprehensive information expression over existing methods of describing matrix structure. Based on the new matrix description method, the number of components is reduced or increased when the mechanism is reconstructed. The change of the type and spatial orientation of the kinematic pair is analyzed, and the mathematical operation formula of the configuration change is given. The motion mode of the reconfigurable mechanism is analyzed and identified by using the configuration change law.

A reconfigurable multi-mode mobile mechanism is used as a case to verify the correctness of the new matrix description method and the feasibility of the mechanism motion mode recognition characteristics. The results show that the theory and method provide a feasible method for reconfigurable mechanism configuration change and structural information feature retrieval automation.

References

1. Dai, J., Jones, J.R.: Mobility in metamorphic mechanisms of foldable/erectable kinds. J. Mech. Des. **121**(3), 375–382 (1999). https://doi.org/10.1115/1.2829470
2. Li, S., Wang, H., Li, X., Yang, H., Dai, J.: Task-orientated design method of practical constraint metamorphic mechanisms. Journal of Mechanical Engineering **54**(03), 26–35 (2018). https://doi.org/10.3901/JME.2018.03.026
3. Zhang, C., Wan, Y., Zhang, D., Ma, Q.: A new mathematical method to study the singularity of 3-RSR multimode mobile parallel mechanism. Math. Probl. Eng. **10**(3), 1563–5147 (2019). https://doi.org/10.1155/2019/1327167
4. Tang, T., Fang, H., Zhang, J.: Conceptual reconfigurable design and kinematic analysis of the Exechon-like parallel kinematic machine. Journal of Tianjin University (Science and Technology) **52**(07), 733–744 (2019). https://doi.org/10.11784/tdxbz201808073
5. Sun, L., Ye, Z., Cui, R., Yang, W., Wu, C.: Compound topological invariant based method for detecting isomorphism in planar kinematic chains. J. Mech. Robot. **12**(5), 1–11 (2020). https://doi.org/10.1115/1.4046840
6. Li, D., Zhang, Z., Dai, J., Zhang, K.: Overview and prospects of metamorphic mechanism. Journal of Mechanical Engineering **46**(13), 14–21 (2010). https://doi.org/10.3901/JEM.2010.13.014
7. Li, S., Dai, J.: Configuration transformation matrix of metamorphic mechanisms and joint-orientation change metamorphic method. China Mechanical Engineering **21**(14), 1698–1703 (2010). CNKI:SUN:ZGJX.0.2010-14-014
8. Li, A., Sun, W., Kong, J., Zhou, Z., Zhang, S.: Improved adjacency matrix description and isomorphism identification of kinematic chain with multiple joints. Mechan. Sci. Technol. Aeros. Eng. **39**(04), 516–523 (2020). https://doi.org/10.13433/j.cnki.1003-8728.20190184
9. Zhou, H., Kong, J., Sun, L., Xiao, Q.: Representation and isomorphism identification of planar kinematic chains with multiple joints on value-added matrix. Mechan. Sci. Technol. Aeros. Eng. **37**(05), 657–662 (2018). https://doi.org/10.13433/j.cnki.1003-8728.2018.0501

Design of a Voice Coil Motor-Driven Multi-DOF Parallel Micropositioning Stage

Yunzhuang Chen and Leijie Lai$^{(\boxtimes)}$

School of Mechanical and Automotive Engineering, Shanghai University of Engineering Science, Shanghai 201620, China
lailj@sues.edu.cn

Abstract. With the rapid development in the field of precision engineering, the demand for large range multi-degrees-of-freedom (DOF) micropositioning stage has been increased recently. To solve the problems of small motion range, local stress concentration and low motion accuracy caused by parasitic motion of the traditional flexure hinge in the multi-DOF micropositioning stage, a kind of large range beam-based flexure spherical hinge (BFSH) is firstly proposed in this paper. Meanwhile, based on the proposed BFSH, a large range 3-DOF $\theta_X \theta_Y\, Z$ spatial micropositioning stage driven by voice coil motor (VCM) is designed by means of parallel branch chains and fully symmetric layout, which realizes the motion decoupling theoretically in structural design. Then, the kinematic equations of the moving platform are derived by geometric method. Finally, finite element analysis (FEA) is carried out to verify the static and dynamic performances of the designed 3-DOF stage. The results show that the stage can achieve a desired large workspace of ± 24.6 mrad $\times$ ± 24.6 mrad $\times$ $\pm 3.50\,\mathrm{mm}$ and the good decoupling.

Keywords: Micropositioning · Flexure mechanism · Multi-DOF

1 Introduction

In recent years, micro-/nanopositioning technology has been widely used in nanoimprint lithography [1], biological cell injection [2], semiconductor manufacturing [3], fast steering mirror [4], scanning probe microscope [5] and other fields. The flexure mechanism transmit force and motion through the elastic deformation of the flexure elements and are widely used as the transmission mechanisms of micro-/nanopositioning stages due to the advantages of no friction, no assembly error and easy machining. At present, multi-DOF micro-/nanopositioning stages can be classified into series and parallel mechanisms [6]. The serial mechanisms are easily constructed by connecting or stacking 1-DOF or few DOFs stages, so that the errors are accumulated and amplified, thus reducing the motion accuracy of the stage. The low load/dead weight ratio and large iner-

© The Author(s), under exclusive license to Springer Nature Singapore Pte Ltd. 2023
H. Yang et al. (Eds.): ICIRA 2023, LNAI 14275, pp. 124–135, 2023.
https://doi.org/10.1007/978-981-99-6504-5_11

tial force are not suitable for high-speed positioning. The parallel mechanism connects the moving and static platforms through parallel branch chains to generate the output pose of the moving platform [7]. Parallel flexure mechanism is widely used in the design of micro-/nanopositioning stage own to its high load, high stiffness, low inertia, high bandwidth and no accumulated error. A large number of studies have been carried out on the structure design and control of the parallel flexure mechanism driven by piezoelectric (PZT) actuator, and good positioning results have been obtained [8]. However, because the stroke of PZT is too small, the micropositioning stage driven by PZT can only be used in small stroke precision motion occasions. The positioning stage with large stroke usually adopts parallel flexure mechanism, which is driven by a large stroke actuator to provide a larger workspace. Voice coil motor (VCM) has become a popular choice of large stroke actuator for micro-/nanopositioning due to its large stroke range, good linear characteristics and fast response speed [9,10].

The large range and multi-DOF precision motion requires the large elastic deformation of flexure element, and also involves the multi-DOF flexure hinge. The commonly used notch flexure hinges, such as straight round, straight beam and oval, take advantage of the deformation of elastic element and make the deformation concentrate on the thinnest position by changing the section size. Although this method has higher rotational accuracy and smaller axial drift error, it also has the problems of stress concentration and small range of motion, which is difficult to be applied in large displacement situations. The integrated design of traditional flexure hinge and amplification mechanism is widely adopted as a compact structure to provide large deformation capability [11,12]. However, in order to achieve this goal, the amplification mechanism needs to be designed together with the linear guide mechanism to generate amplified linear displacement in the motion direction and ensure motion accuracy. In addition, the introduction of amplification mechanism often increases the complexity of the system, and adds difficulties in structural design and system modeling. Therefore, in order to make better use of VCM to achieve large range micropositioning especially for spatial multi-DOF, the decoupling spherical hinge which can be used in the large stroke parallel flexure mechanism is very desirable in many applications [13–15].

In the aspect of configuration design, the common multi-DOF large range micropositioning stages are divided into planar 3-DOF XYZ [16], $XY\theta_Z$ [17–20] and spatial 3-DOF $\theta_X\theta_YZ$ [21] and 6-DOF [22,23]. Over the past few years, numerous studies have been reported on planar large stroke 3-DOF $XY\theta_Z$ recision motion stages, which achieve large stroke and high precision performance requirements through ingenious structural design and control methods. In [24], a novel planar 3-DOF flexure mechanism composed of PPR kinematic chain, based on distributed flexure elements, realizes the large stroke motion of $\pm 3\,\text{mm} \times \pm 3\,\text{mm} \times \pm 3°$ and possesses a high bandwidth over 45 Hz. In [25], a 3-DOF precision positioning stage was designed by using a 3PPR parallel flexure mechanism with VCM as the driving motor. The moving platform could realize large stroke motion of $4.802\,\text{mm} \times 5.236\,\text{mm} \times 82.36\,\text{mrad}$, and the first natural frequency was 30.59 Hz and the resolution is 0.1 μm × 0.1 μm × 2 μrad. In the past few years, other large range XY mechanisms have also been proposed [26].

For the spatial 3-DOF $\theta_X \theta_Y Z$ micropositioning stage to be used in laser communications and fast steering mirrors, many previous works have systematically studied, especially the mechanisms driven by PZT. However, few works have studied the large range 3-DOF $\theta_X \theta_Y Z$ mechanisms driven by VCM in detail. Although some of the current works have designed several 6-DOF long stroke nanopositioning stages driven by VCM, they have their own shortcomings. For example, Choi et al. designed a novel direct-driven 6-DOF nanopositioning stage using crab-leg flexures [27], however, the workspace of the stage is very small because no decoupling mechanism is used. Hopkins et al. proposed a new 6-axes bent-blade-flexure-based positioner, called a hexblade positioner, that can achieve high speeds over large ranges with high precision [28]. Different from conventional decoupled XY mechanism, whose decoupling mechanism and symmetry configuration can be used to realize complete input and output decoupling of two directions, many current designs of 3/6-DOF micropositioning stages have complex kinematics, large crosstalk, and varying stiffness according to the pose of moving platform. Therefore, in order to realize the input and output decoupling of the multi-DOF micropositioning stage like decoupled XY stage, an effective large stroke spherical hinge and the configuration of branch chains symmetrically distributed around the motion axes are required in design of 3/6-DOF decoupled mechanisms.

This paper firstly proposes a kind of large range beam-based flexure spherical hinge (BFSH), and then and designs a 3-DOF $\theta_X \theta_Y Z$ micropositioning stage based on the proposed BFSH by means of parallel branch chains and fully symmetric layout. In the branch chain of micropositioning stage, the VCM is embedded in the parallelogram mechanism composed of two beam flexures to produce a compact design, and the output displacement of VCM is also linearly guided by a parallelogram mechanism. Then, the introduction of large range BFSH and fully symmetric structure make the 3-DOF micropositioning stage realize the decoupling of motion directions theoretically. Using VCM to directly drive the BFSH instead of introducing the common displacement amplification mechanism, reduces the parameters of introducing errors and improves the motion accuracy. The kinematic equations of the stage are derived according to the geometric method. Finally, FEA is conducted to verify the static and dynamic performances of the designed 3-DOF stage. The results show that the 3-DOF micropositioning stage has large working range, and good decoupling performance. The proposed design method can also be further extended to 6-DOF large range parallel micropositioning stage.

The main contents of this paper are organized as follows: the structure design of large range BFSH and 3-DOF large range flexure micropositioning stage driven VCM is described in Sect. 2. The kinematic equations of 3-DOF stage are obtained in Sect. 3. The performances of 3-DOF stage are verified by FEA in Sect. 4. Finally, conclusions and recommendations for future works are discussed in Sect. 5.

2   Mechanism Design

In order to achieve a large motion range with multi-DOF, this paper first proposes a novel kind of spherical hinge based on leaf-spring. The structure and deformation diagram of the BFSH are shown in Fig. 1. The large range BFSH is composed of 7 rectangular beams, which can realize the rotation movements around x, y and z axes and decoupled linear motion in y and z directions. The rectangular beam element with distributed compliance replaces the traditional notch type hinge to effectively increase the workspace. The straight beam structure with constant cross section allows the deformation and stress to be uniformly distributed throughout the beam flexure. The VCM and the BFSH are connected through the parallelogram guiding mechanism to form a driving unit as a branch chain, whose three-dimensional (3D) structure is shown in Fig. 2. In the driving chain, the VCM is embedded in the parallelogram mechanism to produce a compact design.

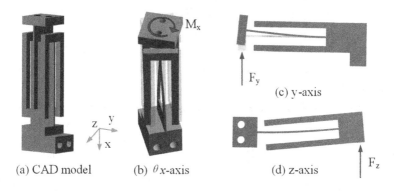

(a) CAD model   (b) θ_X-axis   (c) y-axis   (d) z-axis

Fig. 1. The structure and deformation schematic diagram of the BFSH.

Based on the designed BFSH and the driving chain, a novel 3-DOF $\theta_X \theta_Y$ Z large stroke flexure micropositioning stage is designed by combining the moving platform (end-effector), static platform (base) and four groups of the same driving branch chain, as shown in Fig. 3. The stage is a flexure parallel mechanism that uses VCM as the driving motor in a four-point driving mode. Therefore, the moving platform can realize precise rotational motion in two directions θ_X, θ_Y and precise vertical movement in the Z-axis direction. The four BFSHs A, B, C and D which connected to the moving and static platform are symmetrically arranged at the four corners of the moving platform. When the 3-DOF micropositioning stage works in differential form, the moving platform can realize the decoupling movement around the θ_X and θ_Y directions due to the existence of the BFSHs. During assembly, the static platform is fixed on the vibration isolation platform by pressing plates and bolts to reduce the impact of external vibration on the movement of the moving platform. The prefabricated threaded holes and hollow structure of the moving platform can not only provide operation space for assembly, but also reduce the mass and moment of inertia, which is helpful to improve the dynamic response ability of the moving platform. The stage uses the VCMs to directly drive the BFSHs without introducing the common amplification mechanism which has the advantages of compact structure, short length of the motion chain, fewer parameters of the introduction error, and high precision. If the moving platform is driven directly by VCMs without the BFSHs, the accuracy can be guaranteed, but the moving platform and VCMs will be subjected to lateral torque, which leads to their failure and a short stroke [28].

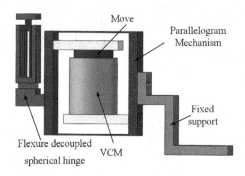

Fig. 2. The 3D view of a single driving unit.

Therefore, the large range BFSHs can effectively avoid the influence of shear force and torque on the VCMs and moving platform. By controlling the elongation of VCMs in the form of differential, the moving platform can precisely rotate around the X-axis or Y-axis. By controlling the elongation of four VCMs at the same time, the moving platform can move precisely vertically along the Z-axis. It is worth mentioning that the BFSH designed in this paper can also be expanded into a 6-DOF precision motion stage, as shown in the transparent part of Fig. 3.

3   Kinematic Analysis of 3-DOF Stage

The kinematic model of the 3-DOF $\theta_X \theta_Y Z$ flexure parallel micropositioning stage is shown in Fig. 4. The coordinate system EXY is a global coordinate system which is located at the geometric center of the moving platform. The parallelogram mechanism driven by VCM is simplified as a moving pair, and d_i ($i = 1,2,...,4$) represents the output displacement of the four VCMs. As the parallelogram mechanism guides the translational motion of the mover of the VCM, and the parasitic displacement in the movement process is very small relative to the output displacement of the VCM, which can be ignored. Moreover, it is also assumed that the BFSH has high sufficient stiffness in the non-functional

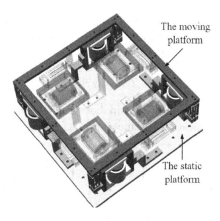

Fig. 3. The assembled view of the 3/6-DOF stage.

direction, that is, there is only the input displacement d_i in the Z direction on the moving platform. The tiny coupled parasitic displacement in the X and Y directions caused by the elastic deformation of the BFSH is also ignored here. $\mathbf{q} = (\theta_X, \theta_Y, Z)^{\mathrm{T}}$ is the end pose of the moving platform relative to the initial position. Only the deflection angle θ_X is represented in Fig. 4, and the deflection angle θ_Y is obtained by similar method. The following geometric relations can be given by

$$\frac{\frac{d_1+d_2}{2} - \frac{d_3+d_4}{2}}{a} = \tan\theta_X \qquad (1)$$

$$\frac{\frac{d_2+d_3}{2} - \frac{d_1+d_4}{2}}{b} = \tan\theta_Y \qquad (2)$$

$$\frac{\frac{d_1+d_2}{2} + \frac{d_3+d_4}{2}}{2} = Z \qquad (3)$$

where a and b are the length and width of the moving platform respectively. The deformation of the BFSH and the rotation amplitude of the moving platform are particularly small for the original size of the mechanism, the above equations can be approximated as follows: $\tan\theta_X \approx \theta_X$, $\tan\theta_Y \approx \theta_Y$. The 3-DOF stage system is a 4-input and 3-output system with input redundancy. Therefore, constraints should be added to achieve uniform distribution of the VCMs force and prevent local overheating. This paper adopts the principle of uniform distribution, that is, the combined thrust generated by the two VCMs on the diagonal is equal, so as to realize the average distribution of current, which can be described as

$$F_{\mathrm{act1}} + F_{\mathrm{act3}} = F_{\mathrm{act2}} + F_{\mathrm{act4}} \qquad (4)$$

$$F_{\mathrm{act}i} = k_{\mathrm{ini}}d_i, i = 1, 2, 3, 4 \qquad (5)$$

$F_{\mathrm{act}i}$ is the driving force generated by each VCM and k_{ini} is the input stiffness of a single branch chain for the stage. As the VCMs are arranged symmetrically in the stage, the input stiffness of each branch chain is equal. The constraint condition of the displacements of four VCMs is obtained from the constraint of the input forces, which is represented as

$$d_1 + d_3 = d_2 + d_4 \tag{6}$$

Therefore, the mapping relationship between the driving displacements of the four VCMs and the pose of the moving platform is

$$\left\{ \begin{array}{l} \begin{pmatrix} d_1 \\ d_2 \\ d_3 \end{pmatrix} = \begin{pmatrix} 0 & \frac{1}{q} & -\frac{1}{a} \\ -\frac{1}{b} & \frac{1}{b} & 0 \\ \frac{1}{2} & 0 & \frac{1}{2} \end{pmatrix}^{-1} \begin{pmatrix} \theta_X \\ \theta_Y \\ Z \end{pmatrix} \\ d_4 = d_1 + d_3 - d_2 \end{array} \right. \tag{7}$$

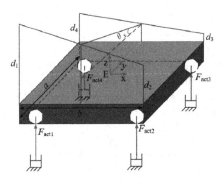

Fig. 4. Kinematic model of 3-DOF flexure parallel micropositioning stage.

4   Ansys Simulation Analysis

The structural parameters are carefully adjusted through the trial-and-error method with the assistance of FEA models. The finally selected parameters for the stage are summarized in Table 1. To verify the static and dynamic performances of large stroke 3-DOF flexure micropositioning stage, this section uses ANSYS Workbench to conduct static and dynamic simulation analysis on the stage. Through the static simulation analysis, the displacement, stiffness in the working direction, maximum stress and its location are obtained. The natural frequencies and modes of the 3-DOF stage are obtained through dynamic analysis. Local mesh refinement of leaf-springs were carried out to ensure the accuracy of calculation. The material was set as aluminum alloy with elastic modulus of 71.7 Gpa, tensile strength of 503 MPa, shear modulus of 26.69 Gpa, density and Poisson's ratio of 2770 kg · m^{-3} and 0.33.

Table 1. Parameters of dimension.

Parameter	l_1	l_2	l_3	p_1	p_2	t_1	t_2	t_3	l_4	l_5	p_6
Value (mm)	10.00	40.00	10.00	7.25	7.25	1.00	1.00	1.00	70.00	25.00	39.50
Parameter	a	b	h	h_1	w_1	w_2	w_3	w_4	t_4	p_5	d
Value (mm)	300	300	8.00	5.00	18.00	3.50	18.00	18.00	1.00	44.50	18.00

(A) Range of motion

In this paper, the VCMs (VCAR0070-0419-00A) are selected as the driver of the stage to generate input displacement, with a maximum stroke of 14.9 mm and a maximum sustained thrust of 40 N. To better reflect the real situation, only the forces of 24 N are analyzed as shown in Fig. 5. It can be seen that the maximum output displacement of the moving platform in the Z-axis direction is 3.50 mm. When the input forces of one pair of VCMs are maintained at 24 N and the input forces of the other pair are -24 N, the maximum and minimum displacement of the moving platform are 3.707 mm and -3.707 mm respectively. The rotation radius of the moving platform is 300 mm, so the deflection angle of the moving platform around the X-axis is ±0.0246 rad ($\pm1.41°$). Similarly, the deflection angle around the Y-axis is also ±0.0246 rad ($\pm1.41°$), which shows that the stage has a good symmetry.

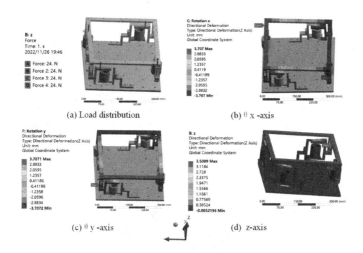

(a) Load distribution   (b) θ x -axis

(c) θ y -axis   (d) z-axis

Fig. 5. The motion range of 3-DOF micropositioning stage.

(B) Maximum stress

In this part, the maximum stress of a 3-DOF micropositioning stage is studied. As shown in Fig. 6, when the input forces are 24 N, the maximum von-Mises stress is 146.84 MPa, which occurred at root of the flexure rectangular beam of the parallelogram mechanism. The stress is far less than the yield strength of the material and could ensure the normal operation. Under the action of differential driving forces, the maximum stress of the 3-DOF micropositioning rotating around the X/Y-axis is 146.42 MPa, which is also less than the yield strength of the material. It can be noted that no matter vertical movement or deflection movement, the BFSHs are subjected to very small stress, which will contribute to the stability of the stage.

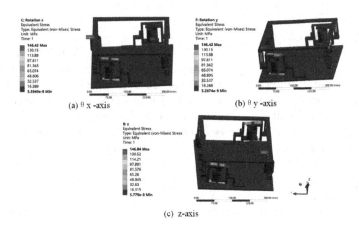

(a) θ x -axis   (b) θ y -axis

(c) z-axis

Fig. 6. The stress analysis of 3-DOF micropositioning stage.

(C) Input stiffness

According to the relationship between input force and displacement, the input stiffness of a single branch chain is also analyzed. By applying a force of 24 N to the parallelogram guide mechanism along the Z-axis, while keeping the other three branch chains unrestricted, the input displacement along the Z direction is 2.90 mm, as shown in Fig. 7. Therefore, the input stiffness of a single branch chain can be calculated as 8.28 N/mm.

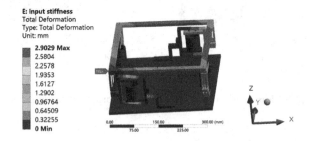

Fig. 7. The input stiffness of a single chain.

(D) Model analysis

In this part, the modal analysis of 3-DOF micropositioning stage is carried out by ANSYS Workbench, and the natural frequencies of the stage can be obtained, as shown in Fig. 8. The first two modes are translations of the moving platform along the X and Y directions, and frequencies are both 31.10 Hz. The third mode is the torsion of the moving platform around the Z-axis, and the frequency is 38.10 Hz. The fourth mode is the working mode of the moving platform. The vibration mode is shown as moving along the Z-axis, and its frequency is 48.95 Hz. The last two modes are the working modes of the moving platform, which represent the moving platform rotating around the X and Y directions, and their frequencies are 55.72 Hz and 55.73 Hz. The six modal shapes of the stage correspond to the 6-DOF motion in space and can provide reference for the design of 6-DOF stage in the future.

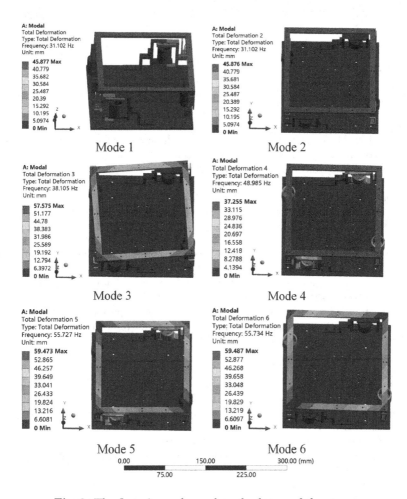

Fig. 8. The first six modes and mode shapes of the stage.

5   Conclusion

In this paper, a kind of large range beam-based flexure spherical hinge (BFSH) together with a VCM-driven 3-DOF $\theta_X \theta_Y Z$ parallel micropositioning stage are designed. The BFSH makes the micropositioning stage realize motion decoupling theoretically by fully symmetrical structural design. The kinematic equations of the moving platform are derived by geometric method. Finally, FEA is carried out to verify the good static and dynamic performances of the designed 3-DOF micropositioning stage. The results show that the 3-DOF parallel micropositioning stage based on the BFSH and fully symmetrical structure has a large working range, and the good decoupling. Future research will focus on the use of large range BFSH by parallel branch chains to achieve 6-DOF large range spatial precision motion.

References

1. Teo, T.J., Yang, G., Chen, I.-M.: A large deflection and high payload flexure-based parallel manipulator for UV nanoimprint lithography: Part I. Model. Anal. Precis. Eng. **38**(4), 861–871 (2014)
2. Zareinejad, M., Rezaei, S., Abdullah, Shiry Ghidary, A.: Development of a piezo-actuated micro-teleoperation system for cell manipulation. Int. J. Med. Robot. Comput. Assist. Surg. **5**(1), 66–76 (2009)
3. Lan, H., Ding, Y., Liu, H., Lu, B.: Review of the wafer stage for nanoimprint lithography. Microelectron. Eng. **84**(4), 684–688 (2007)
4. Xiao, R., Xu, M., Shao, S., Tian, Z.: Design and wide-bandwidth control of large aperture fast steering mirror with integrated-sensing unit. Mech. Syst. Signal Process. **126**, 211–226 (2019)
5. Shi, C., et al.: Recent advances in nanorobotic manipulation inside scanning electron microscopes. Microsyst. Nanoeng. **2**(1), 1–16 (2016)
6. Wu, Z., Xu, Q.: Survey on recent designs of compliant micro-/nano-positioning stages. Actuators **7**(1), 5 (2018)
7. Kucuk, S.: A dexterity comparison for 3-DOF planar parallel manipulators with two kinematic chains using genetic algorithms. Mechatronics **19**(6), 868–877 (2009)
8. Liu, Y., Deng, J., Su, Q.: Review on multi-degree-of-freedom piezoelectric motion stage. IEEE Access **6**, 59986–60004 (2018)
9. Zhao, Y., Yue, H., Yang, F., Zhu, J.: A high thrust density voice coil actuator with a new structure of double magnetic circuits for CubeSat deployers. IEEE Trans. Industr. Electron. **69**(12), 13305–13315 (2022)
10. Xiao, X., Li, Y.: Development of an electromagnetic actuated microdisplacement module. IEEE/ASME Trans. Mechatron. **21**(3), 1252–1261 (2015)
11. Wu, Z., Xu, Q.: Design, fabrication, and testing of a new compact piezo-driven flexure stage for vertical micro/nanopositioning. IEEE Trans. Autom. Sci. Eng. **16**(2), 908–918 (2018)
12. Cui, F., Li, Y., Qian, J.: Development of a 3-DOF flexible micro-motion platform based on a new compound lever amplification mechanism. Micromachines **12**(6), 686 (2021)
13. Yong, Y.K., Moheimani, S., Kenton, B.J., Leang, K.K.: Invited review article: high-speed flexure-guided nanopositioning: mechanical design and control issues. Rev. Sci. Instrum. **83**(12), 802–43 (2012)

14. Li, Y., Xu, Q.: Design and analysis of a totally decoupled flexure-based XY parallel micromanipulator. IEEE Trans. Rob. **25**(3), 645–657 (2009)
15. Kim, H., Kim, J., Ahn, D., Gweon, D.: Development of a Nanoprecision 3-DOF vertical positioning system with a flexure hinge. IEEE Trans. Nanotechnol. **12**(2), 234–245 (2013)
16. Awtar, S., Quint, J., Ustick, J.: Experimental characterization of a large-range parallel kinematic XYZ flexure mechanism. ASME J. Mech. Robot. **13**(1), 015001 (2021)
17. Yu, H., et al.: The design and kinetostatic modeling of 3PPR planar compliant parallel mechanism based on compliance matrix method. Rev. Sci. Instrum. **90**(4), 045102 (2019)
18. Al-Jodah, A., Shirinzadeh, B., Ghafarian, M., Das, T.K., Pinskier, J.: Design, modeling, and control of a large range 3-DOF micropositioning stage. Mech. Mach. Theory **156**, 104159 (2021)
19. Al-Jodah, A., Shirinzadeh, B., Ghafarian, M., Das, T.K., Wei, W.: Development and analysis of a novel large range voice coil motor-driven 3-DOF XYθ micro-positioning mechanism. In: 2019 International Conference on Manipulation, Automation and Robotics at Small Scales (MARSS), pp. 1–6. IEEE (2019)
20. Al-Jodah, A., et al.: Development and control of a large range XYθ micropositioning stage. Mechatronics **66**, 102343 (2020)
21. Pham, M.T., Yeo, S.H., Teo, T.J., Wang, P., Nai, M.L.S.: Design and optimization of a three degrees-of-freedom spatial motion compliant parallel mechanism with fully decoupled motion characteristics. ASME J. Mech. Robot. **11**(5), 051010 (2019)
22. Wang, R., Wu, H.: Design and performance of a spatial 6-RRRR compliant parallel nanopositioning stage. Micromachines **13**(11), 1889 (2022)
23. Chang, Q., Gao, X., Liu, Y., Deng, J., Zhang, S., Chen, W.: Development of a cross-scale 6-DOF piezoelectric stage and its application in assisted puncture. Mech. Syst. Signal Process. **174**, 109072 (2022)
24. Yang, B., Zhang, C., Yu, H., Huang, X., Yang, G., Chen, S.: Design and analysis of a 3-DOF planar flexure-based parallel mechanism with large motion range. In: 2018 IEEE International Conference on Robotics and Biomimetics (ROBIO), pp. 1888–1893. IEEE (2018)
25. Al-Jodah, A., et al.: Modeling and a cross-coupling compensation control methodology of a large range 3-DOF micropositioner with low parasitic motions. Mech. Mach. Theory **162**, 104334 (2021)
26. Zhang, L., Yan, P.: Design of a parallel XYθ micro-manipulating system with large stroke. In: Chinese Control and Decision Conference (CCDC), pp. 4775–4780. IEEE (2016)
27. Kang, S., Lee, M.G., Choi, Y.-M.: Six degrees-of-freedom direct-driven nanopositioning stage using crab-leg flexures. IEEE/ASME Trans. Mechatron. **25**(2), 513–525 (2020)
28. Yang, Z., Lee, R., Hopkins, J.B.: Hexblade positioner: a fast large-range six-axis motion stage. Precis. Eng. **76**, 199–207 (2022)

Structural Design of a Multi Mode Variable Coupling Multi Axis Parallel Mobile Robot

Yiwen Jiang and Chunyan Zhang[✉]

School of Mechanical and Automotive Engineering, Shanghai University of Engineering
Science, Shanghai 201600, China
18930524628@189.cn

Abstract. In this paper, in view of the shortcomings of the parallel robot in dealing with complex terrain, by combining the advantages of the strong coupling mechanism in stiffness, accuracy and other aspects, as well as the advantages of the weak coupling mechanism in kinematics solution and control logic, a multi-mode multi axis mobile variable coupling combined robot is designed. The mechanism adopts two 6R parallel closed loops to form the upper and lower platforms, which are connected by three URU branch chains spaced in pairs. Subsequently, the degree of freedom analysis, gait planning and coupling analysis are carried out, and the feasibility of each mode of motion is verified through simulation.

Keywords: Multimodese · Mobile parallel robot · Structural design

1 Introduction

Parallel moving mechanism refers to a mechanism body composed of one or more branch chain circuits, which has advantages such as flexibility and compactness compared to traditional parallel mechanisms. At the same time, it also has the coupling between the traditional parallel mechanism circuits. This coupling often makes the kinematics, dynamics analysis and control design of the parallel mechanism difficult. When the coupling of the mechanism is low, its kinematics and dynamics analysis are simple, and the control and trajectory planning problems can be simplified.

In recent years, parallel mobile mechanism has been a hot topic in mechanical engineering, control systems and other fields. Dai and others designed a snake shaped robot based on 3-RSR parallel mechanism through the application of bionics. Its flexible, compact and changeable body structure makes it have great prospects in military reconnaissance, geological exploration, disaster rescue and other fields. The modular combined parallel robot model was established by Han et al. using the modularization idea and particle swarm optimization, and the effectiveness of the proposed method was verified by comparing with Moore Penrose method.

However, the parallel mechanism has a strong coupling problem. With the intervention of computer technology and mathematical models, the research on the coupling of the parallel mechanism has also been significantly improved. Gao and others reduced the

H. Yang et al. (Eds.): ICIRA 2023, LNAI 14275, pp. 136–143, 2023.
https://doi.org/10.1007/978-981-99-6504-5_12

coupling effect of the mechanism and improved the control accuracy and motion stability of the mechanism by using the adaptive Sliding mode control method and reasonable control strategies; Zhang et al. designed the uncoupled two mobile parallel mechanism, carried out more detailed analysis and simulation of its coupling, and achieved good results.

2 Introduction to the Organization and Analysis of Degrees of Freedom

2.1 Institutional Introduction

This article proposes a multi mode parallel multi axis mobile robot consisting of two 6R parallel closed loops, consisting of an upper and lower platform, connected by three URU branch chains spaced in pairs. The steering gear at R_{51}, R_{53}, R_{55} drives the three URU branch chains to rotate, so that the axis position of rotating pair $R_{i1}, R_{j2}, R_{k3}, i, j, k = 2, 3, 4$, changes. When the axes of rotating pair $R_{i1}, R_{j2}, R_{k3}, i, j, k = 2, 3, 4$, are parallel to each other, the driving pair at R_{31}, R_{32}, R_{33} is driven to make the three URU branch chains form a straight line. At this time, the parallel moving mechanism is in the six direction moving mode. At the same time, the driving pair $R_{12}, R_{14}, R_{16}, R_{52}, R_{54}, R_{56}$ is driven to make the connecting rod connected to it form a straight line. The upper and lower platforms of the mechanism are equilateral triangular shapes, At this point, the parallel moving mechanism becomes a three way moving mode. When the axes of the rotating pair $R_{i1}, R_{j2}, R_{k3}, i, j, k = 2, 3, 4$, of the three URU branches are not parallel, there is coupling between the three URU branches. By driving the active sub $R_{12}, R_{14}, R_{16}, R_{52}, R_{54}, R_{56}$, the upper and lower platforms can contract, allowing the mechanism to rely on the cylindrical surface for Z-axis crawling. At this time, the mechanism is in wall climbing mode. In the six way movement mode, driving the active pair G can cause the mechanism to overturn. At this time, the servo $R_{12}, R_{14}, R_{16}, R_{52}, R_{54}, R_{56}$ can be driven to roll the mechanism based on the hexagonal shape of the upper and lower platforms. The distance between the upper and lower platforms can be adjusted

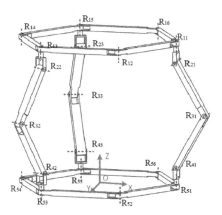

Fig. 1. Schematic diagram of mechanism

by driving the active pair R_{31}, R_{32}, R_{33}, and the mechanism changes to variable pitch rolling mode, as shown in Fig. 1.

2.2 Analysis of Degrees of Freedom in Various Motion Modes

When analyzing the degrees of freedom of multi-mode mechanisms, it is necessary to analyze them one by one according to different modes, and at the same time, the degree of freedom analysis can be used to determine whether the motion mode of the mechanism can be achieved. This article uses the "Spinor Theory" to analyze the degrees of freedom of each motion mode, as shown in Table 1.

From Table 1, it can be seen that the multi mode parallel multi axis mobile robot has two degrees of freedom to rotate around the X and Y axes in the six direction rolling mode; The three way movement mode has the same branch chain as the six way movement mode, so the degrees of freedom are consistent; In the wall climbing mode, the mechanism has 1 degree of freedom to move along the Z-axis; In variable pitch rolling mode, it has 2 degrees of freedom around the Z-axis.Based on the above analysis, it can be concluded that the multi mode parallel multi axis mobile robot can theoretically achieve six direction movement mode, three direction movement mode, wall climbing mode, and variable pitch rolling mode.

3 Active Sub Selection and Motion Logic Design

3.1 Active Secondary Selection

The multi mode parallel multi axis mobile robot needs to add active pairs one by one to the six direction movement mode, three direction movement mode, wall climbing mode, and variable pitch rolling mode. In the six direction movement mode and three direction movement mode, R_{61}, R_{62}, R_{63} is the inclination angle of the active pair control link, and an active pair is set up at R_{51} or R_{52} or R_{53} to control the tilt direction of the link, as shown in Fig. 2 (a); In the wall climbing mode, an active pair is set up at position R_{41}, R_{42}, R_{43} to control the angle between the upper and lower links, and an active pair is set up at positions R_{12}, R_{14}, R_{16} and R_{72}, R_{74}, R_{76} to control the deformation of the upper and lower platforms, as shown in Fig. 2 (b). Add an active pair to control the rolling of the hexagonal mechanism at position R_{12}, R_{14}, R_{16}, R_{72}, R_{74}, R_{76} in the variable pitch rolling mode, as shown in Fig. 2 (c). In summary, the active pair distribution of the multi-mode parallel multi-axis mobile robot is shown in Fig. 3.

Table 1. Analysis of degrees of freedom in various motion modes

Sports mode	Branch chain construction	kinematic screw	constraint equation	degrees of freedom
Six way movement mode		$\$_{11}=\left(0\ 0\ 1;\ 0\ 0\ 0\right)$ $\$_{12}=\left(a\ b\ 0;\ 0\ 0\ 0\right)$ $\$_{13}=\left(a\ b\ 0;\ X_2\ Y_2\ 2Z\right)$ $\$_{14}=\left(0\ 0\ 1;\ X_3\ Y_3\ 0\right)$	$\$_{11}^{r}=\left(0\ 0\ 0;\ -b\ a\ 0\right)$ $\$_{12}^{r}=\left(-Y_3\ X_3\ Z_2;\ 0\ 0\ 0\right)$	2
Three way movement mode		$\$_{11}=\left(0\ 0\ 1;\ 0\ 0\ 0\right)$ $\$_{12}=\left(a\ b\ 0;\ 0\ 0\ 0\right)$ $\$_{13}=\left(a\ b\ 0;\ X_2\ Y_2\ 2Z\right)$ $\$_{14}=\left(0\ 0\ 1;\ X_3\ Y_3\ 0\right)$	$\$_{11}^{r}=\left(0\ 0\ 0;\ -b\ a\ 0\right)$ $\$_{12}^{r}=\left(-Y_3\ X_3\ Z_2;\ 0\ 0\ 0\right)$	2
Wall climbing mode		$\$_{11}=\left(a_x\ b_x\ 0;\ 0\ 0\ 0\right)$ $\$_{12}=\left(a_x\ b_x\ 0;\ X_1\ Y_1\ Z\right)$ $\$_{13}=\left(a_x\ b_x\ 0;\ 0\ 0\ 2Z\right)$	$\$_{11}^{r}=\left(0\ 0\ 0;\ -b_x\ a_x\ 0\right)$ $\$_{12}^{r}=\left(-Y_1\ X_1\ 0;\ -b_x\ a_x\ 0\right)$	1
Variable pitch scrolling mode		$\$_{11}=\left(0\ 1\ 0;\ 0\ 0\ 0\right)$ $\$_{12}=\left(0\ 1\ 0;\ X_1\ 0\ Z_1\right)$ $\$_{13}=\left(0\ 1\ 0;\ X_2\ 0\ Z_2\right)$	$\$_{11}^{r}=\left(0\ 0\ 0;\ b\ a\ 0\right)$	2

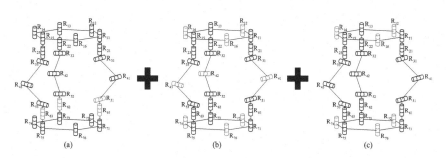

Fig. 2. Active pair distribution of parallel mobile robots in various modes

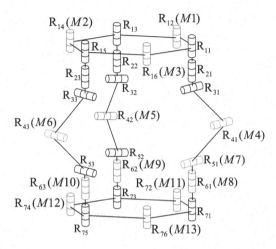

Fig. 3. Active pair distribution of multi-mode parallel mobile robots

3.2 Gait Design for Each Mode

3.2.1 Gait Design in Six Way Movement Mode

In this mode, the active pair M4, M5, M6 controls the connecting rods between the upper and lower platforms to lock at a 180 degree angle. The active pair M1, M2, M3, M11, M12, M13 in the upper and lower platforms locks the connecting rods at a 120 degree angle. At this time, the mechanism begins to execute a six way movement mode. The active pair M8, M9, M10 rotates, driving three branch chains to rotate parallel to one of the connecting rods in the upper and lower platforms. The active pair M7 drives the upper platform to move forward, causing the mechanism to tilt forward after instability. Next, reverse drive the active pair M7 while giving a little acceleration to the lower platform, allowing it to land under the action of inertia. Repeat this method once to restore the mechanism to its original state. In this mode, the mechanism can move in six different directions, hence it is called the six way movement mode, as shown in Fig. 4.

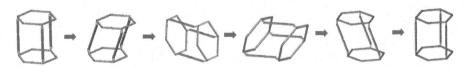

Fig. 4. Gait design in six way movement mode

3.2.2 Gait Design in Three Way Movement Mode

On the basis of the six way movement mode, control the active pair M1, M2, M3, M11, M12, M13 to lock the connecting rod connected to it at a 180 degree angle. At this point, the upper and lower platforms are triangular in shape, and their movement mode is the same as the six way movement mode. It can move in three different directions, hence it is called the three way movement mode,as shown in Fig. 5. Compared to the six way movement mode, it is used in three different directions of motion, which can increase the overall flexibility and range of motion of the robot.

Fig. 5. Gait design in three way movement mode

3.2.3   Wall Climbing Gait Design

When the robot needs to move on the Z-axis, it needs to use the columnar terrain to climb, control the active pair M8, M9, M10 to make the three branch chains form 120° in pairs, and then the mechanism enters wall climbing mode. In this mode, drive the active sub M1, M2, M3 to make the upper platform close to the cylindrical surface, then drive the active sub M4, M5, M6 to fold the upper and lower links, causing the lower platform to rise, drive the active sub M11, M12, M13 to make the lower platform close to the cylindrical surface, and drive the active sub M1, M2, M3 to make the upper platform retract and release. The re driving of the active sub M4, M5, M6 involves the deployment of the upper and lower links, causing the upper platform to rise. Repeat the above steps to move the mechanism along the Z-axis,as shown in Fig. 6.

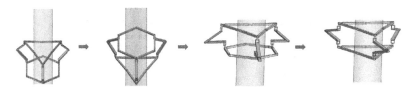

Fig. 6. Gait design in Wall climbing mode

3.2.4   Gait Design for Variable Pitch Rolling Mode

When the robot encounters narrow obstacles during movement, it can tilt forward and backward by driving the active pair M7 on the basis of the six way movement mode. At this time, the robot enters the variable pitch rolling mode. According to the width of the narrow obstacle that can be passed through, the distance between the upper and lower platforms can be controlled by driving the active pair M4, M5, M6, and then driving the active pair M1, M11 to deform the upper and lower platforms, causing the mechanism to tilt forward and backward, By sequentially driving the active pairs M2, M12 and M3, M13 as described above, the robot can perform variable pitch rolling,as shown in Fig. 7.

Fig. 7. Gait design for variable pitch rolling mode

3.3 Design of Mode Switching Between Different Modes

When the robot encounters different terrain structures during its movement, it can switch between six direction movement mode, three direction movement mode, wall climbing mode, and variable pitch rolling mode according to actual needs. The following are the steps to transition from the intermediate configuration to the six way movement mode, three way movement mode, wall climbing mode, and variable pitch rolling mode:

(1) When the robot is in the middle position (Fig. 8a), it drives the active sub to fold the upper platform tightly against the cylindrical terrain, and the robot enters wall climbing mode (Fig. 8b).

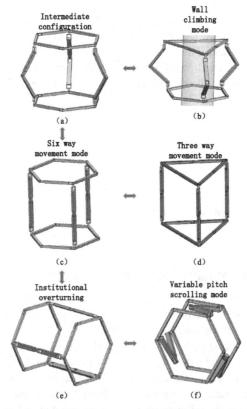

Fig. 8. Switching between multiple modes of robots

(2) When the robot is in the middle position (Fig. 8a), the active auxiliary will drive the upper and lower links in a straight line, and make the three branch chains parallel to each other, the robot enters the six way movement mode (Fig. 8c).

(3) When the robot is in the six way movement mode (Fig. 8c), according to the different needs of the movement direction, the driving active pair causes the connecting rods of the upper and lower platforms to be triangular, and the robot transitions to the three way movement mode (Fig. 8d).

(4) When the robot is in the six way movement mode, the driving active pair causes the robot to overturn (Fig. 8e), and the driving active pair adjusts the appropriate body width, the robot transitions to the variable distance movement mode (Fig. 8f).

4   Conclusion

(1) This article designs a multi mode parallel multi axis mobile robot that consists of two 6R parallel closed loops to form an upper and lower platform. The platforms are connected by three URU branch chains spaced in pairs, and the degrees of freedom of each mode are analyzed through screw theory.

(2) Determine the position of the active pair of the robot based on the degree of freedom of the mechanism, and plan the gait based on the switching conditions between different modes of the robot.

(3) Combining the advantages of strong coupling and weak coupling, and compensating for the shortcomings of strong coupling and weak coupling mechanisms through the multi mode design of robots.

References

1. Wei, W., Zhuang, Z., Tang, Z., et al.: Research on the Configuration Design and Kinematic Performance of Snake Robot Based on 3-RSR Parallel Mechanism. J. Mecha. Eng. **57**(23), 21–33 (2021)
2. Jiang, A., Han, H., Han, C., He, S., Xu, Z., Wu, Q.: Dynamics Modeling and Redundant Force Optimization of Modular Combination Parallel Manipulator. Machines **11**(2), 247 (2023)
3. Fu, T., Gao, G., Fang, Z.: Dual gain adaptive Sliding mode control for overcoming inter chain coupling of parallel mechanisms. Software Guide **21**(11), 44–51 (2022)
4. Zhang, Y., Wu, X.: Structural synthesis of fully decoupled two moving two rotating parallel mechanisms. Journal of Agricultural Machinery (2013)
5. Qu, S., Guo, Z.: Research status and analysis of decoupling mechanisms. Mechanical Transmission **46**(10), 170–176 (2022)
6. Zhang, Y., Wu, X., Liu, H., et al.: Design and analysis of uncoupled 3-degree-of-freedom parallel mechanisms. J. Agric. Machi. **39**(8), 4 (2008)
7. Shen, H., Zhu, Z., Meng, Q., Wu, G., Deng, J.: Kinematics and stiffness modeling analysis of zero coupling space 2T1R parallel mechanism. J. Agricul. Machi. **51**(10), 10 (2020)
8. Chen, Z., Zhang, C., Jiang, X., et al.: Design and analysis of a reconfigurable spatial open/closed 6R mobile parallel mechanism. J. Eng. Design (2021)

Design and Kinematics Analysis of DNA Nanomachines

Lifeng Zhou[✉]

Peking University, Beijing 100871, China
lifengzhou@pku.edu.cn

Abstract. In recent years, the design and fabrication of nanomachines have obtained many significant achievements due to the development of chemical synthesis and bottom-up self-assembly. The rise of DNA nanomachines is one of the essential proceedings that not only broadened the research domain of mechanical science but also opened new doors for developing nanoscale tools that can find many valuable applications in biology, physics, chemistry, biomedical engineering, and nanotechnology. Here, the concept of DNA nanomachines was first introduced. Then, the design and construction of nanoscale kinematic joints were discussed. Following that, the DNA Waterbomb base was used to show the construction of complex nanomachines via hybridizing classic mechanisms and DNA origami concepts. Moreover, based on screw theory, a feasible and practical approach was developed to analyze and verify the DNA Waterbomb base using two-dimensional electron microscopy images.

Keywords: Nanomachines · DNA origami · Kinematics

1 Introduction

Creating and using tools is a critical skill that finally differentiates our ancestors from apes. Those tools, such as stone axes, bone needles, bows and arrows, also sped up the evolution of humans, giving birth to colorful and brilliant human societies and civilizations. Since the first industry evolution, mechanical science was developed by summarizing the studies about machine design, analysis, and fabrication. Schools started to teach courses about mechanical science, and mechanical engineers became the cornerstones of industrialization in many countries. More and more powerful machines were developed, sparked by the second industrial revolution. Due to the development of chip manufacturing, micro, and nanoscale machines started to draw attention to mechanical engineers. Machines are becoming much smaller while internal structures are becoming much more complex, compact, and sophisticated [1, 2]. For many years, top-down fabrication, represented by lithographs used in chip manufacturing, has been the only approach that can create micro/nanoscale machines. However, lithograph needs expensive equipment and professional operations, which are not available in many research groups. Also, the materials, mainly silica, require special treatments, which are also expensive and time-consuming. In addition, it is challenging for lithographs to achieve atom-level precision fabrication.

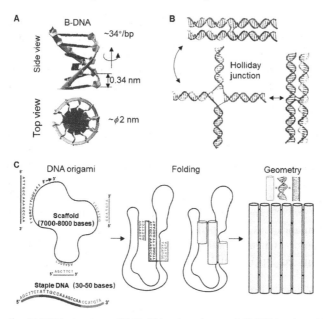

Fig. 1. A) DNA structures, B) Holliday junction, and C) DNA origami [3].

Learning from Nature, living things are built from the bottom up through self-assembly, from the tiny double-stranded DNA molecules and proteins to cells, organs, and the entire body. Biological materials can be used to construct nanostructures from the bottom up with high precision and fascinating functions. Among many biological materials, DNA is the most fundamental and powerful molecule that can be programmed to construct nanostructures due to its primary and concise base-pairing principles, A-T and G-C. Back in the 1950s, the helix structure of DNA was first revealed by two young scientists, Watson and Crick [4] (Fig. 1A). Then, Holliday junction (Fig. 1B), the cross-shaped structure was discovered by British geneticist Robin Holliday in 1964 [5]. People started to realize that DNA molecules can be used to construct junctions that can function as basic elements of larger and more complex nanostructures. In the 1980s, Professor Nadrian Seeman laid down the cornerstones of DNA nanotechnology by developing many DNA-based tiles and junctions that can construct high-order 2D and 3D nanostructures [6]. However, due to the high cost of DNA synthesis, the built DNA nanostructures and nanomachines were simple and impractical. In 2006, Professor Paul Rothemund first introduced DNA origami which can design and build complex DNA nanostructures by folding a long single-stranded DNA with a bunch of short DNA molecules [7] (Fig. 1C). Then, more and more complex 2D and 3D DNA nanostructures were created via DNA origami. DNA nanotechnology became a research hotspot as the cost of DNA synthesis dropped dramatically. In 2012, Professor Hai-jun Su and Carlos E. Castro at the Ohio State University first proposed the concept of DNA origami mechanisms and machines and started to build nanoscale mechanical joints and classic mechanisms via DNA self-assembly [3, 8–10].

Fabrication of DNA nanomachines usually requires thermal annealing, which starts at a high temperature, such as 90 °C, and gradually drops to a low temperature, such as 25 or 4 °C, with precise temperature control. Before thermal annealing, all DNA molecules are mixed with prescribed ratios in the reaction buffer in which cation's concentration, such as magnesium and sodium, are critical for the success of the self-assembly of DNA nanomachines [11–14].

After fabrication, DNA nanomachines can be easily purified via traditional agarose gel electrophoresis and ultrafiltration with molecule weight cutoff spinning centrifugal extraction. As DNA nanomachines are about 100 nm, electron microscopies, and atomic force microscopies are used to image and verify them. Though CryoEM can inspect the 3D structures of the DNA nanomachines, the cost is super high. We developed an easier approach, projection kinematics, for analyzing DNA nanomachines based on two-dimensional images of transmission electron microscopies [15]. Here, a method based on projection kinematics was developed for the analysis of complex DNA nanomachines. The method can dramatically reduce the verification cost and simplify the kinematics analysis with limited experimental data.

2 Design of DNA Kinematic Joints

Similar to the construction of macroscopic kinematic joints, nanoscale DNA kinematic joints can also be fabricated based on the mechanical properties of DNA molecules (Fig. 2). Experiments have demonstrated that a single double-stranded DNA molecule can be modeled as an elastic beam when its length is shorter than 50 nm. When many DNA molecules are assembled parallelly as a bundle, the bending stiffness becomes much bigger, and the entire bundle can be modeled as a rigid link. On the other side, single-stranded DNA molecules are much more flexible and can be used to construct free movable connections. For example, the revolute joint was constructed by two rigid DNA bundles connected with several short single-stranded DNA segments. The design and construction of a DNA prismatic joint are much more difficult as the slide must be assembled on the outside of the frame link. Nevertheless, many experiment conditions and tests have been conducted to obtain well-constructed DNA prismatic joints with high yield [16]. The universal joint is also exceptional as a cross-shaped element connects input and out shafts. Because it is challenging to construct such a rigid cross-shaped element via DNA origami, a simplified universal joint constructed by three rigid parts was developed. The cross-shaped element was replaced by a cubic with two perpendicular edges connected with input and output shafts (Fig. 2). The spherical joint can be constructed by connecting two rigid DNA bundles with a short ssDNA segment. Because the ssDNA segment is so flexible, the two rigid DNA bundles can rotate freely around the connection position.

3 Design and Analysis of DNA Waterbomb Base

Based on the basic DNA kinematic joints, complex nanoscale mechanisms, and machines can be designed and fabricated. Here, as a significant example, the DNA Waterbomb base was used to illustrate the design and modeling process via traditional kinematics analysis methods [17].

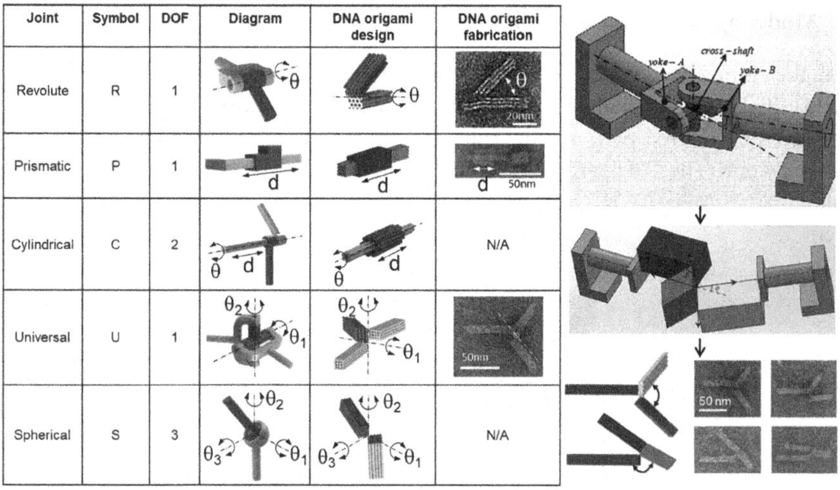

Joint	Symbol	DOF	Diagram	DNA origami design	DNA origami fabrication
Revolute	R	1	θ	θ	20nm
Prismatic	P	1	d	d	d 50nm
Cylindrical	C	2	θ d	θ d	N/A
Universal	U	1	θ_2 θ_1	θ_2 θ_1	50nm
Spherical	S	3	θ_2 θ_3 θ_1	θ_2 θ_3 θ_1	N/A

Fig. 2. DNA kinematic joints. The design of basic DNA kinematic joints (right) and structures demonstrated by TEM images [16] and the simplification of the DNA universal joint and its structure (left). N/A: not available.

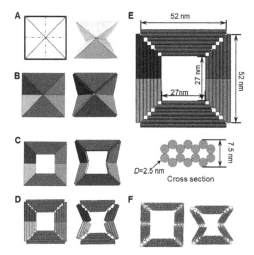

Fig. 3. Design of DNA Waterbomb base. A-C) Simplification and design procedure of the DNA Waterbomb base, E) basic dimensions, and F) molecular models.

Paper origami is a popular approach for constructing expandable and foldable machines of various sizes that can be used in space exploration, surgery, drug delivery, and so on. Waterbomb base is one of the classic paper origami elements that can construct unprecedented geometries with complex functions. Because the diameter of DNA is about 2 nm, the thickness of the DNA Waterbomb base can't be ignored (Fig. 3).

3.1 Modeling of the Waterbomb Base

Then, the entire DNA Waterbomb base can be modeled as a looped six-link mechanism (Fig. 4). Its kinematic analysis can be finished via screw theory. The global coordinate was placed on the red part, and the rotation axes of all six joints can be easily figured out one by one. The D-H parameters of the entire Waterbomb base were summarized in Table 1.

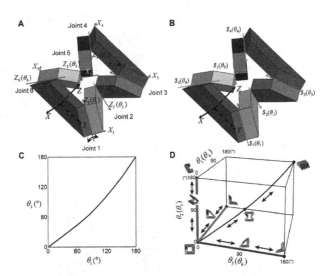

Fig. 4. Modeling and analysis of Waterbomb base. A) Kinematic model, B) screws of all joints, C) relationship between joint angle θ_1 and θ_2, D) transformation.

Table 1. D-H parameters of the Waterbomb base

Joint i	α_{i-1}	a_{i-1}	d_i	θ_i	$\boldsymbol{R}_i$	$\boldsymbol{r}_{i-1}$
1	$\pi/4$	0	0	θ_1	$\boldsymbol{R}_x(\pi/4)\boldsymbol{R}_z(\theta_1)$	$(0,0,0)$
2	$-3\pi/4$	t	0	θ_2	$\boldsymbol{R}_x(-3\pi/4)\boldsymbol{R}_z(\theta_2)$	$(t,0,0)$
3	$-3\pi/4$	$-t$	0	θ_3	$\boldsymbol{R}_x(-3\pi/4)\boldsymbol{R}_z(\theta_3)$	$(-t,0,0)$
6	$-\pi/4$	0	0	θ_6	$\boldsymbol{R}_x(-\pi/4)\boldsymbol{R}_z(\theta_6)$	$(0,0,0)$
5	$3\pi/4$	t	0	θ_5	$\boldsymbol{R}_x(3\pi/4)\boldsymbol{R}_z(\theta_5)$	$(t,0,0)$
4	$3\pi/4$	$-t$	0	θ_4	$\boldsymbol{R}_x(3\pi/4)\boldsymbol{R}_z(\theta_4)$	$(-t,0,0)$

The rotation matrixes about $\mathbf{X}$ and $\mathbf{Z}$ axes are defined as

$$R_X(\alpha) = \begin{bmatrix} 1 & 0 & 0 \\ 0 & \cos\alpha & -\sin\alpha \\ 0 & \sin\alpha & \cos\alpha \end{bmatrix}, \; R_Z(\theta) = \begin{bmatrix} \cos\theta & -\sin\theta & 0 \\ \sin\theta & \cos\theta & 0 \\ 0 & 0 & 1 \end{bmatrix} \tag{1}$$

and the adjoint coordinate transformation matrix is defined as

$$[Ad] = \begin{bmatrix} \mathbf{R} & \mathbf{0} \\ \mathbf{DR} & \mathbf{R} \end{bmatrix} \tag{2}$$

where $\mathbf{R}$ is the rotation matrix of the screw, $\mathbf{D}$ is the anti-symmetric matrix representing the translation vector $\mathbf{r} = (r_x, r_y, r_z)$,

$$\mathbf{D} = \begin{bmatrix} 0 & -r_z & r_y \\ r_z & 0 & -r_x \\ -r_y & r_x & 0 \end{bmatrix} \tag{3}$$

The rotation matrix $\mathbf{R}$ and translation vector $\mathbf{r}$ of all joints were summarized in Table 1.

The screws of the six joints can be calculated as

$$\begin{aligned} \$_1 &= [Ad]_1 \$_0, \; \$_2 = [Ad]_1 [Ad]_2 \$_0, \; \$_3 = [Ad]_1 [Ad]_2 [Ad]_3 \$_0 \\ \$_4 &= [Ad]_6 [Ad]_5 [Ad]_4 \$_0, \; \$_5 = [Ad]_6 [Ad]_5 \$_0, \; \$_6 = [Ad]_6 \$_0 \end{aligned} \tag{4}$$

where $\$_0 = \{0, 0, 1, 0, 0, 0\}$ and $[Ad]_i$ $(i = 1, \cdots, 6)$ can be calculated by using Eqs. (2) and (3) and Table 1.

The relationship between the screws of joint 3 and joint 4 is

$$\$_4 = [Ad]\$_3 \tag{5}$$

where $[Ad]$ was calculated by Eqs. (2) and (3) based on $\mathbf{R} = R_X(\pi/2), \mathbf{r} = (0, 0, 0)$.

Also, due to the symmetry of the entire Waterbomb base, we have

$$\begin{aligned} \theta_1 &= \theta_3 = -\theta_4 = -\theta_6, \\ \theta_2 &= -\theta_5 \end{aligned} \tag{6}$$

From Eqs. (4) and (5), we obtained the relationship between joint angles θ_1 and θ_2

$$-1 + \cos\theta_1^2 + \cos\theta_2 - \cos\theta_1^2 \cos\theta_2 + 2\cos\theta_2 \sin\theta_1^2 - 2\sqrt{2}\cos\theta_1 \sin\theta_1 \sin\theta_2 = 0 \tag{7}$$

3.2 Projection Kinematics Analysis

DNA nanomachines are usually imaged by transmission electron microscopy (TEM) that can obtain tomographic 2D images. We developed the projection kinematic analysis method [15], which can verify the mobility of the nanomachines by statistically investigating many particles on the 2D images. First, the projection plane is defined by using three corner points on three panels P_1 P_2, and P_3 shown in Fig. 5. The projection angles $\bar{\theta}_1$ and $\bar{\theta}_2$ can be calculated by

$$\bar{v} = v - (v \cdot n)n \tag{8}$$

where $\bar{v}$ is the projection vector, v is the true panel edge vector, and n is the normal unit vector of the projection plane. The relationship between the real joint angle θ_1 and its projection angle $\bar{\theta}_1$ is presented in Fig. 5. In addition, the relationship between projection angles $\bar{\theta}_1$ and $\bar{\theta}_2$ is a straight line, which also can be derived from the projection configuration directly $\bar{\theta}_2 = 2\bar{\theta}_1$.

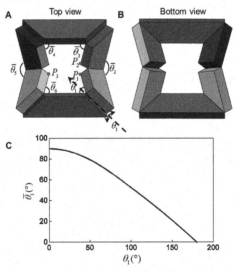

Fig. 5. Projection configurations and analysis of the Waterbomb base model. A) Top view, B) bottom view, and C) relationship between the real and projection angle of joint 1.

Then we measured the inner four angles $(\bar{\theta}_1, \bar{\theta}_3, \bar{\theta}_4, \bar{\theta}_6)$ of 155 DNA Waterbomb bases on 2D TEM images and summarized their average values in Fig. 6. In addition, we picked several examples of Waterbomb bases and plotted their projection angles $(\bar{\theta}_1, \bar{\theta}_2)$. In this way, we found that most of the configurations of DNA Waterbomb bases follow the projection kinematics analysis curve, which demonstrates the fabricated DNA Waterbomb base has the designed mobility.

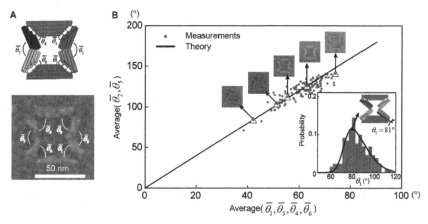

Fig. 6. Projection kinematics anslysis of the DNA Waterbomb base. A) Projection configuration and measured parameters, B) Comparison between the projection analysis and measurements.

4 Conclusion and Discussion

Here, the concept of DNA origami machines and mechanisms was introduced. Basic nanoscale DNA kinematic joints with similar functions as their macroscopic counterparts were discussed. Also, the DNA Waterbomb base also shows the feasibility of constructing much more complex nanomachines using the basic DNA joints. Based on screw theory, the developed projection kinematics analysis can demonstrate mobility of the self-assembled DNA nanomachines with limited imaged data taken by electron microscopies. The developed method presented in this paper can be easily applied to the kinematics analysis of other nanomachines via their 2D images or videos. In the future, much more powerful DNA nanomachines can be designed and fabricated according to the requirements of real-life applications. Those nanomachines can be programmed to conduct complex tasks, such as nanomanipulation, atom scale assembly, cellular surgery, and targeted drug delivery.

References

1. Larsen, U.D., Signund, O., Bouwsta, S.: J. Microelectromech. Syst. **6**, 99 (1997)
2. Hubbard, T., Kujath, M.R., Fetting, H.: In: CCToMM Symposium on Mechanisms, Machines and Mechatronics (2001)
3. Su, H.-J., Castro, C.E., Marras, A.E., Zhou, L.: The kinematic principle for designing deoxyribose nucleic acid origami mechanisms: challenges and opportunities. J. Mech. Des **139**, 062301 (2017)
4. Watson, J.D., Crick, F.H., et al.: Nature **171**, 737 (1953)
5. Holliday, R.: A mechanism for gene conversion in fungi. Genetics Res. **5**, 282 (1964)
6. Seeman, N.C.: Nucleic acid junctions and lattices. J. Theor. Biol. **99**(2), 237−247 (1982)
7. Rothemund, P.W.: Folding DNA to create nanoscale shapes and patterns. Nature **16**, 440(7082), 297−302 (2006)
8. Marras, A.E., Zhou, L., Su, H.J., Castro, C.E.: PNAS 201408869 (2015)

9. Zhou, L.: In Encyclopedia of Robotics, edited by Ang, M.H., Khatib, O., Sicil-iano, B., (Springer, Berlin, Heidelberg, 2020), pp. 1–12 (2020)
10. Huang, C.-M., Kucinic, A., Johnson, J.A., Su, H.J., Castro, C.E.: Nature Mater. **1** (2021)
11. Marras, A.E., Zhou, L., Kolliopoulos, V., Su, H.J., Castro, C.E.: Directing folding pathways for multi-component DNA origami nanostructures with complex topology. New J. Phys. **18**(5), 055005 (2016)
12. Marras, A.E., et al.: Cation-activated avidity for rapid reconfiguration of DNA nanodevices. ACS Nano. **12**(9), 9484–9494 (2018)
13. Zhou, L., Marras, A.E., Su, H.J., Castro, C.E.: DNA origami compliant nanostructures with tunable mechanical properties. ACS Nano. **8**(1), 27–34 (2014)
14. Zhou, L., Marras, A.E., Su, H.J., Castro, C.E.: Direct design of an energy landscape with bistable DNA origami mechanisms. Nano Lett. **15**(3), 1815–1821 (2015)
15. Zhou, L., Su, H.J., Marras, A.E., Huang, C.M., Castro, C.E.: Projection kinematic analysis of DNA origami mechanisms based on a two-dimensional TEM image. Mech. Mach. Theory. **109**, 22–38 (2017)
16. Zhou, L.: In Encyclopedia of Robotics, edited by Ang, M.H., Khatib, O., Siciliano, B., (Springer Berlin Heidelberg, Berlin, Heidelberg, 2020), pp. 1–12 (2020)
17. Zhou, L., Marras, A.E., Huang, C.M., Castro, C.E., Su, H.J.: Paper origami-inspired design and actuation of DNA nanomachines with complex motions. Small**14**(47), 1802580 (2018)

Design and Analysis of a New Type of Solar Panel

Zixuan Liu, Xingyu Liu, Zhen Zhang, and Ziming Chen$^{(\boxtimes)}$

Yanshan University, Qinhuangdao 066000, HB, China
chenzm@ysu.edu.cn

Abstract. In this paper, a new folding mechanism is proposed innovatively from the perspective of origami. The folding model is mainly composed of panels with different shapes, which are successively connected by rotating joints. Firstly, the existing origami model is taken as the research object and the folding model is simplified and improved and the degree of freedom and other theoretical analysis are carried out to ensure that the folding model can be foldable under rigid conditions. Finally, the zero thickness folding model was thickened by the motion synthesis method.

Keywords: origami model · degree of freedom · thickening

1 Introduction

The art of origami has its origins in both China and Japan. During ancient times, its development was primarily through oral transmission rather than being recognized as an art form. In recent times, a notable figure, Mr. Yoshizawa, reintroduced origami to the public by inventing origami symbols and wet folding techniques, thereby revitalizing the practice. Besides Yoshizawa, modern origami artists such as Eric Joisel, Robert Lang, Paul Jackson and others have contributed to the resurgence of origami. This renewed interest in origami has provided people with opportunities to draw inspiration from this art form and apply it in various fields, including aerospace and robotics.

Many researchers have achieved notable advancements in the field of rigid origami. For instance, Chen Yan, et al., from Tianjin University, investigated the reconfigurability of the integrated 8R motion-induced mechanism based on origami and its evolved 6R and 4R mechanisms [1]. They established a connection between origami and linkage mechanisms by utilizing origami as a rotating joint. Additionally, they invented the 8R linkage mechanism and its derivatives, as depicted in Fig. 1 and Fig. 2. Inspire by origami's structure, Rodrigo Luis Pereira Barreto, et al., introduced an innovative spherical mechanism for connecting rods [2]. This approach presents certain limitations to existing origami structures. By employing graph theory and group theory to enumerate spherical mechanisms, other structures that adhere to the flat foldable origami theorem can be discovered, as illustrated in Fig. 1 and Fig. 3. Moreover, deployable wheels constructed using water bomb origami have also been explored. Liu Weiqi, et al., drew inspiration from origami to devise a bispherical 6R connecting rod with space crank rocker characteristics [3]. Furthermore, Yang Mingyuan, et al., from Tianjin University, designed a minimally invasive surgical forceps based on the principles of thick panel origami [4]. In comparison to the previous design of the operating arm in existing minimally invasive surgical robots, the new origami forceps exhibit a significant improvement in interchangeability. These forceps can directly replace the current minimally invasive surgical forceps due to their high level of interchangeability. Furthermore, the new origami forceps offer a mechanical benefit that is 2.5 times greater than the traditional minimally invasive forceps. In addition, animal tests have demonstrated that the clamping performance of the new forceps is more stable and reliable.

Furthermore, various well-established techniques have been developed to enhance the thickness of zero-thickness origami mechanisms [5, 6]. These techniques include the gradient thickness method, axis migration method, crease migration method and the kinematic synthesis of thick panel method. By employing suitable methods, the zero-thickness origami mechanism can be thickened to enable its applicability across different domains. Gu Yuanqing et al. [7] efficiently folded a polyhedron composed of rigid surfaces, providing it with a single degree of freedom. A novel approach for designing origami cubes with rigid foldability, plane foldability and a single degree of freedom was proposed. In the study conducted by Fufu Yang et al. [8], the truss transformation method was utilized to solve the non-over-constrained form of a three-dimensional over-constrained mechanism, which demonstrated successful application in the calculation of rigid origami freedom. Guang Chenhan [9, 10] investigated the single-vertex multi-crease folding mode, taking into account the impact of thickness on its folding ratio. The degree of freedom of the equivalent mechanism was analyzed using the spiral vector method, elucidating its applicability to fixed-surface antennas through a three-dimensional model. Jeremy Shafer's traditional Flasher origami pattern offers advantages in terms of compact folding size and high flexibility. This pattern comprises symmetrical polygons that utilize the rotation of the central module to gradually unfold and achieve a flattened state. Initially employed for folding shading cloth in automobiles, the traditional Flasher origami mode served as the foundation for Zirbel et al. [11] to design a series of similar thick-panel origami mechanisms. These mechanisms were successfully implemented in engineering applications such as folding antennas. Wang Sen et al. [12] proposed a design method for deployable curved rigid origami solar panels in their research. The geometric relationship of the rigid origami in the deployable surface is established and analyzed based on plane projection. Chen Xuesong et al. [13] proposed a new deployable structure design scheme inspired by origami. They considered the planar linkage mechanism as an origami unit with a large deployable capacity. They analyzed the valley crease distribution method of the planar linkage mechanism, identified the physical interference in the folding process from a geometric perspective, and adopted the vertex splitting technique to solve this problem. Finally, they successfully created a structure with a high folding ratio using the derived Mosai pattern. It was found that this structure has considerable potential for future spatial applications.

The above research shows that origami models have great potential to provide creative ideas for many industries. Most of the rigid origami studies mentioned above are based on existing origami models, among which common ones are Miura folding, square twisting, Waterbomb, Flasher, Kresling, etc.

The current Flasher crease pattern exhibits a higher level of complexity, posing challenges in its transformation into a thick panel model. Consequently, it is imperative to simplify the original Flasher crease pattern, followed by the conversion of the streamlined zero-thickness pattern into a thick panel model. This process enables the achievement of radial folding characterized by a single degree of freedom.

In this paper, the Flasher origami structure serves as the foundation for the developed folding method employed to extract the intended folding configuration. However, the existing Flasher crease pattern possesses greater complexity and presents challenges in its direct transformation into a thick plate model. Hence, it becomes necessary to simplify the original Flasher crease pattern and subsequently convert the simplified zero-thickness pattern into a thick plate model. This facilitates the realization of an extension in radial fold with a single degree of freedom.

2   The Proposed Model and the Calculation of Degrees of Freedom

2.1   Model Presentation

In conducting the investigation of the Flasher origami structure, a derived folding form of the Flasher structure was found to be of greater research value. It is shown in Fig. 1.

  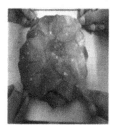

Fig. 1. Flasher origami-derived structure.

However, the aforementioned derivative mechanism proves to be excessively intricate and unsuitable for the design of folding and spreading devices. Therefore, it becomes essential to simplify the structure based on this concept. Subsequently, a four-fold origami structure with eight vertices on both the inner and outer rings is obtained, as depicted in Fig. 2. This structure is centered around an octagon, surrounded by approximately quadrilaterals and triangles, as showcased in Fig. 2(b). While this folding method is comparably simpler than the derived structure, it still poses complications when connecting panels with a certain thickness. Achieving zero thickness in this folding becomes more challenging. Thus, further simplification is necessary, leading to the elimination of the outer ring consisting of eight single-vertex four creases, as demonstrated in Fig. 3. This revised folding method reduces the number of panels in the outer ring, further streamlining the model. The resulting state after folding is presented in Fig. 3(b).

Although the folded form remains largely unchanged compared to the previous model, the overall complexity of the structure has been significantly reduced. Consequently, the analysis is conducted based on this second simplified model, followed by the thickening of the panels.

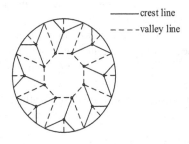

(a) Simplified crease diagram   (b) Folded closed diagram.

Fig. 2. Simplified paper folding diagram of a square octagon.

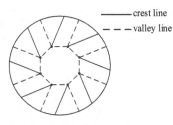

(a) Simplified crease diagram   (b) Folded closed diagram.

Fig. 3. The second simplified diagram of a square octagonal paper folding.

For the simplified graphs in this paper, it is mainly composed of a single-vertex four-crease cell consisting of three valley lines and a peak line. This is shown in Fig. 4. For each cell there are four options for where the peak line is located. It can be at the position of line 2 or at the position of line 1, 3 and 4. However, considering the application area of the folded form, where line 1 and 4 can only be valley line and not peak line, the position of the peak line can be determined at the position of line 2 and 3. Thus the figure of a regular octagon can be composed of two kinds of folded units, the simplified figure in Fig. 4 is only one of the folding forms, which only uses the folding unit with line 2 as the peak line. It is also possible to experiment with folding units in which only line 3 is the peak line and with folding forms in which both folding units are used in common. After folding experiments, it was found that folding with only line 3 as the peak line resulted in large deformations, which obviously did not work in engineering applications. The available folding forms are shown in Fig. 5.

The new structure simplifies the original Flasher crease, reducing the number of creases in the crease diagram from 48 to 24. By significantly reducing the number of creases and vertices in the simplified model, the conversion process from zero-thickness models to thick panels model is greatly facilitated.

Fig. 4. Single vertex four-crease folding unit.

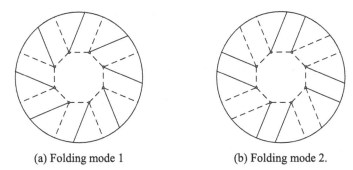

(a) Folding mode 1   (b) Folding mode 2.

Fig. 5. Available in folded form.

2.2 Calculation of Degrees of Freedom

The aforementioned two folding forms are accomplished by folding the origami structure with zero thickness, and they are primarily designed using rigid materials for folding and spreading antennas. Consequently, the flexible origami structure needs to be rigidified and thickened in the subsequent stages. The definitive folding motion is achieved for the thick panel folding structure, maintaining the same folding motions as the zero-thickness origami structure. The analysis of the degrees of freedom in this rigid folding configuration becomes imperative, determining the number of degrees of freedom.

For rigid folded origami structures with multiple closed-loop and redundant folded structures, the application of the modified G-K formula does not guarantee accurate results when calculating the degrees of freedom. Therefore, the conventional methods for calculating degrees of freedom are no longer suitable in such cases. Instead, the adjacency matrix method and the determination of the dimensions of the zero space of the Jacobi matrix are commonly used to calculate degrees of freedom for rigid origami structures. Due to the computational intensity associated with the Jacobi matrix method, in this context, the adjacency matrix method is employed for calculating the degrees of freedom.

To facilitate the subsequent analysis and calculation, the numbering principle is annotated counterclockwise from the non-boundary vertices. As shown in Fig. 6.

For non-boundary vertices the degrees of freedom of each vertex are related as follows:

$$M = m - 3 \tag{1}$$

where M denotes the number of single vertex degrees of freedom and m denotes the number of single vertex creases. For this model the non-boundary vertices are composed of single-vertex four-creases, so $m = 4$ and the vertex degree of freedom M is 1.

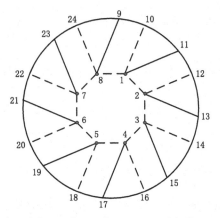

Fig. 6. Folding and spreading structure labeling model.

For the boundary vertices the degrees of freedom of each vertex are related as follows:

$$M = m - 2 \tag{2}$$

where M is the number of boundary vertex degrees of freedom and m is the number of creases owned by each vertex.

In the subsequent determination of the degrees of freedom of the multi-vertex folding structure, the initial adjacency matrix is first defined, where it is recorded as 1 when two vertices are adjacent to each other and 0 when two vertices are not adjacent to each other, thus the initial adjacency matrix is established as follows:

$$
C_0 =
\begin{array}{c}
\\
1 \\
2 \\
\cdots \\
8 \\
9 \\
10 \\
\cdots \\
23 \\
24
\end{array}
\begin{array}{c}
1\ 2 \ldots 8\ 9\ 10 \ldots 23\ 24 \\
\left[
\begin{array}{ccccccccc}
0 & 1 & \ldots & 1 & 1 & 1 & \ldots & 0 & 0 \\
1 & 0 & \ldots & 0 & 0 & 0 & \ldots & 0 & 0 \\
\cdots & \cdots & \cdots & \cdots & \cdots & \cdots & \cdots & \cdots \\
1 & 0 & \ldots & 0 & 0 & 0 & \ldots & 1 & 1 \\
1 & 0 & \ldots & 0 & 0 & 1 & \ldots & 0 & 1 \\
1 & 0 & \ldots & 0 & 1 & 0 & \ldots & 0 & 0 \\
\cdots & \cdots & \cdots & \cdots & \cdots & \cdots & \cdots & \cdots \\
0 & 0 & \ldots & 1 & 0 & 0 & \ldots & 0 & 1 \\
0 & 0 & \ldots & 1 & 1 & 0 & \ldots & 1 & 0
\end{array}
\right]
\end{array}
\tag{3}
$$

The number of 1's in a row or column represents the number of creases in the corresponding vertex. For example, the first row represents vertex 1 which is adjacent to vertices 2, 8, 9 and 10, so the number of 1's in these positions indicates that vertex 1 has four creases. The variable D is introduced to represent the number of inputs required for the motion of each vertex, which can also be called the number of constraints. Each vertex is undefined prior to the analysis, so the initial value of D is set. The analysis is then performed starting from vertex 1, the above analysis shows that vertex 1 is connected to four creases and vertex 1 is a non-boundary vertex, so by Eq. (3) it is shown that the vertex 1 motion requires a crease input, i.e. the motion of the other three creases can be completely determined after any one of them is constrained. Therefore, the motion of vertex 1 can be completely determined.

After analyzing vertex 1, the value assigned to 1 in the matrix changes, indicating that the rotation angle for the associated crease has not been determined yet. Consequently, all the entries in the rows and columns corresponding to the analyzed vertex 1 are set to zero. This procedure necessitates the utilization of an elimination matrix. The elimination matrix is defined as follows:

$$
E_{j,n} = \begin{bmatrix} 1 & 0 & \dots & 0 & 0 & \dots & 0 \\ 0 & 1 & \dots & 0 & 0 & \dots & 0 \\ \vdots & \vdots & & \vdots & \vdots & & \vdots \\ 0 & 0 & \dots & 0_{j,j} & 0 & \dots & 0 \\ 0 & 0 & \dots & 0 & 1 & \dots & 0 \\ \vdots & \vdots & & \vdots & \vdots & & \vdots \\ 0 & 0 & \dots & 0 & 0 & \dots & 1 \end{bmatrix} \tag{4}
$$

The elimination matrix is a diagonal matrix, where the elements of the diagonal are 1 except for the elements of the jth row and column, which are 0. The rest of the positions are complemented by 0 after the elements of the diagonal are determined. The formula when using the elimination matrix for matrix C is as follows:

$$
C_{i+1} = E_{j,n} C_i E_{j,n} \tag{5}
$$

So go on updating C_0 to C_1. The equation is as follows:

$$
C_1 = E_{1,10} C_0 E_{1,10} \tag{6}
$$

So analyzing each vertex in turn, the total degrees of freedom of this folding method is:

$$
M = D_1 = 1 \tag{7}
$$

It turns out that the degree of freedom is just single degree of freedom, which satisfies the design requirements.

3 Transformation from Zero Thickness to Thickness Model

Through the folding experiment, the final zero-thickness folding model is shown in Fig. 7. In this paper, the regular dodecagon folding model is thickened. The folding model when the angle parameter is $\alpha_{12} = 90°$, $\alpha_{23} = 45°$, $\alpha_{34} = 90°$, $\alpha_{41} = 135°$.

As shown in Fig. 8, it consists of an central substrate 1, a basic folding unit 2 and a transitional subpanel 3. The basic folding unit is surrounded by the central substrate, but the adjacent folding unit needs to be connected through the transition panel and each panel surface is connected by a rotating joint.

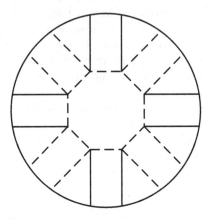

Fig. 7. Folding model of regular octagon.

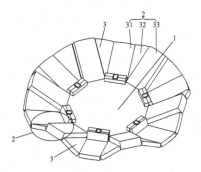

Fig. 8. Folding model of thick panel folding structure.

The basic folding unit is a single-vertex four-crease model, which is connected by kinematic synthesis method, as shown in Fig. 9. The connection principle is completed jointly according to Eq. (8), Eq. (9) and Eq. (10). The folding process of the new folding structure is shown in Fig. 10.

$$a_{12} + a_{34} = a_{23} + a_{41} = \pi \tag{8}$$

$$a_{12} = a_{34}, a_{23} = a_{41} \tag{9}$$

$$\frac{a_{12}}{a_{23}} = \frac{\sin \alpha_{12}}{\sin \alpha_{23}} \tag{10}$$

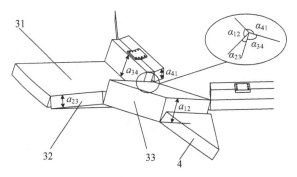

Fig. 9. Basic folding unit connection.

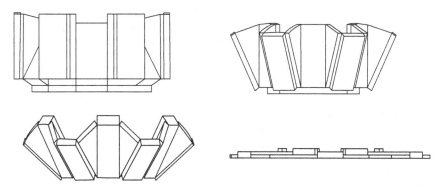

Fig. 10. Folding process.

4   Conclusion

In this paper, a new planar developing structure is designed based on rigid origami. On the basis of the existing origami model, through continuous optimization and analysis, the zero thickness origami model can be rigid folding. Finally, the final application model is obtained by thick-panel processing. Firstly, the existing origami model is simplified and the degree of freedom of the simplified model is calculated by using the adjacency matrix method. Then the zero thickness folding model is thickened by the motion synthesis method to obtain the final rigid folding model. This paper proposes a single-degree-of-freedom thick panel model based on Flasher origami, which can realize radial unfolding of the structure and has a high folding ratio, and can be applied to unfoldable solar panels, unfoldable solid reflective surface antennas, etc.

References

1. Wang, R.Q., Song, Y.Q., Dai, J.S.: Reconfigurability of the origami-inspired integrated 8r Kinematotropic metamorphic mechanism and its evolved 6r and 4r mechanisms. Mech. Mach. Theory **161**(1), 20–25 (2021)

2. Barreto, R.L.P., Morlin, F.V., De Souza, M.B., et al.: Multiloop origami inspired spherical mechanisms. Mech. Mach. Theory **155**(10), 45–50 (2021)
3. Liu, W., Chen, Y.: A double spherical 6r linkage with spatial crank-rocker characteristics inspired by Kirigami. Mech. Mach. Theory **153**(10), 620–635 (2020)
4. Yang, M.Y., Ma, J.Y., Li, J.M., et al.: Minimally invasive surgical forceps based on the theory of thick panel origami. J. Mech. Eng. **54**(17), 36–45 (2018)
5. Yasuda, H., Miyazawa, Y., Charalampidis, E.G., et al.: Origami-based impact mitigation via rarefaction solitary wave creation. Sci. Adv. **5**(5), 56–70 (2019)
6. Chen, Y., Peng, R., You, Z.: Origami of thick panels. Science **349**(6246), 396–400 (2015)
7. Gu, Y., Chen, Y.: Origami cubes with one-dof rigid and flat foldability. Int. J. Solids Struct. **207**(13), 250–261 (2020)
8. Yang, F., Chen, Y., Kang, R., et al.: Truss transformation method to obtain the non-overconstrained forms of 3D overconstrained linkages. Mech. Mach. Theory **102**, 149–166 (2016)
9. Guang, C., Yang, Y.: Single-vertex multicrease rigid origami with nonzero thickness and its transformation into deployable mechanisms. J. Mech. Robot. **10**(1), 60–65 (2018)
10. Guang, C.H., Liu, Y., Yang, Y.: Space folding mechanism inspired by single vertex multi crease origami form. J. Astronaut. **39**(07), 801–807 (2018)
11. Zirbel, S.A., Lang, R.J., Thomson, M.W., et al.: Accommodating thickness in origami-based deployable arrays. J. Mech. Des. **135**(11), 78–88 (2013)
12. Wang, S., Gao, Y., Huang, H., et al.: Design of deployable curved-surface rigid origami flashers. Mech. Mach. Theory **167**(1), 25–30 (2022)
13. Chen, X., Feng, H., Ma, J., et al.: A plane linkage and its tessellation for deployable structure. Mech. Mach. Theory **142**(2), 30–35 (2019)

Cutting-Edge Research in Robotics

Real-Time Monitoring System of Spray-Painting Robot Based on Five-Dimension Digital Twin Model

Wei Wang, Jiahao Zhao[✉], Zhi Chen, and Bin Zi

School of Mechanical Engineering, Hefei University of Technology, Hefei 230009, China
zjh96hfut@163.com

Abstract. The painting operation environment is extremely harsh, and the dust generated during the painting process can lead to poor monitoring using vision. Therefore, a real-time monitoring system for spray-painting robots is proposed based on the digital twin theory. A real-time monitoring scheme for spray-painting robots based on the five-dimension digital twin model is designed. Virtual simulation environments and interactive interfaces of the system are built using Unity3D. The key program of the real-time monitoring system is designed by C# to realize the real-time communication between the real robot and the virtual robot. Real-time follow-up experiments of spray-painting robots were completed using the designed robot experimental platform. By analyzing the collected joint angle data of the real robot and the virtual robot, the experimental results shown that the joint angle deviation at the same time is small and the virtual robot can follow the real robot in time.

Keywords: Spray-painting robot · Five-dimension digital twin model · Real-time monitoring · Real-time follow-up experiment

1 Introduction

With the increase in industrialization and automation, spray-painting robots are gradually developing as an effective alternative to manual operations and are widely used in industrial production [1, 2], ensuring the reduction of manpower and improvement of the working environment [3]. The painting process generates a large number of dust particles, which not only block the view but also cause more harm to the human body, making it difficult to observe the robot operation status from a close distance, so the real-time monitoring of the spray-painting robot is of great significance.

At present, there are two forms of robot motion monitoring [4]. One is to monitor the angle, speed, and acceleration of the robot in motion, which is displayed in the form of curves [5–8]. The second is to visually monitor the robot end effector or part of the robot through a high-definition camera [9–11]. The first form cannot visually observe the robot's motion process and cannot know whether the robot's motion trajectory deviates in real-time. The second form of monitoring cannot know the real-time motion data of

H. Yang et al. (Eds.): ICIRA 2023, LNAI 14275, pp. 165–176, 2023.
https://doi.org/10.1007/978-981-99-6504-5_15

the robot, and the dust particles generated by the spray paint seriously affect the visual observation effect.

The concept of the digital twin was first introduced at the University of Michigan [12] and later introduced and used by NASA for the detection and diagnosis of aerospace systems [13]. Subsequently, more and more research and applications of this technology have been conducted [14] and gradually applied in the fields of production automation such as automotive [15], Internet of Things [16], and manufacturing industry [17]. Wang et al. [18] discussed the requirements of the digital twin fault diagnosis model and proposed a model based on parametric sensitivity analysis. Christos et al. [19] presents a unified framework for the design and development of a passive biped robot and its digital twin. Tao et al. [20] proposed a five-dimension digital twin model, which theoretically describes the working process of the digital twin technology model in a richer way, which refers to physical entities, digital twin, twin data, data connection communication, and services.

The application of digital twin technology to real-time monitoring of spray-painting robots, where the virtual robot reads the spray-painting robot motion data in real-time and reflects it on the virtual robot, provides the advantages of both forms of monitoring and effectively avoids dust particle interference. Therefore, the real-time motion monitoring of the spray-painting robot based on the digital twin is of great practical value and significance.

The structure of this paper is shown as follows: the scheme of the real-time monitoring system for the spray-painting robot is constructed in Sect. 2. The real-time monitoring platform is built by Unity3D in Sect. 3. The effectiveness of the real-time monitoring system is experimentally verified in Sect. 4. Finally, the conclusion is drawn in Sect. 5.

2   Real-Time Monitoring Scheme of Spray-Painting Robot

2.1   Five-Dimension Digital Twin Model of Monitoring System

The principle of real-time monitoring of paint spraying robots is based on the five-dimension digital twin model to establish the software and hardware structure of the robot real-time monitoring system, and realize real-time monitoring of the robot motion process through data communication connection, so as to achieve the purpose of accurate verification and fault detection during the robot operation.

The real-time monitoring system is divided into five parts, which are physical entity dimension, data connection communication dimension, digital twin dimension, twin data dimension, and service dimension.

The physical entity dimension refers to the real-world entity that needs to be analyzed and inspected. The physical entity is a six-axis tandem robot, robot model is Efort ER10–1600. The digital twin is structurally identical to the physical entity, and a virtual entity identical to the physical entity in structure as well as other attributes can be created by 3D modeling software commonly used in industry.

The twin data dimension is all the runtime real-time data within the digital twin system. The communication medium and protocol between the physical entity and the twin constitute the communication dimension of the data connection.

The service dimension in the digital twin system refers to the interface provided to the operator. The service dimension specifically refers to the human-computer interface provided on the upper machine.

2.2 Framework of Real-Time Monitoring System for Spray-Painting Robot

The required monitoring system is built based on the content of the five-dimension digital twin model in real-time robot motion monitoring. The virtual simulation environment is constructed by software tools, which contain the digital twin, the human-machine interface as a service dimension, and the processing of the twin data. This virtual simulation environment is a virtual world mapped to a physical entity. The data of the real-time motion of the physical entity is processed and transmitted to the digital twin so that the digital twin reproduces the motion of the physical entity in real-time. This process enables the monitoring of the real-time motion of the physical entity with remote visualization and global view. The virtual simulation environment and the real robot are connected through the data connection communication dimension. Real-time motion monitoring of the robot can be realized by using the built virtual simulation environment, and Fig. 1 shows the specific scheme of robot real-time motion monitoring.

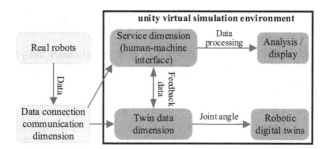

Fig. 1. Robot real-time follow-up monitoring scheme

The service dimension sends a connection request to the robot controller, and the interface of the service dimension starts real-time monitoring after a successful connection, continuously sending data to read requests to the robot controller. The real robot feeds the instantaneous joint angle, velocity, acceleration, and other data to the database as the twin data dimension through the data connection communication dimension. The real-time joint angle data feedback from the robot is then assigned to the virtual robot, allowing it to reproduce the motion of the real robot in real-time in the virtual simulation environment. The corresponding interface of the service dimension reads the robot joint velocity, acceleration, and other data from the twin data for further analysis and display. The purpose of monitoring the real-time motion of the real robot is achieved by processing the twin data in these two parts.

2.3   Kinematics Analysis of Spray-Painting Robot

The human-computer interaction interface usually needs to display the current end position of the virtual robot, which is obtained from the forward kinematic equations. This
section analyzes the forward kinematics of the spray-painting robot.

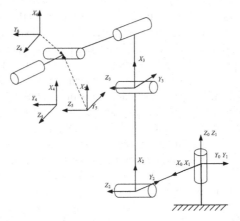

Fig. 2. Schematic diagram of the joint coordinate system of the spray-painting robot

In this paper, the DH parameter method is used to establish the joint coordinate
system of the robot, and the joint coordinate system shown in Fig. 2 can be obtained.
Table 1 lists all DH parameters for this spray-painting robot.

Table 1. DH parameter table of spray-painting robot

joint	a_{i-1}/mm	$\alpha_{i-1}/^\circ$	d_i/mm	$\theta_i/^\circ$	Value range of θ_i /$^\circ$
1	0	0	0	θ_1	$[-165, +165]$
2	195	90	0	θ_2	$[-135, +80]$
3	680	0	0	θ_3	$[-75, +163]$
4	175	90	744.5	θ_4	$[-180, +180]$
5	0	-90	0	θ_5	$[-130, +130]$
6	0	90	0	θ_6	$[-360, +360]$

The poses of the joint coordinate system {i} with respect to the joint coordinate
system {i-1} can be described by a 4 × 4 homogeneous transformation matrix $_i^{i-1}T$.
Each element of the homogeneous transformation matrix can be derived using the DH

parameter, which is calculated as shown in Eq. (1).

$$
{}_i^{i-1}T = \begin{bmatrix} c\theta_i & -s\theta_i & 0 & a_{i-1} \\ s\theta_i c\alpha_{i-1} & c\theta_i c\alpha_{i-1} & -s\alpha_{i-1} & -s\alpha_{i-1}d_i \\ s\theta_i s\alpha_{i-1} & c\theta_i s\alpha_{i-1} & c\alpha_{i-1} & c\alpha_{i-1}d_i \\ 0 & 0 & 0 & 1 \end{bmatrix} \tag{1}
$$

where $c\theta_i = \cos\theta_i$, $s\theta_i = \sin\theta_i$, $c\alpha_{i-1} = \cos\alpha_{i-1}$, $s\alpha_{i-1} = \sin\alpha_{i-1}$, ($i = 1-6$), the same expression is still used in the later equations. By substituting the DH parameters in Table 1 into Eq. (1), the pose matrix of each joint with respect to the previous joint coordinate system can be obtained. By multiplying the obtained matrix right-handedly in turn, the pose of the end of the robot with respect to the reference coordinate system {0} can be found, and thus the forward kinematic equations can be derived.

3 Construction of Real-Time Monitoring System for Spray-Painting Robots

3.1 Overall Structure and Construction of Virtual Simulation Environment

The virtual simulation environment, as the base of other modules, is crucial to the whole system. The virtual simulation environment is built using Unity3D.

The most important part of building a virtual simulation environment is the construction of virtual robots. Other virtual models are built similarly to the virtual robot building process. The virtual robot model built by 3D software is processed and imported into Unity3D. Considering that the tandem robot used has a subordinate relationship between its various motion arms, we use the parent-child relationship in Unity to achieve this device hierarchy. With the create empty object function provided by Unity, each joint is treated as a sub-object of the empty object in turn, and then the poses of each joint coordinate system are adjusted according to the DH parameters.

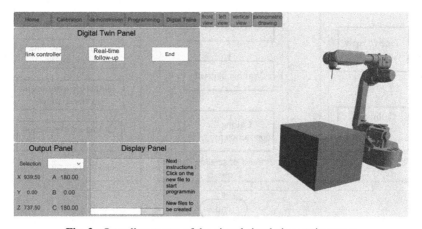

Fig. 3. Overall structure of the virtual simulation environment

Once the virtual robot is built, scripts are created in Unity that perform specific functions and are added to the robot twin, which can then accept the transmitted joint data and perform the corresponding motion to reproduce the motion of the physical robot in real-time.

The main interaction interface of the system is shown in Fig. 3, which mainly includes the demonstration panel, programming panel, digital twin panel, and information display panel. The demonstration panel is mainly used to adjust the individual joints and end movements of the virtual robot; the digital twin panel is used to establish the data communication connection between the robot controllers and to realize the real-time follow-up function; the information display panel is used to display the current end poses of the virtual robot, as well as the current operation information and operation tips.

3.2 Communication Connection Between the Robot and Virtual Environment

Communication at the software level requires the creation of sockets, which provide the Connect method for connecting to a network terminal. The communication protocol is Modbus-TCP, for which the network terminal consists of two parts, one is the server IP and the other is the port number which is fixed to 502. The connection is established by calling the connect method with the IP and port number as parameters. Based on the above principle, the program involves variables such as sockets, IP and port numbers, and network terminals, so the data structure of the program is an object of the Socket class and the IPEndPoint class and a string.

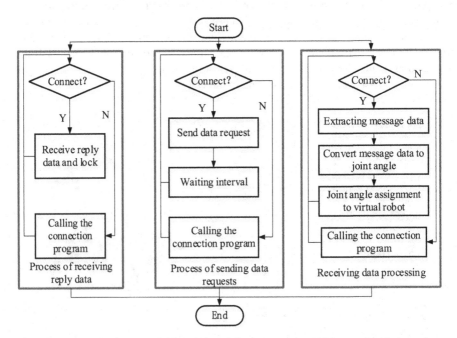

Fig. 4. Schematic diagram of the real-time follow-up program of the spray-painting robot

The program algorithm creates a new string to store the IP and port number values and creates a new IPEndPoint object with these two strings as input parameters. At the same time, a new socket is created and the connect method of the socket is called with the IPEndPoint object as the parameter.

3.3 Real-Time Follow-Up of Virtual and Real Robots

The principle of the real-time follow-up procedure is that by continuously sending a request to the controller to read the joint angle, the controller replies to the robot's current joint angle according to the request; the monitoring system processes the reply information and assigns it to the virtual robot so that the virtual robot motion and the spray-painting robot maintain real-time follow-up. Thus, the operation of the spray-painting robot is monitored.

The program is executed in such a way that the three operations of sending the request, replying to the controller, and processing the data are performed uninterruptedly, while the three operations are performed independently and asynchronously. It is necessary to create a process for each of these three operations in the algorithm, and the three processes are asynchronously scheduled for resources by the operating system.

The three processes are independently and asynchronously performed to ensure that the joint angle data of the real robot can be transmitted to the digital twin in real-time, and the digital twin can real-time monitor the motion process of the real robot. A schematic diagram of the real-time follow-up program of the spray-painting robot is shown in Fig. 4.

4 Real-Time Follow-Up Experiment of Spray-Painting Robot

4.1 Spray-Painting Robot Real-Time Follow-Up Experiment Platform

A spray-painting robot real-time follow-up experiment platform has been built to verify the real-time follow-up function of the spray-painting robot in this paper. The main equipment in this experimental platform includes a six-axis robot, a paint supply system, a spray gun, and a PC.

Figure 5(a) shows the physical diagram of this experimental robot. Kremlin Rexson-Sames A35 automatic spray gun is chosen for the spray gun equipment and the structure of this gun is shown in Fig. 5(b). Figure 5(c) shows the paint supply system.

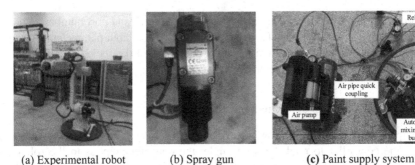

(a) Experimental robot   (b) Spray gun   (c) Paint supply system

Fig. 5. Spray-painting robot real-time follow-up experiment platform

4.2 Real-Time Follow-Up Process and Result Analysis of Virtual and Real Robot

Connect the host computer and robot controller successfully and power up the robot. After checking that there are no faults, configure the Modbus window in the demonstrator and turn on the enable data transfer function. Check that the spraying equipment is working properly. Finally, run the real-time monitoring system in this paper. Transfer the robot test program to the spray-painting robot controller and turn it on in the demonstrator for execution while clicking the real-time follow-up button in the digital twin panel to observe whether the virtual robot and the real robot maintain real-time follow-up with each other.

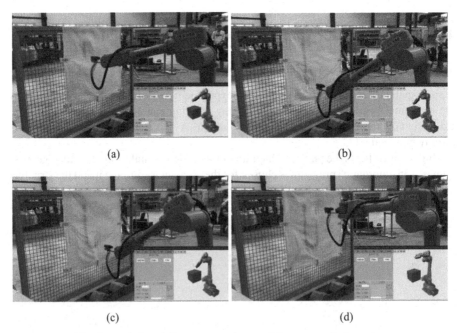

(a)   (b)

(c)   (d)

Fig. 6. Real-time follow-up experiment of the spray-painting robot

After executing the test program, the spray-painting robot starts spray painting on the canvas and the system captures the joint angles of the spray-painting robot in real time while the virtual robot maintains real-time follow-up with the spray-painting robot. Real-time follow-up experiment of the spray-painting robot was shown in Fig. 6. It shows that the motion state of the virtual and real robots is synchronized at each instant.

The test program was executed for 5 s, and the joint angles of the spray-painting robot and the virtual robot were saved at a time interval of 0.02 s during the real-time follow-up experiment, and 250 sets of joint angle data were obtained respectively. The variation curves of the collected joint angle data with time obtained with the help of MATLAB are shown in Fig. 7. From the data results, it can be seen that the angles of each joint of the spray-painting robot and the virtual robot follow the same trend over time, indicating that the virtual robot reproduces the position of the spray-painting robot.

A short delay in the joint angles of the spray-painting robot and the virtual robot can be shown in Fig. 8, and the reason for this phenomenon is that the system processes the collected spray-painting robot joint angle data causing a short delay. Based on Fig. 7, the existing 250 sets of data were collected in a fixed horizontal axis time for analyzing the deviation of the joint angle of the spray-painting robot and the virtual robot at the same moment, and the deviation of the joint angle of the spray-painting robot and the virtual robot at the same moment is shown in Fig. 8.

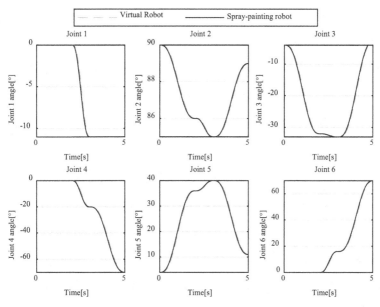

Fig. 7. Angular variation curve of each joint of the spray-painting robot and virtual robot with time.

The maximum value, minimum value, mean value, and standard variance of the angular deviation of joints 1 to 6 at the same time were calculated according to Fig. 13, as shown in Table 2. Statistical table of joint angle deviation between the spray-painting robot and the virtual robot at the same moment. From the table, it can be obtained that the angular deviations of all joints at the same moment of the spray-painting robot and the virtual robot range from −1.874 to 2.024°, while the angular deviations of the first three joints range from −1 to 1°. The first three joints mainly affect the position of the end of the robot, and the deviation is dynamic around 0° as seen from the mean value. Therefore, the deviation of the robot angle at the same moment is within a small range, which meets the requirement of robot real-time monitoring.

Figure 9 shows the rotational speed of robot joint 6, which is in perfect trend with its joint angle deviation, indicating that the deviation of the virtual-real robot joint angle is mainly due to the robot joint rotational speed. To prevent excessive angular deviation in subsequent experiments, the joint rotational speed can be appropriately constrained.

In summary, the virtual robot real-time follow-up process during the spraying process satisfies the real-time monitoring requirements of the operator.

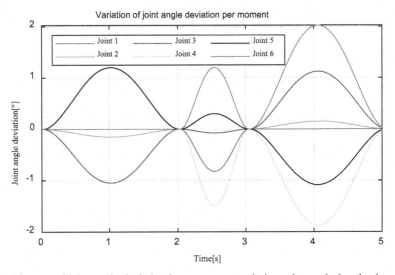

Fig. 8. Diagram of joint angle deviation between spray-painting robot and virtual robot at the same moment

5 Conclusion

This paper constructed a real-time monitoring system for spray-painting robots based on the digital twin theory and described the components of the real-time monitoring system. The virtual robot and the main interaction interface were built by Unity3D. The communication connection program between the real and virtual robots was designed to realize the real-time follow-up of the virtual robot. To verify the performance of the built experimental platform, real-time follow-up experiments of virtual and real robots were carried out. By collecting and analyzing the joint angles of the spray-painting robot and the virtual robot, the fluctuation of the angular deviation is minimal. The experimental results verified that the real-time monitoring system is stable, simple to operate, with good real-time and immersion, and meets the operator's needs for real-time monitoring of the spray painting process.

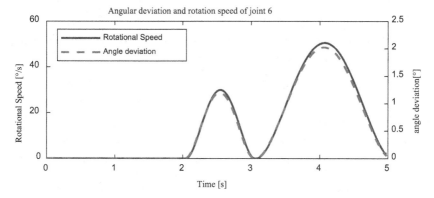

Fig. 9. Angular deviation and rotation speed of joint 6

Table 2. Statistical table of joint angle deviation between the spray-painting robot and the virtual robot at the same moment

Joint serial number	Maximum value /°	Minimum value /°	Mean value /°	Standard variance /°
1	0	−0.8241	−0.0877	0.218
2	0.15	−0.15	−0.00797	0.0878
3	1.125	−1.05	0.00793	0.6206
4	0	−1.874	−0.5577	0.6644
5	1.2	−1.087	0.0558	0.656
6	2.024	0	0.5577	0.6862

Acknowledgment. This work was supported by the National Natural Science Foundation of China (51925502).

References

1. Liu, Y.J., Zi, B., Wang, Z.Y., Qian, S., Zheng, L., Jiang, L.J.: Adaptive lead-through teaching control for spray-painting robot with closed control system. Ro-botica. **41**(4), 1–18 (2023)
2. Zi, B., Xu, F., Tang, K., Wang, Y.F., Sha, W.P.: Trajectory planning for spray-painting robot and quality detection of paint film based on machine vision: a review. Control Decision **38**(1), 1–21 (2023)

3. Kumar, V., Kalita, K., Chatterjee, P., Zavadskas, E.K., Chakraborty, S.: A SWARA-CoCoSo-based approach for spray painting robot selection. Informatica **33**, 35–54 (2022)
4. Wu, Z., Ai, J., Huang, J., Du, Z., Su, B.: A ball-in-ball type self-powered magneto-electric inertial sensor for 3D multi-angle motion monitoring of humanoid robots. Nano Energy **85**, 106016 (2021)
5. Subburaman, R., Kanoulas, D., Muratore, L., Tsagarakis, N.G., Lee, J.: Human inspired fall prediction method for humanoid robots. Robot. Auton. Syst. **121**, 103257 (2019)
6. Wei, M.Y.: Design and implementation of inverse kinematics and motion monitoring system for 6dof platform. Appl. Sci. **11**(19), 9330 (2021)
7. Tao, S., Zhang, X., Cai, H., Lv, Z., Hu, C., Xie, H.: Gait based biometric personal authentication by using MEMS inertial sensors. J. Ambient. Intell. Humaniz. Comput. **9**(5), 1705–1712 (2018)
8. Charvátová, H., Procházka, A., Vyšata, O., Suárez-Araujo, C.P., Smith, J.H.: Evaluation of accelerometric and cycling cadence data for motion monitoring. IEEE Access. **9**, 129256–129263 (2021)
9. Reedha, R., Dericquebourg, E., Canals, R., Hafiane, A.: Transformer neural net-work for weed and crop classification of high resolution UAV images. Remote Sens. **14**(3), 592 (2022)
10. Guo, Y., et al.: Machine learning-based approaches for predicting SPAD values of maize using multi-spectral images. Remote Sens. **14**(6), 1337 (2022)
11. Adil Khan, M., Nawaz, T., Khan, U.S., Hamza, A., Rashid, N.: IoT-based non-intrusive automated driver drowsiness monitoring framework for logistics and public transport applications to enhance road safety. IEEE Access. **11**, 14385–14397 (2023)
12. Grieves, M.W.: Product lifecycle management: the new paradigm for enterprises. Int. J. Prod. Dev. **2**(1), 71 (2005)
13. Tuegel, E.J., Ingraffea, A.R., Eason, T.G., Spottswood, S.M.: Reengineering aircraft structural life prediction using a digital twin. Int. J. Aerospace Eng. **2011**, 1–14 (2011)
14. Zhuang, C., Miao, T., Liu, J., Xiong, H.: The connotation of digital twin, and the construction and application method of shop-floor digital twin. Robot. Comput.-Integr. Manufact. **68**, 102075 (2021)
15. Rolo, G.R., Rocha, A.D., Tripa, J., Barata, J.: Application of a simulation-based digital twin for predicting distributed manufacturing control system performance. Appl. Sci. **11**(5), 2202 (2021)
16. Ma, S., Ding, W., Liu, Y., Ren, S., Yang, H.: Digital twin and big data-driven sustainable smart manufacturing based on information management systems for energy-intensive industries. Appl. Energy **326**, 119986 (2022)
17. Zhang, H., Qi, Q., Tao, F.: A multi-scale modeling method for digital twin shop-floor. J. Manuf. Syst. **62**, 417–428 (2022)
18. Wang, J., Ye, L., Gao, R.X., Li, C., Zhang, L.: Digital twin for rotating machinery fault diagnosis in smart manufacturing. Int. J. Product. Res. **57**(12), 3920–3934 (2019)
19. Vasileiou, C., Smyrli, A., Drogosis, A., Papadopoulos, E.: Development of a passive biped robot digital twin using analysis, experiments, and a multibody simulation environment. Mech. Mach. Theory **163**, 104346 (2021)
20. Tao, F., et al.: Five-dimension digital twin model and its ten applications. Comput. Integr. Manufact. Syst. **25**(1), 1–18 (2019)

A Methodology for Optimization Design of Parallel Manipulators with Similar Stiffness Performance

Chao Yang[1], Fengli Huang[1(✉)], Wei Ye[2], Tianze Sun[1], Yi Zhang[1,2,3], and Qiaohong Chen[3(✉)]

[1] College of Mechanical and Electrical Engineering, Jiaxing University, Jiaxing 314001, Zhejiang, China
{cyang,hfl}@zjxu.edu.cn
[2] Faculty of Mechanical Engineering and Automation, Zhejiang Sci-Tech University, Hangzhou 310018, Zhejiang, China
wye@zstu.edu.cn
[3] School of Information, Zhejiang Sci-Tech University, Hangzhou 310018, Zhejiang, China
chen_lisa@zstu.edu.cn

Abstract. The similar stiffness performance design of parallel manipulators (PMs) is an important prerequisite for scaling the mechanism according to the engineering requirements. Although the scaling problem has been successfully applied in the kinematic performance design of PMs, the scaling problem of the similar stiffness performance of PMs has always been a challenge due to the coupling relationship between the link length and section parameters in the stiffness matrix. This paper proposes a methodology for optimal similar stiffness performance design of PMs based on the characteristic length. The dimensional and sectional parameters of the mechanism are converted into nondimensional design parameters by defining the characteristic length and slenderness ratio. The invariance of optimal nondimensional design parameters under different stiffness indices and characteristic lengths is studied. The 2PRU-PSR PM was taken as the example to implement the proposed method. In order to ensure the robustness of the optimization results, the exhausted search algorithm is adopted in this work. The results showed that the optimal design parameters corresponding to the linear displacement index under different characteristic lengths were consistent, as well as the determinant index. The research results provide a new idea for the stiffness performance design of PMs.

Keywords: parallel manipulator · stiffness index · similar stiffness design · characteristic length

1 Introduction

Compared with the serial mechanism, the parallel manipulator (PM) has attracted the attention of researchers due to its higher stiffness performance [1]. Successful commercial applications include force sensors [2], flight simulators [3], high-speed sorting [4],

H. Yang et al. (Eds.): ICIRA 2023, LNAI 14275, pp. 177–189, 2023.
https://doi.org/10.1007/978-981-99-6504-5_16

parallel kinematic machines [5, 6], etc. Stiffness performance optimization design is one of the main research topics of PMs.

The stiffness optimization mainly consists of two parts. One is to determine appropriate stiffness performance evaluation indices based on the stiffness matrix, such as the determinant index [7], condition number index [8], eigenvalue index [9], and displacement index [10], the other is to determine the appropriate optimization model including design parameters, design space, and constraint space. The traditional stiffness performance design of PMs often maximizes its stiffness performance within prescribed workspace. Chi et al. [11] optimized the x- and y-axes angular stiffness performance and z-axis linear stiffness performance of a 3-DOF PM in a given design parameter space. Yang et al. [12] optimized the comprehensive linear displacement stiffness performance of a 2UPR-RPU PM in a given workspace. However, due to the coupling between dimensional parameters and cross-sectional parameters, the above research is mainly conducted in a dimensional design parameter space, and there is a lack of research on stiffness optimization design in a nondimensional design parameter space. However, a variety of manipulators with different specifications and sizes should be designed to meet the different stiffness performance requirements in engineering, namely a group of similar stiffness mechanisms with a consistent dimension ratio. Meanwhile, which indices are suitable for stiffness performance design and which indices are not, there is a lack of systematic research on these issues.

Theoretically, the reasonable stiffness performance indices of PMs should have a consistent optimal dimension ratio under different manipulator sizes. In other words, although the structural parameters corresponding to the optimal stiffness performance of the manipulator under different sizes are different, their dimension ratios are consistent. It is beneficial to the optimal stiffness performance design of PMs, so that a group of mechanisms with similar stiffness performance can be obtained, which can be scaled to satisfy the engineering environment requirements for the stiffness performance amplitudes. This concept has been proved in the optimal kinematic performance design of PMs. Liu et al. [13, 14] proposed the parameter design space (PDS) method to optimize the nondimensional design parameters for the motion/force transmission index of PMs. The mechanism sizes are determined by assigning the values of normalized factors. Xu et al. [15, 16] established the optimal nondimensional design parameters corresponding to optimal kinematic performance based on the PDS method and then designed the prototype by assigning the normalized factor.

The optimal kinematic similarity mechanism design methodology combining PDS and motion/force transmission index has been accepted by researchers [17]. However, in the above kinematic design model, only equality constraints are considered and inequality constraints are ignored, and the determination of normalized factors is subjective, without considering the influence of the scaling of normalized factors on the magnitude of the manipulator performance. And due to the sectional parameters involved, this methodology has not been successfully applied to the design of the mechanism with similar stiffness performance. Meanwhile, there is a lack of systematic research on which indices are suitable for stiffness performance design and which indices are not.

The main contribution of this work is twofold. First, this work propose a methodology for optimal stiffness performance design of PMs with nondimensional design parameters based on the characteristic length and length-to-diameter ratio, which considered the dimensional parameters, material constants, and sectional parameters of the manipulator. Second, we screened some stiffness indices suitable for the stiffness performance evaluation from whether the ratios of structural parameters corresponding to the optimal stiffness performance under different characteristic lengths are consistent.

The remainder of this work is organized as follows. Section 2 presents the methodology for the optimal stiffness design method of PMs, Sect. 3 presents the stiffness optimization example of the 2PRU-PSR PM. Finally, in Sect. 4, the conclusions are drawn.

2 Methodology for the Optimal Stiffness Performance Design of PMs

The assumptions of the stiffness modeling for the proposed stiffness performance optimization design method of PMs are given as following: 1) the limbs are modeled by rods, the deformation of rods satisfy Hooke's law, that is, in the linear elastic range; 2) All rods are made of the same material; 3) the base and moving platform are assumed to be rigid because they are much stiffer than the rod; 4) flexibility, friction, and clearance of joint are ignored; 5) the effect of gravity is ignored, wherein, assumptions 1) - 3) are reasonable for the stiffness analysis of PMs, while assumptions 4) - 5) are to better present the stiffness design method introduced in this paper.

The overall stiffness matrix should be established before analyzing the stiffness performance. Tsai et al. [18] established the overall stiffness matrix of the 6-SPS PM in the analytical formula of $K = \sum k J_i J_i^T$ by considering the compliance of the joints. Kao et al. [19–21] established the stiffness modeling of PMs by conservative congruence transformation, wherein the links were assumed to be rigid and the effect of the change in geometry due to compliance is captured. In recent years, multiple stiffness modeling approaches were developed to consider the compliance of links, such as matrix structural analysis (MSA), virtual joint method, strain energy, and screw theory. In this work, strain energy and screw theory is adopted to establish the overall stiffness modeling of PMs due to its clear physical meaning [22]. The overall stiffness matrix can be expressed as follows.

$$K = \sum_{i=1}^{n} J_i K_i J_i^T \tag{1}$$

where K is the overall stiffness matrix, J_i is the constraint screw system of the ith limb, and K_i is the stiffness matrix of the ith limb, it's worth nothing that both of the compliance of rods and joints of the ith limb can be considered in the matrix K_i, more details can refer to our previous work [22]. This article focuses on the selection of stiffness performance indices for the design of mechanisms with similar stiffness performance. Therefore, the elasticity of joint is not considered in the stiffness model in the next two case studies.

So far, researchers have proposed many stiffness performance indices, such as determinant index, trace index, eigenvalue index, condition number index, and extreme stiffness index, etc. However, how to use these indices to design a group of mechanisms with similar stiffness performance is always a challenge for PM stiffness design. In this paper, the characteristic length of the mechanism is firstly defined, and then the proportional factor between structure parameters and the characteristic length of the mechanism is defined as nondimensional design parameters. Theoretically, a reasonable stiffness performance index not only meets the definite physical meaning, but also meets the requirement that the corresponding dimension ratio of the optimal stiffness performance of the mechanism under different characteristic lengths should be consistent, that is to say, the stiffness performance of the mechanism under different characteristic lengths is similar. Therefore, one can scale the characteristic length of the mechanism to design the mechanism size that meets the stiffness performance requirements of the engineering environment.

The first and foremost for the optimal stiffness performance design of PMs is to design a set of nondimensional design parameters. In this paper, the distance between the moving platform and the base at the initial installation position is defined as the characteristic length h, the design parameters of the mechanism is defined by

$$x^* = [a_1, \cdots, a_m, \varepsilon_1, \cdots, \varepsilon_n] \tag{2}$$

where x^* is the nondimensional design parameters, a_i ($i = 1, 2, \ldots m$) is the ratio between the structure parameters consist of moving platform size, base size, and rod length, and the characteristic length h; ε_i is the length-to-diameter ratio, namely the ration of rod length and rod diameter.

Stiffness optimization design is to identify the optimal geometry arrangement consists of finding the array x^*_{opt} that maximizes the objective optimization F. Here, F represents the stiffness index attained based on the overall stiffness matrix K.

The limb stiffness matrix is generally obtained by inverting the compliance matrix C_i that is the function of elasticity modulus E, shear modulus G, rod diameter d_i, and rod length L_i. According to the definition in Eq. (2) and $E = \frac{G}{2(1+\mu)}$, the limb stiffness matrix C_i^* based on the nondimensional design parameters and characteristic length can be rewritten as

$$C_i^* = \frac{\varepsilon_i}{Ehc_i(a_1, \cdots, a_m)} N_i^*(\varepsilon_i, h, a_1, \cdots, a_m) \tag{3}$$

where $c_i(\cdot)$ denotes coefficient c_i is the function of argument $(\cdot)$, $N_i^*(\cdot)$ represents that matrix N_i^* is the function of argument $(\cdot)$. It's worth noting that the dimensional parameters are converted to nondimensional parameters in Eq. (3).

It should be noted that the flexibility matrix C_i^* can be decomposed into two parts: matrix external variables and matrix internal variables. The former includes E, h, ε_i, $a_1, \ldots, a_m$, and the latter includes h, ε_i, $a_1, \ldots, a_m$. The elasticity modulus achieves the decoupling from the compliance matrix, while h cannot be separated from the compliance matrix.

Since the constraint screw system J_i is the function of the nondimensional design parameters and characteristic length, thus, the overall stiffness matrix K can be rewritten as

$$K^* = Eh\Omega^*(\varepsilon_1, \cdots, \varepsilon_n, a_1, \cdots, a_m, h) \tag{4}$$

where $\mathbf{\Omega}^*(\cdot)$ denotes that matrix $\mathbf{\Omega}^*$ is the function of argument $(\cdot)$.

Similarly, K^* also consists of two parts, the external variables and the internal variables of the matrix, the former includes E and h, and the latter includes a_m, $\varepsilon_1, \ldots, \varepsilon_n$, h.

According to Eqs. (3) and (4), the following conclusions can be drawn

(1) The elasticity modulus is decoupled from the overall stiffness matrix, and its influence on the stiffness performance of the mechanism varies with the stiffness evaluation index, e.g., it presents an exponential influence on the determinant index and a linear influence on the eigenvalue index.
(2) The stiffness performance of the mechanism increases with the increase of the elasticity modulus and decreases with the length-to-diameter ratio.
(3) It is worth noting that for a mechanism composed of the UPS/SPS limb with equal cross-section, such as the 6SPS PM, the limb stiffness matrix $K_i = EA/L_i$, where, E, ε_i, a_1, h can be decoupled from the limb stiffness matrix. It can be seen from Eq. (1) that the first three rows and the first three columns of the overall stiffness matrix are independent of the characteristic length, that is to say, in this case, the optimal stiffness performance design of the mechanism for the linear displacement stiffness performance under the force load is decoupled from the characteristic length;
(4) In general, it is difficult to decouple the characteristic length from the overall stiffness matrix, and its influence on the stiffness performance of the mechanism should be determined in combination with numerical simulation.

Next, to verify the feasibility of the proposed method, this paper introduces the stiffness performance design method of the mechanism in detail through one example of three degree-of-freedom (DOF) asymmetrical PM, and identifies the suitable performance evaluation index for the optimal stiffness performance design of the mechanism. Finally, a group of similar mechanisms with the same optimal dimension ratio are designed.

3 Example: Optimal Stiffness Performance Design of the 2PRU-PSR PM

Figure 1 shows a 3-DOF 2PRU-PSR PM, the moving platform connected to the three sliders by two PRU limbs and one PSR limb. The one end of each PRU limb is connected to the slider by a revolute joint, while the other end is connected to the moving platform by a universal joint, wherein the R-joints perpendicular to the sliders and parallel to the x-axis, the first axes of two U-joints parallel to the R-joint axis at the other end, and the second axes collinear. The one end of the PSR limb is connected to the slider by a spherical joint, while the other end is connected to the moving platform by a revolute joint, wherein the R-joint axis parallel to second axis of U-joints in PRU limbs. The mechanism motion is obtained by moving the three translational motors mounted on the three sliders. The location of the moving platform relative to the fixed base is described by the position vector p and a rotation matrix R. The 2PRU-PSR PM has three DOFs, namely a translation along the z-axis, a rotation α about the line that pass point A_3 and parallel to the x-axis, a rotation β about the v-axis. $OC_1 = OC_2 = r_1$, $OC_3 = r_2$, oB_1

$= oB_2 = r_3$, $oB_3 = r_4 = r_2r_3/r_1$, $A_1B_1 = A_2B_2 = L_1$, and $A_3B = L_2$. The inverse kinematics of this mechanism can be found in [23].

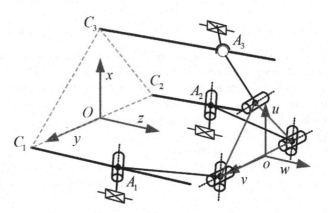

Fig. 1. Schematic diagram of the 2PRU-PSR PM

Consider the distance between A_i and the moving platform as the characteristic length h, the geometric parameters of the mechanism can be expressed based on the characteristic length as

$$\begin{cases} r_1 = a_1h; & r_2 = a_2h; & r_3 = a_3h; & r_4 = a_4h \\ L_1 = a_5h; & L_2 = a_6h \end{cases} \tag{5}$$

It should be noted that the links length are not independent. Once the characteristic length and the radius of the platform and base are specified, the links length are also uniquely determined. Therefore, the following equality constraints should be satisfied

$$\begin{cases} a_5 = \sqrt{1 + (a_1 - a_3)^2} \\ a_6 = \sqrt{1 + (a_2 - a_4)^2} \end{cases} \tag{6}$$

The equal mass constraint is applied to the total mass of the rods, considering the cross section of rods are circular, and the initial slenderness ratio of the rods is $\varepsilon_0 = 9$. The slenderness ratio of rods should satisfy the following equality constraint

$$\varepsilon_3 = \sqrt{\frac{a_6^3}{(\frac{2a_5^3 + a_6^3}{\varepsilon_0^2} - \frac{2a_5^3}{\varepsilon_1^2})}} \tag{7}$$

The inequality constraints for the overall size of the mechanism is given as follows

$$2a_1 + a_2 + 2a_3 + a_4 + 2a_5 + a_6 \leq 7 \tag{8}$$

So far, all the structural parameters of the mechanism are expressed as functions of the characteristic length and nondimensional scale factors

The elastostatic compliance matrix of the PSR limb obtained on the screw theory and strain energy can be expressed as follows [24].

$$C_3 = \begin{bmatrix} \frac{L_2}{GA_3} + \frac{L_2^3}{3EI_3} & 0 \\ 0 & \frac{L_2}{EA_3} \end{bmatrix} \tag{9}$$

Substituting Eqs. (5)–(7) into Eq. (9) one can have

$$C_3 = \frac{4\varepsilon^{\frac{2}{3}}}{\pi E a_6 h} \begin{bmatrix} 2(1+\mu) + 16\varepsilon^{\frac{2}{3}} & 0 \\ 0 & 1 \end{bmatrix} \tag{10}$$

The elastostatic compliance matrices of PRU limbs refer to Ref. [22]. The overall stiffness matrix can be established by Eq. (1)

The mathematical modeling of stiffness optimization design of the 2PRU-PSR PM can thus be established as follows.

$$\begin{cases} \max \quad (\textit{stiffness index}) \\ \text{design parameters} \quad \mathbf{x} = [a_1 \ a_2 \ a_3 \ a_4 \ a_5 \ a_6 \ \varepsilon_1 \ \varepsilon_3] \\ a_1, \ a_2, \ a_3, \ a_4 \in [0.2, \ 1.5]; \quad \varepsilon_1, \ \varepsilon_3 \in [6, \ 12] \\ a_4 = a_2 a_3/a_1; \quad a_5 = \sqrt{1 + (a_1 - a_3)^2}; \quad a_6 = \sqrt{1 + (a_2 - a_4)^2} \\ \varepsilon_3 = \sqrt{\dfrac{a_6^3}{\left(\dfrac{2a_5^3 + a_6^3}{\varepsilon_0^2} - \dfrac{2a_5^3}{\varepsilon_1^2} \right)}} \\ a_1 \geq a_3; \quad 2a_1 + a_2 + 2a_3 + a_4 + 2a_5 + a_6 \leq 7 \end{cases} \tag{11}$$

where stiffness index is the determinant index, condition number index, minimum eigenvalue index, trace index, extreme linear displacement index, or linear displacement homogeneous index. These indices are obtained by averaging the function values of discrete nodes in the plane $z = 1.5$ h and $[\alpha, \beta,] \in [-10°, \ 10°]$.

Similarly, the characteristic length h is uniformly discretized into 30 sets of data in the intervals of $h = 0.1$–5 m to study the influence of the characteristic length on the optimal dimension ratio, so as to identify which index has strong robustness and is suitable for optimal stiffness performance design of the mechanism. Similar to the optimization results of the 2UPR-RPU PM, Table 1 shows that the optimal design parameters for the condition number index, minimum eigenvalue index, or trace index of the mechanism are inconsistent for different characteristic lengths, the robustness of these indices is poor, this further illustrates that these three indices are not suitable for the optimal stiffness performance design of the mechanism due to its unclear physical meaning; the optimal design parameters for the determinant index, extreme linear displacement index, or linear displacement homogeneous index are consistent under different characteristic lengths, which illustrates the strong robustness of these indices again.

Table 1. Optimal design parameters for multiple performance indices of the 2PRU-PSR PM under different characteristic lengths.

		a_1	a_2	a_3	a_4	a_5	a_6	ε_1	ε_3
Trace index	$h = 0.1$ m	0.600	1.400	0.200	0.467	1.077	1.368	7.480	11.996
	$h = 0.3$ m	0.600	1.400	0.200	0.467	1.077	1.368	7.480	11.996
	$h = 0.5$ m	0.240	1.480	0.240	1.480	1.000	1.000	12.000	6.573
	$h = 0.8$ m	0.240	1.480	0.240	1.480	1.000	1.000	12.000	6.573
	$h = 1$ m	0.240	1.480	0.240	1.480	1.000	1.000	12.000	6.573
	$h = 3$ m	0.240	1.480	0.240	1.480	1.000	1.000	12.000	6.573
	$h = 5$ m	0.240	1.480	0.240	1.480	1.000	1.000	12.000	6.573
Condition num-ber index	$h = 0.1$ m	0.880	0.200	0.880	0.200	1.000	1.000	8.160	11.952
	$h = 0.3$ m	0.880	0.200	0.880	0.200	1.000	1.000	8.160	11.952
	$h = 0.5$ m	0.960	0.240	0.800	0.200	1.013	1.001	8.520	10.324
	$h = 0.8$ m	1.000	0.320	0.640	0.205	1.063	1.007	8.920	9.197
	$h = 1$ m	1.000	0.320	0.640	0.205	1.063	1.007	9.120	8.735
	$h = 3$ m	0.960	0.640	0.320	0.213	1.187	1.087	8.440	11.224
	$h = 5$ m	0.760	1.160	0.200	0.305	1.146	1.316	7.840	11.821
Minimum eigen-value	$h = 0.1$ m	0.880	0.200	0.880	0.200	1.000	1.000	8.160	11.952
	$h = 0.3$ m	0.880	0.200	0.880	0.200	1.000	1.000	8.160	11.952
	$h = 0.5$ m	0.960	0.240	0.800	0.200	1.013	1.001	8.520	10.324
	$h = 0.8$ m	1.000	0.320	0.640	0.205	1.063	1.007	8.960	9.096
	$h = 1$ m	1.000	0.320	0.640	0.205	1.063	1.007	9.120	8.735
	$h = 3$ m	1.000	0.560	0.400	0.224	1.166	1.055	8.600	10.442
	$h = 5$ m	0.760	1.160	0.200	0.305	1.146	1.316	7.840	11.821
Determinant index	$h = 0.1$-5 m	0.600	0.800	0.600	0.800	1.000	1.000	9.000	9.000
k_{dfmin}		0.760	1.160	0.200	0.305	1.146	1.316	7.850	11.776
k_{dfmax}		0.52	1.480	0.200	0.569	1.050	1.353	7.450	11.918
δ		0.880	0.920	0.200	0.209	1.209	1.227	8.150	11.820

Figure 2 shows the influence curve of the elasticity modulus E on the extreme linear displacement stiffness performance and linear displacement homogeneous performance under characteristic length $h = 0.5$ m. The elasticity modulus is linearly related to the extreme linear displacement stiffness performance, which means that satisfying Hooke's law. There is a horizontal linear relationship between elasticity modulus and linear displacement homogeneous stiffness performance, which shows the strong robustness of the proposed stiffness design method again.

Figure 3 shows the influence curve of the characteristic length h on the extreme linear displacement stiffness and linear displacement homogeneous performance under the elasticity modulus $E = 180$ GPa. The characteristic length is linearly related and horizontal linear related to the extreme linear displacement stiffness performance and linear displacement homogeneous performance, respectively, e.g., the characteristic length of the mechanism can be designed as $h = 1.9$ m to make the maximum linear displacement stiffness performance of the mechanism achieve $k_{df\text{max}} = 9.219 \times 10^9$ N/m.

The optimal nondimensional design parameters for the homogeneous index deviates greatly from that of the maximum linear displacement index but close to the minimum linear displacement index, which indicates that the homogeneous index is mainly affected by the minimum linear displacement stiffness performance. The design parameters of the 2PRU-PSR mechanism needs to make a trade-off between the maximum linear displacement and the minimum linear displacement stiffness performance according to the requirements of the engineering task.

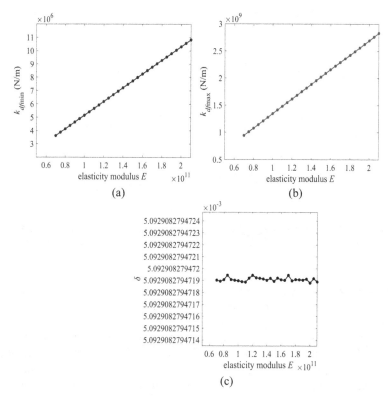

Fig. 2. Influence curve of the elasticity modulus E on the stiffness performance of the 2PRU-PSR PM. (a) $k_{df\text{min}}$, (b) $k_{df\text{max}}$, and (c) δ.

Taking the stiffness design parameters $x = [0.751, 0.751, 0.150, 0.150, 1.166, 1.166, 9, 9]$ proposed in Ref. [20] for comparison, Fig. 4 shows the stiffness performance comparison of the 2PRU-PSR PM in the proposed method and that in Ref. [20] under the characteristic length $h = 0.333$ m and elasticity modulus $E = 180$ GPa. The extreme linear displacement performance and linear displacement homogeneous performance are all improved, which verifies the effectiveness of the proposed stiffness design method in this work (Fig. 3).

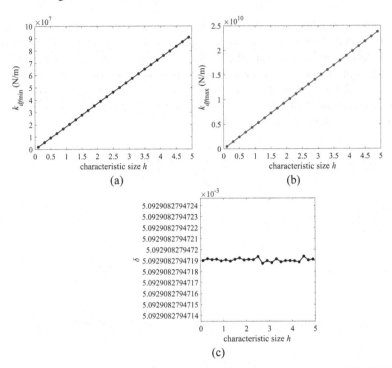

Fig. 3. Influence curve of the characteristic length h on the stiffness performance of the 2PRU-PSR PM. (a) $k_{df\min}$, (b) $k_{df\max}$, and (c) δ.

Compared with traditional stiffness design methods, the advantages of the proposed methodology can be drawn from the above example: (1) Under the constraint of constant mass, the proposed methodology can obtain the optimal dimension ratio of the mechanism (nondimensional design parameters), rather than a set of dimensional optimal solutions; (2) The proposed method can effectively improve the stiffness performance of the mechanism, and can also realize the lightweight design of the mechanism; (3) A group of mechanisms with similar stiffness performance can be obtained through the method presented in this paper, so that the mechanism can be scaled to get the mechanism length that meets the requirements of the engineering environment; (4) From the perspective of whether the optimal structural proportions obtained from the mechanism scaling are equal, the stiffness performance evaluation indices with engineering significance can be selected.

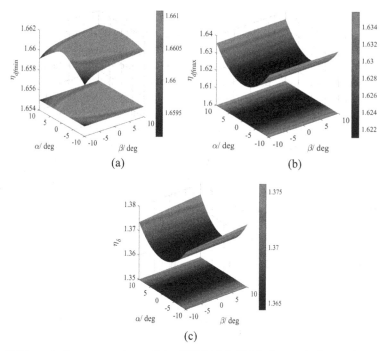

Fig. 4. Stiffness indices comparison of the 2PRU-PSR PM before and after optimization. (a) $\eta_{df\min}$, (b) $\eta_{df\max}$, and (c) η_δ.

4 Conclusions

This paper proposed a methodology for similar stiffness performance design of PMs based on the characteristic length, in which the dimensional and sectional parameters were converted into nondimensional design parameters based on the characteristic length and slenderness ratio. From the perspective of whether the dimension ratio corresponding to the optimal stiffness performance of the mechanism is consistent, which stiffness performance indices are suitable for the similar stiffness performance design of the mechanism and which indices are not applicable were identified. The influence of the characteristic length and elasticity modulus scaling on the stiffness performance of the mechanism was studied, which lays a foundation for determining the mechanism size that meets the engineering environment requirements on the stiffness performance, as well as the lightweight design. To our knowledge, this is the first study on the invariance of the optimal dimension ratio for the stiffness performance design of PMs is presented.

The numerical analysis for the stiffness performance design of the 2PRU-PSR PM was taken as the example to implement the proposed method. The results showed that the robustness of the determinant index and linear displacement index, that is, the optimal nondimensional design parameters of the mechanism are consistent even for different characteristic lengths, which is crucial for the similar stiffness performance design of

PMs; the eigenvalue index, trace index, and condition number index have poor robustness, that is, the optimal nondimensional design parameters of the mechanism is inconsistent in the characteristic lengths space, which is not conducive to the similar stiffness design of PMs. Since the physical explanation for the determinant index is unclear, the extreme linear displacement index is recommended as the stiffness performance design index in this work. The results showed that the elasticity modulus and characteristic length are linearly proportional to the linear displacement performance of the mechanism, but the linear displacement homogeneous performance index is not affected by them. Compared with the structure parameters of the mechanism in the published literature, the stiffness performance of the mechanism obtained by the proposed method in this work were significantly improved with the mechanism mass unchanged. The method presented in this paper provides a new idea for the similar stiffness performance design and scaling problem of PMs. In our future work, the decoupling of characteristic length and stiffness performance indices and lightweight design method considering multiple performance indices constraint will be studied.

Declaration of Competing Interest. The authors declare that there is no conflict of interest.

Acknowledgments. This study was supported by the National Natural Science Foundation of China (NSFC) (grant number 52275036).

References

1. Asada, H.: A geometrical representation of manipulator dynamics and its application to arm design. J. Dyn. Syst.- T. ASME **105**(3), 131–142 (1983)
2. Lu, Y., Wang, Y., Lu, Y.: A novel parallel sensor with six rigid compliant limbs for measuring six- component force/torque. J. Mech. Sci. Technol. **33**(6), 2883–2892 (2019). https://doi. org/10.1007/s12206-019-0536-2
3. Zarkandi, S.: Dynamic modeling and power optimization of a 4RPSP+PS parallel flight simulator machine. Robotica **40**(3), 646–671 (2022)
4. Clavel, R.: Delta, a fast robot with parallel geometry, In: 18th International Symposium on Industrial Robots, pp. 91–100 (1988)
5. Caccavale, F., Siciliano, B., Villani, I.: The Tricept robot: dynamics and impedance control. IEEE-ASME T. Mech. **8**(2), 263–268 (2003)
6. Wahl, J.: Articulated tool head, US Patent (2002 8–13), 6431802
7. Carbone, G., Ceccarelli, M.: Comparison of indices for stiffness performance evaluation. Front. Mech. Eng-Prc. **5**(3), 270–278 (2010)
8. Shin, H., Lee, S., Jeong, J.I., et al.: Kinematic optimization for isotropic stiffness of redundantly actuated parallel manipulators. In: IEEE International Conference on Robotics and Automation, Shanghai, China, pp. 3230–3235 (2011)
9. Li, Y., Xu, Q.: Stiffness analysis for a 3-PUU parallel kinematic machine. Mech. Mach. Theory **43**(2), 186–200 (2008)
10. Courteille, E., Deblaise, D., Maurine, P., et al.: Design optimization of a delta-like parallel robot through global stiffness performance evaluation. In: 2009 IEEE/RSJ International Conference on Intelligent Robots and Systems, St. Louis, MO, USA, pp. 5159–5166 (2009)

11. Chi, Z., Zhang, D.: Multi-objective optimization of stiffness and workspace for a parallel kinematic machine. Int. J. Mech. Mater. Des. **9**(3), 281–293 (2013)
12. Yang, C., Li, Q.C., Chen, Q.H.: Multi-objective optimization of parallel manipulators using a game algorithm. Appl. Math. Model. **74**, 217–243 (2019)
13. Liu, X.-J., Wang, J.: A new methodology for optimal kinematic design of parallel mechanisms. Mech. Mach. Theory **42**(9), 1210–1224 (2007)
14. Wang, J., Wu, C., Liu, X.-J.: Performance evaluation of parallel manipulators: motion/force transmissibility and its index. Mech. Mach. Theory **45**(10), 1462–1476 (2010)
15. Xu, L., Li, Q., Zhang, N., et al.: Mobility, kinematic analysis, and dimensional optimization of new three-degrees-of-freedom parallel manipulator with actuation redundancy. J. Mech. Robot. **9**(4), 041008 (2017)
16. Xu, L., Li, Q., Tong, J., et al.: Tex3: an 2r1t parallel manipulator with minimum dof of joints and fixed linear actuators. Int. J. Precis. Eng. Man. **19**(2), 227–238 (2018)
17. Yang, C., Ye, W., Li, Q.: Review of the performance optimization of parallel manipulators. Mech. Mach. Theory **170**, 104725 (2022)
18. TSAI, L.W.: Robot Analysis and Design: the Mechanics of Serial and Parallel Manipulators. John Wiley & Sons, Inc. (1999)
19. Chen, S.F., Kao, I.: Conservative congruence transformation for joint and cartesian stiffness matrices of robotic hands and fingers. Int. J. Robot. Res. **19**(9), 835–847 (2000)
20. Huang, C., Hung, W.H., Kao, I.: New conservative stiffness mapping for the stewart-gough platform. In: Proceedings of the 2002 IEEE International Conference on Robotics 8 Automation Washington, DC, pp. 823–828 (2002)
21. Kao, I., Ngo, C.: Properties of the grasp stiffness matrix and conservative control strategies. Int. J. Robot. Res. **18**(2), 159–167 (1999)
22. Yang, C., Li, Q., Chen, Q.: Analytical elastostatic stiffness modeling of parallel manipulators considering the compliance of link and joint. Appl. Math. Model. **78**, 322–349 (2020)
23. Xu, L., Ye, W., Li, Q.: Design, analysis, and experiment of a new parallel manipulator with two rotational and one translational motion. Mech. Mach. Theory **177**, 105064 (2022)
24. Yang, C., Chen, Q., Tong, J., et al.: Elastostatic stiffness analysis of a 2pur-psr overconstrained parallel mechanism. Int. J. Precis. Eng. Man. **20**(4), 569–581 (2019)

Collaborative Robot-Oriented Joint Real-Time Control Based on Heterogeneous Embedded Platform

Zhong Chen[1,2](✉), Tianhua Ye[1,2], and Xianmin Zhang[1,2]

[1] South China University of Technology, Guangzhou, Guangdong, China
mezhchen@scut.edu.cn
[2] Guangdong Provincial Key Laboratory of Precision Equipment and Manufacturing
Technology, Guangzhou, China

Abstract. A real-time joint controller oriented on collaborative robots (co-robots) using an embedded multi-core heterogeneous development board is proposed in this paper. The co-robot control system is composed of an ARM core running Linux-RT and a DSP running a real-time RTOS system, which ensures that the system kernel's real-time performance is achieved. The inter-core communication is accomplished using the IPC component provided by Texas Instruments. The co-robot control tasks are assigned to different processors based on their characteristics. Based on this multi-core heterogeneous co-robot control system architecture, a joint compliance control algorithm based on admittance control was designed and discretized. The robot joint compliance control experiment was carried out on a single-joint co-robot platform. The results indicate that good performance on real-time, fast response, and compliance collaboration were achieved by the multi-core heterogeneous co-robot joint controller.

Keywords: multi-core heterogeneous platform · real-time system · admittance control

1 Introduction

Human-robot interaction in the realm of collaborative robots is a subject of great interest in current robot research. To achieve optimal performance in human-robot interaction, it is crucial to design a proper control algorithm, while also considering the impact of the robot control system's performance. This impact is directly related to the real-time performance, stability, and robustness of collaborative robots [1]. The traditional robot controller architecture is composed of a PC/IPC and a motion control card, with developers building Windows programs based on functions libraries provided by motion control card manufacturers. This solution offers a short development cycle and low development difficulty [2]. Since developers do not need to consider the underlying motion control algorithms and hardware design, this solution has been widely used in scenarios that do not require high real-time performance and control precision, such as robot handling, spraying, and other industrial fields.

H. Yang et al. (Eds.): ICIRA 2023, LNAI 14275, pp. 190–201, 2023.
https://doi.org/10.1007/978-981-99-6504-5_17

However, as the demand for robot control performance continues to grow, this traditional control architecture is increasingly unable to meet the demand. For example, in order to ensure the safety of the operator during human-machine cooperation, the robot controller must have the ability to process sensor data in real-time and at high frequency, so that environmental information can be perceived in a timely manner and responded to quickly. Additionally, it is necessary to calculate the robot dynamics and force control strategy, in addition to the traditional robot kinematics. Therefore, the collaborative robot control system is transforming to a distributed control architecture, comprising an industrial computer/embedded device, a real-time operating system, and an industrial field bus [3, 4, 5]. By adopting this distributed control architecture, it becomes possible to achieve high-performance control of collaborative robots, while also ensuring the safety of human operators.

To achieve the desired performance of robot controllers, researchers have developed numerous real-time controllers utilizing different hardware and software architectures. Fedak and colleagues [6] designed a general robot control platform based on superposition control. In this platform, the Host PC is responsible for control command transmission and servo state monitoring, while the MATLAB Simulink module is used for robot trajectory planning and solving inverse kinematics iterative numerical solutions. The Target PC, on the other hand, performs time-critical operations and communicates with the driver in real-time via the CAN bus, achieving a maximum communication speed of 2 ms. Xi and team [7] created a real-time control system for serial robots based on the Xenomai open-source real-time kernel and EtherCAT real-time industrial field bus. In this system, the control task is decomposed into several independent tasks, and the multi-task concurrency method is utilized to ensure the timeliness of task execution, resulting in a control cycle of 5 ms. Zhou and colleagues [8] developed a real-time control system for a snake robot by utilizing the ROS control library and the real-time capabilities of Xenomai. In addition, they created a servo motor drive module and sensor data acquisition module based on FPGA (Programmable Logic Gate Array), which ensures the real-time performance of the control system and achieves a real-time communication rate of 2 ms.

Based on the analysis presented above, this paper proposes the utilization of a multi-core heterogeneous platform to develop a robot control system that can handle computationally intensive tasks while maintaining real-time performance. The control system communicates with servo devices via EtherCAT, which provides precise multi-axis synchronization performance [8].

The paper is structured as follows: In Sect. 2, the robot control system based on an embedded heterogeneous platform is introduced. Real-time operating systems are run on both ARM and DSP, and inter-core communication is implemented using TI IPC. Robot tasks are assigned to different cores to achieve load balancing. In Sect. 3, robot compliant controller is designed and discretized, and the influence of controller parameters on the control performance is discussed. In Sect. 4, compliance control experiments are performed on a single-joint robot platform.

2   Architecture of Real-Time Collaborative Robot Control System

2.1   Software and Hardware Platform

Embedded systems offer several advantages over traditional IPCs, including low power consumption, low cost, high integration, and system customization. The main core of the embedded heterogeneous platform utilized in this paper is ARM and DSP. ARM is a general-purpose processor with strong transaction management abilities, making it suitable for scheduling control tasks, accepting command input, and displaying the status of the control system. As a digital signal processor, DSP has the characteristics of a hardware multiplier, data and address separation (Harvard architecture), and support for pipeline operations, providing it with strong computing power and making it suitable for dealing with time-sensitive tasks. Additionally, TI provides a rich library of DSP mathematical functions, including digital filtering and matrix operations, which greatly reduces the difficulty of developing robot control tasks.

To ensure real-time performance, appropriate operating systems must be selected for ARM and DSP processors. The most common operating system running on ARM is Linux, which is open source, tailored, and easy to transplant, making it widely used in embedded devices. However, Linux does not have real-time features, although process preemption is supported after Linux 2.6. To improve the real-time performance of Linux, developers have proposed two solutions: single-kernel and dual-kernel. Single-kernel involves patching the Linux kernel with PREEMPT_RT, while dual-kernel involves running a real-time kernel on the basis of the Linux kernel, such as Xenomai, RTAI, or RT-Linux.

This paper chooses to run Linux patched with PREEMPT_RT on ARM and run an RTOS on DSP, which constitutes the basic hardware and software architecture of the control system. The open source feature of PREEMPT_RT supports developers in creating real-time systems with enhanced functionality. The proposed approach of utilizing a multi-core heterogeneous platform with a combination of ARM and DSP processors provides a promising solution for achieving high-performance and real-time control in robotic systems.

2.2   Inter-Core Communication

The impact of multi-processor communication on real-time performance is a critical concern that cannot be overlooked in the development of advanced robotic systems. To address this issue, this paper utilizes the IPC component provided by TI to achieve inter-core communication between ARM and DSP. In this setup, ARM serves as the master core, while DSP serves as the remote core. Figure 1 illustrates the flow chart of inter-core communication. IPC encompasses various communication components, and this article utilizes the variable size messaging module, MessageQ. ARM and DSP create their own local message queues, with ARM taking responsibility for initiating inter-core communication and terminating the DSP program. On the other hand, DSP accepts messages from ARM, extracts the message, and sends a reply message accordingly.

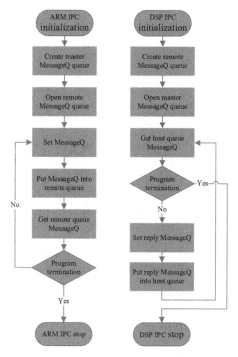

Fig. 1. Inter-core communication flowchart

2.3 Scheduling of Periodic Robot Tasks

The execution of robot control tasks involves both real-time and non-real-time tasks, which are designed as real-time threads and non-real-time threads, respectively. In this paper, the focus is on the scheduling strategy for real-time tasks, which are sensitive to task completion time. Non-real-time threads are assigned to the SCHED_other scheduling strategy and are executed only when the CPU is not occupied by real-time threads. This ensures the priority execution of real-time threads and enhances the real-time performance of the control system.

Real-time tasks mainly include EtherCAT communication between the robot control system and the driver, as well as inter-core communication between ARM and DSP, which are periodic tasks. Figure 2 shows the execution sequence arrangement of these tasks within one period, and $T(n)$ denotes the n-th control cycle of the robot control system. At the start of each communication period, ARM receives feedback data from the driver through EtherCAT frames. ARM then initiates inter-core communication requests with DSP and sends the computation task commands and data of the $T(n)$ period to DSP. ARM waits for a preset time during which the inter-core communication task terminates if it receives the computation result from DSP in the $T(n\text{-}1)$ period or times out. Finally, ARM sends the computation task result of DSP through EtherCAT to the driver, and the cycle repeats.

Successful task scheduling ensures that the robot's periodic control tasks proceed in an organized manner. By running in parallel with both ARM and DSP cores, the load on

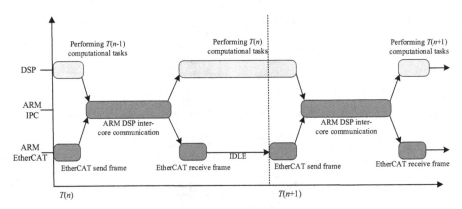

Fig. 2. The control command sequence in robotic tasks

ARM is minimized, and load balancing is achieved. The robot control system operates on a control period of 1 ms, which makes it suitable for real-time control of robotic systems.

3 Joint Compliant Control

Human-robot interaction represents a typical application scenario that necessitates high levels of real-time performance. In order to assess the efficacy of the co-robot control system, a joint compliant controller grounded in admittance control has been developed.

3.1 Compliant Control Based on Admittance Control

The formulation of an effective force control strategy is a pivotal aspect of compliance control in robotics, encompassing both direct and indirect force control approaches. Given the complexities involved in determining torque values for human-robot collaborative tasks, the implementation of indirect force control, specifically through impedance control, has become a popular choice. The dynamic model of impedance control is mathematically expressed through a second-order differential equation, denoted by Eq. (1). Within this equation, the variables x_e and f_e represent position deviation and external force, respectively, while m, b, and k signify the mass, damping, and stiffness coefficients.

$$m\ddot{x}_e + b\dot{x}_e + kx_e = f_e \tag{1}$$

By applying Laplace transform to Eq. (1) and setting torque as input and position as output, the transfer function of the controller can be obtained as

$$G(s) = \frac{X(s)}{F(s)} = \frac{1}{ms^2 + bs + k} \tag{2}$$

The resulting controller, depicted in formula (2), is recognized as admittance control, which is an indirect force control strategy that enables the controlled object to exhibit the dynamic characteristics of a mass-damping-spring system, referred to as the apparent dynamics

By setting different values for the parameters m, b, and k, the robot can exhibit varying dynamic characteristics. When k is not equal to zero, the robot in free space will always return to the equilibrium position after a certain period of time. On the other hand, when k is equal to zero, the robot will move following the direction of external force, and there is no equilibrium position. This function can be utilized for robot drag teaching.

When $k = 0$, set position and velocity as output respectively:

$$G_X(s) = \frac{X(s)}{F(s)} = \frac{1}{ms^2 + bs} \tag{3}$$

$$G_V(s) = \frac{V(s)}{F(s)} = \frac{1}{ms + b} \tag{4}$$

Formula (4) represents a first-order system with a time constant τ of m/b and a gain κ of $1/b$. The gain affects the steady-state value of the system, while the time constant determines the speed at which the system reaches the steady state. To analyze the impact of parameters m and b on the system output, a step signal is used as input in MATLAB, and the resulting time domain response curve is presented in Fig. 3.

Figure 3 (a) and (b) depict the position and velocity response curves, respectively, with the same time constant τ and different gain κ. The output velocity increases with a higher gain κ under the same input, indicating a higher sensitivity of the compliant controller.

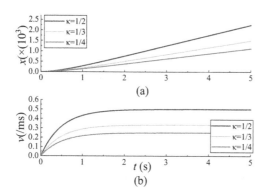

Fig. 3. (a) is the position response curve and (b) is the speed response curve under a step signal input in $\tau = 0.5$.

Figure 4 (a) and (b) depict the position and velocity response curves, respectively, with the same gain κ and different time constant τ. The results show that with a constant gain, a smaller time constant leads to a shorter time for the velocity output to reach the steady state, indicating a better responsiveness of the compliant controller.

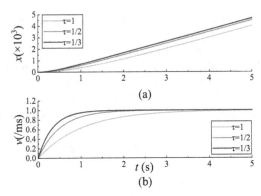

Fig. 4. (a) is the position response curve and (b) is the speed response curve under a step signal input in $\kappa = 1$.

3.2 Discretization of Continuous Controller

The controller described by Eq. (2) is designed for the continuous domain; however, in practical control, the controller can only operate the robot periodically. Therefore, it is necessary to discretize the continuous controller. Common discretization methods for the continuous controller include the forward difference method, the backward difference method, the bilinear transformation method (also known as the Tustin method), among others. While the Tustin method involves greater computational requirements compared to the difference methods, it is more stable. In this study, the Tustin method have been employed to discretize the controller. The transformation operators from the s-domain to the z-domain using the Tustin method are

$$s = \frac{2}{T}\frac{z-1}{z+1} \tag{5}$$

where T denotes the control period. By substituting Eq. (5) into Eq. (2), obtain the transfer function in the z-domain.

$$G(z) = \frac{X(z)}{F(z)} = \frac{a_2 z^2 + a_1 z + a_0}{b_2 z^2 + b_1 z + b_0} \tag{6}$$

in which

$$\begin{cases} a_2 = T^2 \\ a_1 = 2T^2 \\ a_0 = T^2 \end{cases}$$

and

$$\begin{cases} b_2 = 4m + 2bT + kT^2 \\ b_1 = 2kT^2 - 8m \\ b_0 = 4m - 2bT + kT^2 \end{cases}$$

Divide both the numerator and denominator by the highest power of z: z^{-2}

$$G(z) = \frac{X(z)}{F(z)} = \frac{a_2 + a_1 z^{-1} + a_0 z^{-2}}{b_2 + b_1 z^{-1} + b_0 z^{-2}} \tag{7}$$

By substituting the formula $Y(k\text{-}n) = Y(k)z^{-n}$ into Eq. (7), derive the recursive formula for the output value $X(k)$ as shown in Eq. (8). This formula allows us to calculate the output value of the current cycle using the input and output values from the previous two cycles, as well as the input value of the current cycle.

$$X(k) = \frac{a_2 F(k) + a_1 F(k-1) + a_0 F(k-2) - b_1 X(k-1) - b_0 X(k-2)}{b_2} \tag{8}$$

4 Experiments

4.1 Experimental Setup

To validate the performance of the robot control system, the paper constructed a robot experimental platform as shown in the Fig. 5, which consists of a PC, an embedded development board, and a single-joint robot. The PC runs on Windows 11 64-bit operating system, while the development board model is Tronlong TL5728F-EVM-A3. The ARM operating system is Linux-RT-4.9.65, and the DSP operating system is RTOS. Programs running on the ARM and DSP require cross-compilation under PC Linux, which is a virtual machine running on VMware Workstation Pro. The version of the virtual machine is Ubuntu 14.04.3, and the cross-compiler used is provided by TI and integrated into the processor SDK (Software Development Kit). The SDK used for ARM programs is ti-processor-sdk-linux-rt-am57xx-evm-04.03.00.05, while the one used for DSP programs is ti-processor-sdk-rtos-am57xx-evm-04.03.00.05.

The joint servo motor used in the experimental platform is Zeroerr eRob70H100I-BM-18ET, which is equipped with two encoders installed at the input and output ends of the harmonic reducer, respectively. The motor position feedback is obtained from a 19-bit absolute encoder at the output of the harmonic reducer, while the force feedback is estimated by computing the difference between the positions of the two encoders.

The embedded system development board communicates with the servo driver via EtherCAT, with a communication period of 1 ms. The servo drives operate in CSP (Cyclic Synchronous Position) mode.

Fig. 5. The joint compliant control experimental platform

4.2 Experiment of Real-Time Performance of Robot Control System

The determinism of execution time is a fundamental aspect that reflects the real-time performance of a control system, particularly in periodic control tasks. In this context, evaluating the real-time performance of such systems is essential, and one way to do so is to measure the jitter of the control period [9].

To test the real-time performance of our designed robot control system, periodic control tasks were conducted on an ARM device with a control period of 1ms. Additionally, simulated high computational load scenarios by executing the iterative solution of the inverse kinematics of a 6-DOF robot on a DSP device. And employed the high-precision timer of the real-time system on the ARM to measure the control cycle time. The results of the time spent t in each control cycle are presented in Fig. 6.

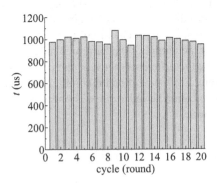

Fig. 6. Control period jitter

According to the results, in the 20-round control cycle, the maximum jitter was 80 us, and the average jitter was 1.5 us. These demonstrate that the designed robot control system exhibits good real-time performance.

4.3 Experiment on Compliant Control of Robot

Drag teaching is accomplished by setting the spring coefficient k = 0, as elucidated in Sect. 3.1. The steady-state speed of the robot during human-robot interaction is determined by the gain κ when interaction torque is constant. And the maximum speed of the servo motor is 260 pulse/ms, with a rated torque of 10 N*m. To ensure the safety of the robot and human, the maximum value of gain κ_{max} is 25 (b_{min} = 0.04). Under such circumstances, the steady-state speed of the robot is 250 pulse/ms when the human-robot interaction torque equals the rated torque. The controller's stability time is governed by the time constant τ. To evaluate the effects of different τ values on the performance of human-robot interaction, experiments were conducted with τ = 0.25, 0.5, and 1, corresponding to m = 0.01, 0.02, and 0.04, respectively.

Despite the use of a lightweight aluminum alloy connecting rod and the negligible inertia force of the joint connecting rod, the feedback torque is estimated by the difference of double encoders, resulting in an uncertain zero drift in the force feedback. This may cause the robot to exhibit unpredictable motion in free space. To prevent this, the paper employs a threshold treatment to the feedback torque value: torque values below the threshold, T_s, are set to 0, while the torque values above T_s remain unchanged.

The experimental results of robot compliance control are presented in Fig. 7: (a)(b)(c) and (d)(e)(f) depict the relationship between robot position and torque, and robot speed and torque, respectively.

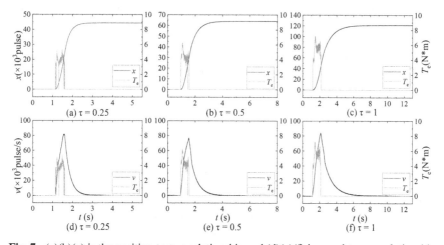

Fig. 7. (a)(b)(c) is the position-torque relationship and (d)(e)(f) is speed-torque relationship

Owing to the challenges associated with maintaining the stability of the artificially applied external torque for an extended duration during the experiment, it was difficult to observe the entire step process. Therefore, the paper primarily focuses on the response process of the controller following the removal of the external force.

As illustrated in Fig. 7(d)(e)(f), it was observed that the response speed of the controller decreases as the time constant τ increases, leading to an increase in the time required for the controller to reach stability. Consequently, the sensation of dragging becomes heavier during the dragging experiment.

Furthermore, it is worth noting that the compliance controller itself functions as a low-pass filter, as demonstrated in Eq. (3) and Eq. (4). Hence, even without applying any additional filtering to the torque signal, the position curve output of the controller remains relatively smooth, resulting in a softer drag sensation. This observation is further supported by the position and speed curve depicted in Fig. 7.

The experiment on robot compliance control corroborated the impact of the control system's real-time factor and control frequency on the controller's actual control performance. The robot control system presented in this paper guarantees uniform and brief sampling and control cycles, thereby assuring the discrete controller's attainment of the intended control effect.

5 Conclusion

To meet the high computational load and real-time requirements of Human-Robot interaction, an embedded heterogeneous platform-based real-time robot control system has been developed. The heterogeneity of the platform is leveraged to distribute the robot control task to each processor core, resulting in a control cycle of 1ms. To evaluate the performance of the control system, a robot compliance controller based on admittance control has been designed and discretized for implementation in the digital control system. The experiment conducted on a single-joint robot demonstrated that the high real-time performance of the control system ensures that the response of the digital controller is consistent with the expected results. Furthermore, the robot displayed good compliance during the dragging and teaching process. Future compliance control experiments will be conducted on the robot to further validate the system's performance.

References

1. Zhao, X., Zhang, J., Qi, S.: Design and research of 6-DOF robot control system based on visual servo. In: 2019 International Conference on Intelligent Computing, Automation and Systems (ICICAS), pp. 556–559 (2019)
2. Xiao, Li., Gong, J., Chen, J.: Industrial robot control systems: a review. In: Wang, R., Chen, Z., Zhang, W., Zhu, Q. (eds.) Proceedings of the 11th International Conference on Modelling, Identification and Control (ICMIC2019). LNEE, vol. 582, pp. 1069–1082. Springer, Singapore (2020). https://doi.org/10.1007/978-981-15-0474-7_101
3. Li, X., Ma, X., Song, W.: Multi-tasking system design for multi-axis synchronous control of robot based on RTOS. In: 2020 15th IEEE Conference on Industrial Electronics and Applications (ICIEA), pp. 356–360 (2020)
4. Delgado, R., Choi, B.W.: Network-oriented real-time embedded system considering synchronous joint space motion for an omnidirectional mobile robot. Electronics 8(3), 317 (2019)
5. Jung, I.K., Lim, S.: An EtherCAT based control system for human-robot cooperation. In: 2011 16th International Conference on Methods & Models in Automation & Robotics, pp. 341–344 (2011)

6. Fedak, V., Durovsky, F., Uveges, R., et al.: Implementation of robot control algorithms by real-time control system. Int. J. Eng. Res. Afr. **18**, 112–119 (2015)
7. Xi, Q., Zheng, C.W., Yao, M.Y.: Design of a real-time robot control system oriented for human-robot cooperation. In: 2021 International Conference on Artificial Intelligence and Electromechanical Automation (AIEA), pp. 23–29 (2021)
8. Chuang, W.L., Yeh, M.H., Yeh, Y.L.: Develop real-time robot control architecture using robot operating system and etherCAT. Actuators (MDPI) **10**(7), 141 (2021)
9. Zhou, Y., Li, Z., Zhang, Y., et al.: The real-time control framework for a modular snake robot. In: 2019 4th International Conference on Robotics and Automation Engineering (ICRAE), pp. 168–172 (2019)
10. Kangunde, V., Jamisola, R.S., Theophilus, E.K.: A review on drones controlled in real-time. Int. J. Dyn. Control 1–15 (2021)

A Novel Sensitivity Analysis Method for Geometric Errors of a Parallel Spindle Head

Liping Wang[1,2], Mengyu Li[1,2], and Guang Yu[1,2(✉)]

[1] State Key Laboratory of Tribology, Department of Mechanical Engineering, Tsinghua University, Beijing 100084, China
gyu@mail.tsinghua.edu.cn

[2] Beijing Key Lab of Precision/Ultra-Precision Manufacturing Equipment and Control, Beijing 100084, China

Abstract. Geometric errors are the main factors affecting the output accuracy of the parallel spindle head, and it is necessary to perform a sensitivity analysis to extract the critical geometric errors. The traditional sensitivity analysis method analyzes the output position and orientation errors independently, and then there are multiple sensitivity indices, which makes it difficult to determine the critical geometric errors. In this paper, we propose a sensitivity index that can comprehensively consider position and orientation errors based on the tool center point (TCP) position error model. First, the configuration of the hybrid machine tool is introduced and the TCP position error model is derived. Then the effective cutting length is introduced and the sensitivity analysis index is defined. After that, the sensitivity analysis of the 3-DOF parallel spindle head is performed using the proposed sensitivity index, and the effectiveness of the proposed method is verified by simulation. The proposed sensitivity analysis method can provide important guidance for machine tool accuracy design.

Keywords: Geometric errors · Parallel spindle head · Sensitivity analysis · Accuracy design

1 Introduction

Parallel mechanisms have been widely used in industrial production, such as machine tool [1, 2], robot [3] and motion simulator [4], because of its theoretical advantages of high stiffness, low inertia and high flexibility. The hybrid machine tool combines the advantages of parallel mechanisms with the large workspace advantage of series mechanisms, making it an ideal configuration to solve the limitations of traditional series machine tools [5]. However, accuracy performance affects the practical application of hybrid machines. The factors affecting the accuracy of machine tools mainly include: geometric errors, thermal errors, structural deformation errors and servo errors [6, 7]. For hybrid machine tools, geometric errors, especially in their parallel mechanisms, are the main contributors to the total error [8]. Therefore, it is necessary to analyze and extract the key geometric errors of the parallel mechanism.

© The Author(s), under exclusive license to Springer Nature Singapore Pte Ltd. 2023
H. Yang et al. (Eds.): ICIRA 2023, LNAI 14275, pp. 202–211, 2023.
https://doi.org/10.1007/978-981-99-6504-5_18

The sensitivity of geometric errors refers to the influence of each error parameter on the output error [9]. The sensitivity analysis can find the key geometric errors of the mechanism and provide a basis for accuracy design [10]. It is also possible to find the errors that have no effect on the terminal or are redundant with each other and eliminate them, thus eliminating the over-parameterization problem of the model. Currently, the error sensitivity analysis of parallel mechanisms is mainly performed by statistical methods, such as Monte Carlo method [11] and stochastic mathematical method [12]. Monte Carlo method carries out enough sampling detection of the error parameters according to a certain probability density, and obtains the pose error bound through the forward kinematics solution, so as to obtain the influence of the error parameters on the output error. The Monte Carlo method can determine the error sensitivity accurately, but it requires a large number of forward solution calculation, and the calculation of the forward solution of the parallel mechanism is complicated, resulting in low solution efficiency.

The stochastic mathematical method set each error parameter as a random variable with definite numerical characteristics according to the structural tolerance, and then calculate the numerical characteristics of the pose error directly through the mapping relationship between the structural error parameters and the pose error at different poses, and then estimate the output error bound. Patel et al. [13] obtained the error sensitivity of the Hexapod parallel mechanism by an approximating linear error mapping. Fan [14] performed a sensitivity analysis of the 3-PRS parallel mechanism using a partial differential method based on the error transformation vector and determined its critical errors. Stochastic mathematical methods are computationally efficient and are currently the main way of sensitivity analysis. However, the output error contains both position and orientation error, and traditional sensitivity analysis methods analyze the elements of the output error vector independently, which results in multiple sensitivity indices, making it difficult to identify critical geometric errors.

In this paper, sensitivity indices that can comprehensively consider both position and orientation errors is proposed based on the error model of the tool center point (TCP) position. The paper is structured as follows: Sect. 1 introduces the configuration of the hybrid machine tool and derives the TCP position error model, Sect. 2 defines the sensitivity indices, Sect. 3 performs the sensitivity analysis of the 3-degree-of-freedom (DOF) parallel spindle head using the proposed sensitivity index, and discusses the simulation results. The proposed sensitivity indices are verified by simulation in Sect. 4. Finally, the conclusions of this paper are given in Sect. 5.

2 Mechanism Configuration and Error Model

The five-axis hybrid machine tool studied in this paper consists of an operating platform and a 3-DOF parallel spindle head mounted on a column, as shown in Fig. 1. The 3-DOF parallel spindle head consists of a base platform, a moving platform and three identical PRRU chains, where P, R and U refer to the prismatic, revolute and universal joints, respectively, as shown in Fig. 2. This paper focuses on the error sensitivity analysis of this 3-DOF parallel spindle head.

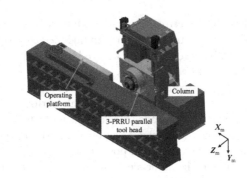

Fig. 1. The configuration of the hybrid machine tool

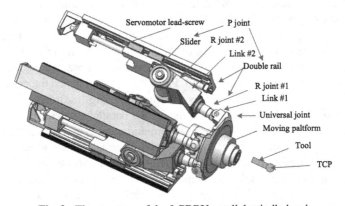

Fig. 2. The structure of the 3-PRRU parallel spindle head

To simplify the error modeling process, this 3-PRRU parallel spindle head can be equivalent to the 3-PRS mechanism as shown in Fig. 3.

For the i-th chain, the closed-loop vector equation can be expressed as

$$H + R_{TT}R_i a_i = R_i b_i + R_i R_{Bi} q_i + R_i R_{Bi} R_{Ci} l_i \tag{1}$$

where a_i, b_i and l_i denote the vector $O'A_i, OB_i$ and C_iA_i. H denotes the position vector of the moving platform, i.e., OO', q_i denotes the input vector of the i-th P joint, R_i denotes the rotation matrix of the i-th chain, and R_{Bi} and R_{Ci} denote the rotation matrices of coordinate systems B_i and C_i. R_{TT} represents the orientation matrix of the moving platform, where the T-T angle is used to decoupled the rotation around the Z' axis from the other two rotations.

$$R_{TT} = \begin{bmatrix} \cos\varphi & -\sin\varphi & 0 \\ \sin\varphi & \cos\varphi & 0 \\ 0 & 0 & 1 \end{bmatrix} \begin{bmatrix} \cos\theta & 0 & \sin\theta \\ 0 & 1 & 0 \\ -\sin\theta & 0 & \cos\theta \end{bmatrix} \begin{bmatrix} \cos\varphi & \sin\varphi & 0 \\ -\sin\varphi & \cos\varphi & 0 \\ 0 & 0 & 1 \end{bmatrix} \begin{bmatrix} \cos\psi & -\sin\psi & 0 \\ \sin\psi & \cos\psi & 0 \\ 0 & 0 & 1 \end{bmatrix} \tag{2}$$

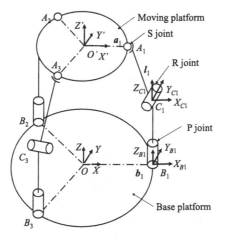

Fig. 3. The equivalent mechanism diagram of the 3-DOF parallel spindle head

When geometric errors are considered, the error model of the 3-DOF parallel spindle head can be expressed as:

$$\boldsymbol{H} + \mathbf{R}_{TT}\mathbf{R}_i(\boldsymbol{a}_i + \Delta\boldsymbol{a}_i) = \mathbf{R}_i(\boldsymbol{b}_i + \Delta\boldsymbol{b}_i) + \\ \mathbf{R}_i\mathbf{R}_{Bi}\mathbf{R}_{\theta Bi}(\boldsymbol{q}_i + \Delta\boldsymbol{q}_i) + \mathbf{R}_i\mathbf{R}_{Bi}\mathbf{R}_{\theta Bi}\mathbf{R}_{Ci}\mathbf{R}_{\theta Ci}(\boldsymbol{l}_i + \Delta\boldsymbol{l}_i) \tag{3}$$

Here the symbol Δ denotes the geometric error of the vector, and $\mathbf{R}_{\theta Bi}$ and $\mathbf{R}_{\theta Ci}$ denote the rotational error matrices of $\mathbf{R}_{Bi}$ and $\mathbf{R}_{Ci}$. The error model contains a total of 42 error parameters, namely $dr = [\Delta a_{ix}\ \Delta a_{iy}\ \Delta a_{iz}\ \Delta b_{ix}\ \Delta b_{iy}\ \Delta b_{iz}\ \Delta q_i\ \Delta l_i\ \Delta\theta_{Bix}\ \Delta\theta_{Biy}\ \Delta\theta_{Biz}\ \Delta\theta_{Cix}\ \Delta\theta_{Ciy}\ \Delta\theta_{Ciz}]$ ($i = 1, 2, 3$). Since the error model of the moving platform has been studied a lot before, the derivation is not performed here. Equation (3) can be alternatively written as

$$\boldsymbol{p} = f(\boldsymbol{q}, \boldsymbol{r}) \tag{4}$$

$\boldsymbol{p}$ denotes the pose error of the moving platform and $\boldsymbol{r}$ denotes the actual geometric structural parameters. By taking partial derivatives of Eq. (4), we can obtain error model of moving platform:

$$d\boldsymbol{p} = \boldsymbol{J}(\boldsymbol{q}, \boldsymbol{r})d\boldsymbol{r} \tag{5}$$

where $d\boldsymbol{r}$ represents the geometric error vector. When a tool of length L is mounted, the TCP position can be expressed as

$$P = H + R_{TT} \cdot [0\ 0\ L]^T \tag{6}$$

The TCP position error model can thus be expressed as:

$$dP = T(q, r, L)dr \tag{7}$$

3 Definition of the Sensitivity Indices

Sensitivity indices are used to evaluate the influence of geometric errors on the output of the mechanism. The sensitivity index is mainly divided into local sensitivity index (LSI) and global sensitivity index (GSI). Here the LSI is used to evaluate the effect of geometric error on the output error in a specific pose; while the GSI is used to evaluate the average effect of geometric error on the output error in the whole working space.

In traditional sensitivity analysis methods, the definition of sensitivity indices is directly related to the output pose error, and a total of six sensitivity indices are generally defined for three position errors and three orientation errors. Too many sensitivity indices can lead to an inability to effectively determine critical geometric errors that have a large impact on output error. For example, a geometric error may have a large impact on orientation error but a small impact on position error, which cannot be evaluated using six sensitivity indices. Here, we define a single sensitivity index based on the TCP position error by introducing tool length. Since the TCP position can reflect both the position and orientation of the moving platform, it is more effective to use the matrix $T(q, r, L)$ for sensitivity analysis, which can solve the evaluation problem of traditional sensitivity indices caused by the non-uniformity of position and orientation units.

The effect of a single geometric error dr_i ($i = 1, 2, \ldots 42$) on the TCP position can be expressed as:

$$e_i = T(q, r, L)dr_i \tag{8}$$

Since the errors in X, Y and Z directions have a similar effect on the machining accuracy in the actual machining process, the modulus length of the TCP position error can be directly taken for evaluation. When the geometric errors are all set to unit values, the modulus length of the TCP position error can then be expressed as:

$$P_{e,i}(q, r, L) = |e_i| = |T_i(q, r, L)| \tag{9}$$

Here T_i means the i-th column of the matrix T. For local sensitivity analysis, q and r are fixed values, so $P_{e,i}$ can be considered as a function of the tool length L. In the actual machining process, the error at any point on the tool within the cutting length has an impact on the machining error. Therefore, by introducing the cutting length, the error parameters can be evaluated uniformly based on the machining accuracy. If there is only position error and no orientation error, the position error of any point in the cutting length is the same, while if there is orientation error, the position error of each point in the cutting length is no longer the same, and the larger the orientation error, the greater the change in position error. Therefore, $P_{Le,i}$ is defined as the integral of the position deviation of each point within the tool cutting length on the tool axis, and $P_{Le,i}$ can reflect the combined effect of the error parameter dr_i on the output accuracy. As shown in Fig. 4, T_0 denotes the tool without error, T_i denotes the tool under the influence of dr_i. A, B, C and D denote the four points on the tool axis and AB denotes the effective cutting length, i.e. L_1-L_0. Then $P_{Le,i}$ can be expressed as

$$P_{Le,i} = \int_{L_0}^{L_1} P_{e,i}(\boldsymbol{q}, \boldsymbol{r}, L)dL \tag{10}$$

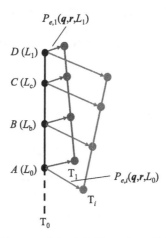

Fig. 4. Diagram of the definition of sensitivity index

Due to the introduction of the cutting length, the value of $P_{Le,i}$ is large and not easy to compare, here $P_{Le,i}$ is normalized to obtain the LSI.

$$LSI_i = \frac{P_{Le,i}}{\sum_{t=1}^{42} P_{Le,t}} \tag{11}$$

Based on the above analysis, the average effect of each geometric error on the output errors in the whole working space can be expressed as

$$W_i = \frac{\int_V P_{Le,i}dV}{\int_V dV} \tag{12}$$

Here, V indicates the full workspace. Again, for comparison purposes, the GSI is obtained here by normalizing W_i.

$$GSI_i = \frac{W_i}{\sum_{t=1}^{42} W_i} \tag{13}$$

4 Sensitivity Analysis of the 3-DOF Parallel Spindle Head

In this section, the geometric error sensitivity of the 3-DOF parallel spindle head is analyzed and the critical error is given based on the proposed sensitivity index. Since we are more concerned with the accuracy characteristics in the full working space, the global sensitivity analysis is performed here using the proposed GSI. Here the 3-DOF parallel spindle head motion range is: $q_i \in [300\ 550]$ ($i = 1, 2, 3$). L_0 is set to 100 mm and L_1 is set to 150 mm. Since the three limbs of this 3-DOF parallel spindle head are perfectly symmetrical, the GSI of the same error on its different limbs is the same, e.g. GSI(Δa_{1x}) = GSI(Δa_{2x}) = GSI(Δa_{3x}). Therefore, it is sufficient to calculate the GSI corresponding to the error parameters of only one of the limbs during the actual calculation. Here, for limb 1, the GSI corresponding to each geometric error parameters are calculated by Eq. (14) under the theoretical parameters of the machine tool. The GSI corresponding to each geometric error parameters are shown in Fig. 5.

$$GSI_i = \frac{W_i}{\sum_{t=1}^{14} W_i} \tag{14}$$

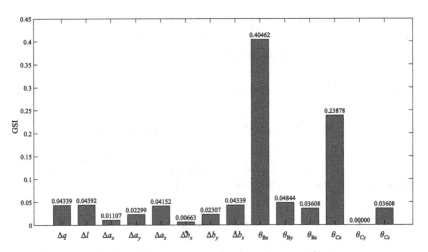

Fig. 5. GSI values corresponding to each geometric error

The GSI corresponding to each error parameters are plotted in the form of a pie chart in order to show their percentage magnitude more clearly, as shown in Fig. 6. Among the geometric errors of the 3-DOF parallel spindle head, $\Delta\theta_{Cy}$ does not affect the terminal accuracy, and Δq and Δb_z as well as $\Delta\theta_{Bz}$ and $\Delta\theta_{Cz}$ have the same effect on the terminal and are redundant errors. Therefore, when oriented to kinematic calibration, $\Delta\theta_{Cy}$ can be directly eliminated, and mutually redundant errors also need to be eliminated. And in the accuracy design, we need to find the critical errors that have a large impact on the terminal. Here, the error with a defined ratio of more than 5% is considered as the critical error, and according to the analysis results, the six critical geometric errors are identified as $[\Delta\theta_{Bix}\ \Delta\theta_{Cix}]$ ($i = 1, 2, 3$).

In order to validate the proposed sensitivity analysis method, the output errors are compared under four different design parameters in Table 1 respectively. Here set all initial position geometric errors to 0.1 mm and all initial geometric angle errors to 0.1°. The maximum, mean and RMS values of the corresponding TCP position errors of L_0 and L_1 are shown in Fig. 7.

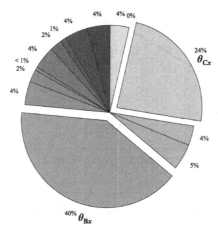

Fig. 6. Pie chart of GSI values

Table 1. Four machine accuracy design parameters used in the simulation.

Case	Critical geometric errors	Other geometric errors
1	Keep the initial value unchanged	Keep the initial value unchanged
2	Reduce by half	Keep the initial value unchanged
3	Keep the initial value unchanged	Reduce by half
4	Reduce by half	Reduce by half

The relative magnitudes of the maximum, mean and RMS values of the corresponding TCP position errors of L_0 and L_1 are the same for the four cases. Taking Max (L_1) as an example, compared with the initial design parameters, the output accuracy is improved by 42.7% after changing the critical geometric errors; while the output accuracy is improved by only 7.2% after changing other geometric errors. Considering the 50.1% improvement in output accuracy when reducing all geometric error parameters, it shows that a good improvement in accuracy can be achieved by reducing the critical geometry errors. At the same time, since the number of critical errors (6) is much smaller than the number of other geometric errors (36), and changing the critical geometric errors achieves better output accuracy improvement, it shows that the critical geometric errors identified in this paper have a significant impact on output accuracy, which verifies the effectiveness of the sensitivity analysis method proposed in this paper.

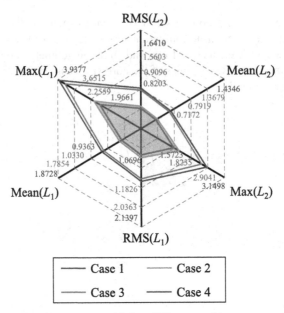

Fig. 7. Comparison of output accuracy with four different machine accuracy design parameters.

5 Conclusion

By combining the TCP position error model and the effective cutting length, this paper proposes a sensitivity index that can comprehensively consider output position and orientation errors. The proposed sensitivity analysis method is used to perform sensitivity analysis of the geometric errors of the 3-DOF parallel spindle head and extract the critical geometric errors. The simulation results show that the critical geometric errors extracted in this paper have a significant impact on the machine accuracy, which verifies the effectiveness of the proposed sensitivity analysis method. The extracted critical geometric errors provide important guidelines for error compensation.

Acknowledgments. This work is supported by the National Natural Science Foundation of China (NSFC) under grants 51975319 and 51905302.

References

1. Yu, G., Wang, L., Wu, J., Gao, Y.: Milling stability prediction of a hybrid machine tool considering low-frequency dynamic characteristics. Mech. Syst. Signal Process. **135**, 106364 (2020)
2. Li, M., Wang, L., Yu, G., Li, W.: A new calibration method for hybrid machine tools using virtual tool center point position constraint. Measurement **181**, 109582 (2021)
3. Pernette, E., Henein, S., Magnani, I., Clavel, R.: Design of parallel robots in microrobotics. Robotica **15**(4), 417–420 (1997)

4. Dong, W., Du, Z., Xiao, Y., Chen, X.: Development of a parallel kinematic motion simulator platform. Mechatronics **23**(1), 154–161 (2013)
5. Wang, L., Kong, X., Yu, G., Li, W., Li, M., Jiang, A.: Error estimation and cross-coupled control based on a novel tool pose representation method of a five-axis hybrid machine tool. Int. J. Mach. Tools Manuf. **182**, 103955 (2022)
6. Ramesh, R., Mannan, M.A., Poo, A.N.: Error compensation in machine tools—a review: part I: geometric, cutting-force induced and fixture-dependent errors. Int. J. Mach. Tools Manuf. **40**(9), 1235–1256 (2000)
7. Ramesh, R., Mannan, M.A., Poo, A.N.: Error compensation in machine tools—a review: part II: thermal errors. Int. J. Mach. Tools Manuf. **40**(9), 1257–1284 (2000)
8. Li, M., Wang, L., Yu, G., Li, W., Kong, X.: A multiple test arbors-based calibration method for a hybrid machine tool. Robot. Comput.-Integr. Manuf. **80**, 102480 (2023)
9. Li, Q., Wang, W., Jiang, Y., Li, H., Zhang, J., Jiang, Z.: A sensitivity method to analyze the volumetric error of five-axis machine tool. Int. J. Adv. Manuf. Technol. **98**, 1791–1805 (2018). https://doi.org/10.1007/s00170-018-2322-1
10. Han, J., Wang, L., Ma, F., Ge, Z., Wang, D., Li, X.: Sensitivity analysis of geometric error for a novel slide grinder based on improved Sobol method and its application. Int. J. Adv. Manuf. Technol. **121**(9–10), 6661–6684 (2022). https://doi.org/10.1007/s00170-022-09777-x
11. Sun, T., Zhai, Y., Song, Y., Zhang, J.: Kinematic calibration of a 3-DoF rotational parallel manipulator using laser tracker. Robot. Comput.-Integr. Manuf. **41**, 78–91 (2016)
12. Zhan, Z., Zhang, X., Jian, Z., Zhang, H.: Error modelling and motion reliability analysis of a planar parallel manipulator with multiple uncertainties. Mech. Mach. Theory **124**, 55–72 (2018)
13. Patel, A.J., Ehmann, K.F.: Volumetric error analysis of a Stewart platform-based machine tool. CIRP Ann. **46**(1), 287–290 (1997)
14. Fan, K.C., Wang, H., Zhao, J.W., Chang, T.H.: Sensitivity analysis of the 3-PRS parallel kinematic spindle platform of a serial-parallel machine tool. Int. J. Mach. Tools Manuf **43**(15), 1561–1569 (2003)

A Novel Prognostic Method for Wear of Sliding Bearing Based on SFENN

Jingzhou Dai$^{(\boxtimes)}$ and Ling Tian

Department of Mechanical Engineering, Tsinghua University, Beijing 100084, China
daijz18@mails.tsinghua.edu.cn

Abstract. Sliding bearings have become essential components in rotating machinery and are widely used in robotics field. Wear is the major failure mode of sliding bearings, while traditional prognostics methods for wear mostly rely on iterative calculations based on physical models, which are time-consuming, inefficient, and have limited practicality. This paper proposes a novel prognostics method for wear based on the Sequential Hybrid of Finite Element and Neural Network (SFENN), which exhibits high accuracy in wear prognostics and instantaneous output capability. The proposed method integrates finite element physical model and deep neural network through a sequential hybrid approach. In the offline phase, we establish the wear physical model of sliding bearing based on wear theory and wear test, then simulated wear data can be obtained through numerical simulations under different conditions. Deep neural network is designed and trained according to the characteristics of simulated data. After SFENN is trained, it can provide instantaneous prognostics of wear profile for new conditions of bearing, overcoming the limitations of traditional methods. The experiment validated the effectiveness of the proposed method, providing a further solution for the digital twin degradation model of mechanical components.

Keywords: Sliding bearing · Wear · Instantaneous prognostics · Hybrid model

1 Introduction

Rotating machinery has become the mainstay of modern industrial equipment and is developing towards complexity, precision, and high speed [1]. A sliding bearing is a mechanical component that utilizes the principle of sliding friction to support rotating parts and allows for relative sliding between bearing surfaces [2]. The advantages of sliding bearings are their simple structure, ability to withstand high axial loads and high-speed rotation while requiring less installation space. Additionally, due to the lack of rolling elements, they experience less inertial force

This work was supported by the National Key Research and Development Project of China [grant number 2020YFB1709103, 2018YFB1700604]; the Beijing Municipal Natural Science Foundation [grant number 3182012].

during high-speed rotation, resulting in smoother, more reliable operation and lower noise levels compared to rolling bearings [3]. Therefore, sliding bearings have a wide range of applications in the field of robotics and related mechanical equipment. Sometimes, hard coatings or woven fabric liners may be added to the inner of bearing to reduce the contact friction [4]. Since sliding occurs on the bearing surface, wear is a common issue and the major failure mode of sliding bearings [5,6]. Therefore, wear prognostics and remaining useful life prediction of sliding bearings are of great significance for equipment reliability.

[7] shows that over half of the machine components fail annually due to wear, and countless incidents of mechanical parts failure are caused by lubrication failure and excessive wear. Scholars at home and abroad have conducted many studies on material wear problems. Archard et al. [8] proposed the Archard wear model in 1953, which has become a classic model for wear problems. Li et al. [9] studied the friction and wear behavior of cobalt-based alloys using a pin-disc sliding model, and established a model of the wear process based on Finite Element Method (FEM). [10] performed force analysis on self-lubricating joint bearings and derived an analytical formula for wear life. Jin [11] conducted wear test on sliding bearings in rotor system and established a wear model based on the improved Archard model, determined the relevant parameters in the wear model based on the amount of wear obtained from experiments under different operating conditions, and obtained a functional expression for the wear life of sliding bearings as a function of rotation speed and torque. Li et al. [12] conducted numerical simulation of wear in self-lubricating bearings using ABAQUS and simulated the wear of the liner during operation. Stankovic et al. [13] determined the wear coefficient of the Archard model through shaft-bearing contact wear test and predicted the wear life of sliding bearing by performing wear numerical simulation using ANSYS. König et al. [14] used the Archard model and the Fleischer model to predict the wear of sliding bearings on a macroscopic scale based on the load conditions and material properties. Pang et al. [15] proposed an improved Archard wear prediction model to characterize the relationship between the torque, speed, and wear rate of sliding bearings.

Generally, numerical models based on physical theory are used to solve wear prediction problems [16]. However, the variation of surface profile leads to changes in contact conditions and stress distribution, making the wear process typically nonlinear and lacking explicit analytical solutions. Therefore, it is often necessary to provide model parameters and solve them through numerical iterations, which requires a significant amount of time and computational resources. Particularly, driven by the concept of Digital Twin, real-time requirements for product reliability maintenance have emerged, rendering the offline numerical iteration methods inadequate to meet the demands of modern product reliability maintenance. This paper proposes a novel prognostics method for wear based on the Sequential Hybrid of Finite Element and Neural Network (SFENN), which offers high-precision prediction capability and real-time output capability. The remainder of this paper is organized as follows: Sect. 2 presents the overview of the method. The establishment of the physical wear model for bearings and the fusion mechanism between the physical model and Deep Neural Network (DNN) are two key points, which are elaborated in Sect. 3 and Sect. 4, respectively. Section 5 conducts experiment and discussion. Finally, Sect. 6 gives the conclusion.

2   Method Overview

This section describes the overall process of the proposed method based on SFENN, as shown in Fig. 1. Firstly, theoretical analysis and sample wear tests are conducted on actual sliding bearings to obtain experimental data that can be used to fit the wear rate model of the bearing material. This model reflects the wear rate of the material under given conditions. Then, considering the geometric features of the bearing, a wear model for the sliding bearing is established based on FEM. Multiple sets of offline inputs are set to represent different types and operating conditions of the bearings. Through the finite element wear model, simulations are performed to obtain corresponding simulated wear data, which is processed to obtain the offline data module required by SFENN. Based on the characteristics of the wear data, DNN is constructed and trained. Once the training is completed, it serves as the online output module, enabling instantaneous output of the wear morphology of the bearing under specified conditions.

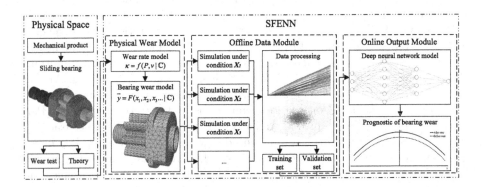

Fig. 1. Structure of SFENN.

The main contribution of SFENN is the successful hybrid of physics-based FEM and data-driven DNN using a sequential mechanism. Its advantages lie in the following aspects:

1) Utilizing FEM as a training data generator rather than directly outputting results, addressing the high cost associated with data acquisition in the mechanical field.

2) Employing DNN as the output module, which avoids the time-consuming nature of traditional FEM methods and enables the capability of instantaneous output that is not typically achievable with conventional approaches.

This hybrid approach allows for the complementary utilization of physics-based and data-driven methods, combining the strengths of both approaches.

The selected sliding bearing is shown in Fig. 2. There are two sliding bearings supporting each end of the gear. The outer surface of the gear shaft has a clearance fit with the inner hole of the sliding bearing. The sliding bearing is made of metal material, while the inner hole is lined with woven fabric liner to provide self-lubrication and reduce the coefficient of friction of the contact surface.

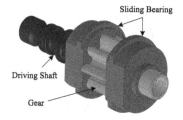

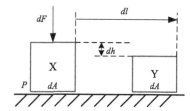

Fig. 2. Assembly of bearing-gear   **Fig. 3.** Illustration of the wear process.

The proposed method has two key points. First, the establishment of an accurate wear model of sliding bearing, which directly determines the accuracy of the model constructed by this method, as described in Sect. 3. Second, the reasonable hybrid of the wear physical model and DNN, which reflects the real-time prediction capability and applicability of the method, and is the innovative aspect of this method, discussed in detail in Sect. 4.

3   Wear Model of Sliding Bearing Based on Physical Mechanisms

Generally, the degradation models derived from physical mechanisms are called physical degradation models. To ensure the effectiveness of the established bearing wear model, this section adopts a physics-based wear modeling approach, combining classical wear theory with actual material wear tests to obtain a material-level wear rate model. Subsequently, a component-level wear model for the bearing is established based on FEM to obtain the required wear physical model.

3.1   Wear Rate Model Based on Archard Theory

The wear process is illustrated in Fig. 3, where a block slides from position X to position Y. This section models the wear rate for sliding bearing materials based on the modified Archard wear model. The wear volume of a material is proportional to the normal pressure between the friction pair contact surfaces and the tangential relative sliding distance between the friction pairs, and inversely proportional to the material hardness [6], and can be expressed as:

$$dV = K\frac{dF \times dl}{H} \tag{1}$$

where K is the dimensionless wear factor, depending on the properties of the material and the contact conditions; V is the wear volume, F is the normal force acting on the contact surface, l is the relative sliding distance, and H is the hardness of the material.

For the terms dV and dF in the equation, they can be further expressed by wear depth h, contact area A, and contact stress P, as follows:

$$dV = dh \cdot dA \tag{2}$$

$$dF = P \cdot dA \tag{3}$$

Putting Eq. (2) and Eq. (3) into Eq. (1) to get the wear depth as follows:

$$dh = K\frac{P}{H}dl \tag{4}$$

Let $\frac{K}{H} = \kappa$, then κ is a dimensioned wear factor, which is related to the friction pair material properties, applied load, sliding speed, working temperature and other factors that affect wear. Therefore, the wear depth expression is obtained:

$$dh = \kappa Pdl \tag{5}$$

In the wear test of this paper, the upper and lower specimens slide reciprocally relative to each other, and the structure of wear tester will be introduced in Sect. 3.2. Assuming that the wear depth of a single stroke is the same after the sample enters the stable wear stage in a single test, the maximum wear depth in one stroke is Δh, which can be obtained:

$$\Delta h = \int_{-\frac{L}{2}}^{\frac{L}{2}} dh = \int_{-\frac{L}{2}}^{\frac{L}{2}} \kappa Pdl \tag{6}$$

where L is the displacement of a single stroke. Δh can be obtained by dividing the maximum wear depth measured after the test by the number of reciprocations during the test, as follows:

$$\Delta h = \frac{h}{2f \cdot 60t} \tag{7}$$

where f is the reciprocating frequency of the testing machine, and t is the test duration.

For the surface-to-surface contact wear test, we consider that the contact stress is constant during a single test, so the wear rate can be considered constant, that is, P and κ are constant, then:

$$\Delta h = \kappa P \int_{-\frac{L}{2}}^{\frac{L}{2}} dl = \kappa PL \tag{8}$$

Combining Eq. (7) and Eq. (8), the calculation formula of wear rate in surface contact test is as follows:

$$\kappa = \frac{h}{120ftPL} \tag{9}$$

3.2   Sample Wear Test

Equation (9) shows that the measured data from wear tests can be used to calculate the material wear rate. In this section, wear tests were conducted under various conditions, and multiple sets of wear rate data were obtained to fit the wear rate model.

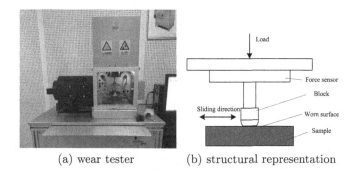

(a) wear tester   (b) structural representation

Fig. 4. The Optimal SRV-4 high temperature tribotester. Under the action of the driving force of the magnetic cylinder, the spindle drives the upper block to reciprocate horizontally, while the lower test sample is fixed.

The sample wear test was carried out on the Optimal SRV-4 high temperature tribotester, which is a standard apparatus widely used in friction and wear tests for performance evaluations of lubricants and additives, as shown in Fig. 4. The lower sample was made of wear material and has a flat wear surface. To conduct face-to-face or line-to-face contact form, the upper block was machined into cylindrical or flat shape.

Table 1. Settings of sample wear test.

Load (N)	Contact form	Stroke (mm)	Frequency (Hz)	Temperature (°C)
150–1500	Line-to-face, face-to-face	0.94–1.88	20	20

In the sample wear test, the contact stress and relative sliding velocity were varied by changing the load and stroke. The settings of wear test were outlined in Table 1. Multiple sets of working conditions were established for the test, and each condition was repeated three times to reduce random error. In the test, the lower specimen was fixed, while the upper specimen performed reciprocating motion. The specimen surface exhibited wear during the test, and the wear depth increased with the progress of the test. The duration of the test is set to 1 h, and the wear depth is measured by 3 Dimensional Confocal Microscope Phase Shift MicroXAM-3D. The wear depth under different settings is shown in Table 2.

Table 2. Data of face-to-face contact wear test.

Contact stress	118.1 mm/s	88.6 mm/s	59.1 mm/s
76.4 MPa	97.6	74.0	53.3
61.1 MPa	80.7	61.3	44.0
50.9 MPa	70.0	52.0	–
40.7 MPa	57.0	41.7	30.0
25.5 MPa	40.0	28.0	20.0
7.6 MPa	15.0	12.3	8.3

The influence of relative sliding speed on wear rate is inapparent, while that of contact stress is significant. Wear rate is calculated using Eq. (9) and fitted to a power function model. A correction factor is provided through the line-to-face contact test, and a wear rate model is finally obtained as follows:

$$\kappa = 8.24 \times 10^{-9} P^{-0.203} \tag{10}$$

3.3 Physical Wear Model of Bearings Based on FEM

After obtaining the wear rate model for the material, it is necessary to further establish the wear model for sliding bearing by considering information such as the geometric structure and material distribution. However, these pieces of information often exhibit nonlinear characteristics, making it difficult to obtain explicit mathematical expression. FEM is widely used for solving model in such cases. The FEM models of the bearing are shown in Fig. 5.

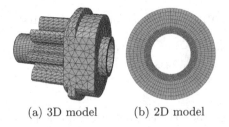

(a) 3D model   (b) 2D model

Fig. 5. Finite element model of sliding bearing.

Ideally, we focus more on the profile changes on the circumferential section of the bearing during the wear process. Therefore, the 3D model can be simplified into a 2D model. There are three analysis steps, involved loading-wear-unloading. Note that an unloading step is necessary to eliminate the node displacement caused by contact elastic deformation because the node displacement is used to reflect the node wear in this method.

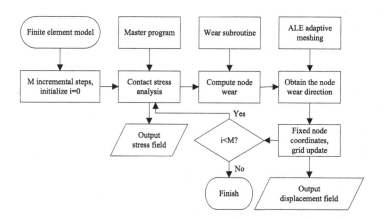

Fig. 6. Process of calculating node wear based on FEM.

The process of using the FEM to solve the node wear amount is shown in Fig. 6. In each increment step, the main program calculates the distribution of the contact stress field, and the node wear amount is calculated in the wear subroutine, where the node mesh is updated using Arbitrary Lagrangian Eulerian (ALE) adaptive meshing algorithm. The node wear depth can be obtained in a single incremental step by Eq. (8) and Eq. (10). Since the wear of the bearing is a cumulative damage process, the actual wear amount in a short period of time is small, and the impact on the profile and stress distribution can be ignored. Therefore, the wear coefficient A is magnified by 1000 times to accelerate the simulation progress (while the simulation time is shortened by 1000 times). Hence, the node wear amount is as follows:

$$\Delta h = 8.24 \times 10^{-6} P^{0.798} v \Delta t \tag{11}$$

where P is the contact stress of the current node, v is the relative sliding velocity that occurs on the current node, and Δt is the duration of the current increment step. The update direction of the local coordinate system in the contact surface is the normal direction, and the local coordinate u_3 of the node in the normal direction is updated as follows:

$$u_3^{(i)} \leftarrow u_3^{(i-1)} - \Delta h \tag{12}$$

It should be noted that for 3D models, the grid node A located at the edge of the contact surface cannot directly define the normal direction and another node B needs to be manually selected to update the coordinates of the target node A using the global coordinates (x_1, x_2, x_3) of node B, as follows:

$$u^{(i)} \leftarrow u^{(i-1)} + M_{trans} \cdot \Delta h \tag{13}$$

where $u^{(i)} = [u_1, u_2, u_3]^T$, and M_{trans} is the coordinate-transformation matrix defined in Abaqus, which can be directly called by the software. $\Delta h = [\Delta h_1, \Delta h_2, \Delta h_3]^T$, specifically:

$$\Delta h_j = \Delta h \cdot \frac{{}^A x_j - {}^B x_j}{\sqrt{\left({}^A x_1 - {}^B x_1\right)^2 + \left({}^A x_2 - {}^B x_2\right)^2 + \left({}^A x_3 - {}^B x_3\right)^2}} \tag{14}$$

After completing the numerical calculation, the wear profile of the bearing can be obtained, as shown in Fig. 7.

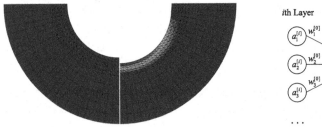

Fig. 7. Comparison of wear profile.

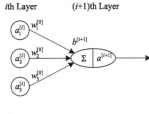

Fig. 8. Structure of neuron.

4   Hybrid Mechanism of SFENN

The hybrid mechanism of SFENN is introduced in this section. SFENN takes inputs such as bearing operating conditions, geometric data, material data, and operating time, and outputs the corresponding surface profile. We adopt the approach of sequential hybrid, where FEM and DNN are connected in sequence.

Within a certain range of input conditions, we select several combinations of input parameters and use the wear model obtained in Sect. 3 to perform offline simulations, generating multiple sets of simulated wear data. According to the data characteristics, we construct a module of DNN and train it using the simulated wear data. Once SFENN is trained, it can provide instantaneous wear pattern predictions for new input conditions. Next, we will discuss the offline data module and the online output module.

4.1   Offline Data Module

The independent variables are defined as $(x_1, x_2, x_3, x_4, x_5, x_6)$, where x_1 represents the inner diameter of the bearing, x_2 represents the radial force, x_3 represents the rotational speed, x_4 represents the wear coefficient A, x_5 represents the wear exponent B, and x_6 represents the operating time. Different values are set for these variables to conduct multiple simulations and collect data, as shown in Table 5. The time step for the wear simulation is uniformly set to 10 s. After completing the simulations, the node wear is obtained as the output, and the independent variables are normalized.

For sliding bearings, when the radial force, rotational speed, operating time, or wear coefficient A is zero, it is evident that the wear depth on each node is also zero. Therefore, an additional dataset $D_0 = \{\boldsymbol{y} | (x_{01}, x_{02}, x_{03}, x_{04}, x_{05}, x_{06})\}$ can be added, where $x_{02} \cdot x_{03} \cdot x_{04} \cdot x_{06} \equiv 0$, and $x_{0i} \sim U(0,1)$ when $x_{0i} \neq 0$, while the label $\boldsymbol{y} = \boldsymbol{0}$.

4.2   Online Output Module

The Universal Approximation Theorem states that a neural network with one hidden layer, containing a finite number of neurons and using a non-constant, bounded, and continuous activation function, can approximate any Borel measurable function from one finite-dimensional space to another with arbitrary precision, provided that the network is given enough hidden neurons and the appropriate weights are learned during training [17]. Therefore, we choose a deep neural network as the output module.

The basic structure of the neural network is shown in the Fig. 8, where each neuron in the i-th layer is connected to neurons in the $(i + 1)$-th layer. Mathematically, this can be expressed as follows:

$$a^{[i+1]} = \sigma(\sum_j w_j^{[i]} a_j^{[i]} + b^{[i+1]}) \tag{15}$$

Due to the constant direction of the bearing radial force, the wear occurs only within the semi-circle range. The model selects the wear depth at five nodes located at 0°, 45°, 90°, 135°, and 180° as the outputs. Therefore, the output layer has 5 neurons, while the input layer has 6 neurons. The neural network architecture is designed as shown in the Table 3.

Table 3. Neural network architecture.

	Number of neurons	Activation function
Input layer	6	–
Hidden layer 1	32	Relu
Hidden layer 2	128	Relu
Hidden layer 3	64	Relu
Dropout	p = 0.5	–
Output layer	5	Relu

5   Experiment and Discussion

In this section, we test the developed SFENN model. Using the datasets of No. 29, No. 30, and No. 31 in Table 5 as the test set, the remaining datasets are randomly divided into training and validation sets in a 4:1 ratio. The training process is conducted with a learning rate of 0.001, batch size of 4096, and 1000 epochs. The mean squared error (MSE) of the node wear depth is used as the loss function.

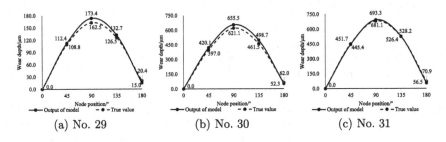

(a) No. 29   (b) No. 30   (c) No. 31

Fig. 9. Results at t = 10000 s.

After completing the training, the test set is used for evaluation. The results at an equivalent time of 10000 s are shown in Fig. 9, and the errors for each node are presented in the Table 4. Due to the unidirectional rotation of the shaft in contact with the bearing inner bore, there is a certain deviation in the direction of bearing wear, which does not strictly align with the radial load direction. This causes the 0° node to have no wear while the 180° node shows wear. Since the wear magnitude at that location is relatively small, it results in a larger relative error.

In terms of bearing life, the focus is on the maximum wear depth, which occurs at the 90° node position. The maximum error is 5.54%, indicating excellent model fitting performance.

Table 4. Relative errors on the test set.

Node position	ERROR		
	No.31	No.32	No.33
0°	0.00%	0.00%	0.00%
45°	7.48%	5.82%	−1.39%
90°	4.27%	5.54%	1.79%
135°	5.26%	8.06%	0.34%
180°	17.11%	−15.65%	−20.31%

Support Vector Regression (SVR) is another regression method that is widely used in some fields. The comparison of the wear depth outputs at the 90° node between DNN and SVR is shown in Fig. 10. SVR uses the rbf kernel function and performs k-fold cross-validation to find the optimal parameters. It can be observed that SVR performs significantly lower than DNN on all three test datasets. Therefore, DNN is suitable for the output module in this context.

It is worth noting that the accuracy of the proposed method is directly influenced by the size of the training dataset. Generally, a larger training dataset, encompassing a wider range of operating conditions, leads to better model fitting. Due to space constraints, this paper refrains from a detailed discussion on this topic.

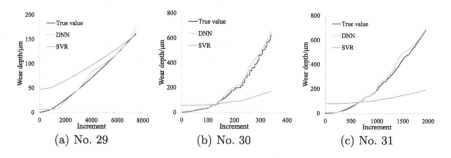

(a) No. 29   (b) No. 30   (c) No. 31

Fig. 10. Comparison of maximum wear depth curves between DNN and SVR.

6   Conclusion

This paper proposes a novel prognostics method for wear of sliding bearing based on SFENN. Specifically, a wear physical model of sliding bearings is established based on classical theories and wear test, and subsequently integrated with DNN through a sequential mechanism to obtain SFENN. Through experiment on the test set, the method demonstrates high-precision wear prognostics capability and enables instantaneous prognostics of wear profile. It addresses the challenges of high costs in experimental data acquisition and long computational time for physical model solving in traditional methods, thus achieving a digital twin solution for the wear degradation of sliding bearings.

Appendix

Table 5.

Table 5. Settings for face-to-face contact wear simulation.

No.	Inner diameter (mm)	Load (N)	Speed (RPM)	Coefficient A	Exponent B
1	10	90	300	2.06E−06	0.399
2	10	180	600	4.12E−06	0.5985
3	10	360	900	8.24E−06	0.798
4	10	540	1200	1.65E−05	0.9975
5	10	540	900	8.24E−06	0.798
6	10	360	1200	8.24E−06	0.798
7	13.5	90	600	8.24E−06	0.9975
8	13.5	360	1200	2.06E−06	0.5985
9	13.5	540	900	4.12E−06	0.399
10	13.5	360	600	8.24E−06	0.798
11	13.5	360	900	8.24E−06	0.798
12	13.5	540	900	8.24E−06	0.798
13	13.5	540	600	8.24E−06	0.798
14	13.5	540	1200	8.24E−06	0.798
15	13.5	360	1200	8.24E−06	0.798
16	13.5	180	1200	8.24E−06	0.798
17	13.5	90	1200	8.24E−06	0.798
18	17	90	900	1.65E−05	0.5985
19	17	360	300	4.12E−06	0.9975
20	17	540	600	2.06E−06	0.798
21	17	540	900	4.12E−06	0.9975
22	17	360	600	8.24E−06	0.798
23	20.5	90	1200	4.12E−06	0.798
24	20.5	180	900	2.06E−06	0.9975
25	20.5	360	600	1.65E−05	0.399
26	20.5	540	300	8.24E−06	0.5985
27	20.5	360	900	1.65E−05	0.798
28	20.5	360	900	8.24E−06	0.798
29	10	300	600	1.65E−05	0.399
30	17	300	1000	8.24E−06	0.798
31	20.5	400	800	1.65E−05	0.5985

References

1. Luo, R.z., et al.: Rotating machinery fault diagnosis theory and implementation. Instrum. Tech. Sensor (3), 107–10 (2014)
2. Yin, Y., et al.: Research progress in sliding bearing materials. Lubr. Eng. **05**, 183–187 (2006)
3. Wang, N.: Numerical calculation to the pressure distribution of journal bearing based on the Matlab. Thesis, Dalian University of Technology (2006)
4. Yang, Y., Zu, D., Huang, S.: Status and development of self-lubricating spherical plain bearings. Bearing (01), 58–61+65 (2009). https://doi.org/10.19533/j.issn1000-3762.2009.01.019
5. Zhao, D., Liu, Z., Ren, Z.: Analysis and experimental study of oil flow characteristics in sliding bearings. Lubr. Eng. **37**(3), 81–84 (2012)
6. Fu, J., Li, K., Li, H., Peng, K., Liu, X.: Optimization design of fuel pump sliding bearing based on the analysis of lubrication characteristics. Tribology **38**(5), 512–520 (2018)
7. Xue, Q.: Progress in Chinese tribology research and application. Sci. Technol. Rev. **26**(23), 3 (2008)
8. Archard, J.F.: Contact and rubbing of flat surfaces. J. Appl. Phys. **24**(8), 981–988 (1953). https://doi.org/10.1063/1.1721448
9. Li, C., Zeng, P., Lei, L., Song, J.: Research on sliding wear behavior of co-based alloy and its simulation prediction. J. Mech. Eng. **47**(21), 97–103 (2011). https://doi.org/10.3901/JME.2011.21.097
10. Lu, J., Qiu, M., Li, Y.: Wear life models for self-lubricating radial spherical plain bearings. J. Mech. Eng. **51**(11), 56–63 (2015). https://doi.org/10.3901/JME.2015.11.056
11. Jin, X.: Experiment study on wear of journal bearing of roted system with torque excitation. Thesis, Taiyuan University of Technology (2017)
12. Li, J., Yin, J.: On the wear simulation of self-lubrication bearings. Lubr. Eng. **43**(11), 120–124 (2018)
13. Stankovic, M., Marinkovic, A., Grbovic, A., Miskovic, Z., Rosic, B., Mitrovic, R.: Determination of Archard's wear coefficient and wear simulation of sliding bearings. Ind. Lubr. Tribol. **71**(1), 119–125 (2019). https://doi.org/10.1108/ILT-08-2018-0302
14. König, F., Ouald Chaib, A., Jacobs, G., Sous, C.: A multiscale-approach for wear prediction in journal bearing systems - from wearing-in towards steady-state wear. Wear **426–427**, 1203–1211 (2019). https://doi.org/10.1016/j.wear.2019.01.036. https://www.sciencedirect.com/science/article/pii/S0043164819300584
15. Pang, X., Xue, X., Jin, X.: Experimental study on wear life of journal bearings in the rotor system subjected to torque. Trans. Can. Soc. Mech. Eng. **44**(2), 272–278 (2019)
16. Du, F.M., et al.: Overview of friction and wear performance of sliding bearings. Coatings **12**(9) (2022). https://doi.org/10.3390/coatings12091303
17. Cybenko, G.: Approximation by superpositions of a sigmoidal function. Math. Control Signals Syst. **2**(4), 303–314 (1989)

Accurate Interpolation Algorithm Based on FIR Filters with Local Dynamic Adjustment

Jun Fang[1,2(✉)], Bingran Li[1,2], Hui Zhang[1,2], and Peiqing Ye[1,2]

[1] Department of Mechanical Engineering, Tsinghua University, Beijing 100084, China
fangj19_thu@163.com
[2] Beijing Key Lab of Precision/Ultra-precision Manufacturing Equipment and Control, Tsinghua University, 100084 Beijing, China

Abstract. In computer numerical control (CNC) machining, the tool-path output by the computer-aided manufacturing (CAM) systems is usually composed of a large number of long and short linear segments. The CNC systems needs to undergo trajectory smoothing, velocity planning, and interpolation to generate smooth interpolation points with high-order velocity continuity. This article proposes a simple finite impulse response (FIR) filter algorithm suitable for three-axis mixed complex trajectory machining. This algorithm firstly establishes contour error model at local corners, and then calculates the corresponding velocity adjustment coefficient. By dynamically adjusting adjacent velocity rectangular-frames, preliminary control of contour error is achieved. Due to the small duration of the rectangular-frame in local areas after velocity adjustment, the contour error at the corners is affected by multiple segments. Therefore, after correcting the contour error again and fine-tuning the velocity, a one-step accurate smooth interpolation point trajectory generation was achieved. Finally, an experimental verification was conducted on an open three-axis machine tool using a section of the Mercedes Benz sample as an example.

Keywords: CNC · Local smoothing · FIR filter

1 Introduction

In the complete computer numerical control (CNC) machining process, computer-aided designing (CAD) systems designs and shapes parts, then computer-aided manufacturing (CAM) systems implements process planning and generates NC files for machining. Finally, CNC outputs interpolation points through trajectory smoothing, speed planning, and interpolation control, achieving control of servo motion.

In surface machining, NC files output by CAM are usually expressed in two ways: i) described through simple instructions such as lines and arcs, which are intuitive and easy to adjust; ii) using complex spline curves such as NURBS curves is highly demanding for CAM, CNC, and machining personnel. Therefore, in the actual production and processing process, the line (G00/G01) and arc (G02/G03) expressions is widely used [1, 2]. In order to ensure machining accuracy and efficiency, CNC usually needs to smooth the trajectory path firstly through the smoothing algorithm, then plan the S-shaped velocity curve, and finally interpolate to obtain interpolation points that meet the requirements. The S-shaped velocity curve represents the continuous acceleration of the trajectory, with bounded jerk.

Traditional smoothing algorithms are divided into local smoothing and global smoothing. Zhang [3] and Gao [4, 5] achieved local smoothing by inserting spline curves and constraining the maximum acceleration of the composite axis at the path transition, improving the transition speed and effectively controlling contour errors, but were unable to achieve cross segment smoothing. Zhang [6] and Park [7] achieved global fitting of trajectory paths through B-spline curves, achieving compression of program segments and high-order continuity of machining paths. However, it is difficult to accurately control contour errors under limited computational conditions. Therefore, in recent years, scholars have proposed using finite impulse response (FIR) filters to achieve one-step smoothing of continuous paths. This algorithm has a simple structure, high contour control accuracy, good smoothness, and can obtain smooth interpolation points in one step, which is beneficial for improving the real-time performance of the CNC system.

Song [8] proved that the velocity curve obtained through FIR filters is equivalent to the velocity curve of the polynomial, that is, the trapezoidal velocity curve is obtained through a first-order FIR filter, and the S-type velocity curve is obtained through a second-order FIR filter. Sencer [9] proposed a path smoothing algorithm for first-order FIR filters by adjusting the dwell time to control the velocity overlap area at local corners, thereby accurately controlling contour errors. Li [10] further derived the contour error control model of the third-order filter and extended the algorithm to third-order continuity. To improve machining efficiency, Tajima [11] derived that under the second-order FIR filter model, precise control of contour error can be achieved by controlling the dwell time and partially reducing the speed at local corners. The above studies are all focused on local smoothing algorithms for long path segments. Furthermore, Sencer [12] proposed a contour error control model under continuous micro-segments, which comprehensively considers the influence of multi-segment trajectories to adjust velocity. Finally, for mixed trajectories, Fang [13] achieved consistency processing by pre-discrete the trajectories, and then adjusted the velocity by solving the micro-segment contour error model. The algorithm implemented the FIR filter interpolation for three-axis mixed trajectories, but its efficiency still needs to be optimized.

This study proposes a local dynamic adjustment second-order FIR filter smoothing algorithm for three-axis complex trajectory machining. By solving the contour error at each corner, the velocity adjustment coefficient is obtained, and then the velocity of the front and rear segments is dynamically adjusted. Finally, the velocity of some continuous micro-segment trajectories is adjusted through contour error verification, ensuring the contour accuracy of the final interpolation points. The structure of this article is as follows. Section 2 introduces the basic principle of FIR filters and the generation of single segment S-shaped velocity curve trajectories; Sect. 3 introduces the establishment of a contour error model and the principles of the algorithm; Sect. 4 verifies the effectiveness of the algorithm through experiments.

2 S-Shaped Velocity Curve Generation Based on FIR Filtering

In three-axis machining, the starting/ending coordinates and feed speed F can be obtained by analyzing each line of G-code, and then the duration T_v of the rectangular-frame can be calculated according to the length L. The velocity curve of the rectangular-frame can be obtained by convolved with an FIR filter with a time constant of T_1, and then convolved with an FIR filter with a time constant of T_2 to obtain the commonly used S-shaped velocity curve in CNC machining, as shown in Fig. 1.

The transfer function (TF) of the 1st order FIR filter defined in Laplace(s) is:

$$M_i(s) = \frac{1}{T_i} \frac{1 - e^{-sT_i}}{s}, \quad i = 1 \dots N \tag{1}$$

where T_i is the time constant for the i-th FIR filter. The transfer function consists of a pure delay element e^{-sT_i} and an integrator $\frac{1}{s}$. The impulse response is obtained by the inverse Laplace(s) transform:

$$m_i(t) = L^{-1}(M_i(s)) = \frac{u(t) - u(t - T_i)}{T_i} \text{ where } u(t) = \begin{cases} 1, t \geq 0 \\ 0, t < 0 \end{cases} \tag{2}$$

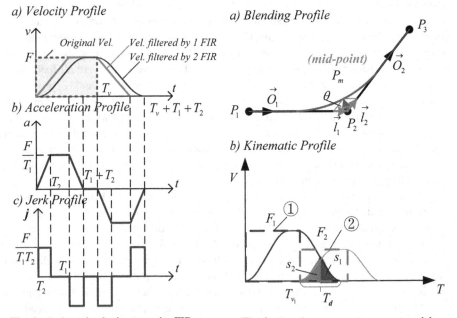

Fig. 1. S-shaped velocity curve by FIR filtering.

Fig. 2. Local corner contour error model.

To obtain the completed seven-segmented S-shaped velocity trajectory, it is necessary to meet $T_v > T_1 + T_2$ and $T_1 > T_2$. The delay time caused by the introduction of the

FIR filters is $T_d = T_1 + T_2$, and the maximum acceleration of the system is $\frac{F}{T_1}$ and the maximum jerk is $\frac{F}{T_1 T_2}$. The speed formula is as follows:

$$v\prime(t) = v(t) * h_1(t) * h_2(t)$$

$$= \begin{cases} \frac{1}{2}\frac{F}{T_1 T_2}t^2 & 0 \le t < T_2 \\ \frac{1}{2}\frac{FT_2}{T_1} + \frac{F}{T_1}(t - T_2) & T_2 \le t < T_1 \\ F - \frac{1}{2}\frac{F}{T_1 T_2}((T_1 + T_2) - t)^2 & T_1 \le t < T_1 + T_2 \\ F & T_1 + T_2 \le t < T_v \\ F - \frac{1}{2}\frac{F}{T_1 T_2}(t - T_v)^2 & T_v \le t < T_v + T_2 \\ F - \frac{1}{2}\frac{FT_2}{T_1} - \frac{F}{T_1}(t - (T_v + T_2)) & T_v + T_2 \le t < T_v + T_1 \\ \frac{1}{2}\frac{F}{T_1 T_2}((T_v + T_1 + T_2) - t)^2 & T_v + T_1 \le t < T_v + T_1 + T_2 \\ 0 & t \ge T_v + T_1 + T_2 \end{cases} \tag{3}$$

* represents convolutional operation.

3 Local Dynamic Adjustment Velocity Algorithm

For continuous paths, each trajectory can be planned into a rectangular-frame with a duration of T_v and a feed rate of F. When the velocity or interval time of the rectangular-frame is not adjusted, the delay time of the filter will inevitably introduce contour errors. The system starts interpolating the trajectory of the second segment before the first segment reaches the endpoint, resulting in overlapping velocity curves and resulting in contour errors at the mixing corner, as shown in the Fig. 2. The meaning of contour error is the deviation distance between the interpolation point track and the G-code point track. Therefore, the key to the continuous path interpolation algorithm based on FIR filters lies in controlling contour errors.

Focusing on a single corner, the maximum contour error ε occurs at the angular bisector $\angle P_1 P_2 P_3$, corresponding to the time $T_b = T_{v_1} + T_d$.

$$\varepsilon = \| \overrightarrow{P_2 P_m} \| = \| \overrightarrow{l_1} - \overrightarrow{l_2} \| \tag{4}$$

From Fig. 2(b), it can be seen that the influence area of rectangular-frame ① on contour error is the shaded area s_1, while the influence area of rectangular-frame ② on contour error is the shaded area s_2.

$$s_1 = \| \int_{T_{v_1} + T_d/2}^{t = T_{v_1} + T_d} v\prime(t)dt \| = \frac{3T_1^2 + T_2^2}{24T_1}F_1 \tag{5}$$

$$s_2 = \| \int_{0}^{t = \frac{T_d}{2}} v\prime(t)dt \| = \frac{3T_1^2 + T_2^2}{24T_1}F_2 \tag{6}$$

Hence,

$$\| \overrightarrow{P_2 P_m} \| = \| s_1 \overrightarrow{t_1} - s_2 \overrightarrow{t_2} \| = \sqrt{s_1^2 + s_2^2 - 2s_1 s_2 (\overrightarrow{t_1} \cdot \overrightarrow{t_2})} \tag{7}$$

As shown in Fig. 2(a),

$$\cos \theta = \overrightarrow{t_1} \cdot \overrightarrow{t_2} \tag{8}$$

Substituting Eqs. (5)-(8) into Eq. (4), so the overall contour error can be obtained as

$$\varepsilon = \frac{3T_1^2 + T_2^2}{24T_1} \sqrt{F_1^2 + F_2^2 - 2F_1 F_2 \cos \theta} \tag{9}$$

Assuming the allowable contour error set by the system is ε, the velocity adjustment coefficient k is

$$k = \frac{\varepsilon_{allow}}{\varepsilon} \tag{10}$$

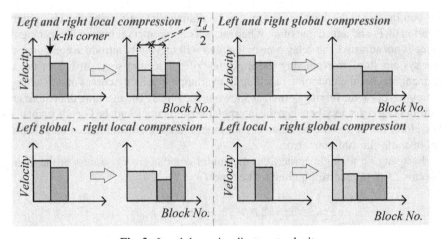

Fig. 3. Local dynamic adjustment velocity.

If the original rectangular-frame is compressed proportionally based on the velocity adjustment coefficient, it may cause the velocity to be compressed too low, greatly affecting the processing efficiency. In fact, from Fig. 2(b), it can be observed that due to the delay time of the filter, only the $\frac{T_d}{2}$ part at the end of rectangular-frame ① and the $\frac{T_d}{2}$ part at the beginning of rectangular-frame ② will affect the contour error. Therefore, the local dynamic adjustment velocity (LDAV) algorithm is proposed to dynamically adjust the rectangular-frame based on the velocity adjustment coefficient, and the implementation effect is shown in Fig. 3.

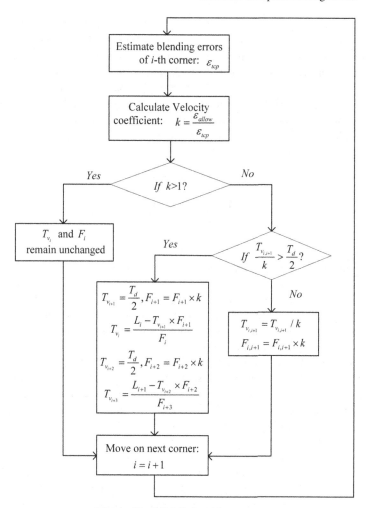

Fig. 4. The LDAC algorithm process.

If $k > 1$, the contour error meets the system requirements and the velocity will not be adjusted. When $k < 1$, if $\frac{T_{v_{i,i+1}}}{k} < \frac{T_d}{2}$, the k was directly applied to the i-th and (i+1)-th rectangular-frames. If $\frac{T_{v_i}}{k} > \frac{T_d}{2}$ or $\frac{T_{v_{i+1}}}{k} > \frac{T_d}{2}$, the rectangular-frame was divided into two rectangular-frames. The duration of the rectangular-frame near the corner is fixed at $\frac{T_d}{2}$, and the velocity is adjusted to $F^* = F \times k$. The velocity of the other part of the rectangular-frame remains unchanged, and the duration is adjusted to $T = (L - F^* \times \frac{T_d}{2})/F$. The schematic diagram of entire algorithm process is shown in the Fig. 4.

It should be noted that for some continuous micro-segment trajectories, after the LDAC algorithm process, the duration of a single rectangular-frame is still less than $\frac{T_d}{2}$, and the contour error of the system will be affected by the cross segments. Therefore, this study proposes an error correction (EC-LDAC) algorithm to further adjust the velocity so that the contour errors of all trajectory points meet the constraints. The principle of error correction is to recalculate the contour error after passing through the LDAC algorithm, and further adjust the rectangular-frame again based on the current contour error ε^* with errors exceeding the tolerance. Ensure that the position remains unchanged, so adjust the rectangular box as follows:

$$\begin{cases} F\prime = F \times \dfrac{\varepsilon_{allow}}{\varepsilon^*} \\ T_v\prime = T_v / \dfrac{\varepsilon_{allow}}{\varepsilon^*} \end{cases} \tag{11}$$

4 Experimental Verification

This section will generate interpolation points through simulation experiments, and then verify the effectiveness of the algorithm on an open three-axis CNC machine tool. The experimental machine tool is a vertical milling machine equipped with Yaskawa's servo drivers, using linear grating as an absolute position detection device, and the control system adopts the 'ELESY-001' CNC system developed by the research group. The Mercedes Benz sample is a standard test sample for three-axis machining in the industry. In this section, one of the precision machining trajectories is selected as the experimental tool-path. This line-cutting is a complex tool-path with multiple features, including long linear segments and micro-segments, arcs, rounded corners, and sharp corners, as shown in Fig. 5. The blue points represent the G-code points, and the red line represents the tool-path.

This article compares the PD-VPC algorithm proposed in Ref. [13] for mixed trajectory machining with the LDAC and the EC-LDAC algorithms proposed in this paper, using second-order FIR filters with filter constants of 20 [ms] and 10 [ms], respectively. Set the maximum feed speed during machining to 3000 [mm/min], and the allowable contour error is 0.01 [mm]. Figure 6 shows the synthesized velocity, acceleration, and jerk profiles obtained by the three algorithms. The PD-VPC algorithm has the longest processing time of 5.678 [s]. The EC-LDAC algorithm took the second place at the time of 5.57 [s], and the processing efficiency improved by 1.9%. As shown in Fig. 6 (a), the speed curve of the EC-LDAC algorithm is sharper and the dwell time in low-velocity zone is shorter, so the efficiency of the algorithm is improved compared with the PD-VPC algorithm. The velocity profile of the LDAC algorithm is basically the same as that of the

EC-LDAC algorithm, as that the blue line is basically covered by the red line, because only the velocity of individual G-code points has been adjusted twice. The acceleration trend and maximum value of the EC-LDAC algorithm and the PD-VPC algorithm are basically similar, but from the acceleration curve, it can be seen that the overall jerk of the EC-LDAC algorithm is relatively small, with a maximum jerk of 293 [m/s^3], while the maximum jerk of the PD-VPC algorithm is 500 [m/s^3]. Because the jerk value of the system is directly positively correlated with the impact and vibration received by the machine tool, the EC-LDAC algorithm effectively reduces the amplitude of the system jerk by 41.4%, which can effectively reduce system vibration and improve machining quality.

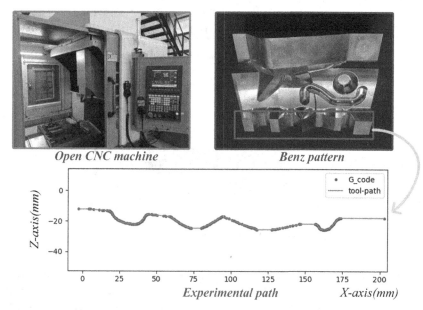

Fig. 5. Open CNC machine tool and experimental tool-path.

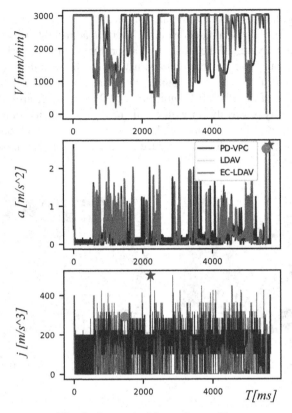

Fig. 6. Composite kinematics profiles.

Figure 7 shows the contour of the single axis velocity, acceleration, and jerk profiles for the X-axis and Z-axis of the system. From the figure, it can be seen that the acceleration of each axis of the system is continuous, and the jerk is bounded. Moreover, the EC-LDAC algorithm effectively reduces the amplitude of the jerk on the X-axis by 31.5%, and the amplitude of the jerk on the Z-axis by 55.8%.

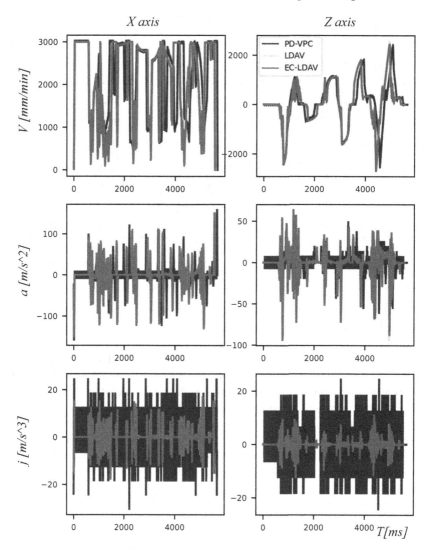

Fig. 7. X axis and Z axis kinematics profiles.

The contour errors of all points in the experimental trajectory are shown in Fig. 8. From the figure, it can be seen that the PD-VPC algorithm satisfies the contour error constraint. However, there are individual points in the LDAC algorithm that exhibit out of tolerance. After the error correction, the EC-LDAC algorithm meets the system contour error constraint in all machining areas.

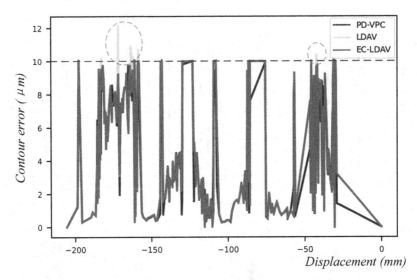

Fig. 8. Contour errors on trajectory.

5 Conclusion

This article proposes a local dynamic adjustment algorithm for three-axis hybrid trajectory error correction based on FIR filters. The experimental results show that this method can effectively constrain contour errors, reduce the amplitude of system acceleration, improve system vibration, and improve machining quality. Compared to the PD-VPC algorithm, the time is reduced by 1.9%, which can improve processing efficiency. Most of the existing algorithms are studied separately for long and micro segments. The EC-LDAC algorithm proposed in this paper is suitable for mixed complex trajectories, and in the future, this algorithm should be studied on the five-axis.

Acknowledgements. The authors did not receive support from any organization for the submitted work.

References

1. Fan, W., Lee, C.H., Chen, J.H.: Real-time repairable interpolation scheme for CNC tool path processing. Int. J. Precis. Eng. Manuf. **17**(12), 1673–1684 (2016)
2. Yang, J.X., Hu, Q., Ding, H.: A two-stage CNC interpolation algorithm for corner smoothing trajectories with geometric error and dynamics constraints. Procedia CIRP **56**, 306–310 (2016)
3. Zhang, Y., Ye, P., Wu, J., Zhang, H.: An optimal curvature-smooth transition algorithm with axis jerk limitations along linear segments. Int. J. Adv. Manuf. Technol. **95**(1–4), 875–888 (2017). https://doi.org/10.1007/s00170-017-1274-1
4. Li, H.B., Gao, X.S., Zhang, L.X., Sun, R.Y.: Discrete interpolation of G01 codes in 2D machining under bounded accelerations. Math. Comput. Sci. **6**(3), 327–344 (2012)

5. Zhang, Q., Gao, X.S., Li, H.B., Zhao, M.Y.: Minimum time corner transition algorithm with confined feedrate and axial acceleration for nc machining along linear tool path. Int. J. Adv. Manuf. Technol. **89**(1–4), 941–956 (2017)

6. Zhang, M., Yan, W., Yuan, C.M., Gao, X.S.: Curve fitting and optimal interpolation on CNC machines based on quadratic B-splines. Sci. Chin. Inf. Sci. **54**(7), 1407–1418 (2011)

7. Park, H.: B-spline surface fitting based on adaptive knot placement using dominant columns. Comput. Aided Des. **43**(3), 258–264 (2011)

8. Song, F., Hao, S., Hao, M., Yang, Z.: Research on acceleration and deceleration control algorithm of NC instruction interpretations with high-order smooth. In: Xiong, C., Liu, H., Huang, Y., Xiong, Y. (eds.) ICIRA 2008. LNCS (LNAI), vol. 5315, pp. 548–557. Springer, Heidelberg (2008). https://doi.org/10.1007/978-3-540-88518-4_59

9. Sencer, B., Ishizaki, K., Shamoto, E.: High speed cornering strategy with confined contour error and vibration suppression for CNC machine tools. CIRP Ann. **64**(1), 369–372 (2015)

10. Li, D.D., Zhang, L.Q., Yang, L., Mao, J.: Accurate interpolation and contouring control algorithm based on FIR filters for the corner transition. Int. J. Adv. Manuf. Technol. **109**(7–8), 1775–1788 (2020)

11. Tajima, J., Sencer, B.: Accurate real-time interpolation of 5-axis tool-paths with local corner smoothing. Int. J. Mach. Tools Manuf **142**, 1–15 (2019)

12. Tajima, S., Sencer, B.: Real-time trajectory generation for 5-axis machine tools with singularity avoidance. CIRP Ann. **69**(1), 349–352 (2020)

13. Fang, J., Li, B.R., Zhang, H., Ye, P.Q.: Real-time smooth trajectory generation for 3-axis blending tool-paths based on FIR filtering. Int. J. Adv. Manuf. Technol. **126**, 3401–3416 (2023)

Investigation of Soft Acoustic Waveguide Dispersion for Wearable Strain Sensing in Human Motion Monitoring

Yuan Lin, Medhanit Alemu, and Peter Shull[✉]

School of Mechanical Engineering, Shanghai Jiao Tong University, Shanghai 201100, China
{lin_yuan,medhanit,pshull}@sjtu.edu.cn

Abstract. Wearable soft strain sensors hold great promise in human-machine interaction and clinical applications, enabling accurate and convenient human motion monitoring. Although a new guided-wave soft strain sensor has been developed, it is still challenging to theoretically model the propagation of guided waves inside the small, soft waveguide and investigate their dispersion behaviors. Therefore, this paper, for the first time, focuses on the theoretical modeling of dispersion behaviors in a soft, small waveguide, utilizing a semi-analytical finite element method to calculate dispersion curves, verifying and explaining the experimentally observed guided wave phenomenon. The study also investigates the impact of different cross-section shapes, materials, and sizes on dispersion behavior. Results indicate that employing Ecoflex0030 with a square cross-section of 1.7 mm side length provides relatively improved performance in reducing signal complexity and enhancing stretchability for strain sensing. Then by characterizing the dynamic response of the optimal waveguide and attaching it to various human joints for motion monitoring, this research showcases the high repeatability and dynamic response of the waveguide in tracking human motions. These findings serve as a foundation for exploring potential solutions to existing barriers in wearable human motion detection, such as insufficient repeatability and time response. Furthermore, this work provides crucial insights for the design of soft, wearable prototypes aimed at developing effective, simple, and soft wearable sensors.

Keywords: Dispersion · Ultrasonic soft waveguide · Semi-analytical finite element method · Wearable strain sensor

1 Introduction

Soft stretchable strain sensors are commonly utilized as intermediary devices that translate external or internal changes in tension, force, and vibration into

This work was supported by the National Natural Science Foundation of China under Grant 52250610217.

measurable strains within the sensor. As a result, these sensors are capable of detecting biological states and regulating machine components where they are installed. Due to their lightweight and flexibility, soft stretchable strain sensors are frequently preferred over hard strain gauges for advanced applications such as human-computer interaction [1], human motion monitoring [2], and electronic skin [3].

The function of various types of stretchable strain sensors varies considerably, and the sensing mechanism underlies this variability. The primary strain sensing mechanisms that have been extensively researched include piezoresistive [4], capacitive [5], inductive [6], piezoelectric [7], triboelectric [8], and optical/visual [9]. These distinctive sensing mechanisms typically result in different performances advantages for the strain sensor. For instance, the resistive type exhibits high stretchability and sensing sensitivity, the capacitive type has a small hysteresis, the inductive type displays extremely high repeatability, the piezoelectric and triboelectric types offer passive detection, and the optical type has a rapid response rate [10].

Despite the benefits of these sensing mechanisms, sensors utilizing them often suffer from key limitations. For example, the resistive type exhibits undesirable hysteresis, the capacitive type lacks sensitivity, the inductive type is susceptible to external electromagnetic interference, and piezoelectric and triboelectric sensors are unable to detect static strain. Moreover, the visual and optical sensors require complex light tracking and processing systems. Additionally, long-term signal stability and complicated manufacturing procedures are common issues encountered with these sensors. Generally, creating soft strain sensors with excellent or well-balanced performance indicators suitable for wearable applications through simple manufacturing processes is challenging, primarily due to limitations introduced by the sensing mechanisms.

To overcome these limitations, the key breakthrough lies in developing possible new mechanisms. Chossat and Shull made an innovative proposal for a strain sensor based on the acoustic waveguide mechanism in their recent work, which showed significant potential for high-precision strain detection [11]. This novel approach exhibits an extremely low strain monitoring hysteresis, thanks to the fact that the electrical properties of the material do not impede the propagation of ultrasound waves, while only its mechanical properties contribute to the minimal hysteresis resulting in an overall hysteresis reduction in the sensor. Additionally, this new type of sensor employs simple and reliable fabrication techniques, utilizing just one material for the waveguide, while maintaining high tensile properties and stability through reliance on ultrasound propagation.

Despite the observation of soft waveguide propagation through experimentation and their potential in strain sensing, there are still limitations to the use of soft ultrasonic waveguides. The most fundamental limitation is the lack of thorough investigation into the theory behind ultrasonic soft waveguides. And one of the main goals of incorporating this theory is to generate dispersion curves that are essential for fully utilizing guided waves in a given waveguide. Dispersion curves allow for the optimization of the structural design of the waveguide by providing a deeper understanding of the propagation of guided waves in soft waveguides. Additionally, they facilitate the analysis of received signals, such as for dispersion compensation, ultimately improving the echo signal-to-noise ratio and the accuracy of strain detection.

Obtaining guided wave dispersion curves is an active area of research, and several theoretical methods have been developed. These include the Global Matrix Method (GMM) [12], Legendre Polynomial Expansion Method (LPEM) [13], and Semi-Analytical Finite Element Method (SAFEM) [14]. These methods can provide valuable insights into the behavior of guided waves in soft waveguides and facilitate the design and optimization of waveguides for strain-sensing applications.

Out of the various methods available, SAFEM is an optimal choice as it balances calculation accuracy and efficiency. SAFEM extracts dispersive solutions via a finite element discretization of the cross-section and conveniently represents displacement along the wave propagation direction as analytical harmonic exponential functions. These solutions enable stable and straightforward extraction of dispersion curves from an eigenvalue problem, obviating the need for root-searching algorithms. SAFEM outperforms other existing methods, making it suitable for calculating dispersive curves for waveguides with any arbitrary cross-sections [15].

Therefore, this paper will, for the first time, focus on obtaining dispersion curves of ultrasonic soft waveguide and to verify the feasibility of ultrasonic waveguide propagation in soft materials. We analyze the results of dispersion curves for soft waveguides crafted from different materials and with varying cross-sectional shapes and sizes. These findings provide a preliminary theoretical basis for choosing appropriate waveguide materials, cross-sectional shapes, and dimensions. To confirm the efficacy of the proposed soft waveguides in wearable human motion monitoring, we fabricate a waveguide with a square cross-section using Ecoflex0030. We perform dynamic testing of the guided wave strain detection to further verify the feasibility of soft waveguides for human motion monitoring. Ultimately, we demonstrate the wearability of the waveguide by incorporating it into a wearable human motion monitoring system.

2   Waveguide Dispersion Curves and Influencing Factors

In this paper, we briefly introduce the mathematical framework of SAFEM [16–19], focusing on an isotropic square cross-section waveguide with traction-free lateral faces. The wave propagates along the z-direction at frequency f and wavenumber k.

In the given coordinate system, the waveguide is of infinite extension in the z-direction, and we set the origin as the center of the front face of the waveguide. At each point in the waveguide, particle displacement vector u, strain vector ϵ, and stress vector σ, can be expressed as:

$$u = \begin{bmatrix} u_x\ u_y\ u_z \end{bmatrix}^T \qquad (1)$$

$$\epsilon = \begin{bmatrix} \epsilon_x & \epsilon_y & \epsilon_z & \gamma_{yz} & \gamma_{xz} & \gamma_{xy} \end{bmatrix}^T \tag{2}$$

$$\sigma = \begin{bmatrix} \sigma_x & \sigma_y & \sigma_z & \sigma_{yz} & \sigma_{xz} & \sigma_{xy} \end{bmatrix}^T \tag{3}$$

The displacement at an arbitrary point can be expressed by:

$$u(x,y,z,t) = \begin{bmatrix} u_x(x,y,z,t) \\ u_y(x,y,z,t) \\ u_z(x,y,z,t) \end{bmatrix} = \begin{bmatrix} U_x(x,y) \\ U_y(x,y) \\ U_z(x,y) \end{bmatrix} e^{i(kz-\omega t)} \tag{4}$$

where $U(x,y)$ is the displacement coefficient function. The displacement expressions in Eq. (4) over the discretized element domain can be represented in terms of the shape functions $N(x,y)$:

$$u^{(e)}(x,y,z,t) = \begin{bmatrix} \sum_{m=1}^{n} N_m(x,y)U_{xm} \\ \sum_{m=1}^{n} N_m(x,y)U_{ym} \\ \sum_{m=1}^{n} N_m(x,y)U_{zm} \end{bmatrix}^{(e)} e^{i(kz-\omega t)} = N(x,y)q^{(e)}e^{i(kz-\omega t)} \tag{5}$$

where $q^{(e)}$ denotes the nodal displacement of the element. And it is a vector with n dimensions (n represents the number of nodes per element). The constitutive relations which connect displacement with strain are given by:

$$\epsilon^{(e)} = \left(L_x \frac{\partial}{\partial x} + L_y \frac{\partial}{\partial y} + L_z \frac{\partial}{\partial z} \right) u \tag{6}$$

where

$$L_x = \begin{bmatrix} 1&0&0 \\ 0&0&0 \\ 0&0&0 \\ 0&0&0 \\ 0&0&1 \\ 0&1&0 \end{bmatrix} \quad L_y = \begin{bmatrix} 0&0&0 \\ 0&1&0 \\ 0&0&0 \\ 0&0&1 \\ 0&0&0 \\ 1&0&0 \end{bmatrix} \quad L_z = \begin{bmatrix} 0&0&0 \\ 0&0&0 \\ 0&0&1 \\ 0&1&0 \\ 1&0&0 \\ 0&0&0 \end{bmatrix} \tag{7}$$

The stress can also be written as:

$$\sigma^{(e)} = C\epsilon^{(e)} \tag{8}$$

where C is an elastic coefficient matrix. According to the virtual work principle:

$$\int_{\Gamma} \delta u^{(e)T} t^{(e)} d\Gamma = \int_{V} \delta u^{(e)T} \left(\rho \ddot{u}^{(e)} \right) dV + \int_{V} \delta \epsilon^{(e)T} \sigma^{(e)} dV \tag{9}$$

where $\delta u^{(e)T}$ denotes the virtual element displacement and $\delta \epsilon^{(e)T}$ is the virtual element strain. And $t^{(e)}$ represents the external traction vector. Γ is the surface of the element, and V is the volume of the element.

To obtain the traction-free state, we can substitute Eq. (5)–(8) into Eq. (9), and then rearrange the equations for all elements by overlapping common nodes together. By doing so, we can simplify the system of equations and obtain a more manageable form that is suitable for analysis:

$$\left[K_1 + ikK_2 + k^2K_3 - \omega^2 M\right]_M U = 0 \tag{10}$$

where K_1, K_2, K_3 and M are the matrices with $M \times M$ dimensions whose values are determined by the waveguide geometry. U is the unknown nodal displacement vector. Equation (10) can further be expressed as an eigensystem for a better calculation to obtain the dispersive curves.

The results can be obtained through the use of COMSOL Multiphysics software within the mathematical framework. For this study, we examined three scenarios for soft waveguide dispersion, which include different cross-sectional shapes, varying waveguide materials, and various cross-sectional sizes. The parameters entered into Comsol Multiphysics were obtained from prior reported studies [20] and the commercial material manual. These material parameters are summarized in Table 1 as follows:

Table 1. Material parameters used for dispersion curves calculation.

	Longitudinal wave Speed (m/s)	Shear wave speed (m/s)	Density (kg/m^3)
Ecoflex 0010	849.2191	3.7978	1040
Ecoflex 0030	1000.6794	4.2139	1070
Ecoflex 0050	1266.6847	5.6646	1070

Influence of Different Cross-Section Shapes. For investigating the effects of two common cross-sectional shapes (square and circular shapes) on guided wave dispersion, we utilized Ecoflex0030 (Smooth-on, Ecoflex, USA) as the soft material.

Overall, the results highlight the complexity of guided wave behavior in soft materials and emphasize the importance of carefully selecting cross-section for designing effective and efficient sensors (Fig. 1(a) & (b)). Several detailed observations can be made from the figures: 1) In soft materials, guided waves have a higher degree of aggregation under different mode curves compared to typical solid materials. This suggests a smaller difference in phase velocities between different modes, which makes identifying guided wave modes in soft materials more challenging. 2) Generally, the trend of waveguide dispersion curves in soft materials is consistent with that of typical solids. Most of the modes exhibit a decrease in phase velocity with increasing frequency, while only a small fraction exhibits an increase in phase velocity. Furthermore, all modes converge at a specific velocity. Additionally, individual modes have cut-off frequencies, some of which occur quite early, as observed in this study (0–2 MHz). 3) The results confirm that ultrasound-guided waves in small soft waveguides are complex. The inset in Fig. 1(a) shows the presence of 11 modes under the target frequency of 0.98 MHz, underscoring the complexity of guided wave signals in small soft waveguides. 4) The square cross-section has fewer modes at the target

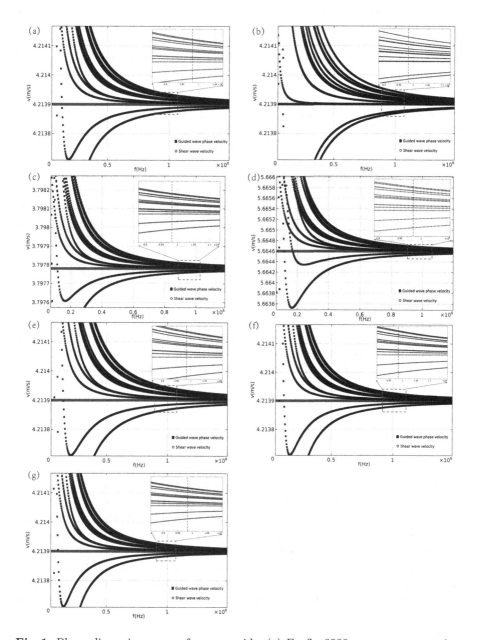

Fig. 1. Phase dispersive curve of a waveguide. (a) Ecoflex0030, square cross-section, 1.7×1.7 mm. (b) Ecoflex0030, circle cross-section, D $= 1.7$ mm. (c) Ecoflex0010, square cross-section, 1.7×1.7 mm. (d) Ecoflex0050, square cross-section, 1.7×1.7 mm. (e) Ecoflex0030, square cross-section, 1.5×1.5 mm. (f) Ecoflex0030, square cross-section, 1.9×1.9 mm. (g) Ecoflex0030, square cross-section, 2.1×2.1 mm.

excitation frequency, which is advantageous since the echo signal will be more stable and the signal-to-noise ratio will be higher. Moreover, the waveguide with a square cross-section is easier to fabricate, and the mold design is simpler compared to a circular waveguide. Hence, we opt to use the waveguide with a square cross-section for further analysis.

Influence of Different Waveguide Materials. In this section, we examine the impact of different materials on waveguide dispersion. We select Ecoflex series materials since they are commercially available and have gained widespread popularity in recent years. Based on existing literature, we focus on the three most commonly used materials within the Ecoflex series, namely: Ecoflex0010, 0030, and 0050.

Overall, these results demonstrate the consistency of dispersion curve trends among different soft materials and the importance of selecting an appropriate material for designing efficient sensors with high signal-to-noise ratios (Fig. 1(a), (c) & (d)). The figures illustrate the following details: 1) The trend of dispersion curves is consistent across different soft materials. Individual modes have cutoff frequencies, and all modes converge to their corresponding wave shear velocities. 2) The complexity of waveguides with different materials remains unchanged. For instance, at the target frequency, at least 11 modes exist for both Ecoflex0010 and Ecoflex0050. 3) Given the aggregation of dispersion curves for Ecoflex0030 at the target frequency, the guided wave packet's signal-to-noise ratio is expected to be better. Moreover, since Ecoflex0030 exhibits higher tensile strength in practical applications, the waveguide with a square cross-section made of Ecoflex0030 is used for subsequent analyses.

Influence of Different Waveguide Cross-Section Sizes. In this section, we examine the impact of cross-sectional sizes on waveguide dispersion. We consider four different sizes (1.5 mm, 1.7 mm, 1.9 mm, and 2.1 mm), with Ecoflex0030 being used for all sizes.

Overall, these results emphasize the importance of selecting appropriate cross-sectional sizes to ensure optimal performance for guided wave sensors (Fig. 1(a), (e), (f) & (g)). Several detailed observations can be made from the figures: 1) Unlike the impact of materials, cross-sectional size has a more significant influence on waveguide dispersion curves. This is mainly reflected in the following aspects: a) The cut-off frequency of each mode decreases as the cross-sectional size increases, indicating that larger cross-sectional sizes result in more modes in the low-frequency range under the study conditions, ultimately leading to the increased complexity of guided waves. b) At the same target frequency, a larger size corresponds to phase velocities closer to shear wave velocity. 2) All waveguides exhibit an equal number of modes at the target frequency for all sizes. 3) Based on signal and fabrication considerations, we select a waveguide with a side length of 1.7 mm for further research and applications. The rationale for this decision is primarily twofold: a) From a signal standpoint, larger sizes entail greater complexity for guided waves. b) In terms of practical fabrication, the waveguide must be stably wrapped around the transducer, making 1.7mm the most suitable choice.

To summarize, the trend of waveguide dispersion curves in soft materials is consistent with that of typical solids. However, guided waves in soft materials have a higher degree of aggregation under various mode curves, which increases the difficulty of identifying guided wave modes in soft materials. The aforementioned studies are the first to calculate the dispersion of small, soft waveguides, providing theoretical support and guidance for the subsequent structural design of soft waveguides and ideas for effective echo signal analysis. Moreover, they illustrate how to conduct dispersion compression effectively to make the wave packet more compact, improving peak detection accuracy and ultimately enhancing strain detection accuracy. For subsequent applications and studies, we will utilize Ecoflex0030 with a square waveguide having a side length of 1.7 mm.

3   Fabrication and Characterization

Based on calculations in the preceding section, the optimal waveguide has a square profile with sides measuring 1.7 mm and a total length of 50 mm. Regarding the fabrication of the soft sensor and hardware system, interested readers can refer to the work [11, 21] for further details. Given that time of flight (TOF) varies under different strains, we can estimate the sensor's strain based on this value. Before algorithms are applied to detect the TOFs, the received echo signal is filtered (Fig. 2) to improve the accuracy of the analysis. The Hilbert transformation is then carried out to obtain the signal envelope. Finally, peak detection algorithms are used to determine the TOFs.

The target application of this sensor is for wearable use. It is crucial to determine whether the sensor can monitor changes induced by human joint movements steadily and continuously. Therefore, the capabilities of the sensors under higher strain rates, such as those encountered during finger motion, have been studied. To evaluate the waveguide sensor accurately, an experiment was carried out using various stretching-releasing rates (10 mm/s, 20 mm/s, 30 mm/s, and 40 mm/s). These different rates can help assess the sensor's performance and determine whether it can detect strain changes in real-time scenarios. By conducting this experiment, we can obtain a better understanding of how the sensor will perform when worn on the body, particularly during activities that involve rapid upper extremity movement.

For the dynamic characterization of the sensor, a 50 mm long specimen was used. To test its performance, a belt-driven linear actuator (YiXuan Tec. Accuracy: 0.05 mm) was employed. To carry out this experiment, the ends of the sensor were fixed between the movable platform and the base of the linear actuator. Ten consecutive stretching-releasing trials were performed at each of the four different strain rates: starting from 10 mm/s and ending at 40 mm/s. These tests were conducted at room temperature, and the sensor was left to relax between subsequent trials. The Python script used for measuring the TOF had a sampling rate of 50 Hz. By analyzing the TOF values obtained during the

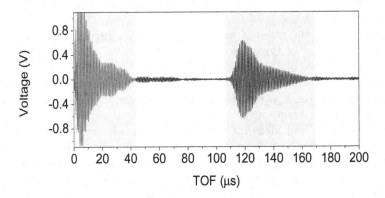

Fig. 2. One echo signal example. (The part under light yellow background is noise, the part under light green background is the target echo packet.) (Color figure online)

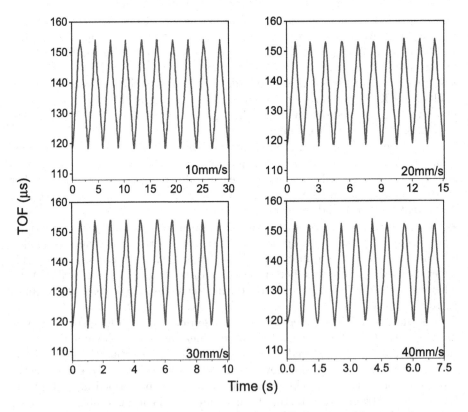

Fig. 3. The sensor TOF signal changes under four different stretching-releasing rates, demonstrating its high dynamic response and repeatability.

stretching-releasing trials, we can evaluate the sensor's dynamic response and determine whether it can detect changes in strain rates accurately and reliably.

The experimental results show that the sensor exhibits high strain detection repeatability regardless of the applied strain rate (Fig. 3). The signal output is steady and detects changes in strain accurately, making it suitable for monitoring human movement. To further validate its performance, the sensor was attached to three different joints on the user's body using double-sided tape: finger joint, wrist joint, and elbow joint. The resulting movement was then monitored by the sensor (Fig. 4). The sensor's ability to produce detectable and stable signal changes when attached to different human joints indicates its potential for use in various applications.

Overall, the results highlight the capability of the novel soft acoustic waveguide-based strain sensor in tracking changes in strain rates during human movement. These outcomes imply promising prospects for advancing and implementing this technology in the realm of wearable devices and other relevant domains, thereby fostering opportunities for further exploration and development.

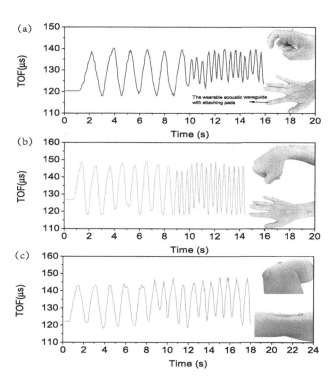

Fig. 4. The sensor TOF signal changes when attaching to (a) the index finger joint, (b) the wrist, and (c) the elbow.

4 Conclusion

This paper mainly focuses on the theoretical modeling, calculation, and application demonstration of soft ultrasonic waveguides. Specifically, we present a comprehensive study on the dispersion behaviors of guided waves within soft, small waveguides and their potential for use in human motion-tracking applications, including finger, wrist, and elbow joint motion monitoring. The dispersive curves were calculated using SAFEM for this soft, small-size waveguide for the first time. The impact of different cross-section shapes, waveguide materials, and cross-section sizes was studied. In terms of signal complexity and stretchability for strain sensing, the result shows that the waveguide can perform relatively better using Ecoflex0030 with a square cross-section of 1.7 mm-side length. Based on a novel acoustic sensing mechanism, the strain-sensing waveguide boasts great repeatability and dynamic response. When worn, the sensor could track human joint movement under varied flexion-extension rates. The sensor exhibits exceptional stretchability and lightweight construction designed to be comfortably worn by the user.

The sensor does not require cleanroom facilities or complex manufacturing processes, making them accessible and inexpensive to manufacture. Moreover, the measuring process and electronics used are inherently scalable. This is particularly attractive compared to most previously reported micro/nano-polymer, fiber, or hydrogel-based strain sensors, and only further their relevance to the soft wearable and motion capture industries.

The work and results serve as a foundation for exploring potential solutions to existing barriers in wearable human motion detection for virtual reality entertainment and clinical applications. It will also provide crucial insights for the design of soft, wearable prototypes as part of an ongoing effort to develop soft sensors. Both time and frequency domains can be employed to extract decoupled signals from simple sensing structures, representing a novel and promising path toward soft, simple, yet effective wearable sensors. In the future, further factors must be taken into account when modeling dispersive behaviors such as damping and prestress. With regard to practical applications, more exploration is required to verify other strain-sensing indicators, such as linearity, hysteresis, and durability.

Acknowledgements. The authors would like to thank the National Natural Science Foundation of China under Grant 52250610217.

References

1. Zhai, K., et al.: High-performance strain sensors based on organohydrogel microsphere film for wearable human-computer interfacing. Adv. Sci. **10**(6), 1–12 (2023)
2. Wang, Y., et al.: Wearable and highly sensitive graphene strain sensors for human motion monitoring. Adv. Func. Mater. **24**(29), 4666–4670 (2014)
3. Oh, H.S., Lee, C.H., Kim, N.K., An, T., Kim, G.H.: Sensors for biosignal/health monitoring in electronic skin. Polymers **13**(15), 2478 (2021)

4. Wan, C., Zhang, L., Yong, K.T., Li, J., Wu, Y.: Recent progress in flexible nanocellulosic structures for wearable piezoresistive strain sensors. J. Mater. Chem. C **9**(34), 11001–11029 (2021)

5. Dong, T., Gu, Y., Liu, T., Pecht, M.: Resistive and capacitive strain sensors based on customized compliant electrode: comparison and their wearable applications. Sens. Actuators A **326**, 112720 (2021)

6. Tavassolian, M., Cuthbert, T.J., Napier, C., Peng, J., Menon, C.: Textile-based inductive soft strain sensors for fast frequency movement and their application in wearable devices measuring multiaxial hip joint angles during running. Adv. Intell. Syst. **2**(4), 1900165 (2020)

7. Ji, Z., Zhang, M.: Highly sensitive and stretchable piezoelectric strain sensor enabled wearable devices for real-time monitoring of respiratory and heartbeat simultaneously. Nanotechnol. Precis. Eng. **5**(1), 013002 (2022)

8. Gogurla, N., Roy, B., Park, J.Y., Kim, S.: Skin-contact actuated single-electrode protein triboelectric nanogenerator and strain sensor for biomechanical energy harvesting and motion sensing. Nano Energy **62**, 674–681 (2019)

9. Belleville, C., Duplain, G.: White-light interferometric multimode fiber-optic strain sensor. Opt. Lett. **18**(1), 78–80 (1993)

10. Souri, H., et al.: Wearable and stretchable strain sensors: materials, sensing mechanisms, and applications. Adv. Intell. Syst. **2**(8), 2000039 (2020)

11. Chossat, J.B., Shull, P.B.: Soft acoustic waveguides for strain, deformation, localization, and twist measurements. IEEE Sens. J. **21**(1), 222–230 (2020)

12. Lou, M., Crampin, S.: Dispersion of guided waves in thin anisotropic waveguides. Geophys. J. Int. **107**(3), 545–555 (1991)

13. Lefebvre, J.E., Zhang, V., Gazalet, J., Gryba, T.: Legendre polynomial approach for modeling free-ultrasonic waves in multilayered plates. J. Appl. Phys. **85**(7), 3419–3427 (1999)

14. Lagasse, P.E.: Higher-order finite-element analysis of topographic guides supporting elastic surface waves. J. Acoust. Soc. Am. **53**(4), 1116–1122 (1973)

15. Aalami, B.: Waves in prismatic guides of arbitrary cross section. J. Appl. Mech. **40**, 1067–1072 (1973)

16. Bartoli, I., Marzani, A., Di Scalea, F.L., Viola, E.: Modeling wave propagation in damped waveguides of arbitrary cross-section. J. Sound Vib. **295**(3), 685–707 (2006)

17. Hayashi, T., Song, W.J., Rose, J.L.: Guided wave dispersion curves for a bar with an arbitrary cross-section, a rod and rail example. Ultrasonics **41**(3), 175–183 (2003)

18. Shorter, P.J.: Wave propagation and damping in linear viscoelastic laminates. J. Acoust. Soc. Am. **115**(5), 1917–1925 (2004)

19. Joseph, L.R., Peter, B.N.: Ultrasonic waves in solid media. J. Acoust. Soc. Am. **107**(4), 1807–1808 (2000)

20. Wang, H., Totaro, M., Blandin, A. A., Beccai, L.: A wireless inductive sensing technology for soft pneumatic actuators using magnetorheological elastomers. In: IEEE International Conference on Soft Robotics (2019)

21. Lin, Y., Chossat, J.B., Shull, P.B.: Wearable water-filled soft transparent pressure sensor based on acoustic guided waves. In: 2022 IEEE International Ultrasonics Symposium (IUS) (2022)

Design and Optimization of Compliant Rotational Hinge Based on Curved Beam

Nianfeng Wang$^{(\boxtimes)}$, Guisheng Shang, Xingyue Liu, Xuewei Zheng,
and Xianmin Zhang

Guangdong Key Laboratory of Precision Equipment and Manufacturing Technology,
School of Mechanical and Automotive Engineering, South China University of Technology,
Guangzhou 510641, China
{menfwang,zhangxm}@scut.edu.cn

Abstract. The compliant hinge is a crucial component of compliant mechanisms, transmitting motion and force through the elastic deformation of the compliant element. It offers advantages such as frictionless, gapless, lubrication-free operation, low cost, and lightweight precision, making it highly desirable for high-resolution and high-precision micro and nano motions. However, conventional compliant hinges have the drawback of axial drift, which hinders precise control of axial motion. We designed a passive-compliant hinge with zero axial drift, no assembly required, and both large travel and integration characteristics to address this issue. Our approach involved modeling the compliance, mechanics, and simulation analysis of the critical structure of the compliant hinge, followed by optimization of the structural parameters. We then performed performance modeling of the compliant elements of the hinge concerning the design parameters and range of motion. Finally, we comprehensively evaluated the optimized structure based on performance indexes of the compliant hinge, yielding superior design results.

Keywords: compliant hinge · compliance modeling · large travel · zero axis drift · performance modeling

1 Introduction

As modern technology continues miniaturizing in many areas, the need for precision mechanisms has increased. A particular type of precision mechanism is called a compliant mechanism, as discussed by Howell and Smith. These mechanisms are widely used in applications requiring high-precision motion over a range. Although the compliant hinge provides only a limited rotation angle, it has a frictionless loss, no lubricity, and hysteresis-free rotational motion [1]. In recent years of research, the compliant hinge is often used as a transfer joint in the design of precision positioning platforms [2, 3] with micro-nano operations [4, 5].

In order to fulfill various usage requirements, various compliant hinges with different structures and properties have been proposed by scholars both domestically and abroad. Among them, notched and straight-piece compliant hinges are the most commonly used

© The Author(s), under exclusive license to Springer Nature Singapore Pte Ltd. 2023
H. Yang et al. (Eds.): ICIRA 2023, LNAI 14275, pp. 250–260, 2023.
https://doi.org/10.1007/978-981-99-6504-5_22

types. Wu [6] utilized NURBS curves to parametrically model a conical notched compliant hinge and obtain an accurate analytical solution of the compliant model. Liu [7] designed a notched compliant hinge consisting of a right-angle circular notch and two parabolic notches and modeled and optimized its performance. Ling [8] derived the compliance of a notched compliant hinge with a neutral axis that is a straight line using the transfer matrix method and the idea of finite element discretization. Based on this, a three-dimensional theoretical model was developed to accurately and generally describe the flexibility and accuracy of notched compliant hinges with straight neutral axes. However, stress concentrations tend to occur around the notch region, which limits their application to a high-precision small range of motion [9]. In recent years, the research on straight-piece type compliant units has been focused on increasing the range of motion while reducing the axial drift of the mechanism and improving its anti-interference capability. Many scholars have made structural innovations by adjusting multiple straight-piece units. Xu et al. [10] designed a multi-reed rotating vice that can achieve a wide range with low axial drift but required a design domain of 100×100 mm to achieve a rotation range of $17°$.

To enhance the overall performance of compliant hinges, Howell [1] introduced the concept of "passive sub" that uses contact or guide structures to constrain the motion behavior of the compliant mechanism. A well-designed passive sub can improve the mechanism's overall performance. Liang et al. [11] developed a finger joint rehabilitation mechanism using a conjugate surface-compliant hinge that enables large displacement motion. Still, they also encountered fatigue failure and friction issues with this structure. Therefore, this paper proposes a compliant passive hinge with a large stroke and zero axial drift, which utilizes a curved sheet beam. The paper calculates and analyzes the relationship between the hinge's range of motion, design domain, and rotational stiffness.

2 Compliant Rotational Hinge Design Based on Curved Beam

This paper aims to design a compliant rotary hinge with large rotational displacement, zero axis drift, and the possibility of integrated wire-cutting processing. This mechanism can be applied in systems of compliant precision positioning stages, rotary joints of space mechanisms, and precision scanning mechanisms. To better measure the performance of the hinge, this paper will design the hinge in the design domain, which is a circular domain with a radius of 20 mm, the thinnest cutting thickness is 0.4 mm, the material used is aluminum 7075, the modulus of elasticity is 72 GPA, and the Poisson's ratio is 0.33.

2.1 Compliant Rotational Hinge Overall Description

The compliant hinge designed in this study has two main parts: the conjugate surface restraint structure and the compliant element. The conjugate surface restraint structure adopts a compliant self-locking design, disengaging and connecting the two ends through elastic deformation. The design reason for this structure is that the wire-cutting process always has a cutting gap of at least 0.3 mm. The conjugates surface constraint structure can reserve the cutting gap, which can realize integrated machining on the one hand; on the other hand, it compensates for the limitation of the cutting gap so that the contact end of the moving sub can achieve gapless rolling and improve the motion accuracy of the compliant hinge. Since the rotary hinge performs circular motion within the design domain of a circle, this chapter uses a circularly shaped thin sheet-like compliant element to improve the flexibility of the compliant element. The designed compliant hinge is shown in Fig. 1. The optimization of these two key components is carried out later.

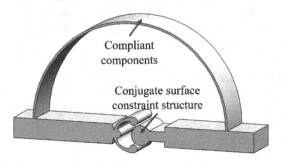

Fig. 1. Overall structure diagram of compliant hinge based on curved beam

2.2 Design of Compliant Rotational Hinge Conjugate Surface Restraint Structure

The conjugate surface-constrained structure has the machining and usage states, as shown in Fig. 2. The left end is the female head, the main component that deforms during the self-assembly process before use, and the right is the male head.

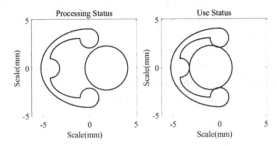

Fig. 2. Two states of the conjugate surface-constrained structure

Before use, the male head moves to the left, causing the two cantilever beams on the upper and lower sides of the female head to move outward. Then, when the diameter of the male head passes through the two circular notches on the upper and lower sides of the female head, the two cantilever beams on the upper and lower sides of the female head begin to reset until the male head moves to the far left. At this point, the preparation work is completed, and the three cylindrical surfaces of the male head and the female head are tangent, with the male head wholly enclosed within the female head, achieving gapless transmission during the male head's rotation. The study focuses on the mechanical changes of the female head during the self-assembly process. Next, the flexibility model of the upper cantilever beam of the female head will be established using Mohr's integral method.

2.2.1 Compliance Modeling and Simulation Analysis

The female head structure is analyzed parametrically, the radius of the three small circles is r, the radius of the large circle of the male head is R, the height of the female head raised during the assembly process is h, the preload distance between the male head and the female head after assembly is d, and the line cutting gap Dt is determined by the actual machining accuracy, which is 0.3 mm. Where the arc segment connecting the three small circles is an ellipse line, and the overall thickness of the structure is set to 10 mm. Four parameters [r, R, h, d] can determine the conjugate surface-constrained structure's overall geometric configuration and dimensions, as shown in Fig. 3.

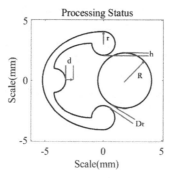

Fig. 3. Parametric analysis of conjugate surface-constrained structures

Next, the compliance matrix of the female head is established, and the mechanical state of the female head at the time of the highest lateral lift is analyzed during the assembly process. First, the neutral layer of the two elliptical lines is found. The ray is made to the two elliptical lines with the origin as the center, intersecting at two points, the midpoint of which is the approximate point on the neutral layer. The influence of the neutral layer offset on the results is considered in calculating the neutral layer by introducing correction parameters.

$$\frac{x^2}{a_1^2} + \frac{y^2}{b_1^2} = 1$$
$$\frac{x^2}{a_2^2} + \frac{y^2}{b_2^2} = 1 \tag{1}$$
$$y = \tan(\theta) \cdot x$$
$$a_1, a_2, b_1, b_2 \in f([r, R, h, d])$$

By combining Eq. (1), we can obtain the trajectory of the neutral layer and the thickness of the neutral layer at each point. By force analysis, we can obtain the bending moment at each force point on the neutral layer, as shown in Eq. (2). Using the Moore integral method, considering only the flexibility in the in-plane directions (x, y, θ), the compliant model can be obtained as shown in Eq. (3).

$$
\begin{aligned}
rr &= abs(point\_Neutral\ layer) \\
M_x(\theta) &= F_x * (rr * (\sin(\theta) - (R - h))) \\
M_y(\theta) &= -F_y * (rr * \cos(\theta)) \\
M_z(\theta) &= M_z \\
\theta &\in (\theta_1,\ \theta_2)
\end{aligned}
\tag{2}
$$

$$
\begin{bmatrix} X \\ Y \\ \theta \end{bmatrix} =
\begin{bmatrix}
\int_{\theta_1}^{\theta_2} \frac{(\bar{M}_x(\theta))^2 \cdot rr}{E \cdot I_z} d\theta & \int_{\theta_1}^{\theta_2} \frac{(\bar{M}_x(\theta) \cdot \bar{M}_y(\theta)) \cdot rr}{E \cdot I_z} d\theta & \int_{\theta_1}^{\theta_2} \frac{(\bar{M}_x(\theta)) \cdot rr}{E I_z} d\theta \\
\int_{\theta_1}^{\theta_2} \frac{(\bar{M}_x(\theta) \cdot \bar{M}_y(\theta)) \cdot rr}{E \cdot I_z} d\theta & \int_{\theta_1}^{\theta_2} \frac{(\bar{M}_y(\theta))^2 \cdot rr}{E \cdot I_z} d\theta & \int_{\theta_1}^{\theta_2} \frac{(\bar{M}_y(\theta)) \cdot rr}{E \cdot I_z} d\theta \\
\int_{\theta_1}^{\theta_2} \frac{(\bar{M}_x(\theta)) \cdot rr}{E \cdot I_z} d\theta & \int_{\theta_1}^{\theta_2} \frac{(\bar{M}_y(\theta)) \cdot rr}{E \cdot I_z} d\theta & \int_{\theta_1}^{\theta_2} \frac{rr}{E \cdot I_z} d\theta
\end{bmatrix}
\begin{bmatrix} F_x \\ F_y \\ M_z \end{bmatrix}
\tag{3}
$$

Next, using the Abaqus software's secondary development, a programmatic simulation analysis will be conducted to verify the accuracy of the compliant model. The input force vector is set to $[F_x, F_y, M_z] = [0, 1, 0]$, and the output displacement in the y direction at the force application point is measured. Finally, the variation trend and relative error between the simulation and calculation results are obtained for the four input parameters, as shown in Fig. 4. It can be seen that the maximum error between the flexibility model established by the Morley integral and the simulation is controlled within 20%, and the calculation results are quite accurate.

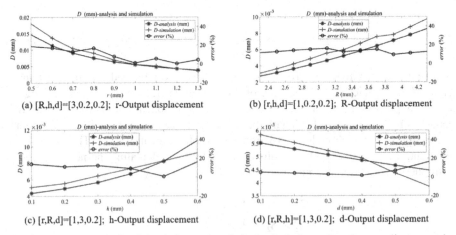

(a) [R,h,d]=[3,0.2,0.2]; r-Output displacement   (b) [r,h,d]=[1,0.2,0.2]; R-Output displacement

(c) [r,R,d]=[1,3,0.2]; h-Output displacement   (d) [r,R,h]=[1,3,0.2]; d-Output displacement

Fig. 4. Accuracy analysis of simulation and analytical calculations when the compliance matrix changes univariately

2.2.2 Stress Modeling and Simulation Analysis

The maximum stress in the conjugate surface restrained structure needs to be controlled to prevent yielding failure during the assembly process. Therefore, a force analysis of the lateral beam on the female head was carried out, as shown in Fig. 5. The state of force at each point was decomposed into radial force, tangential force, and bending moment, considering the neutral layer offset, as in Eq. (4). Subsequently, the stresses they caused were synthesized and calibrated using the third strength theory, as in Eq. (5).

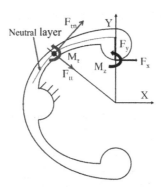

Fig. 5. Force analysis and stress calculation

$$F_{tn} = -(F_x \cdot \sin(\theta) + F_y \cdot \cos(\theta))$$
$$F_{tt} = -F_x \cdot \cos(\theta) + F_y \cdot \sin(\theta)$$
$$M_t = (F_x, F_y)' \cdot (y, x) + M_z \tag{4}$$
$$\theta \in (\theta_1, \ \theta_2)$$

$$\sigma_m = \frac{M_t}{I_z}$$
$$\sigma n = \frac{F_{tn}}{t \cdot w}$$
$$\tau = \frac{F_{tt}}{t \cdot w} \tag{5}$$
$$\sigma = \sqrt{2 \cdot (\sigma_m + \sigma_n)^2 + 4 \cdot \tau^2} \le [\sigma]$$

The stress curve of the female head structure when the structure parameters are [r, R, h, d] = [1,3,0.6,0.2] can be obtained by calculation as shown in Fig. 6. The horizontal coordinates are the line between the stress point and the origin and the angle between the x positive semi-axis. The static model of the structure is obtained by simulation, and the stress distribution trend and the maximum value are basically consistent with those obtained by calculation. The error of the maximum stress point is only 5.07%, and the analytical model is still relatively accurate.

Similar to the previous section, we discuss the calculation results and simulation trends when each of the four structural variables [r, R, h, d] is varied independently. The theoretical modeling and simulation results are consistent and meet the calculation requirements. By combining the compliant model and stress model of the conjugate surface-constrained structure, numerical modeling of the required assembly force during the assembly process can be performed, facilitating subsequent optimization analysis.

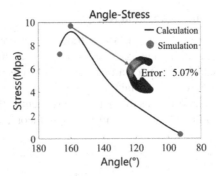

Fig. 6. Analysis of stress distribution and comparison of simulation results

2.3 Compliant Component Design

2.3.1 Compliance Modeling and Simulation Analysis

The compliant element used in this chapter is a circular curved beam, and the same Mohr integral method is used to model the curved beam. As shown in Fig. 7. The curved beam has four structural parameters, t is 10 mm by default, w is 0.4 mm minimum, and the maximum design domain is a circular domain of 20 mm radius. The compliance modeling yields the $\{D\} = C\{F\}$ relation for the flexural element [12], and the subsequent stress analysis of the structure yields the $\{\sigma\} = k\{F\}$ relation, which is still calibrated using the third strength criterion.

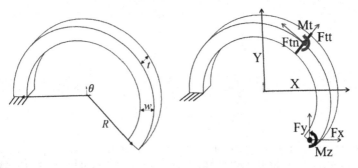

Fig. 7. Parametric modeling and mechanical analysis of compliant components

2.3.2 Range of Motion Calculation

The compliant element acts as a rotational constraint and determines the range of motion of the flexural hinge. In this section, the maximum angular displacement of the structure is predicted by the obtained flexural beam compliance matrix and the force analysis model, and the calculation flow is shown in Fig. 8. When the structure parameters are $[R, w, t, \theta] = [20, 0.4, 10, 180]$, the maximum angular displacement can be obtained as 13.09 degrees by the above calculation process. Currently, the analyzed maximum stress is 318.13Mpa, and the simulated maximum stress is 368.60Mpa, with a relative error of 13.69%, which can be used as a model for stroke calculation of the curved beam.

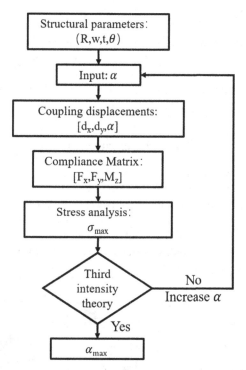

Fig. 8. Calculation process for the maximum range of motion of the compliant element

3   Compliant Rotational Hinge Performance Optimization

3.1   Conjugate Surface-Constrained Structure Optimization Iteration

In the previous section, we obtained the compliant model and stress model of the conjugate surface-constrained structure. As it has a defined geometric motion during assembly, the lateral displacement distance of the male head during assembly can be determined based on the given geometric parameters.

$$D\_install = d_1 + d_2 - d = \sqrt{r + R + D_t^2 - R_1^2} + \sqrt{r + R^2 - R_1^2} - d \qquad (6)$$

$$R_1 = R + r - h; D_t = 0.3 \, \text{mm}$$

Using the three models obtained above, the parametric design of the conjugate surface constraint structure can be transformed into the following constrained, nonlinear optimization problem, where the assembly force refers to the maximum lateral force required during assembly.

Design variables: $X = [x_1, x_2, x_3, x_4] = [r, R, h, d]$.

Objective function: Min {$d_1 = f(r, R, h)$ (minimum assembly distance)}.

Constraints: $\sigma(r, R, h, d) \leq [\sigma]$ (Performance constraint);

{D} = C{F} (assembly force has upper limit: 30N).

$0 \leq r \leq 1.5$; $1 \leq R \leq 5$; $0 < h \leq 0.6$; $0 < d \leq 0.6$ (boundary constraint).

The Matlab optimization function can obtain better design parameters that satisfy the conditions. $[r, R, h, d] = [0.8, 2, 0.1, 0.1]$, the assembly distance is 2.16 mm, the assembly force is 27.00 N, and the calculated stress is 338.17 Mpa. After simulation verification, the maximum stress of simulation is 289.60 Mpa (Maximum allowable stress is 317 MPa), which meets the design requirements.

3.2 Hinge Performance Testing and Experimental Analysis

Optical measurement was carried out on the compliant hinges of the conjugate surface constraint structure, as shown in Fig. 9. After assembly, at least two contact points were used to control the motion, while the other contact position had a gap due to the elasticity of the compliant element. Using a Daheng MERCURY2 camera and ImageJ measurement, the gap was only 100 um and remained constant with the increasing range of motion, indicating controllability. After multiple clockwise and counterclockwise rotations, the transmission rod returned to its original position with good repeatability.

Fig. 9. Experimental measurements of constrained structures on conjugate surfaces

Through the analysis of the conjugate surface-constrained structure and the circular compliant element, the compliant hinge as shown in Fig. 10. Can be obtained by using the optimized structural parameters. The entire process of hinge usage is simulated, and the maximum rotation range is $\pm 5.20°$. Due to the self-assembly process, the actual workspace is smaller than that of a single compliant element, and experimental testing can also achieve this range of motion. The assembly distance is 2.16 mm, and the assembly force is 27.00 N, resulting in a radial stiffness of 12500 N/m. When the maximum range of motion is reached, the torque is 0.10 Nm, resulting in a rotational stiffness of 1.10 Nm/rad. The final performance of the hinge is shown in Table 1.

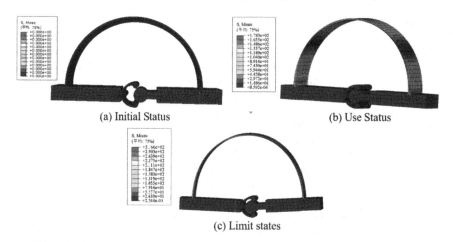

(a) Initial Status   (b) Use Status

(c) Limit states

Fig. 10. Overall structure and working simulation diagram of the compliant hinge

Table 1. Each performance of the hinge

Design Domain (mm²)	Stroke (°)	Assembling force (N)	Rotational stiffness (Nm /rad)	Radial stiffness N/m
$0.5 \cdot \pi \cdot 20^2$	10.4	27	1.1	12.5

4   Conclusion

This paper presents a design for a compliant hinge based on a curved beam, considering the design criteria of large stroke, high accuracy, integrated machining, and actual machining conditions. The design optimization of the conjugate surface restraint structure and performance calculations of the circular curved beam is analyzed. In addition, we provide a detailed analysis of the assembly process and dimensional optimization method for the conjugate surface-constrained structure. The design methods for the compliant hinge are systematically introduced, covering parametric modeling, compliance modeling using Mohr's integral method, and mechanical modeling. The calculation process for the range of motion of the compliant element is established, which can be applied to the general calculation of compliant hinges. The final optimization results show that a design domain with a radius of 20 mm and a working angle of 10.4° can achieve a compliant hinge with integrated processing.

Acknowledgments. The authors would like to gratefully acknowledge the reviewer's comments. This work is supported by the National Natural Science Foundation of China (Grant No. 52075180), and the Fundamental Research Funds for the Central Universities.

References

1. Howell, L.L.: Compliant mechanisms. In: McCarthy, J. (ed.) 21st Century Kinematics, pp. 189–216. Springer, London (2013). https://doi.org/10.1007/978-1-4471-4510-3_7
2. Gräser, P., Linß, S., Harfensteller, F., et al.: High-precision and large-stroke XY micropositioning stage based on serially arranged compliant mechanisms with flexure hinges. Precis. Eng. **72**, 469–479 (2021)
3. Chen, F., Dong, W., Yang, M., et al.: A PZT actuated 6-DOF positioning system for space optics alignment. IEEE/ASME Trans. Mechatron. **24**(6), 2827–2838 (2019)
4. Lyu, Z., Xu, Q.: Recent design and development of piezoelectric-actuated compliant microgrippers: a review. Sens. Actuators A **331**, 113002 (2021)
5. Rong, J., Rong, X., Peng, L., et al.: A new method for optimizing the topology of hinge-free and fully decoupled compliant mechanisms with multiple inputs and multiple outputs. Int. J. Numer. Meth. Eng. **122**(12), 2863–2890 (2021)
6. Wu, J., Zhang, Y., Cai, S., et al.: Modeling and analysis of conical-shaped notch flexure hinges based on NURBS. Mech. Mach. Theory **128**, 560–568 (2018)
7. Liu, M., Zhang, X., Fatikow, S.: Design and analysis of a multi-notched flexure hinge for compliant mechanisms. Precis. Eng. **48**, 292–304 (2017)
8. Ling, M., Yuan, L., Lai, J., et al.: Compliance and precision modeling of general notch flexure hinges using a discrete-beam transfer matrix. Precis. Eng. **82**, 233–250 (2023)
9. Yang, T.S., Shih, P.J., Lee, J.J.: Design of a spatial compliant translational joint. Mech. Mach. Theory **107**, 338–350 (2017)
10. Xu, Q.: Design and implementation of a novel rotary micropositioning system driven by linear voice coil motor. Rev. Sci. Instrum. **84**(5), 055001 (2013)
11. Liang, R., Xu, G., He, B., et al.: Developing of a rigid-compliant finger joint exoskeleton using topology optimization method. In: 2021 IEEE International Conference on Robotics and Automation (ICRA), Xi'an, China, pp. 10499–10504 (2021)
12. Li, C., Wang, N., Chen, B., et al.: Spatial compliance modeling and optimization of a translational joint using corrugated flexure units. Mech. Mach. Theory **176**, 104962 (2022)

A Visual-Inertial Fusion Mapping and Localization System Using AprilTag in GNSS-Denied Scenes

Zhihong Wu, Hao An, Boyu Wu, Huaide Wang, and Ke Lu[✉]

School of Automotive Studies, Tongji University, Shanghai 201800, China
luke@tongji.edu.cn

Abstract. This paper addresses the challenge of achieving precise and long-term positioning for vehicles in GNSS-denied scenes such as indoor parking lots. To tackle this issue, a visual-inertial fusion localization and mapping system using AprilTag is proposed. To meet the requirements of mapping accuracy and real-time positioning, we first employ factor graph optimization to construct a scene tag map based on a complete observation. Then, leveraging the known scene tag map, we employ the Error State Kalman Filter along with vehicle motion constraints to achieve visual-inertial fusion localization in real-time. The system's performance is validated through simulation experiments conducted in a virtual scene and a real-world scene using a ground robot. The results demonstrate that the proposed algorithm can establish an accurate scene tag map and obtain real-time precise positioning results, fulfilling the localization requirements of vehicles operating in GNSS-denied scenes.

Keywords: Indoor Localization · AprilTag · Graph Optimization · ESKF

1 Introduction

In GNSS-denied indoor scenes such as indoor parking lots, relying solely on inertial navigation system (INS) cannot provide stable and accurate positioning results, necessitating the use of alternative localization methods [1]. Localization methods based on ultra wide band (UWB) [2] require prior scene map and device deployment while being susceptible to non-line-of-sight signals. Lidar SLAM [3] can yield satisfactory localization outcomes, but the high cost makes them impractical for widespread deployment. On the other hand, vision sensors, characterized by their compact size and affordability, have found extensive applications in localization solutions [4].

Visual-based localization solutions can be mainly categorized into three main types. The first type is feature-based methods that utilize points [5], lines, and

Supported by the Perspective Study Funding of Nanchang Automotive Institute of Intelligence and New Energy, Tongji University (Grant Number: TPD-TC202211-07).

H. Yang et al. (Eds.): ICIRA 2023, LNAI 14275, pp. 261–272, 2023.
https://doi.org/10.1007/978-981-99-6504-5_23

other features. However, in environments with low texture and repetitive patterns like indoor parking lots, it is challenging to extract reliable features, resulting in poor robustness [6]. The second type is the direct method that utilizes pixel gray-scale information [7]. This method is sensitive to changes in illumination, and scenes with significant lighting variations may affect the accuracy of localization. The third type employs local feature detection methods using reference markers. These methods require the predeployment of tags, and the accuracy of positioning is limited by the number and layout of tags within the camera's field of view. The image-based tags based on QR codes are particularly suitable as positioning references for vehicles in indoor scenes such as indoor parking lots. This is because QR codes have distinct features, and simple encoding and decoding processes. Moreover, when the size of the tag is known, the relative pose between the camera and the tag can be computed with just one observation. Therefore, QR codes are highly suitable for providing accurate positioning for vehicles in indoor scenes.

Currently, there are three types of QR code tags used for tracking and positioning: AprilTag [8,9], ARtag [10], and ArUco [11]. Among these, AprilTag stands out with better localization, orientation estimation results, and detection rates compared to the other two visual tags [12]. In [13], ceiling-mounted AprilTag was used as reference to achieve precise robot localization under both daytime and nighttime conditions. Popović, G [14] proposed a factory personnel localization method that combines visual-inertial navigation system (VINS) and AprilTag map. By fusing the information from two position estimates through graph optimization, accurate personnel positions are obtained. Zhang, W [15] designed a greenhouse localization method for agricultural robots. By utilizing prior AprilTag as landmarks and combining visual geometric constraints between coordinate systems and IMU preintegration, precise localization in agricultural environments is achieved. In [16], under the assumption of accurate knowledge of building parameters, the global position of the camera is obtained by observing tags, enabling real-time accurate positioning of indoor drones. The aforementioned methods utilize the matching results of tags as global localization references fused with other sensors, leading to accurate localization results. However, these methods treated the tag map as prior global localization reference and did not address the issue of establishing an accurate tag map.

This paper presents a visual-inertial fusion localization and mapping system using AprilTag. Considering the requirements of mapping accuracy and real-time localization, the entire system is divided into two parts. Firstly, we propose a graph optimization-based mapping method that establishes an accurate tag map from a complete observation. By simultaneously optimizing the pose of vehicle, velocity, and tag position, the tag map is constructed using factor graph optimization. After obtaining the prior tag map, a visual-inertial fusion localization method is proposed using the prior tag map. To ensure real-time positioning, the Error State Kalman Filter (ESKF) algorithm [17] is employed to correct the accumulated errors of the INS using the globally prior positions of the tag map in GNSS-denied scenes. We also propose an improved AprilTag detection method by adjusting the image contrast to enhance the success rate of tag detection. The accuracy of the established tag map and the performance of the proposed combined localization algorithm are validated in both virtual environments and real indoor scenes.

The main contributions of this paper are as follows:

- A visual-inertial fusion localization and mapping system using AprilTag is proposed. The method addresses the requirements of accurate mapping and real-time positioning. It first establishes an accurate scene tag map using factor graph optimization and then fuses the camera, IMU, and odometer using the ESKF algorithm for localization in real-time.
- A method for tag detection under uneven lighting scenes is proposed. By adjusting the contrast of the image through a nonlinear mapping, the proposed method effectively improves the failure of tag detection caused by uneven indoor lighting, leading to an increased success rate in tag detection.
- A method for fusing multiple tag detection results is proposed. When multiple tags are observed, the proposed method combines the localization results by weighting them based on the distance of each tag and computes the corresponding covariance simultaneously to reduce the influence of measurement errors caused by distant tag detection.

The rest of the paper is organized as follows. System overview and notations are presented in Sect. 2. Section 3 introduces the proposed system. In Sect. 4, the implementation and experimental results are presented. The conclusion is finally given in Sect. 5.

2 Overview

2.1 System Overview

As shown in Fig. 1, the system consists of two components: mapping and localization. The system takes input from three sensors: a camera, IMU, and wheel encoder. Both mapping and localization share a common front-end responsible for tag detection. Here, we propose a method for tag detection under uneven lighting conditions, which significantly improves the detection success rate. To meet the requirements of accuracy and real-time performance, different fusion methods are employed in the back-end for mapping and localization. During the mapping process, a factor graph optimization method is utilized to ensure the accuracy of the tag map. This optimization simultaneously optimizes the vehicle's pose, velocity, and tag position. By incorporating a complete observation, an accurate tag map can be established. In the localization process, the tag detection results are matched with the map. We propose a method for calculating the covariance of visual tag detection results, reducing the influence of measurement errors caused by distant tag detection. To maintain real-time performance during the localization process, the ESKF algorithm is employed to correct the accumulated errors in the IMU using the tag-matching results. Additionally, vehicle motion constraints are applied to further refine the system, yielding precise indoor global localization results.

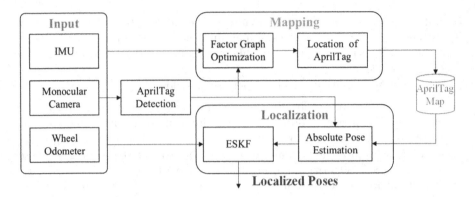

Fig. 1. Overview of the proposed AprilTag-based mapping and localization pipeline.

2.2   Notation

We first define the notation used in this paper. We define $(\cdot)_b$ as the vehicle body coordinate system and $(\cdot)_g$ as the ground coordinate system. $(\cdot)_c$ is the camera coordinate system. $(\cdot)_t$ is the tag coordinate system and $(\cdot)_i$ is the IMU coordinate system. We represent a pose by $T \in SE(3)$ which consists of rotation $R \in SO(3)$ and translation $t \in R^3$. The rotation matrix that transforms points from the tag coordinate system to the camera coordinate system is defined as R_{ct}. Similarly, the origin of the tag coordinate system in the camera coordinate system is defined as p_{ct}. Other variables use similar symbols as well.

3   Proposed System

3.1   Tag Detection Under Uneven Lighting Environment

The tag detection algorithm [9] performs well under ideal lighting conditions, but in real-world scenes, especially in indoor parking lots, there are a lot of areas with uneven lighting that can affect tag detection, as shown in Fig. 2(a). The main reason for this is that the uneven lighting causes the white background around the tags to become darker. When using the original local binarization algorithm of AprilTag, the binarization threshold for pixel blocks in some white background areas becomes larger, leading to the incorrect allocation of the white background as black. This results in blurred boundaries of the tags, and subsequent clustering operations and boundary point detection also fail, ultimately causing the failure of detecting the quadrilateral shape of the tags.

To address the above problem, an improved method based on the tag detection algorithm [9] is proposed. The method involves enhancing the contrast between tags and the white background by applying a nonlinear mapping to the RGB values of the image, thus mitigating the impact of darker regions of the white background on the tag boundaries. The pixel values of each RGB channel in the color image are adjusted according to the mapping relationship given as follows:

$$I_{out} = \begin{cases} I_{out,min} & I_{in} \le I_{in,min} \\ I_{out,min} + \alpha \left(I_{out,max} - I_{out,min} \right) & I_{in,min} < I_{in} < I_{in,max} \\ I_{out,max} & I_{in} \ge I_{in,max} \end{cases} , \qquad (1)$$

where I_{in} is the input pixel values and I_{out} is the output pixel values, α is represented as $\alpha = \left[\left(I_{in} - I_{in,min} \right) / \left(I_{in,max} - I_{in,min} \right) \right]^{\gamma}$.

Using the mapping relationship described above, with the input lower limit, input upper limit, output lower limit, output upper limit, and exponent values set to 0.25, 0.1, 1, 0, and 0.7 respectively, the contrast of the image is adjusted. The result, as shown in Fig. 2(b), demonstrates a significant enhancement in contrast between the tag and the white background after applying the nonlinear mapping. By using the tag detection algorithm on these processed images, accurate recognition can be achieved.

It is important to note that the contrast adjustment method mentioned above is primarily suitable for dark areas with uneven illumination. To ensure the accuracy and stability of the tag detection algorithm, a quadratic detection method is utilized, and the results are combined to obtain the final outcome.

3.2   Mapping with Factor Graph Optimization

The mapping method based on factor graph optimization employs the following variable nodes in the global ground coordinate system: the pose x of the vehicle (including position p and orientation θ), the velocity v of the carrier, and the center point position l of the tag. Constraints between variable nodes are established using the odometry factor, IMU preintegration factor, vehicle kinematics constraint factor, and relative position factor between the vehicle and the tag. The factor graph constructed is depicted in Fig. 3, and incremental solving is performed using iSAM2 [18]. By utilizing a ground vehicle equipped with a wheel odometer, IMU, and camera, a complete observation is made to establish the tag map of the entire scene, and this map is subsequently used for absolute localization. Each of the factors is described below.

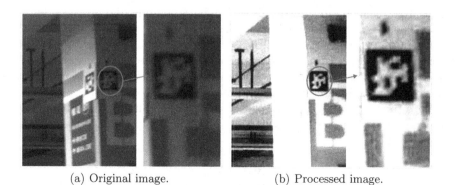

(a) Original image.   (b) Processed image.

Fig. 2. AprilTag in uneven lighting scenes.

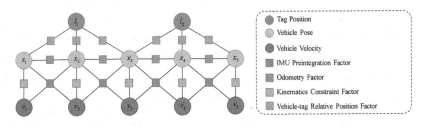

Fig. 3. Illustration of the proposed factor graph optimization.

Odometry Factor. Based on the wheel velocity and the motion model of the vehicle, it can calculate the instantaneous forward velocity v_x^b and yaw rate w_z around the vehicle's Z-axis in the vehicle body coordinate system. By integrating these values over time, we can obtain the relative pose constraint between two consecutive pose nodes of the carrier. For the odometry factor, the measurements are given by the following:

$$h\left(\mathbf{x}_{k-1}, \mathbf{x}_k\right) = \begin{bmatrix} \Delta\mathbf{p} \\ \Delta\theta \end{bmatrix} = \begin{bmatrix} \mathbf{R}_{k-1}^\mathrm{T}\left(\mathbf{p}_k - \mathbf{p}_{k-1}\right) \\ \mathrm{Log}\left(\mathbf{R}_{k-1}^T \mathbf{R}_k\right) \end{bmatrix}, \tag{2}$$

where $\mathrm{Log}\left(\cdot\right)$ denotes the transformation from the Lie group to the Lie algebra.

The Jacobian matrix of the measurement with respect to the variables $\mathbf{x}_{k-1}$ can be expressed as follows:

$$\frac{\partial h}{\partial \mathbf{x}_{k-1}} = \begin{bmatrix} -\mathbf{R}_{k-1}^\mathrm{T} & \left[\mathbf{R}_{k-1}^\mathrm{T}\left(\mathbf{p}_k - \mathbf{p}_{k-1}\right)\right]_\times \\ \mathbf{0}_{3\times 3} & -\mathbf{R}_k^T \mathbf{R}_{k-1} \end{bmatrix}, \tag{3}$$

where $[a]_\times$ is defined as the cross-product matrix of vector a.

The Jacobian matrix of the measurement with respect to the variables $\mathbf{x}_k$ is given by:

$$\frac{\partial h}{\partial \mathbf{x}_k} = \begin{bmatrix} \mathbf{R}_{k-1}^\mathrm{T} & \mathbf{0}_{3\times 3} \\ \mathbf{0}_{3\times 3} & \mathbf{I}_3 \end{bmatrix}. \tag{4}$$

IMU Preintegration Factor. IMU preintegration, initially proposed by Lupton [19], aims to address the problem of repetitive integration of IMU measurements during optimization iterations. It effectively reduces the computational burden during optimization by introducing terms that remain constant throughout each iteration as constraints on the variables. The basic idea is to integrate the incremental changes in position, pose, and velocity between two coordinate systems (including the effects of gravity acceleration) and use them to constrain the pose and velocity nodes in the factor graph. The measurements are given by the following:

$$\begin{aligned} h\left(\mathbf{x}_{k-1}, \mathbf{x}_k, \mathbf{v}_{k-1}, \mathbf{v}_k\right) &= \begin{bmatrix} \Delta\mathbf{p}_{\mathrm{imu}} & \Delta\theta_{\mathrm{imu}} & \Delta\mathbf{v}_{\mathrm{imu}} \end{bmatrix}^\mathrm{T} \\ &= \begin{bmatrix} \mathbf{R}_{k-1}^\mathrm{T}\left(\mathbf{p}_k - \mathbf{p}_{k-1} - \mathbf{v}_{k-1}\Delta t + \frac{1}{2}\mathbf{g}\Delta t^2\right) \\ \mathrm{Log}\left(\mathbf{R}_{k-1}^T \mathbf{R}_k\right) \\ \mathbf{R}_{k-1}^\mathrm{T}\left(\mathbf{v}_k - \mathbf{v}_{k-1} + \mathbf{g}\Delta t\right) \end{bmatrix} \end{aligned} \tag{5}$$

where **g** denotes the local gravitational acceleration.

Vehicle Kinematics Constraint Factor. During the mapping process, the forward velocity of the vehicle at each coordinate system can also serve as a measurement to constrain the velocity variables using the wheel odometer data. Considering the kinematics characteristics of the ground vehicle, the measurement can be expressed to $h(\mathbf{x}_k, \mathbf{v}_k) = \mathbf{v}_{k,b} = \mathbf{R}_k^T \mathbf{v}_k$.

Tag-to-Vehicle Relative Position Factor. When the camera detects tags arranged in the scene, the tag detection algorithm can be used to obtain the position of the tag center in the camera coordinate system. Consequently, the relative position of the tag center with respect to the vehicle can be derived. This information can be utilized to construct measurements that constrain the vehicle's pose node and the tag position node. By incorporating these measurements, the estimation of the vehicle's pose and the positions of the tag can be improved and optimized in the system. The measurements can be expressed as follows:

$$h(\mathbf{x}_k, \mathbf{l}_i) = \mathbf{R}_k^T(\mathbf{l}_i - \mathbf{p}_k), \tag{6}$$

where $\mathbf{l}_i$ the position of the tag numbered i in the camera coordinate system.

The Jacobian matrix of the measurement with respect to the variables $\mathbf{x}_k$ and variables $\mathbf{l}_i$ are given by the following:

$$\frac{\partial \mathbf{h}}{\partial \mathbf{x}_k} = \begin{bmatrix} \frac{\partial \mathbf{h}}{\partial \mathbf{p}_k} & \frac{\partial \mathbf{h}}{\partial \theta_k} \end{bmatrix} = \begin{bmatrix} -\mathbf{R}_k^T & \left[\mathbf{R}_k^T(\mathbf{l}_i - \mathbf{p}_k)\right]_\times \end{bmatrix} \tag{7}$$

$$\frac{\partial \mathbf{h}}{\partial \mathbf{l}_i} = \mathbf{R}_k^T \tag{8}$$

3.3   Visual-Inertial Fusion Localization Using Tag Map

After obtaining the tag map, the prior pose information of the observed tag can be retrieved. By querying the prior absolute pose information of the tag and computing the tag-to-vehicle relative pose information, the absolute position information of the vehicle can be obtained through the coordinate transformation that $\mathbf{p}_b^g = \mathbf{R}_{gt}\mathbf{p}_b^t + \mathbf{p}_t^g$.

The flow of the proposed localization method is shown in Fig. 4. The method first utilizes the accelerometer and gyroscope measurements from the IMU for state prediction. When tags are detected using the proposed detection method, the result of each tag is matched with the tag map to obtain the absolute position. If multiple tags are detected in a single frame, all the localization results are weighted fused as described above. The fused localization result is then used as a measurement to correct the IMU errors within the filter. To enhance inter-frame constraints, the vehicle kinematic constraints described earlier are incorporated to further refine the system's localization errors. By incorporating the vehicle kinematics and the position measurements provided by the prior map, we update the predicted state with the error information. This iterative process allows us to refine the localization estimation and ultimately obtain accurate positioning results.

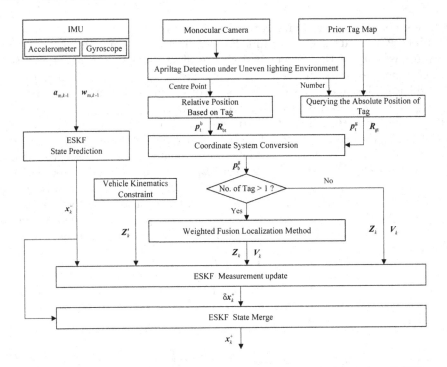

Fig. 4. The flow of visual-inertial fusion localization method based on ESKF.

When multiple tags are simultaneously detected in a camera frame, each detected tag will have its corresponding global localization result. It is necessary to fuse the localization results of multiple tags. We propose a weighted fusion method based on the distance between tags and vehicle. Considering that different sizes of tags may be used in practical applications, the distance factor is designed as follows:

$$\rho_i = s_0 x^b_{t_i} / s_i, \tag{9}$$

where s_0 is the base tag size and s_i is size of the tag numbered i, $x^b_{t_i}$ is the tag-to-vehicle relative position. The localization results can be fused, and the corresponding standard deviation can be constructed as follows:

$$\mathbf{Z} = \sum_i \frac{1}{\rho_i} \mathbf{Z}_i / \sum_i \frac{1}{\rho_i}, \tag{10}$$

$$\sigma = \sum_i \sigma_0 / \sum_i \frac{1}{\rho_i}, \tag{11}$$

where $\mathbf{Z}_i$ is the vehicle localization results $\mathbf{p}^g_b$ provided by the tag numbered i.

4 Experiments

4.1 Implementation

Virtual Scene. We created a virtual parking lot scene using Blender, with dimensions of 33.6 m × 26 m × 3 m. In this scene, 20 tags were placed on the walls. We also created a virtual vehicle model to represent the ego vehicle, which includes a camera with a resolution of 1280 × 720, as well as an IMU and wheel odometer with noise. The ground truth trajectory of the vehicle was recorded for comparison with the localization results.

Real-world Scene. We placed 20 tags in a small indoor parking lot. A self-made ground robot was used as an ego vehicle, equipped with a LiDAR, stereo camera, and wheel odometer. The localization results of LeGO-LOAM [3] were used as the ground truth for the vehicle's pose, and ORB-SLAM2 [5] algorithm was executed to compare the performance of our proposed method.

Procedure. We maneuvered the vehicle around the two scenes separately, attempting to observe all the tags and form loop closures. Using the mapping method described earlier, tag maps of the parking lot with detected tags were created. The errors between the positions of the tag in the map and the ground truth were calculated using root mean square error (RMSE). After obtaining the tag maps, we applied the localization method mentioned earlier to obtain the vehicle's localization in the two scenes. The RMSE between the estimated localization results and the ground truth was also calculated.

4.2 Experiment Results

Mapping. The mapping results in two different scenes are shown in Fig. 5(a) and Fig. 5(b). In the virtual scene, a total of 16 tags were detected, while in the real-world scene, 20 tags were detected. We carefully analyzed the video and confirmed that all the visible tags along the experimental trajectory are detected. The RMSE of the tags' position in the map is shown in Table 1,

Table 1. Position errors of tags in virtual scene and real-world scene.

Scene	No. of detected tags	X. err.(m)	Y. err.(m)	Z. err.(m)
Virtual	16	0.2506	0.0788	0.0183
Real-world	20	0.1774	0.2306	0.0453

It can be observed that the positional accuracy of the tags in the Y and Z directions is lower in the real-world scene compared to the virtual scene. This discrepancy can be attributed to the higher sensor noise in the real-world environment. On the other hand, the X direction error is smaller in the real-world scenario, which can be attributed to the use of larger-sized tags in this scene.

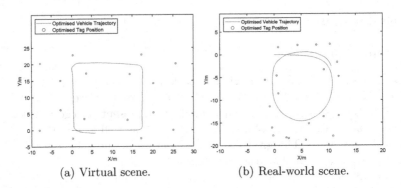

(a) Virtual scene.   (b) Real-world scene.

Fig. 5. Results of mapping in virtual scene and real-world scene.

Both scenes yield tag maps with high accuracy, which can be utilized for subsequent visual and IMU fusion localization.

Localization. The vehicle trajectories in the two scenes were obtained using the localization method described earlier based on the prior tag map in each scene, as shown in Fig. 6(a) and Fig. 6(b) respectively. The vehicle trajectories exhibit loop closures, which improve the accuracy of LeGO-LOAM as the ground truth and also enhance the localization precision of ORB-SLAM2. Both algorithms successfully detected loop closures and optimized the vehicle poses accordingly. The RMSE between the estimated localization results and the ground truth is presented in Table 2.

Table 2. Localization errors of vehicle in virtual scene and real-world scene.

Scene	Method	X. err.(m)	Y. err.(m)
Virtual	Proposed method	0.1873	0.0841
Real-world	Proposed method	0.0701	0.1172
	ORB-SLAM2	0.2845	0.4936

It can be observed that even though the map accuracy is better in the virtual scene, the localization errors are very similar in both scenes due to the fusion of IMU data. This indicates the effectiveness of fusion-based localization. In the real-world scene, our proposed localization method outperforms the ORB-SLAM2 with loop closing. This is because we can real-time correct cumulative errors based on the prior tag map and the inclusion of IMU data enhances the inter-frame constraint. Overall, these results demonstrate the effectiveness of fusion-based localization, as the localization errors are similar in both virtual and real-world scenes.

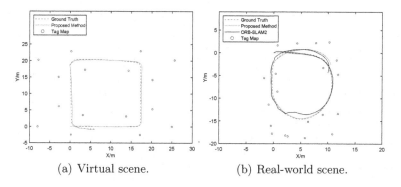

(a) Virtual scene.   (b) Real-world scene.

Fig. 6. Results of localization in virtual scene and real-world scene.

5 Conclusion

In this paper, we proposed a robust and accurate localization and mapping system for vehicles in GNSS-denied scenes. With the improved AprilTag detection method under uneven lighting scenes, a graph optimization-based mapping method that established an accurate tag map using multi-sensor is proposed. During the localization process, the ESKF algorithm is employed to correct the accumulated errors in the IMU using the tag-matching results. The system has been experimentally verified to achieve great mapping and localization results with tags. In the future, we will explore the applicability of the system in more urban GNSS-denied scenes.

References

1. Yassin, A., et al.: Recent advances in indoor localization: a survey on theoretical approaches and applications. IEEE Commun. Surv. Tutor. **19**, 1327–1346 (2017)
2. Feng, D., Wang, C., He, C., Zhuang, Y., Xia, X.-G.: Kalman-filter-based integration of IMU and UWB for high-accuracy indoor positioning and navigation. IEEE Internet Things J. **7**, 3133–3146 (2020)
3. Shan, T., Englot, B.: LeGO-LOAM: lightweight and ground-optimized lidar odometry and mapping on variable terrain. In: 2018 IEEE/RSJ International Conference on Intelligent Robots and Systems (IROS), Madrid, Spain, pp. 4758–4765. IEEE Press (2018)
4. Zhou, X., Huang, R.: A state-of-the-art review on SLAM. In: Liu, H., et al. (eds.) ICIRA 2022. LNCS, pp. 240–251. Springer, Cham (2022). https://doi.org/10.1007/978-3-031-13835-5_22
5. Mur-Artal, R., Tardós, J.D.: ORB-SLAM2: an open-source SLAM system for monocular, stereo, and RGB-D cameras. IEEE Trans. Rob. **33**, 1255–1262 (2017)
6. Qin, T., Chen, T., Chen, Y., Su, Q.: AVP-SLAM: semantic visual mapping and localization for autonomous vehicles in the parking lot. In: 2020 IEEE/RSJ International Conference on Intelligent Robots and Systems (IROS), pp. 5939–5945 (2020)

7. Liang, H.-J., Sanket, N.J., Fermüller, C., Aloimonos, Y.: SalientDSO: bringing attention to direct sparse odometry. IEEE Trans. Autom. Sci. Eng. **16**, 1619–1626 (2019). https://doi.org/10.1109/TASE.2019.2900980

8. Olson, E.: AprilTag: a robust and flexible visual fiducial system. In: 2011 IEEE International Conference on Robotics and Automation, pp. 3400–3407 (2011)

9. Wang, J., Olson, E.: AprilTag 2: efficient and robust fiducial detection. In: 2016 IEEE/RSJ International Conference on Intelligent Robots and Systems (IROS), pp. 4193–4198 (2016)

10. Fiala, M.: ARTag, a fiducial marker system using digital techniques. In: 2005 IEEE Computer Society Conference on Computer Vision and Pattern Recognition (CVPR 2005), vol. 2, pp. 590–596 (2005). https://doi.org/10.1109/CVPR.2005.74

11. Garrido-Jurado, S., Muñoz-Salinas, R., Madrid-Cuevas, F.J., Marín-Jiménez, M.J.: Automatic generation and detection of highly reliable fiducial markers under occlusion. Pattern Recogn. **47**, 2280–2292 (2014)

12. Kalaitzakis, M., Cain, B., Carroll, S., Ambrosi, A., Whitehead, C., Vitzilaios, N.: Fiducial markers for pose estimation. J. Intell. Robot. Syst. **101**, 71 (2021)

13. Hoang, V.T., Tang, Q.N., Truong, X.T., Nguyen, D.Q.: An indoor localization method for mobile robot using ceiling mounted AprilTag. JST **17** (2022)

14. Popović, G., Cvišić, I., Écorchard, G., Marković, I., Přeučil, L., Petrović, I.: Human localization in robotized warehouses based on stereo odometry and ground-marker fusion. Robot. Comput.-Integr. Manuf. **73**, 102241 (2022)

15. Zhang, W., Gong, L., Huang, S., Wu, S., Liu, C.: Factor graph-based high-precision visual positioning for agricultural robots with fiducial markers. Comput. Electron. Agric. **201**, 107295 (2022)

16. Kayhani, N., Zhao, W., McCabe, B., Schoellig, A.P.: Tag-based visual-inertial localization of unmanned aerial vehicles in indoor construction environments using an on-manifold ex-tended Kalman filter. Autom. Constr. **135**, 104112 (2022)

17. Solá, J.: Quaternion kinematics for the error-state Kalman filter. http://arxiv.org/abs/1711.02508 (2017)

18. Kaess, M., Johannsson, H., Roberts, R., Ila, V., Leonard, J.J., Dellaert, F.: iSAM2: incremental smoothing and mapping using the Bayes tree. Int. J. Robot. Res. **31**, 216–235 (2012)

19. Lupton, T., Sukkarieh, S.: Visual-inertial-aided navigation for high-dynamic motion in built environments without initial conditions. IEEE Trans. Rob. **28**, 61–76 (2012). https://doi.org/10.1109/TRO.2011.2170332

An Orientation Measurement Method
for Industrial Robots Based on Laser Tracker

Zhenya He[1,2(✉)], Hongying Zheng[1], Haolun Yuan[1], and Xianmin Zhang[1,2]

[1] Guangdong Provincial Key Laboratory of Precision Equipment and Manufacturing Technology, South China University of Technology, Guangzhou 510640, China
mezhyhe@scut.edu.cn

[2] School of Mechanical and Automotive Engineering, South China University of Technology, Guangzhou 510640, China

Abstract. The end-effector pose accuracy of industrial robots is an important factor influencing their work performance. At present, laser tracker is one of the most popular instruments for position measurement of industrial robots. However, it is more difficult for orientation measurement. Considering the importance of robot's orientation accuracy, this paper presents an orientation measurement method for industrial robots based on laser tracker. Firstly, an additional device with only one spherically mounted reflector (SMR), which has automatic movement function, is designed to measure the orientation of the robot's end-effector. The mounting parameters can be obtained based on the spatial geometric invariance, combining the Lie group theory and the least squares method. And then the orientation information can be calculated by multiplying the rotation transformation matrix. An orientation measurement and compensation experiment was conducted on a 6-DOF industrial robot. It was found that the presented method can reduce the human errors made by manual operation and improve the measurement accuracy and efficiency, and it is simpler and easier to operate without establishing the base coordinate system. The experiment results showed that the mean orientation accuracy of robot's end-effector was increased by more than 86.11% after compensation. Therefore, the orientation measurement method presented in this study is sensible and efficient, and could be used for the error compensation of robots to improve their accuracy.

Keywords: Robot orientation measurement · Laser tracker · Orientation error compensation

1 Introduction

With the extensive application of industrial robot in aerospace, automobile, medical and other fields [1, 2], its position and orientation accuracy has attracted wide attention [3]. Laser tracker is a common device for detecting robot position characteristics due to its high precision and wide range [4–6]. Since the tracker measures orientation of robot inconveniently, it is less frequently used in orientation measurement [7, 8]. However, orientation error cannot be ignored to improve the accuracy of calibration.

© The Author(s), under exclusive license to Springer Nature Singapore Pte Ltd. 2023
H. Yang et al. (Eds.): ICIRA 2023, LNAI 14275, pp. 273–283, 2023.
https://doi.org/10.1007/978-981-99-6504-5_24

Currently, the commonly used method for orientation measurement is to install a calibration plate with multiple positioning holes on the robot's end-effector. The reflector is mounted to the holes and manually moved its relative position to obtain the end orientation, such as Sun [2, 9] and Cheng [10]. In order to achieve simultaneous recording of multiple points, Li [11] adopted tracker machine control probe. Chen [12] adopted three laser trackers to greatly improve the position accuracy compared with a single tracker, and realized the orientation measurement function that was difficult to achieve with a single laser tracker. Liu et al. [13] achieved orientation measurement by aligning coordinate system of the laser tracker and transferring it to coordinate system of the CMM, based on the nine common points. And Nubiola et al. [14] presented an axis-by-axis orientation measurement, where each joint is rotated separately in equal increment. The above methods all need to establish the base coordinate system, and some methods require the use of multiple spherically mounted reflectors (SMR), which would add operation steps, measurement time and cost.

In this paper, in order to meet the demand of the orientation measurement for robot's end-effector, we propose a new orientation measurement method based on laser tracker. It not only avoids building the base coordinate system which streamlines the operation, but also reduces the human errors made by manual operation and improves the measurement accuracy and efficiency. Besides, it has lower requirements for the additional device, because it contains most of error made by the additional device. Therefore, the orientation measurement method could be used to provide a basis for error compensation and improve the accuracy of industrial robots. The paper is structured as follows. Section 2 elaborates the principle of orientation measurement including error analysis. Section 3 shows the experiment and result analysis of the real industrial robot. Finally, Sect. 4 summarizes the main results and contribution of this work.

2   Principle of Orientation Measurement Method

In order to obtain the orientation information accurately and rapidly, a new orientation measurement method for industrial robots is proposed. In this method, the orientation of the robot's end-effector is calculated by multiplying the rotation transformation matrix, considering the mounting errors. The solution of the mounting parameters can be obtained based on the spatial geometric invariance, combining the Lie group theory and the least squares method. The principle of orientation measurement for industrial robots is shown in Fig. 1.

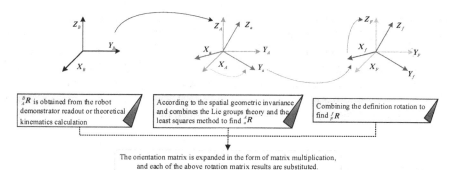

Fig. 1. The principle of orientation measurement for industrial robots

2.1 Calculation of End Orientation

According to the definition of robot orientation and the transformation multiplication rule [15], the rotation matrix can be expanded as follows considering the installation error. Assume that the base coordinate system of the robot is {B}, the actual flange coordinate system under certain robot orientation is {A}, and the tool coordinate system under this robot orientation is {a}; During measurement, the actual flange coordinate system is {F}, and the tool coordinate system under this robot orientation is {f}. The transformation of the actual flange coordinate system in the robot base coordinate system can be obtained by the following formula:

$$^B_F R = {}^B_A R\, ^A_a R\, ^a_f R\, ^f_F R \tag{1}$$

where each rotation matrix represents the rotation transformation of the left subscript coordinate system relative to the left superscript coordinate system, $^B_A R$ is obtained from the robot demonstrator readout or theoretical kinematics calculation; $^a_f R$ is the rotation transformation between the coordinate axis vectors of the additional device; $^A_a R$ and $^f_F R$ is the rotation transformation of the tool coordinate system and flange coordinate system due to the installation error. Because the rotating joint angle does not affect the conversion relationship between the two, $^A_a R$ and $^f_F R$ are reciprocal. By reducing $^A_a R$ to R, the formula (1) can be simplified as following:

$$^B_F R = {}^B_A R\, ^A_a R\, ^a_f R\, ^f_F R = {}^B_A R R\, ^a_f R R^{-1} \tag{2}$$

2.2 Coordinate System Rotation Transformation Based on Additional Device

The X-Y platform of the orientation additional device is composed of X-direction motion axis and Y-direction motion axis. If the initial position of the X-Y platform is set arbitrarily, the spherically mounted reflector (SMR) moves along the X-direction motion axis and Y-direction motion axis respectively to obtain the X- and Y-axis direction vectors in this coordinate system. The Z-direction vector is determined by X cross Y. Finally, the SMR returns to the initial position again and completes the measurement of each direction vector in the coordinate system. The above process is programmed and automatically executed in the actual measurement process. The whole flow chart is shown in Fig. 2. On the one hand, the measurement error of laser tracker with high positioning accuracy has little effect on the experimental results, which can be ignored. On the other hand, the verticality error can be corrected by knowledge of geometry. Firstly, a straight line perpendicular to the plane is obtained by $Z = X' \times Y$, and finally the X-director vector after correcting the verticality error is obtained by $X = Y \times Z$.

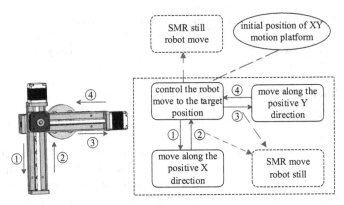

Fig. 2. Movement route of additional device

Suppose the X-, Y- and Z-axis direction vectors of the reference coordinate system $\{S\}$ obtained from the measurement are $\vec{v}_x$, $\vec{v}_y$ and $\vec{v}_z$ respectively, and the direction vectors of the coordinate system $\{H\}$ are $\vec{n}$, $\vec{o}$ and $\vec{a}$ respectively. The direction vectors $\vec{n}$, $\vec{o}$ and $\vec{a}$ of the coordinate system $\{H\}$ are projected on $\vec{v}_x$, $\vec{v}_y$ and $\vec{v}_z$ of the reference coordinate system $\{S\}$ and normalized to obtain the matrix $^{S}_{H}R$ representing the orientation of the object, as shown in Fig. 3. In the Fig. 3, P_{11} and P_{12} represent the first and second points of P_1, respectively, $^{S}_{H}R$ and $^{S}_{H}P$ represent the rotation matrix and translation vector from the coordinate system $\{H\}$ to the reference coordinate system $\{S\}$, respectively.

Suppose the rotation matrix $^{S}_{H}R$ is represented by the following matrix:

$$^{S}_{H}R = \begin{pmatrix} r_{11} & r_{12} & r_{13} \\ r_{21} & r_{22} & r_{23} \\ r_{31} & r_{32} & r_{33} \end{pmatrix} \tag{3}$$

where, the "." in the formula denotes vector multiplication.

$$\begin{cases} r_{11} = \frac{\vec{n}\cdot\vec{v}_x}{|\vec{n}||\vec{v}_x|} & r_{12} = \frac{\vec{o}\cdot\vec{v}_x}{|\vec{o}||\vec{v}_x|} & r_{13} = \frac{\vec{a}\cdot\vec{v}_x}{|\vec{a}||\vec{v}_x|} \\ r_{21} = \frac{\vec{n}\cdot\vec{v}_y}{|\vec{n}||\vec{v}_y|} & r_{22} = \frac{\vec{o}\cdot\vec{v}_y}{|\vec{o}||\vec{v}_y|} & r_{23} = \frac{\vec{a}\cdot\vec{v}_y}{|\vec{a}||\vec{v}_y|} \\ r_{31} = \frac{\vec{n}\cdot\vec{v}_z}{|\vec{n}||\vec{v}_z|} & r_{32} = \frac{\vec{o}\cdot\vec{v}_z}{|\vec{o}||\vec{v}_z|} & r_{33} = \frac{\vec{a}\cdot\vec{v}_z}{|\vec{a}||\vec{v}_z|} \end{cases}$$

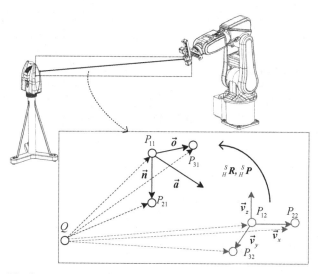

Fig. 3. The additional device coordinate transformation diagram

The orientation of the robot can be represented by three Euler angles α, β and γ, which α is rotation about Z axis, β is rotation about Y axis and γ is rotation about X axis. They can be solved through the following formula:

$$\begin{cases} \beta = \text{A} \tan 2(-r_{31}, \sqrt{r_{22}^2 + r_{21}^2}) \\ \alpha = \text{A} \tan 2(r_{21}/\cos\beta, r_{11}/\cos\beta) \\ \gamma = \text{A} \tan 2(r_{32}/\cos\beta, r_{33}/\cos\beta) \end{cases} \quad (4)$$

2.3 Calibration Method of Additional Device and Robot End-effector

In order to improve the measurement accuracy and avoid the influence of the robot error, a method of measuring the installation error was proposed according to the spatial geometry invariance. According to the invariance of space geometry we get

$$^D_G R = {^D_C R} \, {^C_E R} \, {^E_G R} \quad (5)$$

where, $\{D\}$ is an arbitrary coordinate system, $\{G\}$ is the coordinate system of coordinate system $\{D\}$ after a series of transformations, coordinate system $\{C\}$ and coordinate system $\{D\}$ are relatively static, coordinate system $\{E\}$ is the coordinate system $\{C\}$ after the transformation, namely $^D_C R = {^G_E R}$. Assume that $^D_C R = R_1$, we obtain

$$^D_G R = R_1 {^C_E R} R_1^{-1} \quad (6)$$

where, $^C_E R$ is obtained by measuring the axis vectors of the tool coordinate system before and after rotation; The joint axes are numbered starting from the fixed base of the robot, $j = 1, 2, 3, \dots, k$, and the end joint axis is joint axis k. The robot is controlled to turn a certain angle around the joint axis k and k-1 respectively, and $_G^D R$ is obtained through the conversion relationship between the theoretical kinematics of the robot.

Using the theory of Lie group [16], the solution R_1 in $_G^D R = R_1 {_E^C R} R R_1^{-1}$ is transformed into a least squares problem. Assume that $e^{[d]\theta_1} = {_G^D R}$, $e^{[g]\theta_2} = {_E^C R}$, where the square brackets are added to indicate the skew-symmetric matrix corresponding to the column vectors inside the brackets, and finally $d = R_1 g$ is derived. When there are multiple sets of observed values, the least squares problem is transformed, and its solution is

$$R_1 = \left(M^T M\right)^{-\frac{1}{2}} M^T \tag{7}$$

where, $M = \sum_{i=1}^{k} g_i d_i^T$, d_i and g_i are d and g band of group i.

3 Experiments and Results

3.1 Calibration of Additional Device and Robot End-Effector

As shown in Fig. 4, the robot orientation additional device is fixed on the flange plate, and the X-Y movement platform includes the X-direction movement axis and the Y-direction movement axis. The X-direction movement axis and the Y-direction movement axis are cross connected and the cross linear movement of SMR can be realized by the connection component. The switching plate is connected with the Y-direction movement axis, and the special magnetic nest is fixed on the X-direction movement axis through the connecting plate which suits the SMR of the Leica laser tracker.

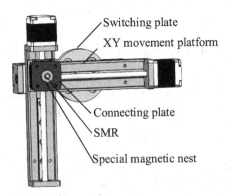

Fig. 4. Robot orientation additional device

The experiment was conducted on an ABB IRB120 robot. The experimental system mainly contained Leica Tracker (AT901-B), the additional device, ABB IRB120 robot, as shown in Fig. 5.

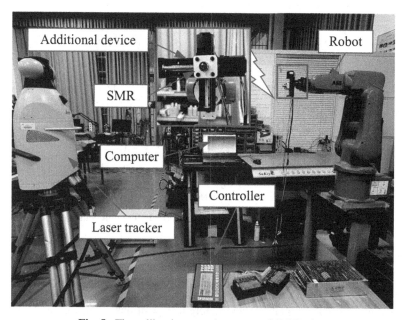

Fig. 5. The calibration experiment on a 6-DOF robot

Before the orientation error measurement, the installation error should be calibrated. During the experiment, the orientation information of 5 points was measured and combined to obtain 10 groups of data. According to the formula (3) and formula (7), the transformation matrix R_1 between flange coordinate system and tool coordinate system was obtained as follow,

$$R_1 = \begin{bmatrix} 0.0054 & -1 & -0.0037 \\ 1 & 0.0054 & -5.25 \times 10^{-4} \\ 5.45 \times 10^{-4} & -0.0037 & 1 \end{bmatrix}$$

3.2 Orientation Error Measurement

The 20 measurement orientations obtained from the common working space of the robot were applied in this experiment, which were programmed into the program in sequence. The reference points of these measurement poses were measured by the laser tracker with the orientation additional device. In the measurement process, the robot waited for 5 s after moving to a point with an orientation to be measured, and the laser tracker started to measure after stabilizing. Then the controller button of the additional device was clicked and 20 sets of position information were measured according to movement route of additional device in Sect. 2.2. The measured orientation errors of the robot end-effector were shown in Fig. 6.

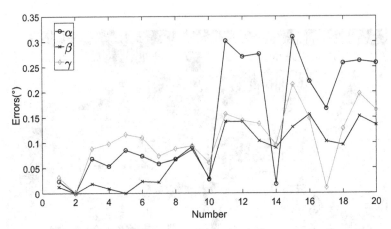

Fig. 6. The orientation errors of the robot before compensation

3.3 Orientation Error Compensation

The measured actual orientations and theoretical positions were used as inputs, and then substituted into the inverse kinematics to obtain the corresponding joint angles. The obtained joint angles were re-input into the robot to re-measure the orientations at this point and checked the errors from the theoretical orientation. The results after compensation were shown in Fig. 7.

Table 1. Orientation errors before and after compensation

Errors	Before compensation/°			After compensation/°			rate/%		
	α	β	γ	α	β	γ	α	β	γ
Mean	0.145	0.076	0.108	0.014	0.007	0.015	90.34	90.79	86.11
max	0.310	0.156	0.215	0.037	0.022	0.046	88.06	85.90	78.60

It can be seen from Fig. 7 and Table 1 that after compensation, the orientation angle error decreased obviously. After compensation, the errors of the robot were reduced from 0.145° to 0.014°, 0.076° to 0.007° and 0.108° to 0.015° with the increase of 90.34%, 90.79% and 86.11% accuracy, respectively. Therefore, through orientation compensation, the mean error of orientation angle was reduced to less than 0.015°, which verified the effectiveness of the method.

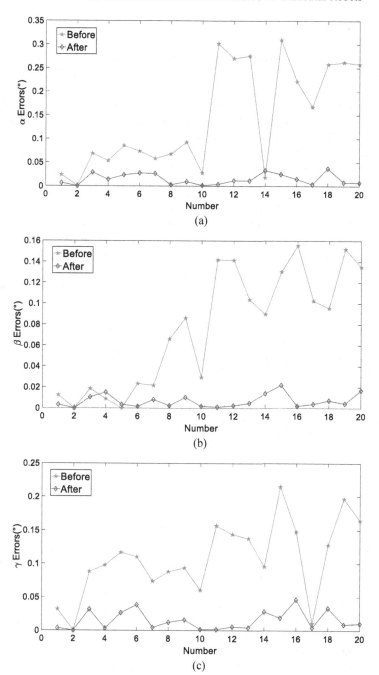

Fig. 7. The orientation errors of the robot before and after compensation (a) α, (b) β, (c) γ.

4 Conclusions

In this paper, we proposed an orientation measurement method for industrial robots based on laser tracker. And an additional device with one SMR having automatic movement function was designed to assist to measure orientation information. According to the spatial geometric invariance, the mounting parameters can be obtained using Lie group theory and least squares method. And then the orientation information can be calculated through the operation of rotation transformation matrix. The method development was carried out on a 6-DOF industrial robot with laser tracker. The feasibility and the effectiveness of the presented method has been verified by experiments. The experimental results bring about the following major conclusions:

a) It doesn't need to establish the base coordinate system and avoid the tedious process of coordinate system establishment using our presented method.
b) The measurement process is automatic with the help of the additional device, which can reduce the human error and improve the measurement accuracy and efficiency.
c) The experiment results show that the end-effector orientation errors of the robot are reduced from $0.108°$ to $0.015°$ after error compensation, with a mean compensation rate more than 86.11%.

Therefore it is reasonable to conclude that the orientation measurement method presented in this paper is sensible and efficient, and that it could be used to provide a basis for error compensation and improve the accuracy of industrial robots.

Acknowledgements. This work was supported by the Science and Technology Project of Guangzhou (No. 202201010072), the Higher Education Teaching Research and Reform Project of Guangdong Province (No. x2jq-C9213027), the National Natural Science Foundation of China (No. 51805172), and the Guangdong Basic and Applied Basic Research Foundation (No. 2019A1515011515).

References

1. Zhu, Z.R., Tang, X.W., et al.: High precision and efficiency robotic milling of complex parts: Challenges, approaches and trends. Chin. J. Aeronaut. **35**(2), 22–46 (2022)
2. Sun, T., Liu, C., Lian, B., Wang, P., Song, Y.: Calibration for precision kinematic control of an articulated serial robot. IEEE Trans. Ind. Electron. **68**(7), 6000–6009 (2020)
3. He, D., Shi, F., Tan, S., Deng, Q.: Research on Inverse kinematics algorithm of 6-DOF industrial robot based on RBF-PID. J. Phys. Conf. Ser. **1624**(4), 042017 (2020)
4. Ma, L., Bazzoli, P., Sammons, P.M., Landers, R.G., Bristow, D.A.: Modeling and calibration of high-order joint-dependent kinematic errors for industrial robots. Rob. Comput.-Integr. Manuf. **50**, 153–167 (2018)
5. Zhang, Y., Zhang, L.: Improving absolute position accuracy method analysis of machining robots by optimizing the posture. In: 8th International Conference on Education, Management, Computer and Society, Shenyang, China, pp. 524–526 (2018)
6. Chen, X., Zhang, Q., Sun, Y.: Non-kinematic calibration of industrial robots using a rigid–flexible coupling error model and a full pose measurement method. Rob. Comput.-Integr. Manuf. **57**, 46–58 (2019)

7. Le, P.-N., Kang, H.-J.: A new robotic manipulator calibration method of identification kinematic and compliance errors. In: Huang, D.-S., Premaratne, P. (eds.) ICIC 2020. LNCS (LNAI), vol. 12465, pp. 16–27. Springer, Cham (2020). https://doi.org/10.1007/978-3-030-60796-8_2

8. Liu, H., Zhu, W., Dong, H., Ke, Y.: An improved kinematic model for serial robot calibration based on local POE formula using position measurement. Ind. Rob. Int. J. **45**(5), 573–584 (2018)

9. Sun, T., Lian, B., Yang, S., Song, Y.: Kinematic calibration of serial and parallel robots based on finite and instantaneous screw theory. IEEE Trans. Rob. **36**(3), 816–834 (2020)

10. Li, C., Wu, Y., Lowe, H., Li, Z.: POE-based robot kinematic calibration using axis configuration space and the adjoint error model. IEEE Trans. Rob. **32**(5), 1264–1279 (2016)

11. Li, G., Zhang, F., Fu, Y., Wang, S.: Kinematic calibration of serial robot using dual quaternions. Ind. Rob. Int. J. Rob. Res. Appl. **46**(2), 247–258 (2019)

12. Chen, Z.W., Zu, H.F., Hong, W., Meng, C.T.: Robot pose accuracy test method based on multi-base station laser tracker. Metrol. Meas. Technol. **41**(01), 10–16 (2021). (in Chinese)

13. Liu, W.L., Li, Y.W.: A novel method for improving the accuracy of coordinate transformation in multiple measurement systems. Meas. Sci. Technol. **28**(9), 095002 (2017)

14. Nubiola, A., Bonev, I.A.: Absolute calibration of an ABB IRB 1600 robot using a laser tracker. Rob. Comput.-Integr. Manuf. **29**(1), 236–245 (2013)

15. Niku, S.B.: Introduction to Robotics: Analysis, Control, Applications, 1st edn. John Wiley & Sons, New York (2020)

16. Park, F.C., Martin, B.J.: Robot sensor calibration: solving AX=XB on the Euclidean group. IEEE Trans. Rob. Autom. **10**(5), 717–721 (1994)

Programming the Motion of Nanofiber Mat Actuator through an Area Selective Epoxy Coating Method

Xiaoting Ma, Hanqian Zhang, Ran Chen[✉], and Fubing Bao

Key Laboratory of Flow Measurement Technology, China Jiliang University, XueYuan Street. 168, Hangzhou, China
yuukyuu.rc@cjlu.edu.cn

Abstract. Nanofiber mat actuators could perform rapid deformations or movements when stimulated by external fields owing to their high surface area and porosity as well as strong mechanical properties. However, nanofiber mat actuators usually perform overall shape-deformations thus require suitable programming methods to achieve complicate motion. Here, through an area selective epoxy coating method, we modify the deformation of specific parts of the nanofiber mat actuator to realize different motion patterns. Compared with nanofiber mat actuators composed of random nanofibers, nanofiber mat actuators built from aligned nanofibers could perform more complicate deformations and better recoveries after epoxy coating, thus are more suitable to realize programmable motions. Our programming method is simple and versatile, thus can be widely used for soft robots, wearable electronic devices and other applications.

Keywords: Nanofiber mat actuator · Motion programming · Epoxy coating · Soft robot

1 Introduction

Owning to their high surface area and porosity as well as strong mechanical properties, nanofiber mat could be used to fabricate actuators which can undergo designate deformation or movement when stimulated by an external field such as electricity [1], light [2], or heat [3]. The nanofiber mat actuators have been widely used in soft robots [4], sensors [5], generator [6, 7], bionic manipulator [8] and so on. Currently, many nanofiber mat actuators use thermos-responsive nanofibers as active layers, thus usually performing overall shape-deformations under temperature excitation. By integrating materials without response to stimulation, deformations of specific parts of nanofiber mat actuators can be achieved, thus resulting in different and programmable motion patterns. For example, a bilayer-structured actuator based on MXene ($Ti_3C_2T_x$)-cellulose composites and polycarbonate membrane has been reported [9]; it can perform programmable specific-part deformation; however, it requires synthesis of special nanosheets and need complex lithography method to realize designate motion patterns. Other programming methods, such as lithography [10] and 3D printing [11], have been applied to design the motion of nanofiber mat actuators, but they also usually require complicated procedure or expensive materials.

In this paper, we report a simple but versatile approach to programming motion of nanofiber mat actuators through an area selective epoxy coating method. The nanofiber mat actuators prepared by this straightforward method undergo deformations only on areas without epoxy, thus resulting in different and programmable motion patterns under temperature triggering. The epoxy used in our coating method is inexpensive and commercially acquirable; this epoxy coating method can be easily applied to modify the motion pattern of existing nanofiber mat actuators.

2   Fabrication of Nanofiber Mat Actuator with Epoxy Coating on Selective Areas

To achieve programmable motion patterns of the nanofiber mat actuator, the concept of the epoxy coating method is shown in Fig. 1. Different areas of nanofiber mat actuators are selected for epoxy coating, thus resulting in different rigidity on different areas. Therefore, the prepared nanofiber mat actuators with different coating could perform different patterns of deformation when immersed into hot water and cold water.

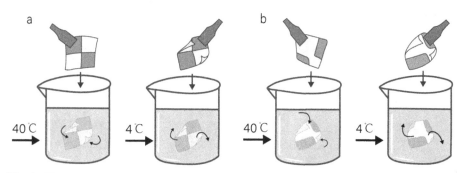

Fig. 1. The concept of motion programming method. The prepared nanofiber mat actuators with different coating could perform different patterns of deformation when immersed into hot water and cold water.

In our experiments, two types of nanofiber mat actuators are prepared by conventional electrospinning method: random nanofiber mat actuators collected by copper plates and aligned nanofiber mat actuators collected by spinning drums. The solution used for electrospinning is prepared by dissolving 3.23 g N-isopropylacrylamide (NIPAM), 0.1 g polyethylene (PEO) (Mw = 1000000), 0.23 g Bis(vinylsulfonyl)propanol (BIS), and 90 mg 2,2'-Azobis(2-methylpropionitrile) (AIBN) in 20 mL 80% ethanol in water. Solution is gently mixed overnight using a magnetic stirrer. Then the obtained solution is spun by electrospinning under the following conditions: the applied voltage is 14 kV; the feeding rate of solution is 1.5 ml/h; the distance from the nozzle to a collector is 80 mm; the rotation speed of the spinning drum is 1000 rpm. After electrospinning, the nanofiber mat actuators are sealed in polyethylene bags and degassed by nitrogen, which subsequently irradiated under UV light for 3 h to ensure the polymerization and cross-linking of nanofiber mat. Subsequently, the nanofiber mat actuators are immersed in water for 2 h to remove PEO and other unreacted residues. The nanofiber mat actuators are dried at 65 °C for 20 min.

The following area selective epoxy coating method is illustrated in Fig. 2. Firstly, the prepared nanofiber mat actuator is cut into square. Then, the polytetrafluoroethylene (PTFE) mask is gently covered on the prepared nanofiber mat actuator (Fig. 2a). Next, an appropriate amount of epoxy (LEAFTOP 9005) poured on the PTFE mask. The epoxy is applied by the scraper from side to side (Fig. 2c). Then, the excess epoxy is scraped away by the scraper, so that the epoxy is evenly covered on the exposed parts of nanofiber mat actuator (Fig. 2d). It usually takes 5 min to crosslink the epoxy. The PTFE mask is removed after the crosslinking of epoxy (Fig. 2e). Finally, a nanofiber mat actuator with an area selective epoxy coating is obtained (Fig. 2f).

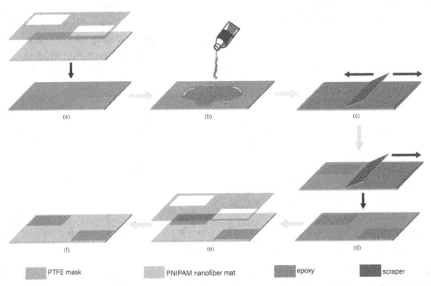

Fig. 2. The schematic shows the area selective epoxy coating method on the nanofiber mat. (a) The PTFE mask is gently covered on the prepared nanofiber mat actuator. (b) The epoxy is poured on the PTFE mask. (c) The epoxy is applied by the scraper from side to side. (d) The excess epoxy is scraped away by the scraper, so that the epoxy is evenly covered on the exposed parts of nanofiber mat. (e) The PTFE mask is removed after the crosslinking of epoxy. (f) A nanofiber mat actuator with an area selective epoxy coating is obtained.

3 Programmed Motion of Nanofiber Mat Actuators with Epoxy Coating on Different Areas

Random nanofiber mat actuators (RNFMAs) and aligned nanofiber mat actuators (ANF-MAs) are divided into 4 × 4 areas and labeled with serial numbers as shown in Fig. 3. The RNFMAs and ANFMAs without epoxy coating are used as control groups; their deformation in hot water at 40 °C and recovery in cold water at 4 °C can be observed in Fig. 3a and 3b respectively. It could be found that the RNFMA and the ANFMA perform similar rolling deformation, but the recovery of ANFMA is better owing to its better fiber orientation.

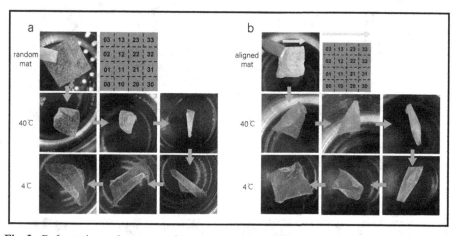

Fig. 3. Deformation and recovery of (a) random and (b) aligned nanofiber mat actuator without epoxy coating in hot water and cold water. Yellow arrows show the orientation direction of aligned nanofiber mat.

The deformation of the RNFMA with different motion patterns is shown in Fig. 4. Figure 4a shows the deformation of the RNFMA with a sandwich shaped area selective epoxy coating. After being put into hot water, the parallel areas with the epoxy coating keep flat, while the other areas of the RNFMA shrink, thus RNFMA deforms to folding state; the RNFMA basically returns to its initial state after being put into cold water. Figure 4b shows the deformation of the RNFMA with a checkerboard shaped area selective epoxy coating. After being put into hot water, the diagonal areas with the epoxy coating keep flat, while the other diagonal areas of the RNFMA without epoxy coating shrink, which shows the wing-like bending; the diagonal areas of the RNFMA without epoxy coating recover but swell a little after being put into cold water. Figure 4c shows the deformation of the RNFMA with a double diamond shaped area selective epoxy coating. After being put into hot water, the RNFMA shows a deformed shape which is curled at the diagonal areas and remains concave-convex in the middle areas; the areas of the RNFMA without epoxy coating swells, but the corners still curl and the RNFMA doesn't recover to its initial state after being put into cold water. Figure 4d shows the deformation of the RNFMA with a 90-degree inverted Z-shaped area selective epoxy coating. After being put into hot water, the diagonal areas of the RNFMA without epoxy coating curls slightly, and some areas of the RNFMA without epoxy coating concave-convex; the areas of the RNFMA without epoxy coating swells and undergoes a degree of recovery, but the corners still curl after being put into cold water.

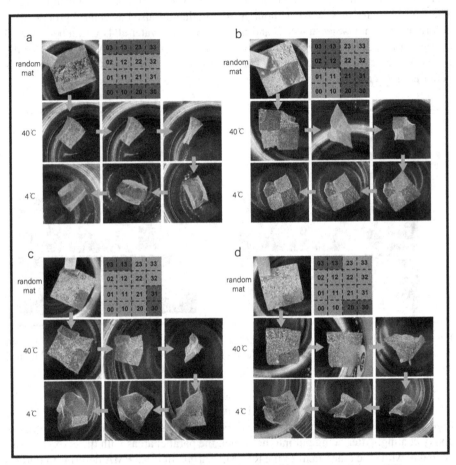

Fig. 4. Deformation of random nanofiber mat actuator with epoxy coating on different areas. (a) coating on the 00,10,20,30,03,13,23,33 areas to form a sandwich shape; (b) coating on the 20,30,21,31,02,12,03,13 areas to form a checkerboard shape; (c) coating on the 20,30,03,13 areas to form a double diamond shape; (d) coating on the 30,31,03,13 areas to form a 90-degree inverted Z shape.

The deformation of the ANFMA with different motion patterns is shown in Fig. 5. Figure 5a shows the deformation of the ANFMA with a sandwich shaped area selective epoxy coating. After being put into hot water, the ANFMA tends to curl along the fiber orientation; but when the epoxy coating is applied to the 00, 10, 20, 30, 03, 13, 23, and 33 areas, the ANFMA doesn't have enough energy to overcome the resistance from epoxy to undergo curling. Figure 5b shows the deformation of the ANFMA with a checkerboard shaped area selective epoxy coating. Because the ANFMA covered by the epoxy possesses stronger stiffness, the deformation of the ANFMA varies in different areas. After being put into hot water, the areas of the ANFMA curls in the direction along the fiber orientation, which is toward the 01, 11, 22 and 32 areas. After being put into cold water, the areas of the ANFMA without the epoxy coating undergo some degree of recovery. Figure 5c shows the deformation of the ANFMA with a double diamond shaped area selective epoxy coating. After being put into hot water, the ANFMA curls in the 20, 21, 22 and 23 areas, while the epoxy-coated areas of the ANFMA keep flat; the corners of the ANFMA are slowly recovering, and the areas without epoxy coating are swelling, thus resulting in a convexity in the middle of the ANFMA after being put into cold water. Figure 5d shows the deformation of the ANFMA with a 90-degree inverted Z-shaped area selective epoxy coating. After being put into hot water, the ANFMA curls in the 10, 11, 12, 21, 22 and 23 areas, while the epoxy-coated areas of the ANFMA keep flat; after being put into cold water, the areas of the ANFMA without the epoxy coating undergo some degree of recovery.

By comparing the deformation of RNFMA and ANFMA, it could be found that they possess different motion patterns even when coated on the same areas. For example, the RNFMA deforms to folding state (Fig. 4a), while the ANFMA keeps flat at all times (Fig. 5a). This is because the ANFMA is anisotropic and it curls along the fiber orientation. Because of the presence of the epoxy-coated areas, the ANFMA doesn't have enough energy to overcome the resistance from epoxy to undergo curling. By comparing the recovery of RNFMA and ANFMA, it could be found that the ANFMA recover better because of its anisotropy. For example, the areas of the RNFMA without epoxy coating swells, but the corners still curl (Fig. 4d); while the areas of the ANFMA without the epoxy coating undergo some degree of recovery (Fig. 5d). This is because the ANFMA recovers along the fiber orientation; while the RNFMA is isotropic, so the RNFMA can't fully recover. The deformation of specific parts of the nanofiber mat actuator is observed in the experiment. This proves that the nanofiber mat actuator achieves programmable motion patterns. Meanwhile, compared with the RNFMA, the ANFMA can perform more complicate deformations and better recoveries.

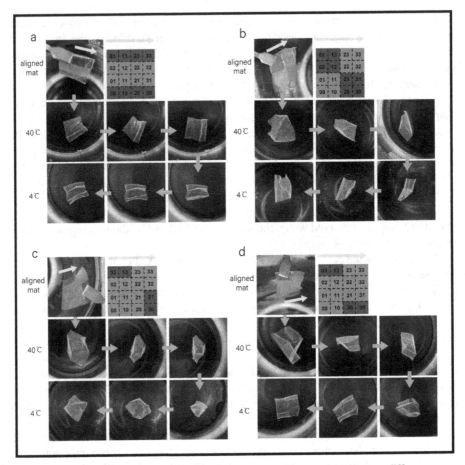

Fig. 5. Deformation of aligned nanofiber mat actuator with epoxy coating on different areas. (a) coating on the 00,10,20,30,03,13,23,33 areas to form a sandwich shape; (b) coating on the 20,30,21,31,02,12,03,13 areas to form a checkerboard shape; (c) coating on the 20,30,03,13 areas to form a double diamond shape; (d) coating on the 30,31,03,13 areas to form a 90-degree inverted Z shape. Yellow arrows show the orientation direction of aligned nanofiber mat.

4   Conclusion

In conclusion, we show a straightforward method to programming motion of nanofiber mat actuators by an area selective epoxy coating method. This method is used to modify the specific-part deformation of the random nanofiber mat actuator (RNFMA) and the aligned nanofiber mat actuator (ANFMA) to achieve different motion patterns. Compared with the RNFMA, the ANFMA can perform more complicate deformations and better recoveries, thus is more suitable to realize programmable motions. This programming method is simple and versatile, thus can be widely used for soft robots, wearable electronic devices and other applications.

Acknowledgements. This work is financially supported by the Zhejiang Provincial Natural Science Foundation of China (LQ21A020005), the National Natural Science Foundation of China (12002333), and the Key R&D Plan Project of Zhejiang Province (2021C01099).

References

1. Pang, D., Alhabeb, M., Mu, X., et al.: Electrochemical actuators based on two-dimensional Ti3C2Tx (MXene). Nano Lett. **19**(10), 7443–7448 (2019)
2. Xianshuo, W., Lian, C., Yifan, W.: An electrospinning anisotropic hydrogel with remotely-controlled photoresponsive deformation and long-range navigation for synergist actuation. Chem. Eng. J. **433**, 134258 (2022)
3. Dompe, M., Cedano-Serrano, F.J., Heckert, O., et al.: Thermoresponsive complex co-acervate-based underwater adhesive. Adv. Mater. **31**(21), e1808179 (2019)
4. Xiao, Y.Y., Jiang, Z.C., Tong, X., Zhao, Y.: Biomimetic locomotion of electrically powered "Janus" soft robots using a liquid crystal polymer. Adv. Mater. **31**(36), 1903452 (2019)
5. Xing, S.T., Wang, P.P., Liu, S.Q.: A shape-memory soft actuator integrated with reversible electric/moisture actuating and strain sensing. Compos. Sci. Technol. **193**, 108133 (2020)
6. Weng, M., Duan, Y., et al.: Electric-fish-inspired actuator with integrated energy-storage function. Nano Energy **68**, 104365 (2020)
7. Yang, C., Su, F., Liang, Y., et al.: Fabrication of a biomimetic hydrogel actuator with rhythmic deformation driven by a pH oscillator. Soft Matter **16**(12), 2928–2932 (2020)
8. Wei, Y., Li, S., Zhang, X.: Smart devices based on the soft actuator with nafion-polypropylene-PDMS/graphite multilayer structure. Appl. Sci. **10**(5), 1829 (2020)
9. Cai, G., Ciou, J.H., Liu, Y.: Leaf-inspired multiresponsive MXene-based actuator for programmable smart devices. Sci. Adv. **5**(7), 7956–7966 (2019)
10. Ma, J.N., Zhang, Y.L., Han, D.D.: Programmable deformation of patterned bimorph actuator swarm. Natl. Sci. Rev. **7**(4), 775–785 (2020)
11. Erb, R.M., Sander, J.S., Grisch, R.: Self-shaping composites with programmable bioin-spired microstructures. Nat. Commun. **4**, 1712–1720 (2013)
12. Stellacci, F.: Towards industrial-scale molecular nanolithography. Adv. Func. Mater. **16**(1), 15–16 (2006)

Design of a Multi-robot Digital Twin System with Bidirectional Motion Synchronization Capabilities

Jinghui He[1,2], Xianmin Zhang[1,2(✉)], and Jian S. Dai[3]

[1] Guangdong Key Laboratory of Precision Engineering and Manufacturing Technology, Guangzhou, China
[2] South China University of Technology, Guangzhou 510640, China
zhangxm@scut.edu.cn
[3] Southern University of Science and Technology, Shenzhen 518055, China

Abstract. This paper presents a multi-robot digital twin (DT) system design for an assembly line and the implementation of bidirectional motion synchronization control. Firstly, the key equipment on the assembly line is introduced. Secondly, we expand from the single-robot DT model and communication scheme to the OPC UA based aggregation server bidirectional communication scheme for multi-robot across the assembly line and introduce the control method in detail during the bidirectional motion synchronization control. Finally, experiments are conducted for the two directions of motion data transmission between the virtual and physical assembly lines to verify the feasibility of the proposed multi-robot DT system.

Keywords: Digital twin · Bidirectional communication · Motion synchronization

1 Introduction

The concept of DT aims to create virtual replicas of physical entities, establishing a seamless connection between the physical and virtual worlds [1]. Its emergence capitalizes on advanced computer technology, effectively integrating extensive data and providing a novel perspective to understand and enhance the production environment. DT is increasingly utilized in actual production environments, including the aerospace field [2,3], industrial manufacturing [4–6], and the product design process [7,8].

The most significant characteristic of DT resides in its ability to establish a communication bridge between physical entities and their virtual twins, thereby facilitating synchronized interaction and coordination. This process entails a real-time collection of operational data from the physical entity during its operation, which is transmitted to the virtual twin, subsequently driving its operation. Concurrently, the virtual twin receives guidance within its virtual environment,

H. Yang et al. (Eds.): ICIRA 2023, LNAI 14275, pp. 292–303, 2023.
https://doi.org/10.1007/978-981-99-6504-5_26

and its operational data is fed back to the physical entity's environment, thus driving its operation within the physical environment. Kousi et al. [9] implemented the ROS (Robot Operating System) as a communication scheme in the automotive industry. Liu et al. [10] focused on industrial robots and employed Unity as the DT platform while utilizing the ROS system as the communication scheme between the physical robot and its DT. Liang et al. [11] utilized ROS topics to receive and send the DT's motion data to the physical robot. In the reverse direction, communication protocols MQTT and TwinCAT ADS were employed to establish and synchronize the systems. Protic et al. [12] utilized the OPC UA (Open Platform Communication Unified Architecture) protocol in the Siemens NX MCD DT system to establish a data channel between the physical and virtual robots. Scholars have proposed various schemes and methods to enable data exchange between virtual and physical entities. However, regarding multi-robot systems, several challenges remain to be addressed. These challenges include the establishment of an efficient and universal DT system and its communication scheme, as well as the implementation of bidirectional motion synchronization control between virtual and physical entities.

The main contributions of this paper are as follows:

1) DT system and communication scheme design: A DT system for assembly line with multi-robot and its symmetric aggregation server communication scheme based on OPC UA are designed.
2) Bidirectional motion synchronization control method: Based on the DT system and communication scheme proposed by 1), a virtual and physical bidirectional motion synchronization control method is proposed.
3) Experimental verification: Based on the proposed DT system scheme and bidirectional motion synchronization control method, an assembly line DT system is constructed, and the effectiveness of the proposed virtual and physical bidirectional synchronous motion control method is verified in the DT system.

The remaining sections of this article are organized as follows: Sect. 2 introduces a typical process assembly line of a mobile phone used for DT. Section 3 introduces the construction of the DT model, the bidirectional communication scheme, and the bidirectional motion synchronization control method of the DT system based on OPC UA. Section 4 validates the feasibility and accuracy of the proposed communication scheme and bidirectional motion synchronization control method we proposed with two experiments. Section 5 gives the conclusion of the article.

2   Brief Description of the Assembly Line

The DT object discussed in this paper represents an assembly line specifically designed for the typical process of assembling mobile phones. The assembly line layout is shown in Fig. 1. The assembly line consists of three SCARA robots, four linear robots, and twelve cameras. The basic design of the SCARA robots on this assembly line is based on our previous work [13].

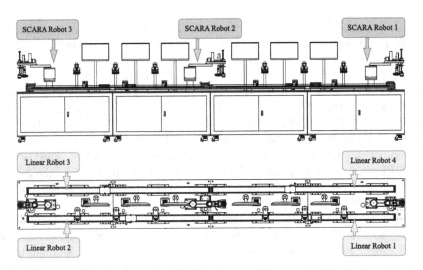

Fig. 1. View of the assembly line

3 Method

3.1 Digital Twin System Scheme

In the DT system, the virtual robot is constructed to replicate the physical robot in a symmetrical scheme. Taking the SCARA robot as an example, the comparison scheme of the physical and virtual robots is illustrated in Fig. 2.

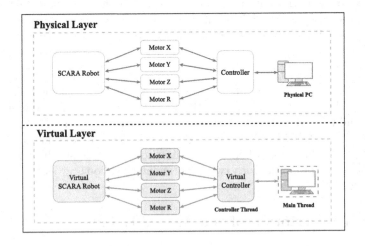

Fig. 2. SCARA robot DT model diagram

The SCARA robot has four motors connected to a controller, which in turn connects to a PC. In the virtual environment, virtual motors and controllers replicate their physical counterparts, with separate threads for each virtual controller to control the virtual motor.

3.2   Communication Scheme

After constructing the virtual model of the DT, an appropriate communication scheme is needed for bidirectional data exchange between the physical and virtual entities. In this part, we use the Client-Server model. Figure 3 illustrates the communication scheme for a single SCARA robot, where each robot has an OPC UA server to convey the feedback data and control commands between the physical and virtual robot.

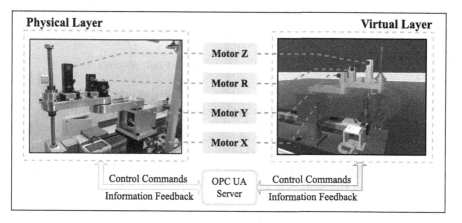

Fig. 3. Communication diagram for a single SCARA robot

The communication scheme of the entire assembly line, based on the aforementioned single robot communication model, is illustrated in Fig. 4. This diagram contains all key devices on the assembly line. The upper and lower layers represent the physical and virtual layers, respectively. At the top are three SCARA robots, four linear robots, and twelve cameras as physical entities on the assembly line. Taking SCARA robot 1 as an example, the Client-Server scheme mentioned earlier is utilized for robot control and information exchange. Similarly, virtual controllers control the virtual counterparts in the virtual layer below. The server-side components of both layers exist within an aggregation server, which contains the server components of all key digitized devices. We can access all the sub-servers by accessing the aggregation server, enabling control over all key devices. Additionally, their connections are bidirectional, allowing data flow from the physical to the virtual layer and vice versa. This symmetric communication structure enhances the scalability of the overall system.

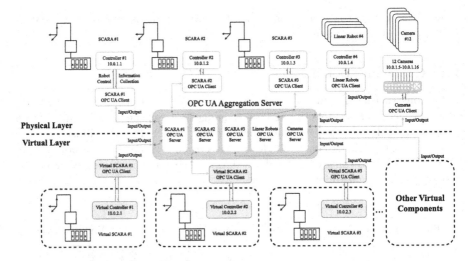

Fig. 4. Communication diagram of the overall assembly line

3.3 Bidirectional Motion Synchronization Control Method

Based on the previously mentioned communication scheme, this section describes how to achieve bidirectional motion synchronization control. Bidirectional motion synchronization control involves two operational directions: the physical entity driving the motion of the virtual entity and the virtual entity driving the motion of the physical entity.

We will propose a physical entity driving the motion of the virtual entity method first. In this scenario, the motion state of the physical robot is transmitted to the virtual layer of the twin to update its state in real-time. The control diagram for this process is depicted in Fig. 5. In this process, the physical robot follows a planned motion path. Each motor's motion data is then associated with the corresponding data node in the OPC UA server, which functions as a sub-server within the aggregation server.

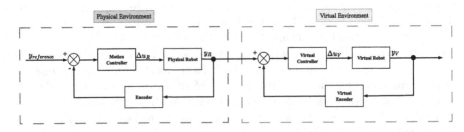

Fig. 5. Control diagram for physical entity driving virtual entity's motion

In the virtual environment, an OPC UA client is created and connected to the aggregation server. By accessing the corresponding data node, the virtual controller retrieves the motion data of each motor. The acquired motion data is subsequently employed as the target trajectory to plan the motion of the virtual robot. Consequently, the motion of the virtual robot is synchronized with the motion of the physical robot.

In the scenario of the virtual entity driving the motion of the physical entity, the motion data of the virtual robot is transmitted to the physical layer to plan and control the motion of the physical robot, which is illustrated in Fig. 6.

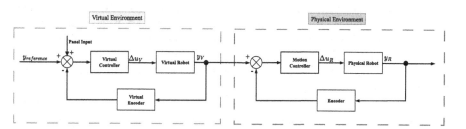

Fig. 6. Control diagram for virtual entity driving physical entity's motion

In this data transmission direction, the motion information can originate from either manual operations or self-generated motion trajectories and strategies learned by the virtual robots within the DT environment. Similar to the motion synchronization from the physical to the virtual robot, on the virtual robot side, a real-time connection is established with the aggregation server to synchronize and store the motion data in the OPC UA server nodes. Subsequently, the physical entity's controller retrieves motion data from the server to guide the movement of physical robots.

In the field of robot trajectory planning, trapezoidal velocity profile (TVP) is one of the lowest computational complexity algorithms. In the standard TVP, with a maximum acceleration of a_{acc}, maximum deceleration of a_{dec}, maximum velocity of v_{max}, target position $x_{absolute}$, and initial position x_{now}, calculate the duration for acceleration t_{acc}, deceleration t_{dec}, and constant velocity t_{vel} phases using the time-optimal strategy as follows:

$$t_{acc} = \frac{v_{max}}{a_{acc}}, \ t_{dec} = \frac{v_{max}}{a_{dec}} \tag{1}$$

$$t_{vel} = \frac{x_{absolute} - x_{now} - \frac{v_{max}^2}{2a_{acc}} - \frac{v_{max}^2}{2a_{dec}}}{v_{max}} \tag{2}$$

If t_{vel} is non-negative, the displacement equation can be calculated as follows:

$$x(\hat{t}) = \begin{cases} x_{now} + \frac{1}{2}a_{acc}\hat{t}^2, & t \in [0, t_{acc}) \\ x_{now} + v_{max}\hat{t} - \frac{1}{2}v_{max}t_{acc}, & t \in [t_{acc}, t_{acc} + t_{vel}) \\ x_{now} + v_{max}\hat{t} & t \in (t_{acc} + t_{vel}, t_{acc} + t_{vel} + t_{dec}] \\ \quad -\frac{1}{2}a_{dec}(\hat{t} - t_{acc} - t_{vel})^2 - \frac{1}{2}v_{max}t_{acc}, & \end{cases}$$

$$(3)$$

In conventional point-to-point trajectory planning using TVP, the trajectory planning is typically performed for each individual point offline. However, in the context of bidirectional motion control between the virtual and physical robot, this paper proposes an on-the-fly TVP strategy to accommodate the online reception of motion target data from either the virtual or physical side, ensuring stable tracking control. This strategy builds upon the TVP planning method but incorporates re-planning of the motion strategy upon receiving new target positions.

Specifically, when a new target position data is received, considering the current robot state with position x_{now2} and velocity v_{now2}, along with the new target position x_{new}, maximum allowable velocity v_{max2}, maximum acceleration a_{acc2}, and maximum deceleration a_{dec2}, the aforementioned problem can be reformulated as giving the initial position x_{now2} and initial velocity v_{now2}, the objective is to plan the TVP to move from the current position to the target position x_{new}. The duration for acceleration t_{acc2}, deceleration t_{dec2}, and constant velocity t_{vel2} can be calculated using the time-optimal strategy for the current target position as follows:

$$t_{acc2} = \frac{v_{max2} - v_{now2}}{a_{acc2}}, \ t_{dec2} = \frac{v_{max2}}{a_{dec2}} \tag{4}$$

$$t_{vel2} = \frac{x_{new} - x_{now2} - \frac{v_{max2}^2 - v_{now2}^2}{2a_{acc2}} - \frac{v_{max2}^2}{2a_{dec2}}}{v_{max2}} \tag{5}$$

Similarly to the previous steps, if t_{vel2} is non-negative, the displacement equation can be calculated as follows:

$$x(\hat{t}) = \begin{cases} x_{now2} + v_{now2}\hat{t} + \frac{1}{2}a_{acc2}\hat{t}^2, & t \in [0, t_{acc2}) \\ x_{now2} + v_{max2}\hat{t} - \frac{1}{2}(v_{max2} - v_{now})t_{acc2}, & t \in [t_{acc2}, t_{acc2} + t_{vel2}) \\ x_{now2} + v_{max2}\hat{t} & t \in (t_{acc2} + t_{vel2}, t_{acc2} + t_{vel2} + t_{dec2}] \\ \quad -\frac{1}{2}a_{dec2}(\hat{t} - t_{acc2} - t_{vel2})^2 - \frac{1}{2}(v_{max2} - v_{now2})t_{acc2}, & \end{cases}$$

$$(6)$$

The velocity equation can be calculated as follows:

$$v(\hat{t}) = \begin{cases} v_{now2} + a_{acc2}\hat{t}, & t \in [0, t_{acc2}) \\ v_{max2}, & t \in [t_{acc2}, t_{acc2} + t_{vel2}) \\ v_{max2} - a_{dec2}(\hat{t} - t_{acc2} - t_{vel2}), & t \in (t_{acc2} + t_{vel2}, t_{acc2} + t_{vel2} + t_{dec2}] \end{cases}$$

$$(7)$$

Utilizing the aforementioned on-the-fly dynamic planning approach makes it possible to input the next desired target position while the robot is still in motion. The current position and velocity are initial conditions to re-plan the motion, satisfying the requirement of continuously inputting new target positions at a specific sampling frequency within the synchronized motion control.

4 Experiment

4.1 Experiment Setup

The experiment is performed using Unity version 2022.2.f1. Following the methodologies described in the previous sections, models of SCARA robots, linear robots, and other assembly line components are created. The completed virtual and physical assembly lines are shown in Fig. 7. Furthermore, based on the construction methods of the OPC UA based aggregation server mentioned in the previous sections, a bidirectional communication is established between the virtual and physical assembly line using the Client-Server model.

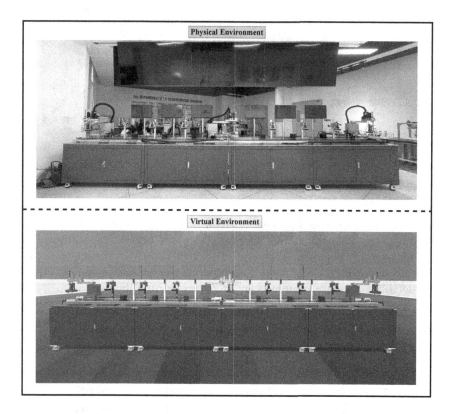

Fig. 7. Completed physical and virtual assembly line

4.2 Experiment Process

The experiment aims to validate two processes. Firstly, we demonstrate the control of the motors Y, Z, and R of the SCARA robot 1 in the virtual assembly line to grip the fixture at the first workstation. The experiment process is briefly shown in Fig. 8. During this motion control process, the virtual robot's motion data serves as the target trajectory. The sampling frequency of the physical and virtual assembly lines is 50 Hz. The experimental result is visualized in Fig. 9.

(a) Process of operating the SCARA robot in the DT system

(b) Positioning results in virtual and physical environments

Fig. 8. Experiment process of SCARA robot in virtual environment

During the operational process of the assembly line, a crucial aspect is the positioning error of various motors throughout the process. Specifically, when reaching assembly points, it is imperative to align them with the reference points as closely as possible. Each motor's positioning average and maximum errors at the assembly points are examined and documented in Table 1.

Table 1. Position result and positioning errors (degree) of the physical robot synchronized with virtual robot

Motor	Virtual position	Physical position	Average error	Maximum error
Motor Y	−95.5400	−95.5487	0.0087	0.0097
Motor Z	100.0000	100.0449	0.0449	0.0545
Motor R	93.5000	93.4216	0.0784	0.0918

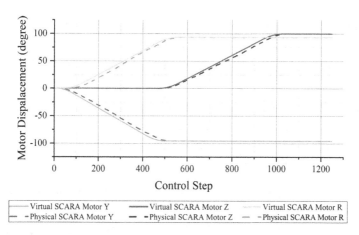

Fig. 9. Motion synchronization result of the virtual assembly line driving the physical assembly line at the first workstation

According to the results presented in Table 1, the average positioning error of the three motors is less than 0.079°. The maximum error is less than 0.092°, which validates the effectiveness and accuracy of the control process and communication scheme when the control commands flow from the virtual environment to the physical environment using the DT system scheme aforementioned.

Furthermore, we perform another experiment to synchronize the motion of the virtual assembly line with the physical assembly line. The overall function of the assembly line is to facilitate the complete assembly process of the phone battery, phone frame, and phone screen. This assembly process involves the utilization of three SCARA robots that are stationed on the assembly line. By performing the assembly process on the physical assembly line, we synchronize the motion data from the physical to the virtual assembly line. The experimental results are illustrated in Fig. 10.

The average and maximum positioning errors of assembly points during motion are evaluated in the aforementioned assembly process. Table 2 comprehensively summarizes the average positioning errors at assembly points during the moving process.

Table 2. Positioning errors (degree) of virtual robot synchronized with physical robot

Robot	Average positioning error				Maximum positioning error			
	Motor X	Motor Y	Motor Z	Motor R	Motor X	Motor Y	Motor Z	Motor R
SCARA 1	0.00068	0.00472	0.02042	0.00141	0.00095	0.00484	0.05665	0.00223
SCARA 2	0.00037	0.00331	0.00953	0.00103	0.00073	0.00452	0.04463	0.00184
SCARA 3	0.00068	0.00253	0.00984	0.00157	0.00130	0.00461	0.01498	0.00214

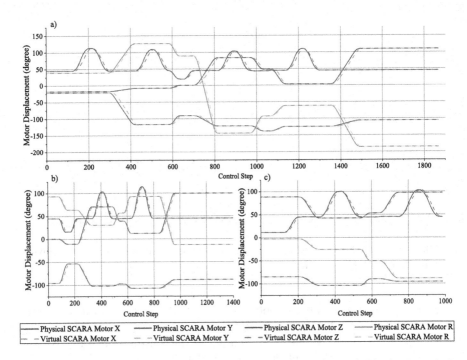

Fig. 10. Motion synchronization result of three SCARA Robots. a), b), c) respectively represent SCARA robot 2, 1, and 3.

The experimental results presented in Table 2 show that the average positioning error of the twelve motors is less than 0.021°, and the maximum error is less than 0.057°. These results show the feasibility and accuracy of the bidirectional control process and communication scheme to achieve synchronization between the virtual and physical robots.

5   Conclusion

In this paper, a multi-robot assembly line DT system is designed. By implementing a symmetric DT communication scheme using OPC UA, bidirectional communication between the virtual and physical environments is actualized. Based on the aforementioned DT system scheme and communication scheme, we achieve bidirectional synchronized motion control by utilizing a trajectory planning method that can be implemented on-the-fly. Experimental verification is conducted in two ways: using the virtual assembly line to drive the physical assembly line and utilizing the physical assembly line to drive the virtual one. In the former, the gripping action at the first workstation is exemplified. In this instance, the virtual robot is manipulated in the virtual environment to perform the gripping motion, which is then synchronized to the physical robot. In the latter, the assembly process is conducted on the physical assembly line, and each robot's motion is synchronized with the virtual robots. These two processes verify the feasibility of bidirectional motion synchronization between physical and virtual environments. Furthermore, the positioning accuracy of the method mentioned above is validated by calculating the average and maximum error at the assembly point. For future work, we intend to implement more responsive tracking based on the robot's dynamics model.

Acknowledgement. This work was supported by the National Key Research and Development Program under Grant No. 2020YFB1713400.

References

1. Grieves, M.: Digital twin: manufacturing excellence through virtual factory replication. White Paper **1**, 1–7 (2014)
2. Glaessgen, E., Stargel, D.: The digital twin paradigm for future NASA and US Air Force vehicles. In: 53rd AIAA/ASME/ASCE/AHS/ASC Structures, Structural Dynamics and Materials Conference 20th AIAA/ASME/AHS Adaptive Structures Conference 14th AIAA, p. 1818 (2012)
3. Tuegel, E.J., Ingraffea, A.R., Eason, T.G., et al.: Reengineering aircraft structural life prediction using a digital twin. Int. J. Aerosp. Eng. **2011**, 1–14 (2011). https://doi.org/10.1155/2011/154798
4. Luo, W., Hu, T., Zhang, C., et al.: Digital twin for CNC machine tool: modeling and using strategy. J. Ambient. Intell. Humaniz. Comput. **10**(3), 1129–1140 (2019)
5. Zhao, H., Liu, J., Xiong, H., et al.: 3D visualization real-time monitoring method for digital twin workshop. Comput. Integr. Manuf. Syst. **25**(06), 1432–1443 (2019)
6. Liu, C., Vengayil, H., Lu, Y., et al.: A cyber-physical machine tools platform using OPC UA and MTConnect. J. Manuf. Syst. **51**, 61–74 (2019)
7. Tao, F., Cheng, J., Qi, Q., et al.: Digital twin-driven product design, manufacturing and service with big data. Int. J. Adv. Manuf. Technol. **94**(9), 3563–3576 (2018). https://doi.org/10.1007/s00170-017-0233-1
8. Lo, C.K., et al.: A review of digital twin in product design and development. Adv. Eng. Inf. **48**, 101297 (2021). https://doi.org/10.1016/j.aei.2021.101297
9. Kousi, N., Gkournelos, C., Aivaliotis, S., et al.: Digital twin for adaptation of robots' behavior in flexible robotic assembly lines. Procedia Manuf. **28**, 121–126 (2019). https://doi.org/10.1016/j.promfg.2018.12.020
10. Liu, H., Zhao, W., Li, S., et al.: Construction method of virtual-real drive systems for robots in digital twin workshops. China Mech. Eng. **33**(21), 2623 (2022)
11. Liang, C.J., McGee, W., Menassa, C.C., et al.: Real-time state synchronization between physical construction robots and process-level digital twins. Constr. Robot. **6**(1), 57–73 (2022). https://doi.org/10.1007/s41693-022-00068-1
12. Protic, A., Jin, Z., et al.: Implementation of a bi-directional digital twin for industry 4 labs in academia: a solution based on OPC UA. In: 2020 IEEE International Conference on Industrial Engineering and Engineering Management (IEEM), pp. 979–983 (2020). https://doi.org/10.1109/IEEM45057.2020.9309953
13. Zhang, J.: Research on automatic conveying SCARA robot for large area screen printing. Master's thesis, South China University of Technology (2018)

Author Index

H. Yang et al. (Eds.): ICIRA 2023, LNAI 14275, pp. 305–306, 2023.
https://doi.org/10.1007/978-981-99-6504-5

Printed in the United States
by Baker & Taylor Publisher Services